WORLD ECONOMIC OUTLOOK

May 1997

**A Survey by the Staff of the
International Monetary Fund**

INTERNATIONAL MONETARY FUND
Washington, DC

World economic outlook (International Monetary Fund)
World economic outlook: a survey by the staff of the International
Monetary Fund.—1980– —Washington, D.C.: The Fund, 1980–

v.; 28 cm.—(1981–84: Occasional paper/International Monetary Fund
ISSN 0251-6365)
Annual.
Has occasional updates, 1984–
ISSN 0258-7440 = World economic and financial surveys
ISSN 0256-6877 = World economic outlook (Washington)
1. Economic history—1971– —Periodicals.   I. International
Monetary Fund.   II. Series: Occasional paper (International Monetary
Fund)

HC10.W7979   84-640155
                              338.5'443'09048—dc19
                                              AACR 2 MARC-S

Library of Congress   8507

Published biannually.
ISBN 1-55775-648-1

*The cover, charts, and interior of this publication
were designed and produced by the IMF Graphics Section*

Price: US$35.00
(US$24.00 to full-time faculty members and
students at universities and colleges)

Please send orders to:
International Monetary Fund, Publication Services
700 19th Street, N.W., Washington, D.C. 20431, U.S.A.
Tel.: (202) 623-7430   Telefax: (202) 623-7201
E-mail: publications@imf.org
Internet: http://www.imf.org

recycled paper

Contents

	Page

Box

Charts

Chapter

CONTENTS

Assumptions and Conventions

A number of assumptions have been adopted for the projections presented in the *World Economic Outlook*. It has been assumed that real effective exchange rates will remain constant at their average levels during March 1–18, 1997 except for the bilateral rates among the European exchange rate mechanism (ERM) currencies, which are assumed to remain constant in nominal terms; that established policies of national authorities will be maintained (for specific assumptions about fiscal and monetary policies in industrial countries, see Box 2); that the average price of oil will be $19.69 a barrel in 1997 and $18.36 a barrel in 1998, and remain unchanged in real terms over the medium term; and that the six-month London interbank offered rate (LIBOR) on U.S. dollar deposits will average 6.0 percent in 1997 and 6.1 percent in 1998. These are, of course, working hypotheses rather than forecasts, and the uncertainties surrounding them add to the margin of error that would in any event be involved in the projections. The estimates and projections are based on statistical information available at the end of March 1997.

The following conventions have been used throughout the *World Economic Outlook*:

. . .   to indicate that data are not available or not applicable;

—   to indicate that the figure is zero or negligible;

–   between years or months (e.g., 1994–95 or January–June) to indicate the years or months covered, including the beginning and ending years or months;

/   between years or months (e.g., 1994/95) to indicate a fiscal or financial year.

"Billion" means a thousand million; "trillion" means a thousand billion.

"Basis points" refer to hundredths of 1 percentage point (e.g., 25 basis points are equivalent to ¼ of 1 percentage point).

Minor discrepancies between sums of constituent figures and totals shown are due to rounding.

*   *   *

As used in this report, the term "country" does not in all cases refer to a territorial entity that is a state as understood by international law and practice. As used here, the term also covers some territorial entities that are not states but for which statistical data are maintained on a separate and independent basis.

Preface

The projections and analysis contained in the *World Economic Outlook* are an integral element of the IMF's ongoing surveillance of economic developments and policies in its member countries and of the global economic system. The IMF has published the *World Economic Outlook* annually from 1980 through 1983 and biannually since 1984.

The survey of prospects and policies is the product of a comprehensive interdepartmental review of world economic developments, which draws primarily on information the IMF staff gathers through its consultations with member countries. These consultations are carried out in particular by the IMF's area departments together with the Policy Development and Review Department and the Fiscal Affairs Department.

The country projections are prepared by the IMF's area departments on the basis of internationally consistent assumptions about world activity, exchange rates, and conditions in international financial and commodity markets. For approximately 50 of the largest economies—accounting for 90 percent of world output—the projections are updated for each *World Economic Outlook* exercise. For smaller countries, the projections are based on those prepared at the time of the IMF's regular Article IV consultations with member countries or in connection with the use of IMF resources; for these countries, the projections used in the *World Economic Outlook* are incrementally adjusted to reflect changes in assumptions and global economic conditions.

The analysis in the *World Economic Outlook* draws extensively on the ongoing work of the IMF's area and specialized departments, and is coordinated in the Research Department under the general direction of Michael Mussa, Economic Counsellor and Director of Research. The *World Economic Outlook* project is directed by Flemming Larsen, Deputy Director of the Research Department, together with Graham Hacche, Chief of the World Economic Studies Division.

Primary contributors to the current issue are Francesco Caramazza, Robert F. Wescott, Staffan Gorne, Mark De Broeck, Paula De Masi, Jahangir Aziz, Kornélia Krajnyák, Ramana Ramaswamy, Phillip Swagel, and Cathy Wright. Other contributors include Paul Armknecht, Tamim Bayoumi, David Ordoobadi, Blair Rourke, Anthony G. Turner, and Andrew Tweedie. The authors of the annex are indicated on its first page. The Fiscal Analysis Division of the Fiscal Affairs Department computed the structural budget and fiscal impulse measures. Sungcha Hong Cha, Toh Kuan, and Michelle Marquardt provided research assistance. Shamim Kassam, Allen Cobler, Nicholas Dopuch, Isabella Dymarskaia, Gretchen Gallik, Mandy Hemmati, and Yasoma Liyanarachchi processed the data and managed the computer systems. Susan Duff, Caroline Bagworth, and Margaret Dapaah were responsible for word processing. Juanita Roushdy of the External Relations Department edited the manuscript and coordinated production of the publication.

The analysis has benefited from comments and suggestions by staff from other IMF departments, as well as by Executive Directors following their discussion of the *World Economic Outlook* on March 31 and April 2, 1997. However, both projections and policy considerations are those of the IMF staff and should not be attributed to Executive Directors or to their national authorities.

I

Global Economic Prospects and Policies

World economic growth quickened during 1996 following widespread deceleration of activity in 1995 (Chart 1). Economic and financial conditions are generally propitious for the global expansion to continue in 1997 and the medium term at rates at least matching those seen in the past three years (Chart 2). There are few signs of the tensions and imbalances that usually foreshadow significant downturns in the business cycle: global inflation remains subdued, and commitments to reasonable price stability are perhaps stronger than at any other time in the postwar era; fiscal imbalances are being reduced with increasing determination in many countries, which should help contain real long-term interest rates and foster higher investment; and exchange rates among the major currencies appear to be generally consistent with broader policy objectives.

In many countries, structural reforms are enhancing the role of market forces and thereby strengthening the basis for sustained, robust growth. The process of trade integration continues to deepen and is being supported by growing liberalization of external payments. Also, changes in the role of the state through privatization and deregulation are raising efficiency and spurring private sector activity in a growing number of successfully managed economies in all regions.

The favorable global economic conditions are underscored by the continued robust growth performance with low inflation in the United States and the United Kingdom, the pickup in growth in Japan in 1996, and improved prospects for a strengthening of the recoveries in continental Europe and Canada. In many of the dynamic emerging market countries, there was a desirable moderation of growth and inflation in 1996, which should allow their expansions to be sustained in the period ahead. Growth has picked up in those developing countries in the Western Hemisphere that were particularly affected by the financial crisis in Mexico in 1995. Activity has also strengthened in the Middle East and Africa, while the transition countries, as a group, are expected to register positive growth in 1997 for the first time since the collapse of central planning.

Nevertheless, despite these grounds for optimism, it is important to recognize that contrasts in economic performance across countries have become starker in recent years. There are also a number of risks to the central scenario. First, in much of the European Union

Chart 1. World Industrial Production[1]
(Percent change from a year earlier)

Following a marked slowdown in 1995, the pace of world industrial activity quickened during 1996.

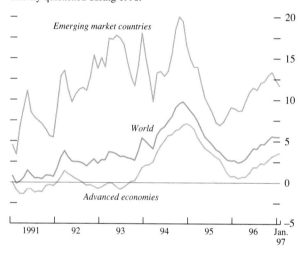

[1]Data are for output in manufacturing in 30 advanced and emerging market economies representing 75 percent of world output; three-month centered moving average.

1

Chart 2. World Indicators[1]

(In percent a year)

The global expansion is expected to continue with the growth of world output and trade above trend, while inflation should remain contained in the advanced economies and slow further in the developing countries.

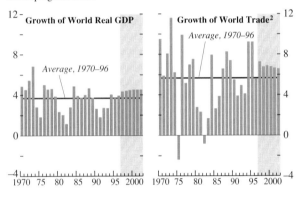

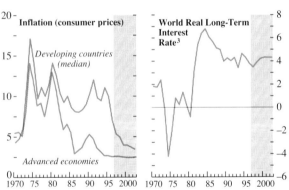

[1]Shaded areas indicate IMF staff projections.

[2]Volume of goods and services.

[3]GDP-weighted average of ten-year (or nearest maturity) government bond yields less inflation rates for the United States, Japan, Germany, France, Italy, United Kingdom, and Canada. Excluding Italy prior to 1972.

(EU), unemployment has risen further to new postwar peaks, and neither prospective growth nor the progress made with labor market reforms gives reason to expect any significant decline in joblessness in the near future. High unemployment and weak growth could make it difficult for EU members to fully meet the fiscal deficit targets associated with the plan for monetary union, affect expectations about the likelihood of the project going ahead on time, and lead to turbulence in financial markets.

Second, stock markets. The strength of equity prices in the United States and many other countries in the period up to early March was a reflection of investors' positive assessment of the business outlook. But recent declines in equity prices have underscored the risk of a more significant correction, especially if earnings expectations were to be downgraded or a reemergence of inflationary pressures were to require a marked rise in interest rates. The potential for a market correction large enough to contribute to a cyclical downturn depends partly on the extent to which the rise in stock prices has been an element in a broader buildup of demand pressures. In contrast to the run-up in asset prices in the late 1980s, especially in Japan but also in the United States and several other countries, a generalized overvaluation of asset prices, leveraged by increased indebtedness, does not appear to be present in most countries with strong stock markets. Nevertheless, a significant decline in stock prices could undermine confidence in some countries.

Third, capital flows to emerging market countries. The surge in such flows in recent years reflects both the growing shift to a more open global financial system and the successful economic policies of many recipient countries. But caution is warranted since both the global availability of these flows and their cost are vulnerable to higher global interest rates and to adverse developments affecting systemically important capital-importing countries. While the aggregate global flows do not seem excessive, the reliance on capital inflows by some countries, and the associated narrowing of their interest rate spreads, may not be sustainable.

Finally, fragile banking systems are of concern in a broad spectrum of countries. These problems often stem from excessive credit expansion in the past under conditions of inadequate prudential supervision. In some emerging market countries, banking sector difficulties linked to significant exposure to foreign exchange risk have become more apparent following the reversal of capital flows from abroad. Among transition countries, bank loans have often allowed enterprises to delay restructuring, and as a result many firms have become increasingly unable to service their debt. Large portfolios of nonperforming loans, the erosion of banks' capital bases, and outright banking crises can affect countries' economic performance by obstructing banks' ability and willingness to lend, by constraining the operation of monetary policy, and because of the budgetary costs of rescuing and restructuring ailing financial institutions.

* * *

It is becoming increasingly clear that the benefits of a favorable global economic environment do not accrue automatically to any country. In fact, remarkable differences persist in the degrees of success that countries have had in taking advantage of the opportunities for strengthening their economic performance.

- Among the advanced economies, developments have been mixed and cyclical positions differ widely. Prospects for recovery have improved in continental western Europe following disappointing performances in 1995 and much of 1996. But unemployment is expected to remain at or near record levels in France, Germany, Italy, and several other countries. In Japan, growth was stronger than expected in 1996, and there is upside potential for activity in 1997 although there remains uncertainty in financial markets, in particular, as to whether the momentum of Japan's recovery will be maintained in the period ahead. The uncertain prospects and lack of confidence characteristic of these economies in recent years contrast with the favorable performance of the United States and the United Kingdom as well as a number of smaller countries including Australia, Denmark, Ireland, New Zealand, and the Netherlands. These contrasts reflect both cyclical and structural factors, including policies.

- An increasing number of developing countries in all regions are reaping the benefits of the steadfast pursuit of sound financial policies and outward-oriented, market-based structural reforms. This is reflected in large inflows of foreign direct investment, rapid expansion of both exports and imports, and solid growth prospects. But some countries have experienced setbacks and others are vulnerable to changes in investor sentiment. While economic conditions have clearly been improving in a growing number of low-income countries, many of the poorest countries have continued to fall behind, facing the risk of marginalization from the mainstream of global economic progress.

- Among the transition countries, the contrasts in performance have also widened between some of the early, relatively successful reformers and countries that have started adjustment and reform later and with less determination and consistency. Between these two extremes, which, to be sure, also reflect widely different starting conditions, there are wide ranges of policy effort and economic success.

Motivated in part by these contrasts, the Interim Committee in its September 1996 "Declaration on Partnership for Sustainable Global Growth" set out a range of broad policy principles to promote the full participation of all economies in the global economy. These principles stress the need to implement sound macroeconomic policies that consolidate success in bringing inflation down, strengthen fiscal discipline, enhance budgetary transparency, and improve the quality of fiscal adjustment; to foster financial and exchange rate stability and avoid currency misalignments; to maintain the impetus toward trade liberalization and current account convertibility; to tackle labor and product market reforms more boldly; and to ensure the soundness of banking systems and promote good governance in all its aspects. The complementary and mutually reinforcing roles of macroeconomic and structural policies were given particular emphasis.[1]

The uneven performance across countries and uneven distribution of rewards within them are frequently linked to the phenomenon of *globalization*— the rapid integration of economies worldwide through trade, financial flows, technology spillovers, information networks, and cross-cultural currents. There is no doubt that globalization is contributing enormously to global prosperity. At the same time, however, public debate often focuses on perceived negative aspects of globalization, including the effects on employment and real wages, especially of the low skilled, in the advanced economies. Globalization, like any form of technological or structural change, may adversely affect the living standards of some in the short run. However, it does not seem to be the principal force behind the unfavorable developments in employment and income distribution observed in some advanced economies.

Another widespread perception is that globalization may, at some cost, limit the autonomy of policymakers at the national level. It is argued in this report that while it does appear that globalization increases the costs of economic distortions and imbalances, policy related or otherwise, it clearly enhances the rewards of sound policies. In this way, globalization may be contributing to the apparent polarization between successful countries and those that are falling behind in relative, and sometimes even absolute, per capita income positions. Globalization is not, however, a zero-sum game with some economies winning at the expense of living standards and employment elsewhere. If policies are adapted to meet the requirements of integrated and competitive world markets, then all countries should be better able to develop their comparative advantages, enhance their long-run growth potential, and share in an increasingly prosperous world economy.

---

[1]See *World Economic Outlook,* October 1996, p. xii.

Globalization is not a new phenomenon. Highly integrated markets contributed to the rapid growth of trade and output during the period of the gold standard prior to World War I. But two world wars, the Great Depression, the adoption of central planning in a substantial part of the world economy, and the pursuit of protectionist and interventionist policies in many countries seriously disrupted international economic and financial interactions. The liberalization of trade and financial flows over the past fifty years has gradually resulted in a level of integration similar in some respects to that known at the beginning of the century—with plenty of scope for further integration as the next century approaches. This issue of the *World Economic Outlook* particularly focuses on the opportunities arising from globalization and on how countries may best meet the challenges of a rapidly changing and highly integrated world economy.

Advanced Economies

Recent indicators point to a moderate firming of output growth in the advanced economies in 1997–98 following a slowdown in a number of countries, particularly in Europe, in 1996 (Table 1). Long-term interest rates have come down significantly in many countries with inflation remaining generally subdued, and the danger of overheating has subsided in the newly industrialized economies of Asia following policy tightenings (Box 1). External imbalances are projected to remain relatively well contained, although a few large surplus and deficit positions may not be sustainable. And exchange rates of the major currencies appear to be reasonably consistent with fundamentals, taking into account cyclical conditions.

Despite the many positive developments, long-standing differences in the advanced economies' ability to achieve and maintain high levels of employment have become even starker in recent years. In much of continental Europe, rates of unemployment have recently risen to postwar record levels, and widespread resort to work sharing and early retirement is not only adding to the underutilization of labor resources but in many cases is raising business costs and budgetary expenditures. The growing imbalance between the inactive population and those employed may require further increases in already very heavy tax burdens. It also undermines future economic growth and living standards and threatens the viability of public pension systems. This situation is particularly striking compared with the impressive ability of the United States to create jobs for a rapidly expanding labor force and the progress achieved by the United Kingdom and a number of smaller countries in reversing earlier increases in trend unemployment. Addressing the malfunctioning of labor markets has clearly become the

---

Box 1. Revised Country Classification

Beginning with the current issue of the *World Economic Outlook,* a number of newly industrialized economies in Asia (Hong Kong, Korea, Singapore, and Taiwan Province of China), as well as Israel, are considered together with the group of countries traditionally known as industrial countries. The reclassification reflects the advanced stage of economic development these economies have now reached. In fact, they all now share a number of important industrial country characteristics, including per capita income levels well within the range indicated by the group of industrial countries, well-developed financial markets and high degrees of financial intermediation, and diversified economic structures with relatively large and rapidly growing service sectors. Rather than retaining the old industrial country label, the expanded group is labeled the "advanced economies" in recognition of the declining share of employment in manufacturing common to all of these economies.

---

most pressing economic policy issue of the late 1990s for many advanced economies.

Both macroeconomic and structural policies need to be strengthened to improve growth and labor market performance. For fiscal policy, as discussed below, the priority remains the need to further reduce budgetary imbalances, which are still excessive in many cases. This is a key requirement for restoring higher sustainable rates of economic growth in the medium term. As discussed in the May 1996 *World Economic Outlook,* the short-term effects on output and employment of fiscal consolidation depend partly on the composition of fiscal adjustment measures. Also, in countries with unsustainable fiscal imbalances credible steps to improve the fiscal outlook can have positive effects on confidence and activity relatively quickly. Normally, some short-run costs tend to be associated with implementing budgetary retrenchments, but progress toward fiscal consolidation and the achievement of reasonable price stability provide added scope for monetary policy to support activity in countries with significant margins of slack. This has been generally recognized by monetary authorities, which have appropriately eased official interest rates to support demand when price stability would not seem to be threatened. Even so, official interest rates could have been adjusted more rapidly in some European countries in recent years in response to widespread signs of cyclical weakness, without compromising the credibility of monetary policy. This would have helped to put the recovery on a stronger footing.

The greatest need for policy action to strengthen Europe's economic performance is in the structural area (which is also true of Japan, as discussed below).

Table 1. Overview of the *World Economic Outlook* Projections

(Annual percent change unless otherwise noted)

	1995	1996	Current Projections		Differences from October 1996 Projections	
			1997	1998	1996	1997
World output	**3.7**	**4.0**	**4.4**	**4.4**	—	**0.2**
Advanced economies	2.5	2.5	2.9	2.9	—	0.1
Major industrial countries	2.0	2.2	2.6	2.6	—	0.1
United States	2.0	2.4	3.0	2.2	—	0.6
Japan	1.4	3.6	2.2	2.9	—	−0.5
Germany	1.9	1.4	2.3	3.0	0.1	−0.1
France	2.2	1.3	2.4	3.0	0.1	—
Italy	3.0	0.7	1.0	2.4	−0.4	−1.2
United Kingdom	2.5	2.1	3.3	2.8	−0.1	0.4
Canada	2.3	1.5	3.5	3.4	0.1	0.3
Other advanced economies	4.2	3.7	3.8	4.1	—	−0.1
Memorandum						
Industrial countries	2.1	2.3	2.7	2.7	—	0.2
European Union	2.5	1.6	2.4	2.9	—	−0.1
Newly industrialized Asian economies	7.4	6.3	5.7	6.1	−0.3	−0.9
Developing countries	6.0	6.5	6.6	6.5	0.2	0.5
Africa	2.9	5.0	4.7	4.8	—	−0.4
Asia	8.9	8.2	8.3	7.7	0.2	0.7
Middle East and Europe	3.8	4.5	3.9	3.9	0.7	0.6
Western Hemisphere	1.3	3.5	4.4	5.1	0.5	0.5
Countries in transition	−0.8	0.1	3.0	4.8	−0.7	−1.0
Central and eastern Europe	1.6	1.6	3.0	4.7	−0.5	−1.2
Excluding Belarus and Ukraine	5.0	3.4	3.3	4.7	−0.8	−1.4
Russia, Transcaucasus, and central Asia	−4.0	−1.9	3.0	4.9	−0.9	−0.8
World trade volume (goods and services)	**9.2**	**5.6**	**7.3**	**6.8**	**−1.1**	**0.2**
Imports						
Advanced economies	8.7	5.3	5.9	6.1	−0.5	−0.1
Developing countries	11.6	8.3	10.7	8.4	−2.9	0.6
Countries in transition	15.9	7.7	9.8	6.8	−4.2	1.8
Exports						
Advanced economies	8.4	5.0	6.9	6.7	−0.2	0.2
Developing countries	11.2	7.0	11.0	8.0	−3.3	0.5
Countries in transition	13.5	4.7	6.9	7.0	−5.8	1.1
Commodity prices						
Oil[1]						
(In SDRs)	1.9	24.3	1.4	−6.4	6.4	9.0
(In U.S. dollars)	8.0	18.9	−3.6	−6.7	5.8	4.0
Nonfuel[2]						
(In SDRs)	2.1	3.1	5.2	0.1	−1.7	7.7
(In U.S. dollars)	8.2	−1.3	—	−0.3	−1.9	2.5
Consumer prices						
Advanced economies	2.6	2.4	2.5	2.5	—	−0.1
Developing countries	21.3	13.1	9.7	8.5	−0.2	−1.1
Countries in transition	119.2	40.4	30.7	11.6	1.4	14.1
Six-month LIBOR (in percent)[3]						
On U.S. dollar deposits	6.1	5.6	6.0	6.1	—	—
On Japanese yen deposits	1.3	0.7	1.0	2.8	−0.3	−1.4
On deutsche mark deposits	4.6	3.3	3.3	3.8	—	−0.5

Note: Real effective exchange rates are assumed to remain constant at the levels prevailing during March 1–18, 1997, except for the bilateral rates among ERM currencies, which are assumed to remain constant in nominal terms.

[1]Simple average of spot prices of U.K. Brent, Dubai, and West Texas Intermediate crude oil. The average price of oil in U.S. dollars a barrel was $20.42 in 1996; the assumed price is $19.69 in 1997 and $18.36 in 1998.

[2]Average, based on world commodity export weights.

[3]London interbank offered rate.

There has been some progress in reforming the complex web of regulations, benefits, and taxes that discourage job creation and job search, but efforts to date have been piecemeal and inadequate in many cases. Opposition to more comprehensive reforms stems from fears that changes in Europe's social welfare system would reduce job security, widen wage differentials, and threaten living standards. Mounting evidence that labor market regulations and high benefit levels are major contributing factors to high and persistent unemployment, excessive tax burdens, chronic fiscal imbalances, and lack of economic dynamism is too often ignored.

It is therefore essential to strengthen the public's understanding of the economic forces that are at work. At the same time, there is a continued need to persevere with comprehensive reforms to reduce overly generous levels of unemployment compensation, tighten eligibility criteria, reduce taxes on employment, and facilitate not only job search and training but also restructurings and layoffs—and thereby hirings. Such reforms would allow market forces a greater role in helping to clear the labor market at much lower levels of unemployment. Tax and transfer systems also will need to be reformed so that they may better meet equity objectives and safeguard a reasonable level of social protection without the negative implications for incentives and employment that are clearly associated with present arrangements. Reducing unemployment would in itself alleviate a major source of income inequality and social exclusion.

To what extent can the difficulties in labor markets in the advanced economies—whether in the form of unemployment or widening wage differentials—be attributed to pressures from globalization? As discussed in this *World Economic Outlook,* there is little indication that increased trade with low-cost countries has contributed significantly to the declining share of employment in manufacturing, which is the principal tradable goods sector. Nor does it seem to explain much of the relative decline of low-skilled wages. The claim that these phenomena stem from globalization and could be alleviated through trade protection and other inward-looking policies does not appear to be supported by the evidence. The relative decline of employment in manufacturing has occurred in spite of relative stability in the distribution of expenditures between manufactures and services at constant prices; it seems attributable mainly to the relatively rapid growth of labor productivity in manufacturing, as a result of technical progress and the normal process of capital deepening. Although the share of manufacturing employment has been declining in these countries—a development referred to as deindustrialization—the trend of industrial output remains positive in most of them.

As economies mature, it seems likely that the share of employment in industry will continue to fall while the importance of services increases further. However, whereas many service industries attract highly qualified labor into well-paid jobs, some service jobs are in activities with low value added and paying correspondingly low relative wages. This is one of the ways in which technological change appears also to have affected wage differentials. The precise mix of service jobs created, however, is likely to depend on the quality of the labor available. Better education and training, therefore, should be of high priority in dealing with both the unemployment problem and the tendency for wage differentials to widen as technical progress demands new skills. In many countries, governments are appropriately pursuing policies whereby those who benefit the most from these developments contribute to the assistance of those less well positioned. However, in designing such policies it is important to avoid creating poverty traps while promoting incentives to enhance skills and to seek out better employment opportunities.

The need for fiscal consolidation is another key policy priority in many advanced economies. There has been welcome progress in many cases and structural fiscal imbalances have been brought down, on average, from 3½ percent of GDP in 1990 to about 2 percent of GDP in 1996. Nevertheless, fiscal imbalances are still excessive in a large number of countries, with the prospective aging of populations and the attendant pressures on health and pension outlays adding to the urgency of fiscal reforms. The need to restore and safeguard sound public finances has led a number of countries to consider introducing codes of fiscal transparency as exemplified by New Zealand's Fiscal Responsibility Act and the Charter of Budget Honesty that is expected to be enacted in Australia. Similar concerns have stimulated interest in rules for the conduct of fiscal policy, as reflected in the Stability and Growth Pact that has now been agreed among members of the European Union, and the discussions of balanced budget constitutional amendments in the United States and Switzerland.

The introduction of fiscal rules is one approach to achieving greater fiscal discipline and to avoiding the "deficit bias" that has emerged from discretionary policy or from the unintended consequences of social insurance programs adopted under more favorable economic circumstances. Sustained and committed efforts to contain fiscal imbalances through discretionary actions could equally achieve the same objective. Opponents of fiscal rules argue that they could unduly constrain the conduct of fiscal policy during cyclical downturns. But this does not need to be the case. In fact, the increased discipline involved in the adherence to such rules may well permit a greater stabilizing role for fiscal policy than has been possible in most countries for a long time. It is of course essential that fiscal rules be well designed and provide reasonable room to accommodate cyclical fluctuations. A requirement to balance revenues and expenditures every year would necessitate immediate adjustments of the level of outlays or taxes in response to cyclical variations in revenue and expenditure, which would be neither feasible nor desirable. Moreover, to be effective, any fiscal rule would need to be supported by increased transparency of off-budget transactions, unfunded pension liabilities, and other future commitments.

The year 1997 is especially important for Europe—the test year for deciding, by the spring of 1998, which members of the EU meet the criteria for initial participation in the planned Economic and Monetary Union (EMU). This project has already achieved much, notably in terms of promoting a sustained decline in inflation and an impressive start on fiscal consolidation. Public sector deficits, which averaged 6.5 percent of GDP in 1993, had been reduced to 4.4 percent of GDP by last year, when 6 of the 15 members were in compliance with the 3 percent reference value for budget deficits that forms part of the eligibility criteria for participation in EMU. Indeed, had it not been for the relatively large output gaps, it is estimated that all but four of the members would have met that reference value last year (Chart 3). Despite continuing output gaps, virtually all members are aiming to satisfy the deficit criterion in 1997, and a fortiori in 1998 and beyond. The policy achievements that have been accomplished set the stage for stronger economic performance in the future. But the run-up to EMU is nonetheless exacting a toll, both because of the short-term consequences of fiscal consolidation and also by contributing to uncertainties and hesitancies in business and consumer confidence that have fed back into demand and activity. It is critical to get through this period promptly by bringing the project to term within the agreed time frame. To this end, governments need to continue to follow through on their policy commitments and objectives, in both the fiscal and structural areas. A strong foundation is being laid, and it is time to begin to reap the fruits.

The EMU project reflects the political will to forge ever-closer links among the member countries of the EU. From an economic perspective, the attractiveness of monetary union includes the prospect of greater economic and financial stability among the participants, associated with a strong commitment to price stability, to be implemented by one independent central bank, and increased efforts to achieve and safeguard fiscal balance. This should help contain real interest rates, especially in countries where risk premiums have been high. In addition, the monetary union is likely to foster deeper capital market integration in Europe and help increase efficiency in financial markets. The introduction of a single currency will also eliminate the potential for tensions to develop among the members' currencies, which in the past have often accentuated the effects of asymmetric economic and financial disturbances.

Of course, disturbances may still affect countries unevenly, and a need to promote a smooth adjustment to such shocks will remain. Since monetary policy will be determined by areawide considerations, fiscal policy will have to play some role, subject to the constraints agreed in the framework of the Stability and Growth Pact. In some instances, financial assistance from the EU budget may be warranted, as indicated in the Maastricht Treaty, to help a country address severe difficulties caused by exceptional occurrences beyond its control. Most critical for the success of the EMU project, and for the dynamism of the European economies, is the need to improve the functioning of European labor markets. From this perspective, most members of the EU must strive to make much more progress irrespective of their plans to participate.

Changes in the exchange rates among the major currencies during the past 18 months have been generally consistent with underlying fundamentals and relative cyclical positions and constitute a substantial correction of the misalignments of spring 1995. These exchange rate changes are a reflection of, and are helping to reinforce, the policy stances that are needed from a cyclical perspective—in the United States and the United Kingdom to restrain inflationary pressures, and in Japan, Germany, and France to support fragile recoveries. However, they should not be viewed as fully substituting for adjustments of monetary policies that may be needed for domestic reasons. Over the medium term, some of the recent appreciation of the dollar and depreciation of the yen may not be compatible with further reduction of external imbalances, and these currency movements may be reversed as cyclical positions become less uneven.

* * *

With regard to prospects and policies in individual countries, the *United States* has been remarkably successful in maintaining a high level of employment while reducing its fiscal deficit and safeguarding low inflation. The economy expanded by 2½ percent in 1996, and price pressures remained subdued despite high resource utilization, including a tight labor market. In 1997, real GDP is expected to increase by 3 percent, somewhat faster than envisaged in the October 1996 *World Economic Outlook*. To reduce the risk of rising inflation the Federal Reserve raised short-term rates slightly in late March. Given the strong underlying growth momentum, a moderate further firming of monetary conditions may soon be needed and is assumed in the forecast (the policy assumptions underlying the projections are set out in Box 2). Continued efforts are also needed to balance the budget over the medium term and to avert a rise in the deficit in the longer run due to the rapid growth in spending on pensions and medical care for the elderly. Enhancing national saving performance through a stronger fiscal position would help sustain future

Chart 3. European Union: General Government Budget Positions[1]
(In percent of GDP)

Expected progress toward reducing underlying budgetary imbalances is masked to some extent by large cyclical components in fiscal deficits.

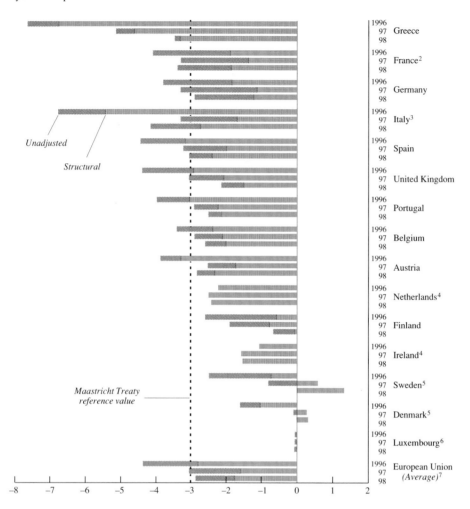

[1]The detailed assumptions underlying the fiscal projections are set out in Box 2. The ordering of countries is based on the projected unadjusted budget positions in 1997, except that where the differences between projections are not significant the ordering is alphabetical.

[2]The projection for 1998 is based on the assumption that, in the absence of official measures, most categories of primary expenditures will increase in line with potential output. Therefore, it does not take into account the planned decrease in general government financing needs of 0.65 percent of GDP for 1998 (i.e., the same target as for 1997) that the French authorities have officially announced. Full implementation of the government's policy intentions would yield a deficit below 2.9 percent of GDP.

[3]The projection for 1998 is made on a "current services" *(tendenziale)* basis. It therefore does not take into account any possible effects of the announced review of pension and welfare spending.

[4]The unadjusted budget positions for Ireland and the Netherlands are not shown separately because they are about equal to the structural balance, given that output is estimated to be close to potential in both countries.

[5]The unadjusted budget position for Sweden is projected to show a surplus of 0.3 percent of GDP in 1998. Denmark's unadjusted budget position is projected to be in balance in 1998.

[6]Structural budget positions are unavailable and unadjusted budget positions are expected to be in approximate balance in 1996–98.

[7]Excludes Luxembourg.

growth. It would also be the best way, from both a domestic and global perspective, to address the chronic external deficit.

In *Canada,* after a disappointing performance in 1995 and early 1996, economic activity picked up in the second half of last year; unemployment has begun to decline, and the economy is poised for solid growth in 1997 and 1998. The general government fiscal deficit, which reached 7½ percent of GDP in 1992, has been reduced progressively and is expected to disappear next year. This has helped restore financial market confidence, which together with subdued inflation has allowed official interest rates to be reduced well below U.S. money market rates without undermining the credibility of the authorities' commitment to price stability or weakening the exchange rate.

The recovery in *Japan* became more broadly based in 1996 and the economic climate improved under the influence of supportive fiscal and monetary policies and a correction of the excessive appreciation of the yen through the spring of 1995. GDP growth picked up in the fourth quarter reflecting strong domestic demand as well as the effects of yen depreciation on net exports. Easy monetary conditions and improving labor market conditions are expected to underpin continued recovery at a moderate underlying pace in 1997. Although there is potential for growth to turn out stronger than expected, uncertainties remain about the impact of fiscal consolidation measures and the effects of strains in the financial system. Thus monetary policy will need to remain easy until an autonomous recovery is firmly established. Fiscal consolidation should proceed at a sustained pace without undermining prospects for continued recovery.

The sluggish performance of the Japanese economy in recent years reflects not only weak demand related partly to financial sector difficulties but also the lack of progress in many areas of structural reform. This is apparent in the divergences that have built up over time between the performances of the tradable and nontradable goods sectors. The latter have remained overregulated, subject to a low degree of competition, relatively inefficient, and characterized by very high cost and price levels. As in other mature economies, however, the tradable goods sector accounts for a declining share of total employment so that jobs and living standards increasingly have to be supported by more dynamic service sectors. It will therefore be important to translate quickly into substantive reforms the growing consensus on the need for further deregulation.

In both *Germany* and *France,* growth slowed to about 1½ percent in 1996 and is expected to be in the range of 2–2½ percent in 1997. In Germany, strong exports should eventually spill over into domestic demand, which will also benefit from lower interest rates. M3, the principal monetary aggregate monitored by the Bundesbank, has expanded relatively strongly.

However, confidence indicators are still quite mixed, unemployment has risen to postwar records, and the pace of fiscal consolidation is set to strengthen in 1997. In the structural area, Germany is confronted both with the need to enhance the flexibility of its labor and product markets and with the special challenges posed by the dependence of the eastern Länder on transfers and subsidies. In France, the business climate has improved somewhat, but consumer confidence is still weak, and the projected pickup in business investment seems fragile. Moreover, it remains necessary to implement more comprehensive labor market, tax, and public sector reforms in order to foster job creation and entrepreneurship.

Short-term interest rates have been reduced considerably in both Germany and France to help offset recessionary forces. In combination with the absence of inflationary pressures, and the recent helpful depreciation of the deutsche mark and the franc against the U.S. dollar and some other European currencies, the easing of monetary conditions has helped to contain long-term interest rates in the face of higher bond yields in the United States. All these developments provide good reasons to expect the recovery to gain some momentum. While there is upside potential, however, there remain downside risks, and it is too early to conclude that the process of monetary easing has fully run its course.

In *Italy,* after relatively strong growth in 1995, recovery stalled in 1996 and activity is now expected to remain subdued in 1997, mainly owing to an accelerated pace of fiscal consolidation and the lagged effects of the lira's appreciation. Considerable progress has been made in reducing inflation to the levels of Italy's EU partners and in strengthening the credibility of the authorities' commitment to reduce the budget deficit. This contributed in 1996 to a marked narrowing of the premium in long-term interest rates over those of Germany and to the correction of the earlier excessive depreciation of the lira, which permitted its return to the European exchange rate mechanism (ERM) in November. Lower debt-servicing costs and the strengthening of fiscal plans, including the recent additional package, are expected to bring the fiscal deficit close to the Maastricht reference value in 1997. The authorities have announced the start of a thorough review of pension and welfare spending, which should help ensure that the progress recorded to date is sustained in 1998 and beyond.

The *United Kingdom*'s solid upswing, now in its fifth year, is expected to continue in 1997 on the strength of consumption and a projected pickup in business investment. The recent appreciation of sterling is helping to dampen inflationary pressures and seems to pose no immediate threat to the expansion, but the forces supporting growth may be tilting too much toward domestic demand. Wage increases have picked up as unemployment has continued to fall, and

Box 2. Policy Assumptions Underlying the Projections

Fiscal policy assumptions for the short term are based on official budgets adjusted for any deviations in outturns as estimated by IMF staff and also for differences in economic assumptions between IMF staff and national authorities. The assumptions for the medium term take into account announced future policy measures that are judged likely to be implemented. Both short-term and medium-term projections are based on information available up to the end of March 1997. In cases where future budget intentions have not been announced with sufficient specificity to permit a judgment about the feasibility of their implementation, an unchanged structural primary balance is assumed, unless otherwise indicated. For selected advanced economies, the specific assumptions adopted are as follows (see Tables 4–5, and A15–A16 in the Statistical Appendix for the projected implications of these assumptions).

United States: For the period through FY 1999, fiscal revenues and outlays at the federal level are based on the administration's February 1997 budget proposal, after adjusting for differences between the IMF staff's macroeconomic assumptions and those of the administration. For FY 2000 onward, the federal government's structural primary balance as a proportion of GDP is assumed to remain unchanged from its projected FY 1999 level.

Japan: The projections take account of policies announced in the 1997 budget, in particular an increase in the consumption tax rate from 3 percent to 5 percent and an end to the temporary income tax cut. Reflecting likely moves toward fiscal consolidation, public investment is assumed to total ¥570 trillion between FY1995 and 2004, rather than the ¥630 trillion assumed in the medium-term public investment plan and earlier WEO projections. The projections assume that the 1994 pension reform plan is fully implemented.

Germany: The 1997 revenue and expenditure projections take into account the effects of the government's consolidation package (comprising measures at the federal, state, and local levels, and the social security funds) and the 1997 Tax Act as passed by parliament in December. The difference with the official deficit projec-

tion of 2.9 percent is mainly due to a slightly less sanguine view of the macroeconomic environment, the financial position of social security funds, and tax revenues; it also reflects available information on fiscal developments so far in 1997. In 1998, and over the medium term, IMF staff projections assume an unchanged structural primary balance.

France: Budget projections for 1997 reflect the government's plans for the state budget (a freeze of nominal expenditure, some income tax relief, and a special transfer from France Télécom) and assume that the social security expenditure ceilings will be respected. The blocking of F 10 billion in state expenditure announced in early March is also included, as is the expected deterioration in the finances of the unemployment insurance fund. For 1998, it is assumed that the ratio of revenue to GDP drops by 0.3 of 1 percentage point (the revenue ratio in 1997 having been boosted by the special transfer mentioned above) and that most categories of primary expenditure grow in line with potential output. For the medium term, the projections assume an unchanged structural primary balance.

Italy: The projections take into account measures that have already been implemented as part of the 1997 budget and the supplementary "effort for Europe," as well as the additional package announced in March 1997. In the absence of an updated plan for 1998–99 following the strengthening of the 1997 effort, the projections for those years are made on a current services *(tendenziale)* basis and reflect also the phased resumption of tax refund payments postponed from 1997. Projections beyond 1999 are based on an unchanged structural balance.

United Kingdom: The budgeted three-year spending ceilings are assumed to be observed. Thereafter, noncyclical spending is assumed to grow in line with potential GDP. For revenues, the projections incorporate, through the three-year budget horizon, the announced commitment to raise excises on tobacco and road fuels each year in real terms; thereafter, real tax rates are assumed to remain constant.

Canada: Federal government outlays for departmental spending and business subsidies are assumed to conform

there is a risk that inflation will again exceed the authorities' target (of 2½ percent or below) in 1998 and beyond unless further action is taken to rein in demand. This would need to be achieved in the first instance through an early tightening of monetary policy. While the fiscal deficit has been reduced substantially in recent years, the November budget tightened the fiscal stance only slightly further in the near term, and more fiscal action is needed to help restrain demand and alleviate the burden on monetary policy.

Many of the smaller advanced economies have enjoyed robust growth in recent years and several have

taken measures to reduce the risk of overheating, generally with considerable success. In fact, official interest rates in *Australia* have declined recently in response to moderating inflation. *Korea* and *Singapore* experienced a moderation of growth in 1996 as a result of a slowdown in exports and, in Korea, some policy tightening. With the transfer of sovereignty over *Hong Kong* to China proceeding smoothly, and apart from the short-term effects of labor unrest in Korea, the prospects for the newly industrialized economies in Asia remain bright, even though their future growth may be somewhat slower than the rapid pace of catch-to the medium-term commitments announced in the February 1997 budget. Other outlays and revenues are assumed to evolve in line with the IMF staff's projected macroeconomic developments. The projections include a contingency reserve for 1997/98 through 1998/99 and assume a reduction of 10 cents in the employment insurance premium in 1998/99 and a reduction of 5 cents a year thereafter. The fiscal situation of the provinces is assumed to be consistent with their stated medium-term targets.

Australia: Projections are based on the Commonwealth government's 1996–97 midyear economic and fiscal outlook, adjusted for any differences between the economic projections of the IMF staff and the authorities. Unchanged policies are assumed for the state and local government sector from 1997.

Belgium: The 1997 projections are based on the 1997 budget and the IMF staff's macroeconomic projections; an allowance is made for some slippage in social security expenditure, but this is offset by lower-than-budgeted interest payments. For 1998, the decline in the deficit reflects mainly lower interest payments and a partial closing of the output gap. Beyond 1998, the structural primary balance is assumed unchanged.

Israel: The fiscal assumptions are in line with the government's medium-term fiscal plan, which establishes annual targets for the budget deficits until 2001.

Korea: Projections for 1997–2002 assume that the central government budget remains broadly in balance and that small surpluses continue to be recorded at the general government level.

Netherlands: The 1997 projections are based on the 1997 budget and IMF staff estimates for interest rates and economic activity; they assume that a portion of the higher-than-anticipated revenues recorded in 1996 was structural in nature. The 1998 projections reflect the government's expenditure norm, with no further tax cuts. Beyond 1998, the structural primary balance is assumed constant.

Spain: Fiscal projections for 1997 assume that the budget is implemented as passed by parliament but allow for

differences in macroeconomic assumptions and some expenditure overruns that are partially offset by lower interest payments. For 1998 and beyond, it is assumed that there is no major change in tax policy, the wage freeze ends, public sector wages grow at roughly the rate of increase of wages in the private sector, and goods and services purchases remain constant as a share of GDP.

Sweden: The medium-term projections are based on the government's multiyear consolidation program approved by parliament in 1995 and augmented by additional measures incorporated into the 1997 budget.

Switzerland: Projections for 1997–2000 are based on official estimates for current services. Thereafter, the general government structural primary balance is assumed to remain constant.

* * *

Monetary policy assumptions are based on the established framework for monetary policy in each country, which in most cases implies a nonaccommodative stance over the business cycle. It is generally assumed that official interest rates will firm when economic indicators suggest that inflation will rise above its acceptable rate or range and ease when indicators suggest that prospective inflation will not exceed the acceptable rate or range, that prospective output growth is below its potential rate, and that the margin of slack in the economy is significant. For the exchange rate mechanism (ERM) countries, which use monetary policy to adhere to exchange rate anchors, official interest rates are assumed to move in line with those in Germany, except that progress on fiscal consolidation may influence interest differentials relative to Germany. On this basis, it is assumed that the London interbank offered rate (LIBOR) on six-month U.S. dollar deposits will average 6 percent in 1997 and 6.1 percent in 1998; on six-month Japanese yen deposits, it will average 1.0 percent in 1997 and 2.8 percent in 1998; and on six-month deutsche mark deposits, 3.3 percent in 1997 and 3.8 percent in 1998. Changes in interest rate assumptions compared with the October 1996 *World Economic Outlook* are summarized in Table 1.

ing up sustained in the past. In *Israel,* which has also been grappling with overheating, the planned tightening of the fiscal stance is needed to relieve the burden on monetary policy, reduce the external deficit to a more sustainable level, and help bring inflation into the low single digits typical of other advanced economies. In Europe, *Ireland* and *Norway* are expected to continue to expand rapidly. In both cases, vigilance is needed to prevent overheating; investments abroad through Norway's "petroleum fund" should help reduce upward pressure on the krone associated with large oil revenues. In *Denmark* and the

Netherlands also, action may be needed to contain relatively buoyant domestic demand; because of the continued easy monetary stance warranted in Germany, fiscal policy should provide the necessary degree of restraint in both of these ERM countries.

In other EU countries, where margins of slack are still significant, fiscal consolidation is helping to relieve the burden on monetary policy and is improving the economic outlook. In *Spain,* thanks also to an impressive drop in inflation, both short-term and long-term interest rates have come down sharply. In *Sweden* and *Finland,* solid recoveries from serious downturns early in the decade are set to continue, supported by subdued inflation, improving fiscal positions, and a marked narrowing of interest differentials vis-à-vis Germany. Activity has also picked up in *Austria, Belgium,* and *Portugal.* Outside the EU, there are still no clear signs of recovery in *Switzerland* from a protracted recession that left the economy stagnant in 1996 for the sixth successive year. However, an easier monetary stance and correction of the earlier excessive appreciation of the Swiss franc have improved the prospects for a turnaround.

Developing Countries

In the developing countries as a group, growth picked up to 6½ percent last year from 6 percent in 1995, as stronger activity in Africa, Latin America, and the Middle East offset a moderate slowdown in parts of Asia. Data on trade and industrial production indicate that aggregate activity slowed in the course of 1995 but picked up speed again during 1996. The apparent synchronization of the developing countries' business cycle in 1995–96 with that of the advanced economies contrasts with the experience of the early 1990s when the buoyancy of developing country growth helped maintain global expansion while many advanced economies suffered recessions (see Chart 1). The recent abatement of overheating pressures in many of the most successful developing countries has enhanced the chances of their expansions being sustained, and the growth projection for the developing countries overall in 1997 has been marked up to 6½ percent.

The *Mexican* economy is continuing to recover following the 1995 crisis, and the return of financial market confidence has allowed Mexico to prepay a substantial part of the emergency loans obtained in support of its adjustment efforts. The expansion is expected to maintain its momentum in 1997 provided financial policies and structural reforms remain on track. The recovery in *Argentina* is also expected to continue in 1997, with inflation remaining close to zero. In *Brazil,* growth strengthened in 1996 while inflation fell to 9 percent by the end of the year, the lowest in three and a half decades. But a widening deficit on current account and a policy mix characterized by a weak fiscal stance and tight monetary conditions carry risks. In *Chile,* the most successful economy in the region, inflation fell to a 36-year low of 6½ percent at the end of 1996, and demand pressures have eased in response to tighter monetary policies. Output growth remains strong, however, and the external deficit, affected by the decline in copper prices, is quite large so that further restraint may be warranted. To avoid stimulating capital inflows, fiscal policy should provide the bulk of this restraint.

Among the developing countries in Asia, those that have had to deal with risks of overheating have generally been successful in dampening the growth of domestic demand. The slowdown in the region's export growth in 1996 helped to contain inflationary pressures, although it has exacerbated external imbalances in some cases. *Thailand* saw a significant slowdown in growth in 1996, largely as a result of a disappointing export performance; concerns about the large current account deficit as well as fragilities in the financial system have given rise to exchange market pressures in recent months. *Malaysia* appears to have weathered the slowdown in foreign demand relatively well; the possibility of a rebound in demand pressures in 1997, as well as concerns about asset-price inflation, warrant a cautious policy stance. In *Indonesia,* inflation has begun to diminish and growth has slowed moderately; the reliance on foreign saving will need to be contained through a stronger fiscal position. The *Philippines* saw a further strengthening of economic performance in 1996 and is expected to continue to reap the fruits of its intensified stabilization and reform efforts.

Like many other rapidly growing economies in Asia, *China* has taken measures to reduce overheating, and real GDP growth moderated to just under 10 percent in 1996 with retail price inflation slowing further to 6 percent, down from 22 percent in 1994. The soft landing has set the stage for continued expansion, but sustaining rapid growth with low inflation will require tangible progress in restructuring and raising efficiency in state enterprises (including by diversifying ownership), addressing weaknesses in the financial sector, and enhancing budget revenue. The strong external sector provides the opportunity to accelerate significantly the process of trade liberalization, which is critical for China to benefit fully from the recent and welcome implementation of current account convertibility.

India's quite strong expansion moderated somewhat in 1996, and inflation also slowed, as a result of both policy measures and a marked slowing of export growth in line with trends in the rest of Asia. In 1997, growth is expected to be sustained at a moderate pace, helped by the easing of monetary policy since mid-1996, but limited progress in reducing the fiscal deficit remains a risk for inflation and a constraint on growth. Further trade liberalization, reform of domestic product markets, and enterprise reform are needed to put India on a higher sustainable growth path. In *Pakistan,* which experienced severe balance of payments difficulties in late 1996, there is a continued need for strong stabilization measures and a wide range of structural reforms.

Growth in the Middle East and Europe region in 1996, at 4½ percent, was stronger than expected, partly as a result of economic reforms introduced in recent years, but also reflecting the higher-than-projected level of oil prices. For 1997, expected output growth has also been marked up. The temporary character of the recent tightness in oil markets underscores the continued need for structural reforms to lessen the dependence on oil revenues and enhance long-term growth prospects. Higher oil revenues and public expenditure restraint contributed to an improvement in economic conditions in *Saudi Arabia* last year, which is expected to continue in 1997. In *Egypt,* recent actions to consolidate macroeconomic stabilization and deepen the process of structural reform should strengthen growth further and promote the reorientation of the economy. *Jordan* is setting a prominent example in the region through its progress with stabilization and reform policies as underscored by declining internal and external imbalances, low inflation, and robust economic growth. In contrast, the economic outlook in *Turkey* remains subject to significant downside risks owing to lax fiscal and monetary policies and rampant inflation.

Africa's growth performance in 1996 was particularly encouraging: real GDP is estimated to have risen by about 5 percent, the strongest growth rate in 20 years, and nearly twice the average growth rate observed since the early 1970s. There are signs that the implementation of stronger macroeconomic and structural policies and improvements in governance have begun to produce higher growth in an increasing number of countries. For example, *Benin, Côte d'Ivoire, Senegal,* and other CFA franc zone countries are seeing continued recovery following the adjustment to a more realistic exchange rate since 1994 and the adoption of appropriate reforms. *Ghana, Kenya, Malawi,* and *Uganda* are also achieving growing success from allowing market forces a greater role in an environment of macroeconomic discipline. In *South Africa,* downward pressure on the exchange rate emerged in 1996, while growth, at 3 percent, was somewhat weaker than expected. Sustained reform and stabilization policies, in accordance with the authorities' announced strategy, would enhance future growth. Stronger oil revenues have improved the near-term outlook for *Nigeria* but medium-term prospects remain uncertain. In *Algeria,* which has shown impressive stabilization gains, public enterprise restructuring and privatization are needed to enhance the medium-term outlook, although the security situation greatly complicates the tasks of economic policy. *Morocco* and *Tunisia* also need to step up the pace of structural reform to further enhance their growth prospects. In both Algeria and Morocco, however, high unemployment, while making economic growth all the more important, also constitutes a difficult social setting for stronger reform efforts. Overall, Africa's recovery remains fragile and, in spite of recent successes, it is still a great challenge for Africa and the international community to reverse the decline in the region's living standards over the past quarter century.

Sharply contrasting economic trends have emerged during the past decade or so in the developing world. Some countries, such as Chile and Malaysia, have benefited considerably from strong macroeconomic policies and outward-oriented, market-based reforms, which are enabling them to integrate rapidly into the global economic and financial system. With their already relatively high per capita income levels, these countries are firmly on the road to joining the ranks of the advanced economies along with the newly industrialized economies. Other emerging market economies like China, Thailand, and Indonesia are similarly showing impressive achievements even though convergence will, of course, take longer given their lower levels of income. The economic success of all of these economies reflects the mutually reinforcing effects of sustained progress in many areas of economic policy. Their major policy challenge for the future is to continue to deregulate product, labor, and financial markets, while guarding against domestic and external imbalances and financial sector fragility. If these conditions are met, the benefits of economic reforms should continue to be reinforced by the forces of globalization.

A large part of the developing world, however, has not yet reaped the benefits of globalization: many countries have seen their living standards grow only modestly and have continued to lose ground in relation to the advanced economies. This is the case, for example, in the Indian subcontinent, and much of the Middle East and Latin America. Although there is no simple recipe for improving economic performance, there are strong indications that these countries have made inadequate progress in improving the policy environment. Policy shortcomings are in many cases not across the board but in some critical areas such as the failure to sustain macroeconomic stability, delays in liberalizing foreign trade, or inadequate progress in deregulating domestic product markets, establishing market-based institutions, and improving governance. Many of these countries are increasingly realizing the need for more comprehensive strategies and are beginning to see the fruits of their efforts as illustrated, for example, by the recent experiences of Argentina, Jordan, the Philippines, and Uganda.

Some of the poorest countries, especially in Africa, have fallen behind not only in relative but also in absolute terms. These countries are facing a general need to open their economies, reform government, establish financial markets, and maintain internal and external financial stability. To help them cope with the enormous challenges they are facing, the international community needs to provide well-targeted assistance and to lessen external debt burdens, which have risen to unsustainable levels in some cases. In addition to special low-cost lending facilities to support the adjustment efforts of the poorer countries, the IMF and the World Bank have launched a joint initiative, which will provide further assistance to help reduce the debt burden of heavily indebted poor countries that have followed sound policies but for whom traditional debt-relief mechanisms have failed to secure a sustainable external position.

Transition Countries

The transition countries also display sharp contrasts in performance. Those that are the most advanced in the transformation process are now reaping the rewards of comprehensive reform and stabilization policies pursued with determination over several years. These include Poland, the Baltic countries, Croatia, the Czech Republic, Hungary, the Slovak Republic, and Slovenia. Most of these are experiencing relatively robust economic growth, moderate inflation, and promising progress in their reintegration into the world economic and financial system. In fact, several are now experiencing some of the policy challenges that come with successful reforms, including the need to manage large capital inflows, contain the associated external current account deficits, and deal with other signs of overheating. These problems can best be addressed by pursuing strong stabilization policies and continued structural reforms, including privatization and financial market reforms.

Those that are less advanced in the transition are struggling with a number of policy challenges. Several have made good progress, and in Armenia, Azerbaijan, Georgia, Kazakstan, and the Kyrgyz Republic, inflation fell considerably and growth picked up in 1996 with prospects of continued expansion in 1997. In Russia and Ukraine, inflation has also fallen, but a clear turnaround in output has yet to emerge. All of these countries need to consolidate progress with stabilization, including by reforming tax systems, improving revenue performance, redefining public expenditure priorities, and dealing with the pervasive problems of arrears and nonpayment. Greater progress is also generally needed in structural reform, especially privatization, the establishment of market-based institutions, and the strengthening of property rights. Many of these countries also need to deal with fragile

banking systems. Measures to address Bulgaria's serious financial crisis are now being implemented in the context of a stabilization program supported by the IMF.

The reintegration of the transition countries into the global economy through trade and financial flows is critical for the success of the transformation process. At the same time, reintegration is bound to take time. Most progress has been made in the liberalization of trade and payments arrangements, which has been reflected in a marked reorientation of trade flows. However, there has been considerable variation across countries in the pace and extent of trade liberalization, and in the ability to take advantage of new market opportunities. Progress in financial market integration is necessarily less far advanced and will require the establishment of a stable, investor-friendly environment. Even so, foreign direct investment already plays an important role in the most advanced transition countries and private portfolio inflows have also increased sharply in a number of cases.

Financial market integration provides both challenges and benefits for the transition countries. Increased financial linkages with the world economy tend to amplify the effects of sound policies by promoting capital inflows and lower interest rates. These benefits can be misused: a country may borrow more merely to increase consumption. But if there is such a lack of self-discipline in policies, open financial markets will eventually impose their own discipline, possibly at considerable cost. This threat should help promote necessary policy changes. Capital inflows also allow the countries in transition to sustain the high levels of investment needed to revitalize industries and replace obsolete capital equipment. At the same time, it needs to be recognized that large-scale capital inflows can complicate macroeconomic management and that there is a need to guard against excessive external current account deficits and changes in investor sentiment. Because of such concerns, liberalization of capital account transactions is likely to be gradual and will depend on progress in other areas.

II

World Economic Situation and Short-Term Prospects

World output growth is expected to increase further, to about 4½ percent, in 1997 and to remain at this rate in 1998, projections that are slightly higher than those in the October 1996 *World Economic Outlook*. Relatively solid growth is expected in the United States and the United Kingdom, although in both countries there is a risk of inflationary pressures emerging. In Canada, where there is considerable economic slack, the expansion is expected to gain momentum. In Japan, recovery is expected to continue at a moderate pace. Declines in interest rates over the past two years and the return of exchange rates to more competitive levels are expected to support recovery in Germany, France, and elsewhere in continental Europe, although continuing fiscal consolidation and weaknesses in consumer and business confidence pose downside risks. Growth in the newly industrialized economies of Asia should also pick up slightly in 1998, as exports recover from the recent slowdown.

Activity is projected to strengthen among the developing countries of the Western Hemisphere, as the recovery from the 1995 Mexican crisis continues, while growth in Africa should remain close to its improved rate in 1996, reflecting further progress with stabilization and reform. Sustained growth at about 8 percent is expected in the developing countries of Asia, while recovery is likely to weaken slightly in the Middle East and Europe region, where conditions remain mixed. For the countries in transition, the growth outlook for 1997 is somewhat weaker than perceived last October, but recovery is still expected to broaden as an increasing number of countries reap the benefits of sustained stabilization and reform efforts.

Inflation remained subdued during 1996 in the advanced economies and declined further in the developing and transition countries, despite a sharp increase in oil prices. The IMF's index of commodity prices rose by about 5 percent in U.S. dollar terms in 1996, with an increase of about 20 percent in the price of crude petroleum partly offset by a 1 percent decline in the prices of nonfuel primary commodities (Chart 4).[2]

---

[2]Measured in SDRs, the IMF's index of commodity prices rose by nearly 10 percent in 1996, reflecting a 24 percent increase in crude petroleum and a 3 percent increase in nonfuel primary commodities. The smaller increases in terms of U.S. dollars reflect the appreciation of the U.S. currency against most other major currencies during 1996.

Chart 4. Commodity Price Indices[1]
(In U.S. dollars; 1990 = 100)

Petroleum prices increased during 1996 but are expected to be lower in 1997.

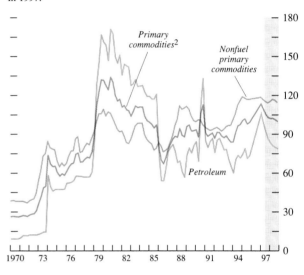

[1]Shaded area indicates IMF staff projections.
[2]The weights are 57.7 percent for the index of nonfuel primary commodities and 42.3 percent for the index of petroleum prices.

15

Chart 5. Major Industrial Countries: Output Gaps[1]
(Actual less potential, as a percent of potential)

Recently, greater differences have emerged in the relative cyclical positions of the major industrial countries.

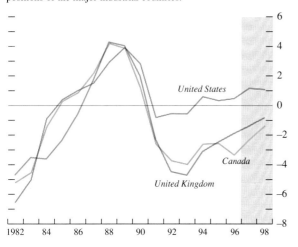

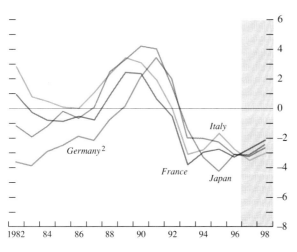

[1]Shaded areas indicate IMF staff projections. The gap estimates are subject to a significant margin of uncertainty. For a discussion of the approach to calculating potential output, see *World Economic Outlook,* October 1993, p. 101.

[2]Data through 1991 apply to west Germany only.

For petroleum prices, the low levels of stocks in the aftermath of the unusually harsh 1995–96 winter season in the Northern Hemisphere exacerbated the impact of increased demand for heating oil, particularly in the second half of 1996 (Box 3). After peaking in mid-January 1997, petroleum prices fell by about 23 percent by the end of February owing to stronger world oil production and improved inventory levels, and remained near this level through the end of March. With no other upward pressures evident, petroleum prices by the end of 1997 are expected to be about 20 percent lower than at the end of 1996.

Economic Activity, Inflation, and Policy Stances in Advanced Economies

Following the 1995 slowdown in most major industrial countries, a more uneven pattern of economic growth developed in 1996 (Chart 5). In the United States, hesitant growth during 1995 gave way to more solid expansion in 1996, in part reflecting the response to lower interest rates. In Japan, the economic recovery gained momentum in late 1995 and early 1996 and while erratic maintained a moderate underlying pace. In Canada, expansion picked up in the second half of 1996 after 18 months of weak growth; markedly lower interest rates and improved confidence are helping to spur the recovery. In the United Kingdom, growth during 1996 was significantly stronger than in the preceding year, raising concerns about the buildup of inflationary pressures. In contrast, 1996 brought renewed sluggishness in economic activity for continental Europe. In a number of countries, including Germany and France, weak consumer and business confidence persisted, industrial production stagnated, and unemployment continued to increase to new postwar records. By year-end, however, with lower interest rates and the return of exchange rates to more competitive levels, conditions for a pickup appeared to be in place. In other advanced economies, including Korea, Singapore, and Hong Kong, growth in 1996 slowed from above-trend rates, reflecting a weakening in exports and, in some cases, a tightening of monetary conditions.

Growth in the advanced economies is expected to firm to almost 3 percent in 1997, a projection that has changed little from the October 1996 *World Economic Outlook,* and to remain at this rate in 1998 (Table 2). Although growth is expected to improve in 1997 in Europe, its projected pace of 2½ percent will be insufficient to make any significant dent in the high level of unemployment.

Safeguarding price stability is critically important for ensuring continued economic expansion and requires careful monitoring of underlying price pressures. To illustrate the considerations involved, Table 3—introduced in the October 1996 *World Economic*

Box 3. Rising Petroleum Prices in 1996

After remaining fairly steady at about $17 a barrel during most of 1994–95, the price of petroleum rose to about $21 a barrel by April 1996, subsequently receded, but climbed higher by year-end.[1] Between 1995 and 1996, petroleum prices increased on average by about 20 percent. The spot price peaked in the second week of January 1997 at about $25 a barrel and declined by about $6 a barrel by the end of February reflecting the less severe winter weather—as compared with a year earlier—in Europe and North America, rising global oil production, particularly the resumption of oil export shipments by Iraq, and the strengthening of the U.S dollar.

The upward trend in petroleum prices in 1996 can be explained by the interaction between low inventories of crude oil and petroleum products and weather-related demand for heating oil. Inventories of crude petroleum and petroleum products are usually run down by the end of the Northern Hemisphere's winter season, with replenishment beginning in May and June before the summer maintenance period in the North Sea and well in advance of the next winter season. However, following the relatively severe 1995/96 winter, early stock replenishment was more limited than usual, and there was little additional accumulation until late October. As a result, stocks were lower at the beginning of the 1996/97 winter season than at the beginning of the 1995/96 winter season.

The low level of stocks was partly attributable to the reluctance to accumulate sizable inventories given the continued expectation of lower prices in the not too distant future. During most of 1995 and throughout 1996, the prices for distant deliveries of crude oil were at substantial discount to prices for near deliveries, reflecting expectations of increased supplies, mainly from Iraq but also from other sources. In September 1996, for example, futures prices for West Texas crude for September 1997 delivery were about $3.50 a barrel (about 15 percent) below prices for December 1996 contracts (see chart). This price pattern created little incentive to increase private stocks above the levels required to meet immediate consumption demand. Thus, each time unexpected adverse weather increased demand for heating oil, there was little supply buffer, and prices rose sharply. The Organization of Petroleum Exporting Countries (OPEC) appears to have had little to do with the rise in petroleum prices in 1996 and early 1997. In fact, trade journals have reported that a number of countries have been producing in excess of their OPEC quotas, with Venezuela and Nigeria exceeding the quotas regularly and by substantial margins.[2]

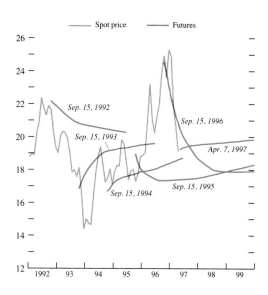

West Texas Oil Prices: Spot and Futures Contracts[1]
(In U.S. dollars a barrel)

[1]Spot prices are monthly averages.

Agreement was reached in December between Iraq and the United Nations on the implementation of an oil-for-food sales plan, which allows Iraqi oil exports of up to $1 billion in each 90-day period. World oil production is expected to be stronger—through continued exports from Iraq, and higher exports from the North Sea and several other sources—which should restore inventories to more normal levels, thereby loosening the supply constraint that helped to drive prices upward in 1996. Prices quoted on futures markets indicate that average 1997 prices will be about 5 percent lower than average 1996 prices, and prices at the end of the year will be about 20 percent lower than at the end of 1996. In fact, nearly all of the correction in oil prices reflected in recent futures contracts seemed to have occurred by mid-February, earlier than had been anticipated by the markets.

---

[1]The average petroleum price referred to is the simple mean of prices for U.K. Brent, Dubai, and West Texas crude petroleum.

[2]Crude oil production by OPEC members in the fourth quarter of 1996 is reported in trade journals to have been 26.3 million barrels a day (mbd) compared with 25.9 mbd in the third

quarter. December crude oil production by these countries is estimated at 26.6 mbd, including 0.85 mbd in Iraq. These levels of production compare with the total OPEC quotas of 25.033 mbd. See, for example, International Energy Agency, *Oil Market Report,* January 14, 1997.

Table 2. Advanced Economies: Real GDP, Consumer Prices, and Unemployment Rates
(Annual percent change and percent of labor force)

	Real GDP				Consumer Prices				Unemployment			
	1995	1996	1997	1998	1995	1996	1997	1998	1995	1996	1997	1998
Advanced economies	**2.5**	**2.5**	**2.9**	**2.9**	**2.6**	**2.4**	**2.5**	**2.5**	**7.3**	**7.3**	**7.2**	**7.0**
Major industrial countries	2.0	2.2	2.6	2.6	2.3	2.2	2.3	2.3	6.9	6.9	7.0	6.7
United States[1]	2.0	2.4	3.0	2.2	2.8	2.9	2.9	3.0	5.6	5.4	5.5	5.5
Japan	1.4	3.6	2.2	2.9	−0.1	0.1	1.3	1.2	3.1	3.3	3.1	3.0
Germany	1.9	1.4	2.3	3.0	1.8	1.5	1.8	2.0	9.4	10.3	11.3	10.6
France	2.2	1.3	2.4	3.0	1.8	2.0	1.6	1.8	11.6	12.4	12.8	12.3
Italy	3.0	0.7	1.0	2.4	5.4	3.9	2.4	2.0	12.0	12.1	12.3	12.0
United Kingdom[2]	2.5	2.1	3.3	2.8	2.8	2.9	2.6	2.5	8.2	7.5	6.2	6.0
Canada	2.3	1.5	3.5	3.4	2.2	1.7	1.7	1.8	9.5	9.7	9.4	8.8
Other advanced economies	4.2	3.7	3.8	4.1	3.7	3.3	3.1	3.0	8.5	8.4	8.2	7.9
Spain	2.8	2.2	2.8	3.4	4.7	3.5	2.5	2.3	22.9	22.1	21.4	20.7
Netherlands	2.1	2.7	3.0	2.9	2.0	2.1	2.7	2.5	8.3	7.6	7.1	6.3
Belgium	1.9	1.4	2.3	2.2	1.5	2.1	2.0	2.0	12.9	12.6	12.8	12.6
Sweden	3.6	1.1	2.0	2.5	2.5	0.5	2.3	2.2	7.7	8.1	7.2	6.7
Austria	1.8	1.1	1.7	2.8	2.2	1.9	1.9	1.9	4.6	4.7	4.8	4.8
Denmark	2.7	2.4	2.7	2.5	2.1	2.1	2.5	2.7	10.3	8.8	8.2	8.1
Finland	4.5	3.2	4.4	3.4	1.0	0.6	1.3	1.6	17.2	16.3	15.1	14.0
Greece	2.0	2.6	3.0	3.1	9.3	8.5	6.9	6.0	10.0	9.8	9.6	9.3
Portugal	2.3	3.2	3.3	3.5	4.1	3.1	2.5	2.3	7.2	7.3	7.4	7.5
Ireland	10.3	7.0	6.3	5.6	2.5	1.6	2.2	2.1	13.4	12.4	11.6	11.0
Luxembourg	3.5	3.7	3.7	3.5	1.9	1.8	2.0	2.0	2.8	2.8	2.8	2.8
Switzerland	0.1	−0.7	0.7	2.3	1.8	0.8	1.0	1.5	4.2	4.7	5.5	5.5
Norway	3.3	4.8	4.2	3.2	2.5	1.3	2.5	2.5	4.9	4.8	4.0	3.8
Israel	7.1	4.4	4.8	4.8	10.0	11.3	7.9	6.6	6.3	6.7	6.8	6.5
Iceland	2.1	5.5	3.0	2.4	1.7	2.3	2.8	2.5	5.0	4.3	4.1	4.0
Korea	8.9	7.1	5.6	6.3	4.5	5.0	4.4	4.1	2.0	2.1	2.2	2.2
Australia[3]	3.2	4.0	3.2	3.7	2.7	2.7	2.1	2.8	8.5	8.6	8.4	8.0
Taiwan Province of China	6.0	5.6	6.0	6.3	3.7	3.1	3.4	3.3	1.8	2.6	2.5	2.4
Hong Kong	4.8	4.5	5.0	5.0	9.0	6.0	7.1	6.5	3.2	2.9	2.9	2.8
Singapore	8.8	7.0	6.6	6.1	1.7	1.4	1.8	2.0	2.7	3.0	3.0	3.0
New Zealand[3]	3.4	2.7	3.7	3.0	2.4	2.4	1.9	1.6	6.3	6.2	6.0	5.9
Memorandum												
European Union	2.5	1.6	2.4	2.9	3.0	2.5	2.2	2.1	11.2	11.3	11.3	10.8

[1]The projections for unemployment have been adjusted to reflect the new survey techniques adopted by the U.S. Bureau of Labor Statistics in January 1994.

[2]Consumer prices are based on the retail price index excluding mortgage interest.

[3]Consumer prices excluding interest rate components; for Australia also excluding other volatile items.

Outlook, and updated to reflect recent changes—seeks to answer a number of questions about various signs of inflationary pressure in each of the major industrial countries. In general, policymakers' credible commitment to reasonable price stability has played an important role in taming inflation and will remain essential to keeping inflation down. In the United States and the United Kingdom, where resource use is high, inflation remains subdued, although some recent evidence suggests a risk of price pressures in both countries. Relatively large output gaps arising from delayed or weak recoveries in Canada, France, Germany, Italy, and Japan indicate that there is little risk of a resurgence of inflation as growth firms in the year ahead.

Similarly, in a number of other advanced economies where signs of recovery have recently emerged, including Austria, Belgium, Finland, and Sweden, con-siderable slack can also be expected to dampen inflationary pressures. Moderating economic growth in 1996 in Australia and New Zealand has allayed earlier concerns about the possibility of overheating. The highest inflation rates in the advanced economies are in Greece, Hong Kong, and Israel, each of which is expected to see inflation of 7–8 percent over the next year. Overall, therefore, inflation remains subdued in most of the advanced economies and, taking into account recent and projected movements in primary commodity prices, including recent declines in petroleum prices, is expected to remain at about 2½ percent through 1998.

The overall growth and inflation projections mask considerable differences in the pace and phase of, and in the risks to, economic expansion among the advanced economies. Growth in 1997 is expected to

Table 3. Major Industrial Countries: Questions About Inflationary Pressures[1]

(Italics indicate a change since the October 1996 World Economic Outlook *)*

	Canada	France	Germany	Italy	Japan	United Kingdom	United States
1. Is inflation outside a range the country's authorities consider to be consistent with price stability?	No	No	No	*No*	No	Slightly above	No
2. Does the IMF forecast that inflation will pick up in 1997?	Only slightly	No	*Only slightly and in part due to increases in administered prices*	No	Yes, but increase mainly reflecting higher consumption taxes	No (excluding mortgage interest)	Only slightly
3. Do private forecasters expect inflation to pick up in 1997? (*Consensus Forecasts*, Consensus Economics, Inc.)	Only slightly	No	Only slightly	No	Yes	Only slightly (headline rate)	Only slightly
4. Is there concern about money growth?	No	No	No	No	No	Yes	No
5. Has the output gap been closing?	*Yes*	No	No	No	Yes, but remains relatively large	Yes	Yes
6. Is excess capacity being taken up too quickly?	No	No	No	No ·	No	*Perhaps*	Little, if any, remaining slack?
7. Are labor market conditions tight?	No	No	No	No	No	*Becoming so*	Yes
8. Do yield curves or changes in market interest rates suggest a rise in inflation expectations?	No[2]	No	No	No	No[2]	No	No
9. Is exchange rate weakness stimulating inflation?	No	*Only slightly*	*Only slightly*	No	*Yes, but prospective inflation still low*	No	No
10. Do external accounts show signs of overheating?	No	No	No	No	No	No	*Possibly*
11. Have equity prices risen rapidly?	*Somewhat*	*Yes*	*Yes*	*Yes*	No	Yes, through 1996	Yes
12. Have real estate prices recently been rising rapidly?	No	No	No	No	No	Recovering after long stagnation	No

[1]This table is intended to provide a broad cross-country survey of inflationary pressures and reflects IMF staff judgments. For individual countries, various indicators will differ in the extent to which they contribute to the inflationary process.

[2]Yield curve has steepened but this appears unlikely to reflect increased inflation expectations.

edge somewhat above potential in the United States and the United Kingdom, two countries that are into their fifth or sixth year of economic expansion. Although inflation is expected to remain relatively subdued in both countries, the high level of resource use implies a growing risk of overheating.

In the *United States,* the economy continued to operate near capacity during 1996, with further improvements in business and consumer confidence. The unemployment rate fell to 5¼ percent in midyear and subsequently remained close to that level, below most estimates of the natural rate. Despite high resource use, the core rate of inflation has remained subdued at just above 2½ percent;[3] there has, however, been some acceleration of wages. Following a 3 percent rate of expansion in 1997, growth is expected to moderate to

[3]Some recent studies have drawn attention to the possibility that inflation is overestimated by official price data (Box 4).

19

Box 4. United States: Sources and Implications of Bias in the Consumer Price Index

Changes in the consumer price index (CPI) provide the most commonly used measure of inflation in all countries. In a recent study, the U.S. Advisory Commission to Study the Consumer Price Index estimated that the U.S. CPI overstated inflation by 1.1 percentage points in 1996, and by slightly more in each of the previous twenty years.[1] Thus, whereas the official 1996 rate of inflation was 2.9 percent, the true rate of inflation may have been in the neighborhood of 1.8 percent. This upward bias arises because the CPI methodology does not adequately capture shifts in consumer purchases when relative prices move, or the effects of changes in quality, or the introduction of new products, or the increasing number of discount stores. While some experts have disputed that the upward bias is as large as suggested by the Commission, there is a growing consensus that there may be significant bias.

Upward bias in the official inflation rate has important implications. First, real wage growth may have been significantly higher over the past two decades than suggested by official data, which indicate that they have hardly grown at all.[2] Second, in the area of fiscal policy, upward bias has considerable budgetary cost: expenditures indexed to the CPI rise more than needed to offset inflation; and tax brackets are overadjusted by the CPI, reducing tax

Sources of Bias in the U.S. Consumer Price Index, 1996

Sources of Bias	Percentage Points
Quality change/new product bias	0.6
Substitution bias	0.4
Outlet substitution bias	0.1
Total	**1.1**
(Plausible range)	(0.8–1.6)

revenues. Recent estimates indicate that if the current inflation bias continues for the next ten years, the federal government deficit will increase on this account alone by $140 billion by the end of the period, and more than $650 billion will be added to the U.S. national debt.

The Commission's report identified and quantified three sources of bias, all of which arise because of limitations in the methodology of how the CPI is calculated (*see table*).

(1) *Quality change and new product bias,* the largest source of bias, arises because the CPI does not adequately take into account improvements in the quality of goods and services and the introduction of new products. If changes in quality are not taken into account, changes in the CPI will not show true inflation, because they will partly reflect changes in the characteristics of products. New products need to be incorporated into the CPI on a timely basis so that the early declines in price that are a normal part of the product life cycle are captured.

(2) *Substitution bias* occurs because the CPI assumes that consumers purchase a constant mix (in terms of quantities) of various goods and services despite changes in relative prices. In actuality, if the price of one good rises relative to that of another good, consumers will tend to sub-

---

[1] *Toward a More Accurate Measure of the Cost of Living,* Final Report to the Senate Finance Committee from the Advisory Commission to Study the Consumer Price Index, December 4, 1996. The report notes that the 1.1 percentage point estimate of bias falls within a plausible range of 0.8 to 1.6 percentage points.

[2] Preliminary evidence suggests that the GDP deflator also suffers from upward bias implying that real GDP growth and productivity may have been understated over the last two decades. The magnitude of this bias, however, remains to be fully documented.

---

about the rate of potential in 1998, and inflation to remain close to 3 percent. A pickup in inflation and the need for a stronger tightening of monetary policy than is assumed remain a risk to the forecast. The federal budget deficit declined to 1½ percent in fiscal year 1996, the lowest ratio to GDP since 1974, reflecting expenditure restraint as well as the strong cyclical position of the economy (Table 4). The Federal Reserve left the target federal funds rate unchanged at 5¼ percent between February 1996 and late March 1997, but then increased it by 25 basis points to restrain persistently strong demand and avert the risk of inflationary pressure. In late January 1997, for the first time, the U.S. Treasury issued inflation-indexed securities, auctioning just over $7 billion of such securities with a ten-year maturity, at a real yield of 3½ percent. The differential with respect to the yield on nonindexed bonds of comparable maturity provides a rough indication of the market's inflation expectations over the

medium term.[4] At the time of the auction, this differential was about 3¼ percent.

Growth in the *United Kingdom,* having moderated during 1995, strengthened to rates close to or above potential during 1996 as private consumption rebounded. By early 1997, unemployment had fallen to 6¼ percent, one of the lowest rates in Europe, although in the current cyclical upswing unemployment has fallen significantly more than employment has risen, partly owing to changes in the unemployment benefit system. The rate of inflation remained above its 2½ percent target throughout 1996, rising above 3 percent temporarily in the final quarter. Increasing tightness in the labor market (reflected in an acceleration of labor earnings to 5 percent annual growth in early 1997), a significant pickup in house prices, and

---

[4] See October 1996, *World Economic Outlook,* pp. 118–19.

stitute away from the relatively higher priced good. Because the weights of goods in the CPI are adjusted infrequently (revisions occur about once every ten years), substitution is not taken into account, creating an upward bias.

(3) *Outlet substitution bias* occurs because the CPI does not adequately take into account the extent to which new discount-type stores have offered lower prices and enticed consumers away from the more traditional outlets that tend to be more fully represented in the CPI basket.

To eliminate the various biases, the Commission recommends replacing the method used in calculating the CPI with one that more accurately takes into account changing spending patterns.[3] Other changes recommended include adopting new procedures for annual updates of weights and revisions to historical data; changing the price data and methods of collection; and establishing a committee of outside experts to review and advise on statistical issues.

The Commission's conclusions have been subject to some criticism. There is widespread agreement among economists that an upward bias in the CPI exists, but its magnitude remains controversial. The largest uncertainties surround the magnitudes of quality and new product bias. Measuring quality improvements is particularly difficult because direct quantitative evidence is scarce and no new substantive information on this issue was provided in the report. Some critics have noted that the report does not take into account the fact that for some goods and services quality has deteriorated.

Although the debate about upward bias in the CPI has been most active in the United States, the findings of the

Commission's study are relevant more generally, as many countries use methodologies having much in common with that used in the United States. Analyses of the Canadian CPI suggest that there may be an upward bias in the range of ½–1 percentage point, somewhat lower than in the United States, reflecting in part the more frequent updating in Canada of the weights of the goods and services in the CPI market basket.[4] A study on the United Kingdom's retail price index (RPI) suggests a plausible range of bias of about 0.35–0.8 percentage point, although further work is under way to assess whether the bias may be larger.[5] More generally, the magnitude of bias in other countries depends on, among other factors, the frequency with which the CPI weights and items sampled are updated; the extent to which new and improved products are brought to market; the formula used in estimation; and the extent to which quality adjustments are made. For example, countries such as Norway, Sweden, and the United Kingdom, where weights are updated annually, are likely to be less susceptible to substitution bias. Although most industrial countries—including the United States—make some attempt to allow for quality changes, they are not successful in eliminating this form of bias entirely. In most of the developing and transition countries, however, no quality adjustments are made, suggesting that this form of bias may be important, particularly when newly opened markets increase the variety and quality of goods and services available to the consumer.

---

[3]This would entail switching from the currently used base-weighted price index to a chain-superlative formula. By taking into account both current and previous purchasing patterns, the latter method would substantially eliminate substitution bias.

[4]See, for example, A. Crawford, "Measurement Bias in the Canadian CPI," Technical Report No. 64 (Ottawa: Bank of Canada, 1993). This study suggests that the bias is not more than 0.5 percentage point.

[5]Alastair Cunningham, "The Measurement Bias in Price Indices: An Application to the U.K.'s RPI," Bank of England Working Paper No. 47 (March 1996).

rapid monetary expansion may be viewed as early warning signals that inflationary pressures are building. The 1997 growth projection has been revised up to 3¼ percent, reflecting the renewed strength in private consumption, and an expected pickup in investment spending. The threat posed to the United Kingdom's inflation target by the growing momentum in the economy prompted the authorities in October 1996 to raise the minimum lending rate by 25 basis points to 6 percent. The appreciation of sterling since August should also have a dampening effect on demand and price pressures. Fiscal slippages during 1995–96, accounted for mainly by revenue shortfalls, slowed the pace of fiscal consolidation, and the budget presented in November tightened fiscal policy only slightly further in the near term. Thus, during 1996 the planned path of deficit reduction toward medium-term balance was put back a year. The general government deficit for 1997 is projected to be close to 3 percent.

The pace of economic expansion in *Australia* moderated over the course of 1996 as consumption spending slowed. An improvement in the outlook for inflation provided room for the authorities to lower interest rates in the latter part of 1996, which should help sustain growth through 1997. In *New Zealand,* economic expansion slowed to about 2¾ percent in 1996, the slowest growth in four years but a welcome development as it reduced the risk of overheating. Economic activity is expected to strengthen in 1997 owing to a pickup in consumption, reflecting recent and planned future tax cuts.

In contrast to the countries that are in advanced stages of their current expansions, in *Japan* recovery did not get under way in earnest until late 1995. Since then growth has fluctuated, around a moderate underlying pace. Domestic demand growth has remained modest, with increases in business fixed investment largely offset by small declines in private consumption

Table 4. Major Industrial Countries: General Government Fiscal Balances and Debt[1]

(In percent of GDP)

	1980–90	1991	1992	1993	1994	1995	1996	1997	1998	2000	2002
Major industrial countries											
Actual balance	−2.9	−2.7	−3.8	−4.3	−3.5	−3.4	−3.0	−2.3	−2.1	−1.5	−1.4
Output gap	—	0.7	−0.2	−1.7	−1.3	−1.4	−1.4	−1.0	−0.7	−0.1	0.3
Structural balance	−2.8	−3.1	−3.5	−3.3	−2.7	−2.6	−2.2	−1.6	−1.6	−1.4	−1.6
United States											
Actual balance	−2.6	−3.3	−4.4	−3.6	−2.3	−2.0	−1.4	−1.5	−1.3	−1.1	−1.1
Output gap	−0.4	−0.8	−0.5	−0.5	0.6	0.4	0.5	1.2	1.1	0.9	0.7
Structural balance	−2.4	−3.1	−4.1	−3.4	−2.5	−2.1	−1.6	−1.9	−1.7	−1.5	−1.3
Net debt	35.4	46.7	50.0	52.1	52.9	53.9	53.8	53.3	52.8	51.5	50.0
Gross debt	49.4	62.1	64.6	66.4	66.0	66.2	67.0	66.5	65.8	64.1	62.3
Japan											
Actual balance	−1.1	2.9	1.5	−1.6	−2.3	−3.7	−4.6	−2.9	−2.7	−2.2	−3.1
Output gap	0.3	4.1	1.5	−1.4	−3.3	−4.2	−3.1	−3.2	−2.6	−1.1	—
Structural balance	−1.2	1.5	0.9	−1.1	−1.1	−2.0	−3.3	−1.7	−1.6	−1.8	−3.1
Net debt	20.9	4.8	4.2	5.2	8.0	11.8	16.0	18.5	20.6	23.9	28.1
Gross debt	66.5	66.7	70.0	75.1	82.4	90.1	94.9	98.8	101.2	106.4	112.7
Memorandum											
Actual balance excluding social security	−4.0	−0.7	−2.0	−4.8	−5.4	−6.5	−7.3	−5.5	−4.9	−5.4	−5.8
Structural balance excluding social security	−4.1	−2.0	−2.5	−4.3	−4.3	−5.1	−6.3	−4.5	−4.1	−5.0	−5.7
Germany[2]											
Actual balance	−2.1	−3.3	−2.8	−3.5	−2.4	−3.5	−3.8	−3.3	−2.9	−1.8	−1.3
Output gap	−1.3	3.4	2.0	−2.0	−2.0	−2.2	−3.1	−3.1	−2.4	−0.7	—
Structural balance	−1.5	−5.2	−3.8	−2.3	−1.2	−2.2	−1.8	−1.1	−1.2	−1.3	−1.3
Net debt	21.0	21.4	27.7	35.4	40.7	49.1	51.5	53.0	53.5	52.9	51.4
Gross debt	40.1	41.1	44.1	48.2	50.4	58.1	60.3	61.5	61.6	60.2	58.2
France											
Actual balance	−1.9	−2.0	−4.0	−5.8	−5.8	−5.0	−4.1	−3.3	−3.4	−2.7	−2.0
Output gap	0.6	0.6	−0.5	−3.8	−3.0	−2.7	−3.3	−2.7	−2.1	−0.9	0.3
Structural balance	−2.2	−2.4	−3.5	−3.3	−3.7	−3.2	−1.9	−1.4	−1.8	−2.0	−2.1
Net debt[3]	22.0	27.1	30.2	34.4	40.2	43.5	46.9	48.4	49.5	50.6	50.2
Gross debt	29.6	35.8	39.7	45.7	48.6	52.9	56.3	57.8	58.9	60.0	59.6
Italy[4]											
Actual balance	−10.9	−10.2	−9.5	−9.6	−9.0	−7.1	−6.8	−3.3	−4.1	−3.6	−2.9
Output gap	2.6	1.9	—	−3.1	−2.8	−1.7	−2.7	−3.5	−3.0	−1.5	−0.2
Structural balance	−12.0	−11.2	−9.6	−8.1	−7.6	−6.2	−5.4	−1.7	−2.7	−2.9	−2.8
Net debt	73.4	96.3	103.0	111.8	117.3	116.8	116.4	115.0	113.0	108.9	102.0
Gross debt	79.0	101.4	108.5	119.3	125.5	124.9	123.0	121.5	119.3	115.0	107.8
United Kingdom											
Actual balance	−2.0	−2.5	−6.3	−7.8	−6.8	−5.6	−4.4	−3.1	−2.1	−0.4	0.1
Output gap	−0.6	−2.3	−4.5	−4.7	−3.1	−2.5	−1.9	−1.4	−0.8	−0.7	—
Structural balance	−1.3	−2.7	−3.8	−4.3	−3.9	−3.6	−2.9	−2.1	−1.5	0.2	0.3
Net debt	40.3	26.7	28.1	32.5	37.7	40.9	43.9	45.7	43.1	41.3	37.2
Gross debt	48.0	33.6	34.8	40.4	46.0	47.3	49.3	49.4	49.6	47.8	43.7
Canada											
Actual balance	−4.5	−6.6	−7.4	−7.3	−5.3	−4.1	−1.8	−0.3	0.3	1.4	2.1
Output gap	0.1	−2.6	−3.7	−4.0	−2.6	−2.6	−3.3	−2.3	−1.4	−0.1	0.3
Structural balance	−4.4	−4.9	−4.8	−4.6	−3.6	−2.7	—	0.9	1.0	1.4	1.9
Net debt	30.1	49.7	56.9	61.9	64.7	67.5	68.7	66.3	62.9	55.3	47.1
Gross debt	60.2	79.4	86.9	92.5	94.6	98.3	99.9	96.5	91.7	81.5	70.9

Note: The budget projections are based on information available through March 1997. The specific assumptions for each country are set out in Box 2. See also notes to Chart 3.

[1]The output gap is actual less potential output, as a percent of potential output. Structural balances are expressed as a percent of potential output. The structural budget balance is the budgetary position that would be observed if the level of actual output coincided with potential output. Changes in the structural budget balance consequently include effects of temporary fiscal measures, the impact of fluctuations in interest rates and debt-service costs, and other noncyclical fluctuations in the budget balance. The computations of structural budget balances are based on IMF staff estimates of potential GDP and revenue and expenditure elasticities (see the October 1993 *World Economic Outlook,* Annex I). Net debt is defined as gross debt less financial assets, which include assets held by the social security insurance system. Estimates of the output gap and of the structural budget balance are subject to significant margins of uncertainty.

[2]Data before 1990 refer to west Germany. For net debt, the first column refers to 1986–90. Beginning in 1995, the debt and debt-service obligations of the Treuhandanstalt (and of various other agencies) were taken over by the general government. This debt is equivalent to 8 percent of GDP and the associated debt service to ½ of 1 percent of GDP.

[3]Figure for 1980–90 is average of 1983–90.

[4]Data from 1996 onward reflect a new accounting methodology.

and the initial effects of an unwinding of the earlier surge in public investment. With the official discount rate at ½ of 1 percent since September 1995, monetary policy has been set so as to provide important stimulus to economic recovery (Chart 6). With fiscal policy also supporting economic activity, the general government deficit (excluding social security) reached 7¼ percent of GDP in 1996, of which 6¼ percentage points were structural. The structural deficit is expected to decline to about 4½ percent of GDP in 1997 as a result of further reductions in public investment expenditures, the unwinding of temporary cuts in income taxes, and a rise in the consumption tax. The recovery in labor earnings and rising net exports are expected to sustain growth, outweighing the effects of the withdrawal of fiscal stimulus. The 1997 growth projection for Japan has been revised down slightly to 2¼ percent partly to reflect the possible adverse effects of recent stock market weakness and lower confidence. The inflation rate is expected to rise slightly in 1997 albeit largely due to the increase in the consumption tax.

In *Canada,* following a reasonably strong upswing in 1993–94, the economy slowed considerably in 1995. A revival of activity emerged in the second half of 1996, but growth for the year amounted to only 1½ percent. Domestic demand, particularly increases in residential construction and investment in machinery and equipment, has fueled the recent pickup. Unemployment has remained in the 9½–10 percent range for most of the period since late 1994; and core inflation eased further to about 1½ percent last year, within the lower half of the official target range of 1 to 3 percent. In this context of low inflation, a large output gap, and upward pressure on the Canadian dollar, the Bank of Canada lowered short-term interest rates by close to 3 percentage points during 1996, thereby maintaining an accommodative monetary policy stance. This easing of monetary conditions, the return of confidence, and continued progress in reducing the fiscal deficit helped lower long-term interest rates. The strength of fundamentals in Canada bodes well for continuing recovery in 1997–98, with inflation remaining within the target range.

In contrast with the sustained growth in countries such as the United States and the United Kingdom, the continuing moderate upturn in Japan, and the promising recovery in Canada, growth in continental Europe has been more modest and prospects remain uncertain. Nevertheless, a number of improvements that have occurred in the economic environment are expected to contribute to a strengthening of activity in 1997. The mix of economic policies has shifted since 1995 in a direction that is more conducive to sustainable growth in the medium term. A high degree of price stability and continued efforts at fiscal consolidation have allowed a more accommodative stance of monetary policy, and monetary conditions, broadly defined to in-

Chart 6. Three Major Industrial Countries: Policy-Related Interest Rates and Ten-Year Government Bond Yields[1]
(In percent a year)

Policy-related interest rates in Japan and Germany remain low.

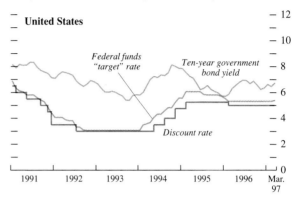
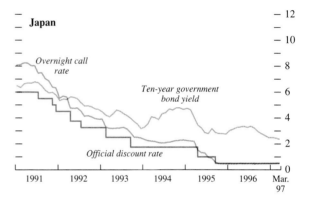
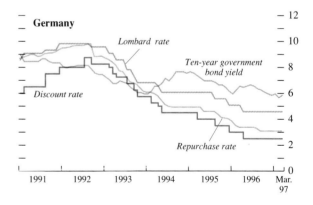

[1]The U.S. federal funds "target" rate, Japanese overnight call rate, German repurchase rate, and all ten-year government bond yields are monthly averages. All other series are end of month.

Chart 7. Major Industrial Countries: Monetary Conditions Indices[1]

An easing of monetary conditions—broadly defined to take account of changes in both interest rates and exchange rates—in Germany and France is expected to support a resumption of growth.

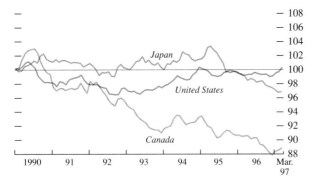

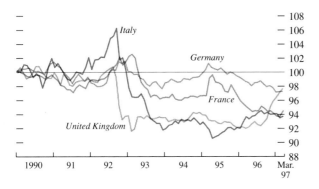

[1]For each country, the index is defined as a weighted average of the percentage point change in the real short-term interest rate and the percentage change in the real effective exchange rate from a base period (January 1990). Relative weights of 3 to 1 are used for Canada, France, Italy, and the United Kingdom, 4 to 1 for Germany, and 10 to 1 for Japan and the United States. The weights are intended to represent the relative impacts of interest rates and exchange rates on aggregate demand; they should be regarded as indicative rather than precise estimates. For instance, a 3-to-1 ratio indicates that a 1 percentage point change in the real short-term interest rate has about the same effect on aggregate demand over time as a 3 percent change in the real effective exchange rate. Movements in the index are thus equivalent to percentage point changes in the real interest rates. The lag with which a change in the index may be expected to affect aggregate demand depends on the extent to which the change stems from a change in the interest rate or the exchange rate, and varies depending on the cyclical position; the lag also differs across countries. No meaning is to be attached to the absolute value of the index; rather, the index is intended to show the degree of tightening or easing in monetary conditions from the (arbitrarily chosen) base period. Small changes in the relative weights may affect the value of the index but not the qualitative picture.

clude the effects of exchange rate changes, have eased considerably since early 1995, particularly in France (Chart 7). Short-term interest rates in Germany were cut by 75 basis points during 1996, following larger reductions in each of the three preceding years, and a number of other European countries lowered their rates in tandem. Commitment to fiscal consolidation has also contributed to declines in long-term interest rates, and exchange rates vis-à-vis key non-ERM currencies have returned to more competitive levels from their positions of early 1995, providing stimulus to net exports and the opportunity to take advantage of solid world demand.

With this favorable climate, there would seem to be some upside potential to the 1997 European growth projection of 2½ percent, but this conjecture is balanced by a number of considerations working in the opposite direction. A convincing revival of domestic demand remains to be seen particularly in Germany, France, and Italy (Chart 8). Record levels of unemployment have eroded consumer confidence and weakened consumer spending (Chart 9). Large margins of slack may mean that sluggishness in business investment will continue for some time to come. Moreover, further efforts to achieve fiscal consolidation and meet the 3 percent Maastricht reference value for budget deficits are likely to have a dampening effect on domestic demand (Table 5).[5] At the same time, however, failure to reach the deficit target could heighten uncertainty about EMU and further undermine business and consumer confidence. In addition to macroeconomic factors, structural rigidities in European labor markets have also been contributing to the lack of dynamism, creating a vicious circle of prolonged underutilization of resources, erosion of human capital, and rising levels of already high structural unemployment. Structural unemployment, which will not decline through economic recovery alone, probably accounts for close to three-quarters of the 11¼ percent unemployment rate in Europe.

Indicators of economic activity in *Germany* remain mixed. Real GDP rebounded quite strongly in the second and third quarters of 1996 but growth slowed to a virtual halt in the fourth quarter. The export sector has been the main source of strength, and business confidence has rebounded; but domestic demand growth has remained modest, consumer confidence has yet to recover, and unemployment rose to a new seasonally adjusted peak of 11¼ percent in January before falling slightly in February. Inflation remains subdued, at about 1½ percent, with wage settlements in 1996 gen-

---

[5]The reductions in fiscal deficits in 1997 shown in Tables 4 and 5 exaggerate the projected fiscal adjustment in a number of cases, particularly France and Italy, because they include accounting measures with no impact on underlying fiscal positions and one-off measures whose reversal is expected to increase deficits subsequently.

erally below 2 percent, and settlements thus far in 1997 of about 1 percent.

In contrast with the easing of monetary conditions referred to above, the stance of fiscal policy in Germany is being tightened in 1997, correcting the slippages that occurred in 1995 and making up for the lack of progress in 1996. From a general government deficit of about 4 percent of GDP in 1996, the fiscal program for 1997 aims to reduce the budget deficit to below 3 percent of GDP to meet the Maastricht criteria, although fully achieving this objective may be difficult without additional policy action. With monetary conditions supportive of moderate recovery, growth of 2¼ percent is projected for 1997, with continuing strong expansion of exports helping to revive investment in machinery and equipment. Consumption is expected to pick up later in the year. Reflecting the considerable output gap, inflation is projected to remain subdued. Weaker-than-expected investment and consumption could, however, delay prospects for recovery.

In *France,* economic activity in 1996 as a whole remained sluggish, with real GDP increasing by about 1¼ percent. Despite weak income growth and very low consumer confidence, consumer spending as well as net exports contributed positively to growth. Investment, however, remained flat, and destocking continued to be a drag on growth. Unemployment reached a new peak of 12¾ percent in early 1997. Inflation remained firmly under control. The fiscal deficit was held to the government's 1996 target of 4 percent of GDP, following the adoption of a supplementary budget in November. Fiscal plans for 1997 entail keeping central government spending unchanged in nominal terms and strict limits on social security expenditure; but additional measures appear necessary to bring the deficit below 3 percent of GDP on a durable basis. Since the Deutsche Bundesbank last lowered short-term interest rates in August, the Bank of France has reduced its operating rates by between 15 and 25 basis points; while the franc has remained stable against the deutsche mark, it has depreciated against the dollar and in effective terms.

Growth in 1997 is expected to strengthen to almost 2½ percent, as the underlying expansion of private consumption is maintained and exports continue to expand. Unemployment is expected to exceed 13 percent by midyear, and inflationary pressures are likely to remain negligible. Though growth could be stronger if exchange rates remain near their levels in early 1997, there is at least an equal risk that rising unemployment could undermine consumption and that sluggishness in European growth could hinder the expansion of exports.

In *Italy,* activity stagnated in 1996, reflecting in part the strengthening of the lira since mid-1995 and the weakness of key export markets in Europe. Industrial production declined during the year, and unemploy-

Chart 8. Selected European Countries: Real Total Domestic Demand
(Percent change from four quarters earlier)

A convincing revival of domestic demand remains to be seen in continental Europe.

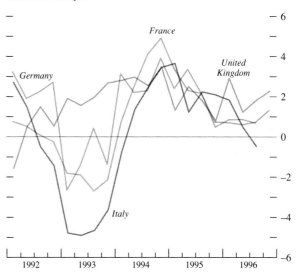

Chart 9. European Union and the United States: Indicators of Consumer Confidence[1]

Consumer confidence remains particularly weak in the countries of the European Union.

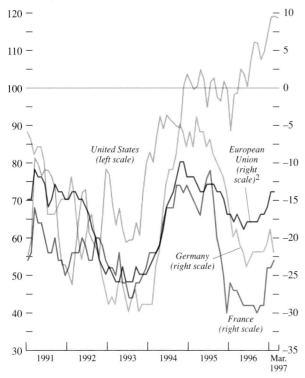

United States (left scale)

European Union (right scale)[2]

Germany (right scale)

France (right scale)

Sources: For the United States, the Conference Board; and the European Commission.

[1]Indicators are not comparable across countries.

[2]Percent of respondents expecting an improvement in their situation minus percent expecting a deterioration.

ment was relatively stable at about 12 percent. Inflation has been the main bright spot of recent performance, falling from 6 percent in November 1995 (on a 12-month basis) to 2¼ percent in March 1997. Modest growth of 1 percent is expected in 1997. Apart from the direct effects of fiscal tightening, growth remains dampened by the lagged effects of the lira's appreciation and depressed private sector demand. Inflation is expected to remain subdued and in line with the official target for the year of 2½ percent.

The substantial headway made in reducing Italy's fiscal imbalances in 1992–95 stalled in 1996, owing to inadequate expenditure control as well as weak growth. Despite the corrective measures taken at midyear, the general government deficit, at 6¾ percent of GDP (inclusive of all accounting revisions), exceeded the official target by a considerable margin. For 1997, the government's objective of early EMU participation will require a comparatively large fiscal correction, for which additional measures were recently taken, along with the announcement of a forthcoming review of pension and welfare spending. The additional package should serve to reduce the deficit to close to the Maastricht reference value in 1997. However, the considerable reliance in 1997 on one-off measures would—in the absence of additional measures—lead to a rebound of the deficit in subsequent years. Hence it is important that the forthcoming review of social transfers leads to structural cost-saving measures to ensure the sustainability of adjustment in 1998 and the medium term. Increased market confidence in the authorities' commitment to reduce the budget deficit and bring down inflation has contributed to a marked reduction in long-term interest rates over the past two years. The performance of the lira in the ERM, which it rejoined in November 1996, and continued subdued inflation allowed a reduction of 75 basis points in official interest rates in late January 1997, following a similar reduction in October 1996.

Evidence of economic recovery is apparent in a number of the smaller economies of Europe. In *Sweden,* economic activity picked up around the middle of last year, primarily fueled by the external sector and investment spending. Monetary policy was eased significantly during 1996 with cuts in the repurchase rate. Growth is expected to strengthen further in 1997. A pickup in exports has also contributed to tentative recoveries in Austria, Finland, and Spain. In *Austria,* the external sector and business fixed investment are expected to support stronger growth during 1997 and 1998. Further fiscal consolidation, however, aimed at reducing the fiscal deficit by about 1 percent of GDP in 1997 may keep economic activity somewhat subdued. In *Finland,* the strengthening of exports during 1996 has contributed to a resumption of growth. Continued buoyancy of consumption and investment is also supporting growth, which is expected to exceed

Table 5. European Union: Convergence Indicators for 1995, 1996, and 1997

(In percent)

	Consumer Price Inflation			General Government Balance/GDP				Gross Government Debt/GDP[3]			Long-Term Interest Rates[4]
	1995	1996	1997	1995	1996	1997[1]	1997[2]	1995	1996	1997	March 1997
Germany[5]	1.8	1.5	1.8	−3.5	−3.8	−3.3	−2.9	58.1	60.3	61.5	5.8
France	1.8	2.0	1.6	−5.0	−4.1	−3.3	−3.0	52.9	56.3	57.8	5.7
Italy	5.4	3.9	2.4	−7.1	−6.8	−3.3	−3.0	124.9	123.0	121.5	7.6
United Kingdom[6]	2.8	2.9	2.6	−5.6	−4.4	−3.1	...	47.3	49.3	49.4	7.5
Spain	4.7	3.5	2.5	−6.6	−4.4	−3.2	3.0	65.3	69.5	69.0	7.1
Netherlands	2.0	2.1	2.7	−4.0	−2.3	−2.2	...	79.7	78.8	76.1	5.7
Belgium	1.5	2.1	2.0	−4.1	−3.4	−2.9	−2.9	133.5	130.0	127.1	5.9
Sweden	2.5	0.5	2.3	−7.9	−2.5	−0.8	−2.6	78.2	78.6	76.6	7.1
Austria	2.2	1.9	1.9	−5.3	−3.9	−2.5	−3.0	69.3	69.8	68.1	5.7
Denmark[7]	2.1	2.1	2.5	−1.9	−1.6	−0.1	0.2	72.2	69.9	67.3	6.5
Finland	1.0	0.6	1.3	−5.2	−2.6	−1.9	−1.4	58.5	58.0	58.7	6.1
Greece[8]	9.3	8.5	6.9	−9.2	−7.6	−5.1	−4.2	111.8	110.7	107.7	10.3
Portugal	4.1	3.1	2.5	−4.9	−4.0	−2.9	−2.9	71.7	70.8	69.2	6.9
Ireland	2.5	1.6	2.2	−2.4	−1.0	−1.6	−1.5	84.8	76.4	72.3	6.3
Luxembourg	1.9	1.8	2.0	0.4	−0.1	−0.1	...	5.4	5.9	5.7	6.1
All EU[9]	3.0	2.5	2.2	−5.2	−4.4	−3.1		72.1	73.2	73.0	6.6
Reference value[10]	**2.9**	**2.4**	**3.1**	**−3.0**	**−3.0**	**−3.0**		**60.0**	**60.0**	**60.0**	**7.9**

Sources: National sources; and IMF staff projections.

Note: The table shows the convergence indicators mentioned in the Maastricht Treaty, except for the exchange rate. The three relevant convergence criteria are (1) consumer price inflation must not exceed that of the three best-performing countries by more than 1½ percentage points; (2) interest rates on long-term government securities must not be more than 2 percentage points higher than those in the same three member states; and (3) the financial position must be sustainable. In particular, the general government deficit should be at or below the reference value of 3 percent of GDP. If not, it should have declined substantially and continuously and reached a level close to the reference value, or the excess over the reference value should be temporary and exceptional. The gross debt of general government should be at or below 60 percent of GDP or, if not, the debt ratio should be sufficiently diminishing and approaching the 60 percent value at a satisfactory pace. The exchange rate criterion is that the currency must have been held within the normal fluctuation margins of the ERM for two years without a realignment at the initiative of the member state in question.

[1]Based on information available up to the end of March 1997.

[2]Official targets or intentions. The IMF staff's fiscal projections shown in the preceding column are in some cases based on different growth, inflation, or interest rate assumptions from those used by national authorities and do not take into account further consolidation measures that are planned by EU governments in accordance with their convergence programs but which have not yet been announced. See Box 2 for the IMF staff's fiscal assumptions.

[3]Debt data refer to end of year. They relate to general government but may not be consistent with the definition agreed at Maastricht.

[4]Ten-year government bond yield or nearest maturity.

[5]While some other EU countries have adopted supplementary fiscal actions for 1997 (e.g., France and Italy), the German authorities have not yet announced additional measures to achieve the Maastricht fiscal deficit criterion.

[6]Retail price index excluding mortgage interest.

[7]Government deposits with the central bank, government holdings of nongovernment bonds, and government debt related to public enterprises amounted to some 20 percent of GDP in 1995.

[8]Long-term interest rate is 12-month treasury bill rate.

[9]Average weighted by GDP shares, based on the purchasing power parity (PPP) valuation of country GDPs for consumer price index, general government balances, and debt.

[10]The Treaty is not specific as to what methodology should be used to calculate reference values for inflation and the interest rate beyond noting that they should be based on the three lowest-inflation countries. For illustrative purposes, a simple average for the three countries is used in calculating the reference values.

4 percent in 1997. In *Spain,* exports and equipment investment are the driving forces behind the emerging recovery. Employment growth has been stronger than in previous economic cycles, but unemployment of over 22 percent remains Spain's greatest economic challenge.

Elsewhere in continental Europe, revivals of domestic demand are contributing to recoveries from the 1995 slowdown. Activity strengthened in early 1996 in *Denmark,* with notable increases in construction and in private consumption, and also in the *Netherlands,* reflecting gains in employment and more buoyant consumer spending. Growth of exports coupled with continued buoyancy in domestic demand is expected to sustain relatively solid growth in both countries in the year ahead. In *Portugal* also, growth picked up in 1996 as both consumption and investment improved. Activity is expected to firm over the next year as investment strengthens further. Similarly in *Belgium,* a recovery in business fixed investment is expected to support stronger growth. In *Greece,* despite consolidation plans to reduce the structural fiscal

27

Chart 10. Selected Asian Countries: Growth in Export Revenues[1]

(Percent change from 12 months earlier; three-month moving averages)

Exports in U.S. dollar terms from a number of Asian countries slowed markedly during 1995–96; in a number of countries, the slowdown was less pronounced in SDR terms.

U.S. dollars ———   SDRs ———

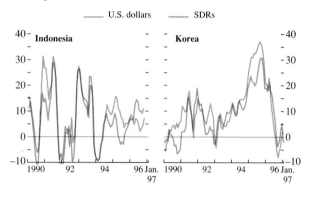

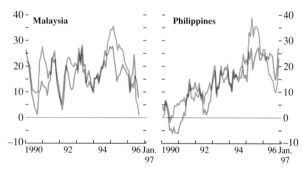

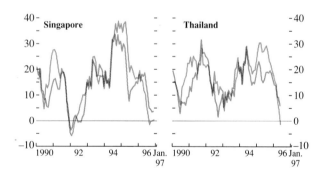

[1]Trade in goods and services.

deficit substantially in 1997, economic growth is expected to pick up, led by investment. In contrast, domestic demand in *Switzerland* remains weak, and real GDP in 1996 contracted by ¾ of 1 percent. With monetary policy now having been eased substantially, real GDP is projected to expand, but by less than 1 percent in 1997, supported mainly by the partial reversal of the earlier excessive appreciation of the Swiss franc.

Robust economic recoveries in Ireland, Norway, and Israel have slowed, or are expected to slow, to a more sustainable pace. Growth in *Ireland* moderated to 7 percent in 1996 after peaking at over 10 percent in 1995, and inflation has also decelerated. The strong and broadly based economic upswing in *Norway* continued, with real GDP accelerating to 5 percent growth in 1996. Although the expansion is expected to moderate somewhat in 1997, the marked tightening of the labor market in the current upswing and the recent easing of monetary policy, motivated by exchange rate considerations, indicate a risk of rising inflation. In *Israel,* six years of rapid economic growth with widening budget deficits culminated in a sharp increase in the current account deficit during 1995–96, with inflation near 10 percent. The projected tightening of fiscal policy, if successfully implemented, should allow growth to continue at a more sustainable pace, the external imbalance to narrow, and inflation to moderate.

In several of the advanced economies of Asia, growth slowed during 1996, and growth projections for 1997 have been revised downward somewhat. The slowdown, which represented a mild cyclical correction following the above-trend growth rates of 1994–95, resulted partly from appropriate policy tightening intended to diminish the risk of overheating. At the same time, exports slowed owing to losses in the external competitiveness of currencies tied to the appreciating U.S. dollar, weaker import demand from other advanced economies and from within the region, and the general deceleration in world industrial activity, which was particularly pronounced in the global electronics market. The slowdown in the growth of export revenues in U.S. dollar terms was particularly marked, reflecting the appreciation of the U.S. dollar; in SDR terms, the slowing of export revenues was less pronounced (Chart 10). A recovery in exports is expected in 1997, as global demand firms. In *Hong Kong,* growth in private consumption and continuing rapid growth in China are expected to support somewhat stronger growth in 1997. In *Singapore,* improvements in the external sector are expected to offset a moderation in both public consumption and private investment—which made considerable contributions to GDP growth last year—resulting in growth of about 6½ percent in the year ahead. In *Taiwan Province of China,* a recovery in domestic demand should support activity in 1997. In *Korea,* the slowdown in growth to 7 percent has reduced the risk of overheating. The short-term outlook for growth appears favorable, although labor unrest and uncertainties associated with the recent Hanbo bankruptcy imply some downside risk.

Economic Situation and Prospects in Developing Countries

In the developing countries, growth in output firmed to 6½ percent in 1996, marking the fifth consecutive year of expansion of around 6 percent, and the median inflation rate slowed to about 7 percent, the lowest rate in nearly a quarter century (Table 6). Sustained growth close to 6½ percent, with further declines in inflation, is expected in the period ahead.

Among the developing countries of the *Western Hemisphere,* growth picked up to 3½ percent in 1996—a somewhat better performance than projected last October—and inflation declined further. Growth in the region is expected to reach almost 4½ percent in 1997 as recoveries in several countries gain momentum, and inflation is projected to moderate further. In Mexico, the economic recovery in 1996 exceeded most expectations, with real GDP increasing by 5 percent. Strong export performance and a pickup in domestic investment—reflecting improved confidence and lower interest rates—are expected to sustain recovery this year. Tight fiscal and monetary policies should help to lower inflation to below 20 percent. Economic recovery also gathered strength in Argentina, with GDP increasing by about 4½ percent in 1996 after a comparable decline in output in the preceding year; inflation was virtually zero. With a pickup in growth in the second half of the year, Brazil's economy expanded by 3 percent in 1996, and inflation declined to about 11 percent, its lowest rate in many years. Reflecting the success of the real plan, a further strengthening of growth and decline in inflation are expected in the year ahead. In Chile, high real interest rates and weaker exports associated with the fall in world copper prices reduced growth to 7 percent in 1996, and a further slowdown is projected for the year ahead. Nevertheless, Chile's growth rate in 1997, at about 5¾ percent, will again be one of the highest in the region. Although the adjustment measures taken in early 1996 in Venezuela contributed to a 1 percent decline in output, they succeeded in improving financial stability: the exchange rate stabilized, and inflation began to decline in the second half of the year. Economic activity is expected to rebound this year, supported by higher oil prices and buoyant foreign direct investment in the newly privatized oil and mining sectors.

With an increasing number of countries in *Africa* making significant progress with macroeconomic stabilization and structural reform efforts, the upturn in economic growth that began in 1994–95 broadened

further in 1996. In fact, the 5 percent expansion seen in 1996 was Africa's best growth performance in two decades, and reflected strong activity in the primary products sector—agriculture, in particular, with a number of countries recovering from earlier adverse weather—and in some cases, manufacturing. Growth is expected to average about 4¾ percent in 1997. In South Africa, the government's commitment to fiscal responsibility and structural reform is gaining increasing credibility, but efforts to stabilize the economy and remaining uncertainties are likely to constrain the pace of growth in the near term. In Morocco, the rate of expansion is expected to slow, mainly because of weaker performance in the agricultural sector. In many other countries in Africa, however, growth prospects are quite encouraging, with further declines expected in inflation. Adjustment efforts in Kenya have continued in many areas, including fiscal consolidation, but a weakening of growth is likely in 1997 reflecting the impact of a drought and a slowing of structural reform. Robust growth in Uganda continues to be fueled partly by capital inflows, and by investment in manufacturing and construction, all of which reflect increased confidence. In Ethiopia, growth surged to almost 8 percent in 1996, owing to strong performance of the agricultural sector, and inflation declined to about 1 percent. Tight monetary policy and further strong output growth should keep inflation at a similar level in 1997. Rapid growth driven by agricultural production and exports continued in Malawi during 1996, while inflation declined substantially. After the 1995 drought, output growth picked up in Zambia, largely owing to recoveries in agricultural and copper production, and is projected to strengthen further in 1997. Some limited progress was made during 1996 to restore economic stability in Nigeria, but inflation, while easing, remained high. A recovery in output and a further fall in inflation are expected in 1997.

Following the 1994 devaluation of the CFA franc and the implementation of associated structural adjustment programs, growth in the countries of the CFA franc zone registered a turnaround in 1995. During 1996, economic activity gathered strength, resulting in growth rates of about 5 percent. Output growth is projected to remain relatively strong in 1997, and inflation to remain low or to decline further. In Senegal, the rebound in agricultural production and continued expansion in the output of the industrial and construction sectors contributed to growth of 5 percent in 1996. In Côte d'Ivoire, robust growth in 1996 was largely driven by expansion of exports, especially cocoa and petroleum, which partly reflected improved competitiveness. Inflation continued to abate despite further price liberalization measures.

Among the developing countries of *Asia,* growth in 1996 moderated to 8¼ percent. This aggregate outcome, however, masks diverse developments across the region. The weakening of export growth, noted

29

Table 6. Selected Developing Countries: Real GDP and Consumer Prices

(Annual percent change)

	Real GDP			Consumer Prices		
	1995	1996	1997	1995	1996	1997
Developing countries	**6.0**	**6.5**	**6.6**	**21.3**	**13.1**	**9.7**
Median	**4.1**	**4.3**	**4.7**	**10.0**	**7.0**	**5.4**
Africa	**2.9**	**5.0**	**4.7**	**32.1**	**24.8**	**12.0**
Algeria	3.9	4.0	5.0	21.9	15.1	7.0
Cameroon	3.3	5.0	5.1	26.9	6.4	3.5
Côte d'Ivoire	7.0	6.5	6.0	14.3	6.6	3.0
Ghana	4.5	5.0	5.0	59.5	45.6	21.5
Kenya	4.9	4.2	3.8	1.7	9.0	8.0
Morocco	−7.6	10.3	3.0	6.1	3.0	3.5
Nigeria	2.5	2.1	4.7	70.0	29.3	14.1
South Africa	3.4	3.1	2.2	8.6	7.4	10.2
Sudan	4.5	4.0	4.0	57.0	85.0	55.0
Tanzania	3.8	4.5	5.0	34.0	25.7	15.0
Tunisia	2.5	7.5	7.0	6.3	5.0	4.5
Uganda	9.8	7.0	7.0	7.4	5.0	5.0
SAF/ESAF countries[1]	4.9	6.0	5.5	22.0	15.7	7.4
CFA countries	4.6	5.2	5.7	15.3	6.0	3.2
Asia	**8.9**	**8.2**	**8.3**	**11.8**	**6.6**	**6.2**
Bangladesh	4.9	5.0	5.0	6.3	3.5	3.3
China	10.5	9.7	9.5	14.8	6.0	6.0
India	7.4	6.9	6.6	10.2	7.0	8.0
Indonesia	8.2	7.8	8.0	9.4	7.9	7.3
Malaysia	9.5	8.4	8.0	3.4	3.5	3.8
Pakistan	4.4	6.0	5.0	12.1	10.3	11.0
Philippines	4.8	5.5	6.3	8.1	8.4	6.5
Thailand	8.7	6.7	6.8	5.8	5.8	4.5
Vietnam	9.5	9.5	9.5	12.8	6.0	7.0
Middle East and Europe	**3.8**	**4.5**	**3.9**	**33.8**	**24.5**	**21.0**
Egypt	3.2	4.3	5.0	9.4	7.2	6.2
Iran, Islamic Republic of	3.1	4.2	3.8	49.4	23.0	15.7
Jordan	6.9	5.2	6.5	2.4	6.5	4.0
Kuwait	1.6	1.6	0.8	0.7	0.9	1.2
Saudi Arabia	0.0	2.5	2.0	5.0	1.0	1.0
Turkey	7.5	6.4	3.9	93.6	82.3	75.0
Western Hemisphere	**1.3**	**3.5**	**4.4**	**36.0**	**20.4**	**12.9**
Argentina	−4.6	4.4	5.0	3.4	0.1	1.1
Brazil[2]	4.2	3.0	4.5	. . .	11.1	8.0
Chile	8.5	7.2	5.8	8.2	7.4	6.0
Colombia	5.4	3.0	3.4	20.9	20.8	18.0
Dominican Republic	4.8	7.3	5.0	12.5	5.4	5.0
Ecuador	2.3	1.8	3.0	23.0	24.4	30.4
Guatemala	4.9	3.1	4.0	8.4	10.6	9.5
Mexico	−6.2	5.1	4.5	35.0	34.1	17.3
Peru	7.0	2.8	5.0	11.2	11.5	9.9
Uruguay	−2.4	4.8	4.5	42.3	28.3	19.3
Venezuela	3.4	−1.2	3.9	59.9	99.9	46.6

[1]African countries that had arrangements, as of the end of 1996, under the IMF's Structural Adjustment Facility (SAF) or Enhanced Structural Adjustment Facility (ESAF).

[2]"Consumer prices" are based on a price index of domestic demand, which is a weighted average of the consumer price index, the wholesale price index, and a price index for construction activity. The average year-on-year increase in 1995 in this price index was 59.6 percent, which largely was the result of carryover effects from the high inflation rate prevailing prior to the introduction of the real on July 1, 1994. Consequently, the inflation rate from December 1994 to December 1995, which was 14.8 percent, better reflects the underlying rate during 1995. From December 1995 to December 1996, the inflation rate was 9.3 percent.

earlier in the context of the advanced Asian economies, was also visible in a number of the fast-growing developing countries of the region. In some countries, such as Indonesia, Malaysia, and Thailand, the impact of the export slowdown on output coincided with the effects of tighter domestic financial policies aimed at reducing the risk of overheating. The decline in export growth affected activity in Thailand more than in other East Asian countries, although real GDP still grew by nearly 7 percent in 1996, with the current account deficit remaining large. In contrast, in Indonesia, the export slowdown was limited and partially offset by continued buoyancy of domestic demand, in part reflecting large capital inflows. As a consequence, growth remained close to 8 percent. In Malaysia, slower export growth, combined with a tighter monetary policy, helped contain overheating pressures. While labor markets in Malaysia are tight and rates of expansion in private credit, real estate sales, and investment demand have remained high, pressures on capacity should be eased by the tightening of fiscal policy announced in the 1997 budget. The economic recovery that began in 1994 continued in the Philippines, with a further strengthening of output. Deregulation and liberalization are helping by producing supply-side benefits and growth is projected to strengthen slightly further in 1997 as investment and exports pick up.

In China, after three years of double-digit inflation, a soft landing was successfully achieved in 1996. While inflation declined to 6 percent, GDP growth was well maintained at about 9½ percent. The outlook for 1997 remains favorable, with growth roughly unchanged and inflation remaining in the single digits. In India, strong agricultural output partly offset a slowdown in the industrial sector so that real GDP growth slowed only moderately to about 7 percent in 1996, while inflation declined to 7 percent. In Pakistan, after economic activity started to pick up in early 1996, the fiscal position worsened and a balance of payments crisis ensued later in the year as the trade deficit widened and capital inflows slowed. The adjustment required is expected to lead to slower growth in 1997 but will help improve the medium-term outlook.

Solid performance continues in the Asian developing countries undergoing transition from central planning to market-based systems. Cautious fiscal and monetary policies in Vietnam succeeded in lowering inflation in 1996, while solid growth was maintained. Continued robust growth is expected in the year ahead, with only a slight increase in inflation. The economic recovery under way in Cambodia continued in 1996, although growth slowed somewhat reflecting the adverse impact of recent floods on rice output, and further progress was made in reducing inflation. In the Lao People's Democratic Republic, growth remained buoyant owing to strong construction and services activity, which offset a slump in export-based manufacturing.

For almost a decade, the performance of many economies in the *Middle East and Europe* region has been disappointing. While the region has been periodically beset by political tensions and fluctuating oil revenues, inadequate economic policies also help explain the weak economic conditions. In recent years, however, a number of countries have implemented reform programs, albeit with varying degrees of commitment and subsequent success. Reflecting the continued progress toward macroeconomic stabilization and deregulation of the economy in the past few years, growth in Egypt increased to about 4 percent in 1996 and inflation was contained at about 7 percent. Prudent monetary and fiscal policies in Jordan have been supporting robust growth, which is expected to continue in the year ahead. Gradual fiscal consolidation has been the centerpiece of Saudi Arabia's reform efforts during the past decade. Improved fiscal and external positions, buoyed by higher oil export revenues, contributed to increased private sector confidence and a pickup in economic activity in 1996. In contrast, overheating pressures continued in Turkey last year. Inflation accelerated to around 80 percent, the fiscal deficit climbed to over 9 percent of GDP, and interest rates reached over 120 percent.

Developments and Prospects in Transition Countries

For the countries in transition, considered as a group, the contraction in economic activity seems to have bottomed out in 1996 after six years of deep decline. Also last year, inflation fell to 40 percent on an annual average basis, its lowest rate since the transition began, and to lower levels on a 12-month basis by the end of the year (Table 7 and Chart 11). Output is expected to expand by 3 percent in 1997—with all but five countries registering growth of 2 percent or higher—and inflation to slow further. It should be emphasized that output data for these countries may underestimate actual growth because they may not take full account of various forms of economic activity, particularly the output of new enterprises and activity in the informal service sector (Box 5).

The *countries more advanced in the transition process* have generally continued to make progress in macroeconomic stabilization and structural reform.[6] By the end of 1996, inflation had declined to 20 percent or less in each of these countries, and to 10 percent or below in the Czech Republic, the Slovak Republic, Croatia, and Slovenia. Output growth, although still quite strong, moderated somewhat in the Czech Republic, Estonia, Poland, and the Slovak Republic, mainly reflecting weaker exports to the EU. Nevertheless, overheating remains a risk in both the Czech Republic and the Slovak Republic, where relatively high wage increases are helping to fuel domestic demand. Despite a slowdown in growth in Hungary in 1996, tight fiscal and monetary policies have estab-

---

[6]See Chapter V, Table 21, for lists of countries considered to be more and less advanced in transition.

Table 7. Countries in Transition: Real GDP and Consumer Prices
(Annual percent change)

	Real GDP			Consumer Prices[1]		
	1995	1996	1997	1995	1996	1997
Countries in transition	**–0.8**	**0.1**	**3.0**	**119**	**40**	**31**
Median	**1.5**	**2.7**	**4.0**	**46**	**24**	**16**
Central and eastern Europe	1.6	1.6	3.0	68	36	38
Excluding Belarus and Ukraine	5.0	3.4	3.3	24	30	41
Albania	8.9	8.2	2.0	8	13	20
Belarus	–10.2	2.0	0.0	709	52	30
Bulgaria	2.6	–9.0	–4.8	62	123	769
Croatia	1.5	5.0	5.5	2	3	4
Czech Republic	4.8	4.2	4.5	9	9	8
Estonia	3.2	3.1	4.4	29	23	17
Hungary	1.5	1.0	2.0	28	24	18
Latvia	0.4	2.5	4.0	25	19	12
Lithuania	3.1	3.5	4.5	39	25	12
Macedonia, former Yugoslav Rep. of	–1.4	1.1	5.0	16	2	2
Moldova	–3.0	–8.0	3.0	30	24	11
Poland	6.5	5.5	5.5	28	20	16
Romania	7.1	4.1	–1.5	32	39	109
Slovak Republic	6.8	7.0	6.0	10	6	6
Slovenia	3.9	3.5	4.0	13	10	8
Ukraine	–12.0	–10.0	2.7	376	80	25
Russia	–4.0	–2.8	3.0	190	48	14
Transcaucasus and central Asia	–3.9	1.6	2.8	260	70	52
Armenia	6.9	6.6	5.5	177	19	8
Azerbaijan	–11.0	1.3	5.2	412	20	9
Georgia	2.4	10.5	10.0	163	40	12
Kazakstan	–8.9	1.0	2.0	176	39	21
Kyrgyz Republic	1.3	5.6	6.9	53	30	27
Mongolia	6.3	3.0	5.0	57	50	39
Tajikistan	–12.5	–7.0	–5.3	610	443	32
Turkmenistan	–8.2	–3.0	1.7	1,005	992	153
Uzbekistan	–0.9	1.6	2.0	305	54	87

[1]Average annual percent changes in consumer prices can differ significantly from during-the-year changes. See Chart 11 for monthly data for selected countries in transition.

lished important conditions for robust and sustainable growth; indeed signs of a pickup in activity emerged in the second half of 1996. Progress with structural reforms continues in these countries, although often at a slower pace than previously, reflecting the relatively difficult tasks now being addressed, including enterprise restructuring, the rehabilitation and rebuilding of infrastructure, and the establishment of robust financial and legal institutions.

For a number of *countries less advanced in transition,* efforts at macroeconomic stabilization were rewarded in 1996 with sustained and sharp declines in inflation and, except for Russia and Ukraine, significantly improved growth performance. Inflation fell markedly in 1996 in Armenia, Azerbaijan, Georgia, Kazakstan, Russia, and Ukraine and remained broadly stable in the Kyrgyz Republic and Moldova owing in part to the increased stability of nominal exchange rates. Positive growth emerged in 1996 in Azerbaijan, Kazakstan, and the former Yugoslav Republic of

Macedonia, while Armenia and the Kyrgyz Republic recorded growth above 5 percent and Georgia above 10 percent. The recent economic performance of Russia and Ukraine has been mixed. Both countries made substantial progress in bringing down inflation during 1996—with end-of-year annual inflation declining to 22 percent in Russia and to 39 percent in Ukraine. However, both countries have yet to record positive growth in output since the start of the transition. The government's fiscal position in Russia remains fragile, with revenue collection particularly weak, but recent indicators suggest that the long-awaited recovery of output may materialize in 1997. In particular, private investment is expected to begin to pick up in response to reforms and progress with macroeconomic stabilization. In Ukraine, progress has been made with privatizing large- and medium-scale enterprises in the last two years, but the pace has slowed down in early 1997, and regulatory uncertainty continues to impede market activity.

In other countries less advanced in transition, including Albania, Bulgaria, Romania, and Uzbekistan, macroeconomic stabilization has slipped, and there have been significant increases in inflation in recent months. The situation has been particularly difficult in Bulgaria, where the banking system came under severe pressure in late 1996. In early 1997, the Bulgarian and Romanian governments both adopted far-reaching stabilization and reform programs. Inflation in Bulgaria has since declined sharply and the exchange rate has stabilized. Albania was confronted in early 1997 with a financial crisis caused by the collapse of "pyramid" investment schemes. The crisis led to civil strife and the breakdown of law and order in the country. Uzbekistan has taken steps backward in the reform process, notably by reimposing restrictions on current account convertibility. Civil unrest has continued in Tajikistan, while already limited structural reform efforts have been partly reversed in Belarus. In Turkmenistan, the inflation rate has remained the highest among all the countries in transition.

Financial and Foreign Exchange Markets

Developments in the foreign exchange and financial markets of the advanced economies since the October 1996 *World Economic Outlook* have reflected changing perceptions of the near-term growth prospects for individual countries, of the outlook for continued low global inflation, and of progress with fiscal consolidation and toward monetary union in Europe. Short-term interest rates have in most cases either remained broadly unchanged or declined, the most notable exceptions being the United Kingdom and the United States, where they were raised slightly in October 1996 and March 1997, respectively. Long-term interest rates continued on a downward trend until early December in the United States and Canada and until mid-February in most other countries, with the higher-yielding bond markets in Europe recording the largest overall declines. Renewed concerns about inflation risks in the United States combined with signs of stronger activity in Europe and some increase in EMU-related uncertainty prompted significant increases in long-term rates in most countries except Japan in late February and March. Movements in exchange rates, for the most part, have maintained the trends prevailing since mid-1995, with the U.S. dollar appreciating further against most other major currencies, although a marked acceleration in the appreciation of the pound sterling in late 1996 and early 1997 was a notable new development. The exchange rate mechanism (ERM) of the European Monetary System was generally free of significant tensions, with the Finnish markka joining the ERM in October and the Italian lira reentering in November. The environment of low inflation, stable or falling interest rates, and

Chart 11. Selected Transition Countries: Inflation

In countries more advanced in transition, inflation has come down steadily. In those less advanced in transition, inflation has been reduced in the countries that have maintained tight financial policies.

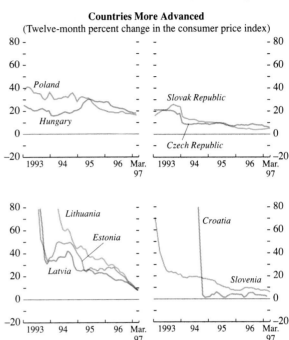

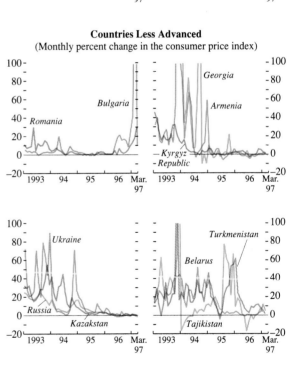

Box 5. Problems in Measuring Output in Transition Countries

Real output in the transition economies declined sharply in the initial phase of the transformation. Output is officially reported to have fallen cumulatively by more than one-half in the early years in a number of countries of the former Soviet Union. While by 1996 output growth had resumed in most transition countries, official reports show another year of decline in five countries of the former Soviet Union, including Russia and Ukraine. There are indications, however, that the actual size and consequences of the decline in output have been less severe than the official numbers suggest. Official measures of output are likely to overstate the decline for a number of reasons, including a tendency to exaggerate output before the transition began; methodological problems in constructing real output indicators; and incomplete coverage and underreporting of certain economic activities. Moreover, it is difficult to assess the welfare effects of output changes following such a shift in economic regime, and the decline in output is likely to overstate significantly the deterioration of living standards during the transition.

The statistical authorities in the transition economies, while gradually beginning to compile GDP statistics on the basis of the 1993 System of National Accounts, encountered numerous methodological problems in the derivation of real output indicators. The difficulties were compounded by the effects of high inflation and persisting distortions in relative prices, as measuring the changes in real output involves valuation issues such as the choice of the appropriate weighting scheme to aggregate sectoral physical output indicators and the computation of the share of intermediate consumption in gross output; these issues have often not been adequately addressed. With statistical systems having improved sub-stantially and inflation having fallen to more moderate levels, the methods to derive measures of aggregate real output have become more sound; however, the flawed estimates for the initial years of the transformation still await revision in many cases.

The traditional statistical methodology, based on exhaustive reporting of production by state-owned and mainly large-scale enterprises, was not well equipped to deal with privatization and the rapid increase in new, and for the most part small, private enterprises. As a result, many enterprises and activities are still not covered or are reported inadequately. Households involved in small-scale private activities, such as retail trade and agriculture, and private firms that would not be included in business registers, do not report at all. In addition, a large number of enterprises that are covered by the reporting system seem to underreport their activities, often to avoid taxes. To the extent that new forms of economic activity in particular are poorly measured, the reported data also tend to overestimate the share of the declining sectors inherited from central planning relative to the new and expanding private sectors. Statistical authorities in the transition countries have long recognized that incomplete coverage and underreporting are major issues and have started to make upward adjustments to the output data provided through the traditional reporting channels and to prepare estimates of the magnitude of unreported activity. For instance, a recent statement by the Russian State Statistical Committee indicated that in 1996 only about 85 percent of industrial output and around 45 percent of trade activity was actually reported to the statistical authorities.

A consensus is emerging that the cumulative output decline in the early years of the transition has been overesti-

---

moderate or improving growth prospects in most countries laid the basis for further large gains in major industrial country equity markets, with the notable exception of Japan, in the period until early March before a partial correction occurred that appeared to be prompted mainly by concerns about rising interest rates, particularly in the United States.

Since early September, monetary authorities in most industrial countries have either held short-term interest rates steady or lowered them. The most notable exceptions are the United Kingdom, where official rates were raised by 25 basis points in October to help counter the inflation risks associated with a consumer-led upswing in activity, and the United States, where the Federal Reserve raised the target federal funds rate by 25 basis points in late March in response to the persisting strength of demand and increasing risk of rising inflation (Chart 12). Short-term rates have remained unchanged in Japan (since September 1995) and Germany (since August 1996). The Bank of France made four modest cuts in official rates,

amounting to 15–25 basis points, in the closing months of 1996 and early 1997, and as a result French and German short-term rates had converged by late February compared with a differential of over 100 basis points in favor of French rates a year earlier.

Elsewhere in Europe, the Bank of Italy's discount rate was cut on two occasions, in October and January, by a cumulative 150 basis points as inflation in Italy fell below 3 percent, activity remained weak, and plans were announced for a substantial fiscal tightening in 1997. Fiscal consolidation and favorable inflation developments also provided scope for official rate cuts in Portugal, Spain, and Sweden, where short-term rates have fallen by 90–150 basis points since early September, while the Norwegian central bank cut the overnight lending rate by 125 basis points between November and January in an effort to curb upward pressures on the exchange rate. Conversely, in the Netherlands, the central bank raised the special advances rate by a cumulative 40 basis points on two occasions in late February and early March. Outside

mated. A recent detailed revision of Russia's national accounts found that the cumulative decline in real GDP was about 35 percent during 1990–94, compared with an initial estimate of around 47 percent.[1] The revision reflects both methodological corrections (including correction of the underlying data for 1991) and more accurate estimates of value added, as well as improvements in the coverage of trade and other services. Similarly, the cumulative output decline in Kazakstan during 1990–94 was recently revised from 51 percent to around 35 percent. Reassessments for other countries, especially countries of the former Soviet Union, while not yet available, are likely to result in comparable revisions for this period.

Despite significant improvements in methodology and coverage, the authorities may still be conservative in their estimates of underreporting. For Russia, the IMF staff estimates that after taking proper account of increasing tax avoidance the output decline in 1996 was 2.8 percent rather than the officially reported 6 percent. In a number of other cases, for instance Azerbaijan and the Kyrgyz Republic in 1995, the IMF staff has also made upward adjustments to the official output data. Without proper adjustment for problems of incomplete coverage and underreporting, the output recovery in countries where growth has resumed is similarly underestimated. The real

GDP data for the transition countries reported in the *World Economic Outlook* reflect the IMF staff's current best estimates.

There is clearly a need to continue to improve the quality of the national accounts estimates in the transition countries by strengthening the standard survey processes, combining information from separate sources, such as household budget surveys, and developing methods for estimating activities that are difficult to measure.[2] At the same time, it should be recognized that not only will implementing these improvements take time, but also the increasing share of activities that go untaxed and unrecorded reflects underlying problems. Such activities are a response to inefficient tax collection practices, high tax burdens and nontransparent tax laws, poor implementation of laws and regulations, and general macroeconomic instability.[3] Experience in a number of central and eastern European countries shows that the role of activities outside the normal fiscal and regulatory framework diminishes as progress with the transformation process continues, including through the redefinition of the role of and limits on government intervention in the economy. However, tax evasion can be a serious problem even in advanced economies and will be difficult to curtail completely.

---

[1] See State Statistics Committee of the Russian Federation and the World Bank, Russian Federation: Report on the National Accounts (Washington: The World Bank, October 1995); this revision confirms the argument and computations in Evgeny Gavrilenkov and Vincent Koen, "How Large Was the Output Collapse in Russia? Alternative Estimates and Welfare Implications," *Staff Studies for the World Economic Outlook* (IMF, September 1995), pp. 106–19.

[2] See Adriaan M. Bloem, Paul Cotterell, and Terry Gigantes, "National Accounts in Transition Countries: Distortions and Biases," IMF Working Paper 96/130 (November 1996).

[3] See Daniel Kaufman and Aleksander Kaliberda, "Integrating the Unofficial Economy into the Dynamics of Post-Socialist Economies: A Framework of Analysis and Evidence," World Bank Policy Research Working Paper No. 1691 (Washington: World Bank, December 1996).

Europe, Canadian short-term rates fell by a further 100 basis points in October and early November as the Bank of Canada cut official rates to offset the tightening of monetary conditions associated with the rise of the Canadian dollar. The Australian and New Zealand central banks have also permitted short-term rates to fall since early September by about 100 and 200 basis points, respectively, in response to slower growth and an improved outlook for inflation.

Following the divergent movements in long-term interest rates in the previous six months, bond yields fell virtually across the board in major industrial countries in the period from early September until early December. Yields fell by 60–90 basis points in many countries and by 150–200 basis points in a few cases, reflecting reduced concerns about global inflation, as price pressures remained subdued or eased further in many countries, and as the moderation of growth in the United States in the third quarter became clearer in the data. In addition, bond yield spreads continued to narrow in Europe in response to further conver-

gence in inflation performance and progress on fiscal consolidation, which also contributed to positive market assessments of prospects for EMU. Additional factors contributing to the yield declines were cuts in official interest rates in several countries and expectations that the highly accommodative monetary stance in Japan would be maintained for longer than perceived earlier given the hesitant progress of the recovery. The largest declines were recorded in Italy, Portugal, and Spain on lower inflation and intensified efforts to meet the criteria for EMU participation. Long-term interest rates also fell by 100–150 basis points in several other higher-yielding bond markets, notably Australia, Canada, and Sweden.

Between early December and early April, long-term rates rebounded by about 90 basis points in the United States as the renewed strength of activity in the fourth quarter became more apparent to markets and as data became available indicating continued growth above potential in the first three months of 1997. Rates in Canada rose by a similar amount, reflecting the upturn

**Chart 12. Major Industrial Countries:
Nominal Interest Rates**

(In percent a year)

In most countries, short-term interest rates have remained steady or declined, and long-term rates have continued on a downward trend.

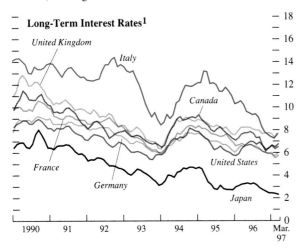

Long-Term Interest Rates[1]

United Kingdom

Italy

Canada

France

Germany

United States

Japan

1990 91 92 93 94 95 96 Mar. 97

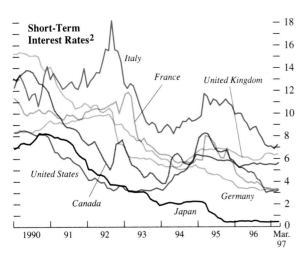

**Short-Term
Interest Rates[2]**

Italy

France

United Kingdom

United States

Canada

Germany

Japan

1990 91 92 93 94 95 96 Mar. 97

Sources: WEFA, Inc.; and Bloomberg Financial Markets.
[1]Yields on government bonds with residual maturities of ten years or nearest.
[2]Three-month maturities.

in the Canadian economy as well as the spillover effects of higher U.S. rates. In Europe, bond yields mostly continued to move downwards until mid-February before turning up partly in response to the rise in U.S. rates but also owing to signs of stronger activity in continental Europe and some market reassessment of the probabilities of early participation by certain countries in EMU. In contrast, long-term rates continued to decline in Japan, reaching historic lows around 2.1 percent in early April. By that time, long-term rates in the United States had returned to their early September levels, but in most other countries they remained lower, particularly in Canada and in the higher yielding European markets. As a result of these movements, the premium of U.S. over German and French yields has widened to close to a full percentage point after having been negative in most of 1995 and early 1996. This change in differentials is a particularly welcome development, reflecting the lower underlying inflation rates in continental Europe, the relative cyclical positions of the U.S. and key continental economies, and the correction of the overly strong exchange rate of the deutsche mark in terms of the U.S. dollar.

In *foreign exchange markets,* the U.S. dollar strengthened further against most other major currencies since last September but weakened against the pound sterling and barely changed in value against the Canadian dollar (Chart 13). By early April, the dollar was about 15 percent higher than in early September in terms of the Japanese yen, the deutsche mark, and the French franc, and more than 20 percent higher against the Swiss franc. On the other hand, it was about 3 percent weaker against sterling. Reflecting these partly offsetting movements, the dollar was about 10 percent higher in nominal effective terms than in early September 1996 and about 19 percent above its trough of April 1995. The yen weakened by a further 9 percent in nominal effective terms between early September 1996 and early April 1997, taking the cumulative depreciation since April 1995 to 30 percent. During the fourth quarter of 1996 the pound sterling rose against all other major currencies, strengthening by 10 percent against the deutsche mark and in nominal effective terms, before weakening slightly in January but strengthening again in February. The Italian lira has weakened in effective terms by about 2 percent, while the Canadian dollar has strengthened by about 3 percent.

These exchange rate movements are partly attributable to the continued disparities in relative cyclical positions among the major economies, which have been reflected in interest rate differentials given the subdued inflation environment in these countries. Thus the appreciation of the U.S. dollar has been supported by the continued relatively strong performance of the U.S. economy and by associated interest differentials in favor of dollar-denominated assets. Interest differentials favoring sterling-denominated assets and expectations that higher interest rates may be needed in the United Kingdom to avoid higher inflation also contributed to the rise of sterling. In contrast, the yen has continued to weaken as concerns over the robustness of the Japanese economic recovery have contributed to expectations that domestic interest rates will remain low for some time. Similarly, low interest rates in Switzerland and weak domestic growth prospects have contributed to the marked depreciation of the Swiss franc.

These currency realignments have for the most part been helpful responses to relative demand pressures in the major economies given their different cyclical positions, redistributing demand among countries in ways that are generally conducive to sustainable growth, and seemingly not taking exchange rates to levels that would be clearly out of line with medium-term requirements for balance of payments sustainability. In the case of the dollar, recent movements have more than reversed the sharp depreciation that took it to its low point in April 1995 and by early April 1997 had taken the real exchange value of the dollar to its highest level since 1989. Similarly, by early April, the real effective value of the yen had returned to its level prior to the large run-up beginning in 1993, while the deutsche mark returned to the level prevailing in late 1994, and sterling had reversed most of the losses following its withdrawal from the ERM in mid-1992. Following their meeting in early February, finance ministers of the seven major industrial countries released a statement noting that the earlier misalignments in exchange markets had been corrected and that there was agreement to monitor exchange market developments and to cooperate as appropriate. Subsequently, the exchange rates of the major currencies generally traded within fairly narrow ranges in February and March.

Stock market prices rose strongly in most industrial countries in the period between early September and early March, extending the gains recorded earlier in 1996. By mid-March, equity prices in the United States, Canada, and several major European markets were about 30–45 percent higher than at the end of 1995. Subsequently, in late March and early April, most major markets underwent downward corrections on the order of 10 percent in the United States and Canada and somewhat less in Europe in response to the rise in bond yields.

Prior to the subsequent correction, the rise in the U.S. stock market to new peaks in late 1996 and early 1997 had prompted official expressions of concern. The total value of the U.S. equity market is estimated to have reached nearly 140 percent of GDP in early 1997, which is well above the levels seen in the past three decades. The rise in equity prices in recent years is clearly related to the strong growth of corporate earnings (profits), which rose from about 8 percent of

Chart 13. Major Industrial Countries: Effective Exchange Rates
(1990 = 100; logarithmic scale)

As the dollar has risen to levels not seen earlier in the 1990s, the yen has declined to the levels of early 1993.

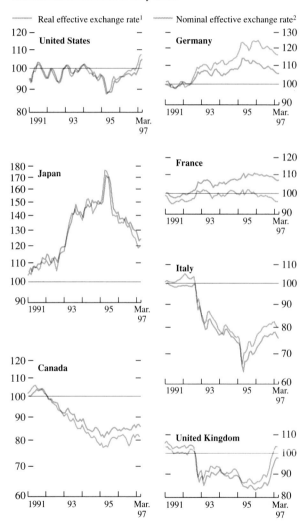

[1]Defined in terms of relative normalized unit labor costs in manufacturing, as estimated by the IMF's Competitiveness Indicators System, using 1989–91 trade weights.
[2]Constructed using 1989–91 trade weights.

Chart 14. United States: Stock Market Indicators

With the strong increase in U.S. equity prices in recent years, market capitalization has reached a high; price-earnings ratios have increased; and dividend yields have declined to low levels; but the yield gap vis-à-vis bonds has remained below recent peaks.

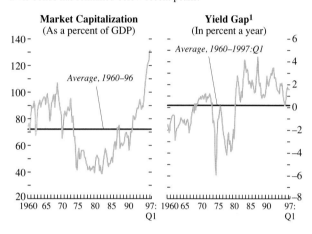

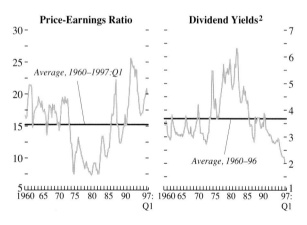

Sources: WEFA, Inc.; and Bloomberg Financial Markets.

[1]The equity yield gap is defined as the difference between the yield on ten-year government bonds and the inverse of the price-earnings ratio of S&P's 500 price index.

[2]Dividend yields are calculated as a ratio of gross dividends to share prices.

GDP in 1990–91 to 11 percent in 1996. The rise in price-earnings ratios has therefore been less dramatic than the rise in equity prices; but price-earnings ratios nevertheless have risen to levels well above the averages of the past three decades (Chart 14). There has been a corresponding decline in dividend yields to levels well below recent historical averages. The decline in equity yields and rise in price-earnings ratios may be attributed partly to declines in yields on alternative assets, owing in particular to declines in interest rates and inflation. Thus the yield gap between bonds and equities, though becoming wider (in favor of bonds) than the average since 1960, has remained significantly lower than peaks reached in recent years, for example, immediately prior to the 1987 market drop. The rise in the U.S. equity market in recent years may therefore be attributed in large part to strong fundamentals—strong earnings growth and lower interest rates, in particular. But this indicates that the market would be vulnerable both to increases in interest rates and to downward revisions of expectations of future profit growth, and both of these factors seemed to underlie the partial correction of prices that subsequently occurred in late March and early April.

Equity markets in Canada and Europe mostly lagged behind the U.S. market prior to 1996, and their more recent upswing appears to reflect improved growth prospects in many countries combined with lower bond yields. The main exception to this trend has been Japan, where equity prices fell 13 percent in the period between early September and early April on concerns about the outlook for growth and corporate profitability, combined with concerns about weaknesses in bank balance sheets and uncertainties about the pace and extent of financial deregulation. Concerns about corporate indebtedness and its effects on the financial sector also contributed to a further fall in equity prices in Korea, where growth has slowed and exports have weakened.

Against a background of continued strong capital flows to emerging markets, *foreign exchange markets in developing countries* remained relatively stable in the second half of 1996, with occasional periods of turbulence in particular countries generally not having significant spillover effects on other markets.[7] After several months of relative stability, the Mexican peso weakened by about 6 percent in October as a result of uncertainty concerning the announcement of the economic policy program for 1997 and investor concerns linked to the privatization of public enterprises, among other factors. However, the peso quickly stabilized after the central bank tightened monetary policy and

---

[7]Capital inflows to emerging market countries and related issues including policy options in managing these flows have been discussed extensively in previous issues of the *World Economic Outlook*. For example, see Annex IV, October 1996 *World Economic Outlook*.

agreement was reached with business and labor leaders on policy targets for 1997; financial markets in Mexico have since rebounded. In mid-January, the Chilean central bank widened the exchange rate band and revalued the peso, in terms of its reference exchange rate, by about 4 percent against the U.S. dollar. In Brazil, the real continued to depreciate gradually within its band, while reserve accumulation slowed in response to lower interest rates and measures taken in early 1996 to dampen capital inflows. The trading band for the real against the U.S. dollar was depreciated by about 7 percent in February 1997. In Venezuela, higher oil prices and an improved capital account contributed to a $6 billion rise in reserves in 1996, and the bolívar stabilized following exchange rate unification and the adoption of an IMF-supported program in April. In Colombia, reserves rose strongly toward the end of 1996 as the authorities sought to contain upward pressure on the peso.

Strong capital inflows contributed to further substantial reserve accumulation in several Asian countries in 1996. Most countries maintained broadly stable exchange rates against the U.S. dollar, which entailed appreciation in real effective terms given inflation differentials and the rise of the dollar especially against the Japanese yen. In China, reserves rose by a further $30 billion following comparably large increases in the previous two years. In Indonesia, the authorities have continued gradually to lower the intervention band for the rupiah in terms of the dollar and have also allowed somewhat greater flexibility by widening this band on three occasions during 1996. In Malaysia, the authorities allowed the ringgit to rise moderately in nominal effective terms in early 1997 in response to continued strong capital inflows. Thailand encountered downward pressures on its currency in 1996 and early 1997, partly reflecting concerns about its current account deficit. Although the Thai baht depreciated only slightly against the U.S. dollar, the authorities intervened substantially to support the currency on three occasions—in July, December, and January–February. In late October, the Pakistan rupee was devalued by 8½ percent as part of a package of measures to address widening macroeconomic imbalances and a sharp fall in foreign exchange reserves.

Among other emerging market economies, the South African rand came under renewed downward pressure in October on concerns about higher inflation and disappointment with progress toward the macroeconomic plan announced earlier in the year; the pressure was resisted by a hike in interest rates. The rand depreciated by about 28 percent in 1996 but rebounded somewhat in early 1997. In Turkey, the lira maintained its path of steady but rapid depreciation broadly in line with inflation. In central and eastern Europe, with the exceptions of Bulgaria and Romania, all countries saw their currencies appreciate in real terms. The Czech koruna appreciated even in nominal effective terms,

reflecting a tightening of domestic monetary conditions intended to dampen inflationary pressures and contain a widening in the current account deficit.

In contrast to the performance of industrial country markets, there was a variety of equity price movements in emerging market countries in the second half of 1996. Price gains overall were modest, with the International Finance Corporation (IFC) composite index rising only 7½ percent in 1996 as a whole (Chart 15). However, the flat overall picture disguises sharp movements in some individual countries. In China, prices rose between two- and threefold prior to a partial correction in December prompted by official expression of concern about illegal speculation, which was accompanied by a tightening of regulations. In contrast, stock market prices fell sharply in Thailand as growth slowed in response to earlier monetary tightening and the rapid downturn in exports. Improved investor confidence following the successful implementation of stabilization measures saw equity prices roughly double in U.S. dollar terms in Hungary, Russia, and Venezuela in 1996. In most other emerging market countries, price gains in dollar terms were modest, with price falls recorded in the second half of the year in Chile, the Czech Republic, and South Africa. Following the subdued overall performance in 1996, equity markets in most developing countries recorded significant gains in early 1997 with the IFC composite index rising 10 percent in the period through early April.

External Payments, Financing, and Debt

The expansion of world trade slowed markedly in 1996 following the exceptionally rapid growth of the two preceding years (Chart 16). Some decline in trade growth both absolutely and relative to output growth was projected in the October 1996 *World Economic Outlook.* But the decline that occurred last year exceeded expectations, taking the elasticity of trade with respect to output to its lowest level since the mid-1980s. This elasticity nevertheless remained higher than the averages of both the 1970s and the 1980s. Even though the growth of world output increased in 1996, sluggish demand for imports in some of the advanced economies—arising in some cases from efforts to reduce excessive inventories—and moderating growth in a number of Asian countries appear to have contributed to the disproportionate slowing of trade.[8]

---

[8]The IMF staff's estimate that the expansion of world merchandise trade slowed to 5½ percent in 1996 may be compared with the World Trade Organization's (WTO) estimate that it slowed to about 4 percent. The discrepancy between these estimates is largely attributable to differences in underlying data sources, with the IMF using balance of payments trade data and the WTO using customs statistics.

Chart 15. Emerging Market Countries: Equity Prices

(In U.S. dollars; logarithmic scale; January 1990 = 100)

Stock markets have been more stable for most of this year compared with the turbulence in 1995.

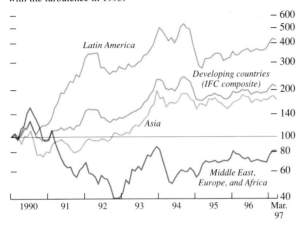

Sources: WEFA, Inc.; and International Finance Corporation, Emerging Market Data Base.

Chart 16. Elasticity of World Trade with Respect to World Output[1]

The elasticity of world trade with respect to world output declined markedly in 1996 but remained higher than the averages for the 1970s and 1980s.

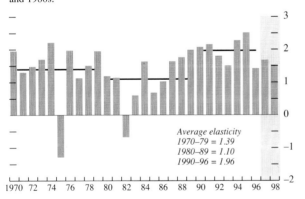

Average elasticity
1970–79 = 1.39
1980–89 = 1.10
1990–96 = 1.96

[1]The growth in world trade (which refers to goods and services) is calculated as the average of annual percent changes for world exports and imports. The elasticity is calculated as the annual percent change in world trade divided by the annual percent change in world GDP. Shaded area indicates IMF staff projections.

Within the overall slowdown, Japan, Germany, and France experienced small declines in their shares of world exports, while the other major industrial countries and the emerging market economies maintained or increased their shares (Table 8). Progress with multilateral trade negotiations continued with the first Ministerial Conference of the World Trade Organization concluding an agreement in December to liberalize global trade in information technology products.

Current account imbalances in the major industrial countries have in most cases remained moderate, and smaller than those seen in a number of countries in the mid-1980s. The recent pattern of imbalances reflects the improved alignment of exchange rates among the major currencies that has emerged in recent years, although relative cyclical developments have also had important effects (Table 9). In Japan, the appreciation of the yen in the period up to early 1995, in combination with continuing structural changes, helped to reduce the current account surplus to 1½ percent of GDP in 1996; a modest widening to 1¾ percent of GDP is projected for this year. In the United States, the current account deficit widened slightly in 1996 as the domestic economy grew relatively strongly, and the recent appreciation of the dollar is expected to outweigh the effect of a prospective pickup in growth in other advanced economies, resulting in a further slight increase in the deficit this year. Current accounts reached virtual balance in 1996 in Canada and the United Kingdom, but in the latter case a moderate deficit is expected to emerge this year reflecting strong growth of domestic demand and the recent appreciation of sterling. Pickups in exports in 1996 slightly reduced the current account deficit in Germany and modestly increased the surplus in France, and these trends are expected to continue in 1997. Italy's current account surplus widened further to 3½ percent of GDP in 1996 as the slowdown in domestic demand resulted in weaker imports; a slightly larger surplus is expected this year.

Among other advanced economies, current account deficits in New Zealand and Australia are expected to remain broadly unchanged in 1997. In Korea, the sharp drop in export prices and appreciation of the won against the yen resulted in a widening of the current account deficit to almost 5 percent of GDP last year, even though export volumes grew strongly. Slower import growth is expected to contribute to a narrowing of the deficit in 1997.

Among the developing countries of Asia, changes in current account positions in 1996 reflected a variety of factors. In Malaysia, the current account deficit narrowed to 6 percent of GDP as a tightening of monetary policy reduced import demand, more than offsetting a slowdown in exports. Current account deficits remained roughly unchanged both in Indonesia, at about 3½ percent of GDP, with a slowdown

Table 8. Selected Economies: World Export Market Shares

(In percent of world exports of goods and services)

	1970–79	1980–89	1990–94	1995	1996	Projections 1997	Projections 1998
United States	12.4	12.2	13.1	12.6	12.8	13.2	13.2
Japan	6.3	7.9	8.1	7.9	7.2	6.8	6.7
Germany	10.3	9.7	10.3	9.8	9.4	8.8	8.7
France	7.0	6.6	6.4	5.9	5.7	5.4	5.4
Italy	4.4	4.4	4.9	4.8	5.0	4.8	4.7
United Kingdom	6.0	5.6	5.3	5.0	5.1	5.2	5.1
Canada	4.0	3.7	3.4	3.4	3.4	3.5	3.5
Hong Kong	1.0	1.6	3.0	3.4	3.4	3.6	3.8
Korea	0.7	1.5	1.9	2.4	2.4	2.5	2.6
Singapore	0.7	1.3	1.9	2.4	2.4	2.5	2.5
Taiwan Province of China	0.7	1.5	1.9	2.0	2.0	2.2	2.2
China	0.7	1.1	1.7	2.4	2.4	2.6	2.7
Indonesia	0.6	0.8	0.8	0.9	0.9	1.0	1.0
Malaysia	0.5	0.7	1.0	1.3	1.3	1.4	1.5
Thailand	0.3	0.4	0.9	1.1	1.1	1.1	1.2
Argentina	0.5	0.4	0.3	0.4	0.4	0.4	0.4
Brazil	0.9	1.0	0.8	0.8	0.8	0.8	0.9
Mexico	0.6	1.0	1.0	1.1	1.2	1.3	1.4
Czech Republic	0.5	0.4	0.3	0.5	0.4	0.5	0.5
Poland	0.9	0.5	0.4	0.5	0.5	0.6	0.6
Russia	2.5	2.7	1.5	1.5	1.5	1.6	1.5

in non-oil export receipts offset by stronger oil exports and low growth in imports, and in Thailand, at about 8 percent of GDP, with a decline in imports offset by higher foreign interest payments on short-term bank liabilities. Indonesia's deficit could widen further in 1997. In China, the current account remained in approximate balance in 1996, moving from small surplus to small deficit owing to a narrowing of the trade surplus and further increases in outward profit remittances.

With recovery taking hold in a number of Latin American countries, current account deficits expanded in 1996 reflecting faster growth of imports, particularly capital goods. Mexico's current account deficit increased slightly in 1996 to ½ of 1 percent of GDP and is projected to widen to 1¼ percent of GDP in 1997. In Argentina, the current account deficit is also expected to increase modestly in 1997, and in Brazil to narrow slightly. Mostly owing to significant declines in the prices of copper and other commodities, Chile's current account shifted from near balance in 1995 to a deficit of 4 percent of GDP in 1996. In Venezuela, higher oil prices in 1996 boosted exports, resulting in an increase in the current account surplus, despite higher imports.

Declines in various commodity prices resulted in a widening of current account deficits in a number of African countries in 1996. A slight deterioration is projected for the region in 1997. The overall picture masks significant diversity among countries. Current account deficits are expected to widen in Ethiopia and

Zambia, owing to further deteriorations in terms of trade, but to improve or remain broadly unchanged in several other countries, including a number in the CFA franc zone, and Kenya and Tanzania. In contrast, higher oil prices in 1996 eliminated current account deficits in Nigeria and Algeria.

Also aided by higher oil prices, Saudi Arabia's oil export revenues grew by 17 percent in 1996, enabling the current account to return to approximate balance after deficits of close to 15 percent of GDP in 1992 and 1993, which were progressively brought down to just over 5½ percent by 1995. Jordan's current account deficit as a proportion of GDP fell by about 1 percentage point to 3 percent in 1996, as a rise in workers' remittances more than offset the increase in the trade deficit brought about by higher imports of food and transport equipment.

Current account balances deteriorated in 1996 in many countries in transition. In the Czech and Slovak Republics deficits widened to about 8 percent of GDP, as imports surged and capital inflows contributed to real exchange rate appreciations. Tight financial policies in Hungary helped narrow the current account deficit.

Net private capital flows to developing countries reached a record high of about $200 billion in 1996, with flows to China alone reaching about $40 billion (Table 10). This level of net capital inflows reflects relatively low interest rates in industrial countries, the continued development of capital markets, particularly bond and equity markets, in many emerging market

41

Table 9. Selected Economies: Current Account Positions

(In percent of GDP)

	1993	1994	1995	1996	1997
Advanced economies					
United States	−1.5	−2.1	−2.0	−2.2	−2.3
Japan	3.1	2.8	2.2	1.4	1.8
Germany	−0.7	−1.0	−0.9	−0.7	−0.5
France	0.7	0.5	1.1	1.3	1.6
Italy	1.1	1.5	2.5	3.5	3.7
United Kingdom	−1.7	−0.4	−0.5	—	−0.9
Canada	−4.0	−3.0	−1.4	−0.2	—
Australia	−3.4	−5.0	−5.3	−3.7	−3.6
Austria	−0.4	−0.9	−2.0	−1.8	−1.6
Finland	−1.3	1.3	4.3	3.4	3.4
Greece	−0.4	0.2	−1.5	−1.4	−2.0
Hong Kong	7.4	2.0	−2.0	1.3	1.1
Ireland	3.9	2.7	2.4	1.1	1.3
Israel	−1.7	−3.1	−4.5	−5.2	−3.8
Korea	0.1	−1.2	−2.0	−4.9	−4.1
New Zealand	−1.2	−3.0	−4.3	−5.5	−5.8
Norway	3.0	2.4	3.1	7.2	8.5
Singapore	7.2	15.9	17.7	15.7	15.8
Spain	−1.1	−1.4	0.2	0.5	0.6
Sweden	−2.0	0.4	2.1	2.5	4.3
Switzerland	8.4	6.9	6.9	6.6	6.2
Taiwan Province of China	3.0	2.6	1.9	2.7	2.4
Developing countries					
Algeria	1.6	−5.3	−5.3	0.4	−0.4
Argentina	−3.1	−3.6	−1.4	−2.1	−2.7
Brazil	−0.1	−0.3	−2.5	−3.3	−3.1
Cameroon	−5.2	−4.2	−0.4	−2.4	−2.4
Chile	−4.6	−1.2	0.2	−4.1	−3.5
China	−2.7	0.6	0.2	−0.1	−0.7
Côte d'Ivoire	−11.0	−1.0	−4.7	−4.9	−4.9
Egypt	4.7	0.4	1.2	−0.6	−1.9
India	−0.7	−0.8	−1.5	−1.7	−2.0
Indonesia	−1.5	−1.7	−3.4	−3.6	−3.9
Malaysia	−4.8	−6.3	−8.5	−6.0	−4.8
Mexico	−5.8	−7.0	−0.3	−0.5	−1.2
Nigeria	−2.9	−3.2	−1.7	5.0	11.9
Pakistan	−7.7	−3.7	−3.7	−6.9	−5.9
Philippines	−5.5	−4.6	−4.4	−4.3	−4.3
Saudi Arabia	−14.6	−8.7	−5.5	−0.2	2.0
South Africa	1.6	−0.3	−2.1	−1.6	−1.1
Thailand	−5.9	−5.6	−8.1	−8.2	−7.4
Turkey	−3.5	2.0	−1.4	−3.8	−3.4
Uganda	−1.5	−2.2	−1.8	−1.6	−1.8
Countries in transition					
Czech Republic	2.2	−0.1	−3.0	−7.9	−8.2
Hungary	−9.0	−9.5	−5.6	−3.8	−3.7
Poland[1]	−0.1	2.3	3.3	−0.8	−2.2
Russia	1.4	3.8	1.2	1.7	0.6

[1]Based on data for the current balance, including a surplus on unrecorded trade transactions, as estimated by the IMF staff.

countries, and the progress made by many of them with privatization and other structural reforms.

Within private capital flows, the trend away from bank loans toward foreign direct investment and portfolio investment has continued, particularly in Latin America and Asia. Over the past five years, these last two types of inflows ranged between 2 percent and 4 percent of developing country GDP, compared with less than 1 percent in years prior to 1990. Bond issues have also been on the rise, including in some transition countries. In Russia, for example, the recent issuance of Eurobonds amounting to $1 billion represented the largest ever debut issue by a sovereign government. The cost of capital to emerging market countries has also declined since early 1995. Spreads on Brady bonds in Latin America have narrowed considerably in

Table 10. Developing Countries: Capital Flows[1]

(Annual average, in billions of U.S. dollars)

	1983–88	1989–95	1991	1992	1993	1994	1995	1996
Developing countries								
Net private capital flows[2]	15.1	107.6	136.1	127.4	141.2	118.3	151.2	200.7
Net direct investment	10.4	41.8	26.7	34.3	50.2	69.5	72.5	90.7
Net portfolio investment	3.4	44.0	36.1	53.0	89.3	83.6	16.9	44.6
Other net investments	1.3	22.1	73.2	41.6	2.3	−35.0	61.7	64.9
Net official flows	29.0	21.4	20.8	14.3	23.3	20.4	31.0	−3.8
Change in reserves[3]	8.4	−42.7	−49.7	−45.7	−40.0	−42.2	−60.7	−82.3
Africa								
Net private capital flows[2]	3.5	7.2	5.5	5.7	4.7	12.7	13.6	9.0
Net direct investment	1.1	2.3	2.4	1.9	1.2	3.4	2.3	5.1
Net portfolio investment	−0.9	−0.2	−1.6	−0.7	0.9	0.4	1.9	0.7
Other net investments	3.3	5.1	4.7	4.5	2.5	8.8	9.4	3.2
Net official flows	5.0	6.0	5.9	8.6	6.2	5.5	4.0	6.4
Change in reserves[3]	0.2	−2.3	−3.2	2.4	−1.0	−5.8	−2.2	−4.4
Asia								
Net private capital flows[2]	11.9	43.6	32.4	21.8	52.7	63.2	89.2	94.7
Net direct investment	3.6	25.0	12.1	17.7	34.0	43.6	49.5	54.8
Net portfolio investment	1.2	5.2	0.5	1.8	11.7	10.0	10.2	9.2
Other net investments	7.1	13.6	19.8	3.7	7.6	9.2	29.4	30.1
Net official flows	7.6	8.4	10.6	10.7	10.1	6.2	5.6	7.2
Change in reserves[3]	−2.2	−23.8	−26.7	−15.1	−25.3	−47.4	−28.3	−43.2
Middle East and Europe								
Net private capital flows[2]	1.8	23.9	73.2	44.5	22.0	−2.4	12.6	19.4
Net direct investment	1.1	1.3	1.4	1.9	1.5	0.9	0.8	0.8
Net portfolio investment	4.2	13.5	22.6	21.2	15.6	12.2	12.2	7.6
Other net investments	−3.4	9.0	49.2	21.3	4.9	−15.6	−0.5	10.9
Net official flows	6.7	1.4	1.1	−3.0	5.9	10.3	−1.3	−5.8
Change in reserves[3]	9.9	−4.4	−4.3	−11.7	6.1	−0.1	−6.5	−13.9
Western Hemisphere								
Net private capital flows[2]	−2.0	33.0	24.9	55.5	61.7	44.9	35.7	77.7
Net direct investment	4.7	13.2	10.9	12.9	13.4	21.5	19.9	29.9
Net portfolio investment	−1.1	25.4	14.5	30.6	61.1	60.8	−7.5	27.1
Other net investments	−5.7	−5.6	−0.5	12.0	−12.8	−37.5	23.3	20.7
Net official flows	9.7	5.7	3.2	−2.0	1.1	−1.7	22.7	−11.6
Change in reserves[3]	0.5	−12.2	−15.5	−21.3	−19.9	11.2	−23.6	−20.8

[1]Net capital flows comprise net direct investment, net portfolio investment, and other long- and short-term net investment flows, including official and private borrowing.

[2]Because of data limitations other net investment may include some official flows.

[3]A minus sign indicates an increase.

the aftermath of the Mexico crisis, reflecting restored confidence in adjustment programs. Elsewhere, spreads have declined by less, but recently dropped below 100 basis points for Poland and the Philippines. While in many cases reflecting improvements in economic conditions and policies in recipient countries, the narrowing of spreads has been such as to suggest that in some cases, expected returns may be overestimated, and risks underestimated.

Net private capital flows to developing countries are likely to maintain and perhaps exceed their recent levels in the period ahead. Demand for infrastructure finance is expected to increase with economic growth, particularly in Asia. However, capital flows remain vulnerable to increases in interest rates and equity market developments in major industrial countries and to contagion effects from adverse developments in

some emerging market countries. While the aggregate flows as a whole seem sustainable under current market conditions, some countries may be adversely affected by changes in financial market sentiment. In particular, countries where there is insufficient fiscal consolidation, and therefore excessive reliance on short-term interest rates to restrain domestic demand (and overheating pressures), may be more vulnerable to changes in financial market sentiment. The IMF staff's assessment of the outlook for capital flows assumes continued progress with the implementation of reforms and stabilization policies in developing countries.

The solid and steady economic expansion in the developing countries as a group and the gains in stabilization and reform in the countries in transition resulted in a further easing of the overall burden of

Chart 17. Developing Countries and Countries in Transition: External Debt and Debt Service[1]

(In percent of exports of goods and services)

The burden of external debt eased further in 1996.

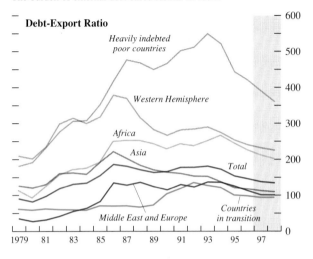

Debt-Export Ratio

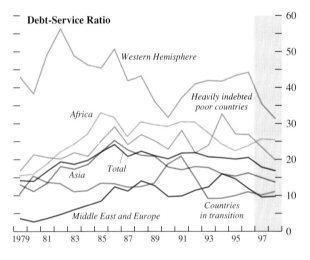

Debt-Service Ratio

[1]Debt service refers to actual payments of interest on total debt plus actual amortization payments on long-term debt. The projections (shaded areas) incorporate the impact of exceptional financing items.

external debt in 1996 for the fifth consecutive year (Chart 17). The ratio of debt to GDP is projected to decline to 29 percent in 1997, and the ratio of debt to export earnings to 139 percent—the lowest level since 1984.[9] Many poor countries, particularly in sub-Saharan Africa, continue to suffer heavy external debt burdens. For some of these countries, traditional debt-relief mechanisms are unlikely to make debt burdens sustainable in the medium term even with continued policies of adjustment and reform. To ensure that all heavily indebted poor countries (HIPCs) that pursue appropriate policies can attain debt sustainability, the World Bank and the Fund approved and are in the process of implementing the "HIPC Initiative," which involves concerted action by all creditors of qualifying countries to reduce their total debt to sustainable levels.

Since the October 1996 *World Economic Outlook,* a number of countries have completed debt and debt-service agreements with official and commercial creditors. Under the aegis of the Paris Club, flow reschedulings on Naples terms involving a 67 percent reduction in the net present value (NPV) of debt were agreed with Mozambique in November 1996; with Niger in December 1996; with Ethiopia and Tanzania in January 1997; and with Guinea in February involving a 50 percent NPV reduction of all arrears. Agreement was also reached in October 1996 with Benin on a stock-of-debt operation with a 67 percent NPV reduction of all eligible debt. Other countries have made progress in completing debt and debt-service agreements with commercial banks. Agreement was reached with Côte d'Ivoire on highly concessional terms for $5.4 billion of debt in November 1996, and with Vietnam for a $900 million repayment package—which will clear arrears accumulated since the late 1970s—in January 1997.

---

[9]In addition, the ratio of debt service to export earnings is projected to decline from 23 percent in 1996 to 20 percent in 1997—also the lowest level since the early 1980s.

III

Meeting the Challenges of Globalization in the Advanced Economies

Globalization refers to the growing economic interdependence of countries worldwide through the increasing volume and variety of cross-border transactions in goods and services and of international capital flows, and also through the more rapid and widespread diffusion of technology. It presents economies and policymakers with both new opportunities and new challenges. On a broad level, the welfare benefits of globalization are essentially similar to those of specialization, and the widening of markets through trade, emphasized by classical economists. By enabling a greater international division of labor and a more efficient allocation of savings, globalization raises productivity and average living standards, while broader access to foreign products allows consumers to enjoy a wider range of goods and services at lower cost. Globalization can also confer other benefits by, for instance, allowing a country to mobilize a larger volume of financial savings (as investors have access to a wider range of financial instruments in various markets) and increasing the degree of competition faced by firms.

International commerce and competition, and hence globalization, are, like technological progress, fundamental sources not only of economic growth but also of structural change in economies. Market economies are dynamic systems engaged in a continuous process of structural change. Economic progress is in large part a result of successful adaptation and adjustment to such change. It entails not only the growth of overall production but also a continuous reproportioning of the sectors of the economic system and of the structure of employment, along with changes in income distribution. While society as a whole benefits from this process of economic development, the gains are unlikely to be evenly distributed. Some groups may initially gain a great deal, while others may benefit only gradually or suffer setbacks. A question that has been raised about globalization is whether it adversely affects large segments of society.

Thus the increasing integration of both developing and transition countries into the global economy has sparked concerns that competition from "low-wage economies" will displace workers from high-wage manufacturing jobs to lower-wage service employment, and in doing so depress living standards in the advanced economies. A related concern is that globalization will decrease the demand for less-skilled labor in the advanced economies, thereby adversely affecting the distribution of income by widening the gap between the wages of less-skilled and more-skilled workers, as well as by raising unemployment among the less skilled. Yet other perceived undesirable consequences of globalization, especially financial globalization, are that it may erode the capacity of national authorities to manage economic activity and constrain governments' choices of tax rates and tax systems.

This chapter examines two sets of issues related to the increasing integration of the world economy that are of particular interest to the advanced economies. One, how has globalization affected wages, the sectoral shares of employment, and income distribution in the advanced economies? And what are its implications for labor market policies and social safety nets? Two, to what extent has globalization increased policy interdependence and reduced national policy sovereignty?

Features of Modern Globalization

Economic integration among nations is not a new phenomenon. Indeed, the increasing integration of the world economy in recent decades can in many ways be seen as a resumption of the intensive integration that began in the mid-1800s and ended with World War I. During that period, artificial barriers to economic exchange among countries were few; as a result, the flows of goods and capital across borders, as well as migratory flows, were large (see Annex). That earlier period was also characterized by dramatic economic convergence in per capita incomes among today's industrial countries.[10]

In some respects, however, the recent process of global integration is qualitatively different from that of the earlier period. A larger part of the world and a larger number of independent countries are participating in it. New technological advances have sharply reduced transportation, telecommunication, and computation costs, greatly increasing the ease with which national markets may be integrated at the global level

---

[10]See Jeffrey G. Williamson, "Globalization, Convergence, and History," *Journal of Economic History*, Vol. 56 (June 1996), pp. 277–306, and Kevin H. O'Rourke, Alan M. Taylor, and Jeffrey G. Williamson, "Factor Price Convergence in the Late Nineteenth Century," *International Economic Review*, Vol. 37 (August 1996), pp. 499–530.

Table 11. Costs of Air Transportation, Telephone Calls, and Computer Price Deflator

(In 1990 U.S. dollars unless otherwise indicated)

Year	Average Air Transportation Revenue per Passenger Mile	Cost of a Three-Minute Call, New York To London	U.S. Department of Commerce Computer Price Deflator (1990 = 1,000)
1930	0.68	244.65	. . .
1940	0.46	188.51	. . .
1950	0.30	53.20	. . .
1960	0.24	45.86	125,000
1970	0.16	31.58	19,474
1980	0.10	4.80	3,620
1990	0.11	3.32	1,000

Source: Richard J. Herring and Robert E. Litan, *Financial Regulation in the Global Economy* (Washington: Brookings Institution, 1995), p. 14.

(Table 11). Economic distances have shrunk and coordination problems have diminished to such an extent that in many cases it has become an efficient method of industrial organization for a firm to locate different phases of production in different parts of the world. The structure of foreign trade has increasingly become intra-industry and intrafirm, and foreign direct investment (FDI) serves as an important vehicle of globalization. More and more, countries depend on each other for technology transfer and learn from each other manufacturing methods, modes of organization, marketing, and product design. Research and development (R&D) spillovers are thus another aspect of economic linkages among countries (Box 6). Moreover, these various elements of globalization—trade, direct investment flows, technology transfers—have become more closely linked and interconnected, and the world economy is becoming, more and more, the relevant context for economic decisions.

Two groups of factors have played an important role in the growing integration of the world economy. One is technological advances, particularly in information and communications, which allow firms to coordinate production activities in different locations in cost-effective ways, allow new technologies or know-how to spread more quickly and widely, and generally reduce frictions to world commerce. The influence of technological advances in overcoming the natural barriers of space and time that separate national markets has been most evident in financial markets. Policies have also played a role in the integration of national economies. Countries have lowered artificial barriers to the movement of goods, services, and capital. The Bretton Woods institutions, the Organization for Economic Cooperation and Development (OECD), and the General Agreement on Tariffs and Trade (GATT) (now WTO) framework of multilateral trade liberalization have played pivotal roles in encouraging a growing number of countries to adopt open, market-based economic systems. An indication of countries'

increasing orientation toward open economic systems is provided by the rising number of countries that have accepted the IMF's Article VIII obligations of convertibility of currencies for current account transactions. That number has risen sharply from 35 in 1970 (30 percent of the membership) to 137 in early 1997 (76 percent of the membership).

Extent of Globalization

How globalized have markets become? This question mainly concerns the integration of product and capital markets. Labor markets remain highly segmented by immigration policies and by language, cultural, and other barriers to the international movement of labor. Although residents born abroad, as a share of total population, have been increasing in many advanced economies, their number is still below 5 percent in most countries and exceeds 10 percent in only four. It does not appear that labor markets have become more integrated in recent decades.[11]

One measure of the extent of product market integration is provided by the ratio of trade to output. By this measure, product market integration has doubled since 1950 and has risen significantly in the past decade. This measure likely understates the degree of integration, however, because an increasing share of output in advanced economies consists of services, a large proportion of which are nontradable. The importance of international trade appears to be much greater when merchandise trade is measured in proportion to the production of tradable goods.[12] Another way of assessing the degree of product market integration is to examine the extent to which prices for internationally traded products converge across countries. Empirical studies have consistently found large and persistent deviations from the law of one price for a wide range of traded goods, except for some highly homogeneous commodities, such as gold. This may be attributed to various adjustment costs and trading frictions, including transportation costs, tariff and nontariff barriers, and information costs. Thus, even though international goods markets are becoming increasingly integrated, they are clearly not yet as integrated as domestic goods markets.[13]

---

[11]Measured by the number of workers moving across borders, labor markets were much more integrated in the early part of the century than they are today.

[12]For instance, for the United States, merchandise exports as a share of total output rose from 3.6 percent in 1950 to 7.3 percent in 1992, while as a share of tradables output they rose from 8.9 percent to 34.8 percent over the corresponding period.

[13]For a review of the empirical evidence on absolute and relative purchasing power parity, see Kenneth Rogoff, "The Purchasing Power Parity Puzzle," *Journal of Economic Literature*, Vol. 34 (June 1996), pp. 647–68. Some estimates of the economic significance of the national border relative to physical distance in explaining deviations from the law of one price is provided by Charles Engel and John H. Rogers, "How Wide Is the Border?" *American Economic Review*, Vol. 86 (December 1996), pp. 1112–25.

Capital markets have also become more integrated, especially over the past two decades or so. The degree of capital market integration is discussed in greater detail below. Here, it is simply noted that despite the phenomenal growth of cross-border flows and the rapid progress toward the integration of financial markets, financial globalization seems to be confined to heavily traded, highly liquid financial assets, while countries' overall investment performance continues to be determined predominantly by their domestic saving rates rather than by net capital inflows. International capital mobility is sufficiently high, nonetheless, and the highly integrated segment of the capital market is sufficiently large to exercise tighter constraints than in the past on the conduct and effectiveness of macroeconomic policies.

Causes and Implications of Deindustrialization

Manufacturing employment as a share of total employment has declined continuously in most advanced economies since the beginning of the 1970s. This decline—a phenomenon often referred to as deindustrialization—has coincided with the growing global integration of markets and economies. The perception is common that deindustrialization is a consequence of increased openness and trade. Contrary to popular perceptions, however, deindustrialization is not a result of globalization, nor is it a negative phenomenon; rather, as argued below, it is a normal feature of technological progress and economic development in advanced economies, and trade with the developing countries has had relatively little to do with it. The following analysis first considers the case of the "old" industrial countries; the more recent experience of the newly industrialized economies is considered subsequently.

For the industrial countries as a whole, the share of manufacturing employment declined from about 28 percent in 1970 to about 18 percent in 1994 (Chart 18). The extent of the decline varies across countries, as does the time at which the process of deindustrialization started. Deindustrialization began as early as the mid-1960s in the United States, and the trend there has been one of the most pronounced, with the share of manufacturing employment declining steeply from about 28 percent in 1965 to 16 percent in 1994. In the European Union countries as a group, the share of manufacturing employment began declining later, but the fall became just as steep as in the United States, from over 30 percent in 1970 to 20 percent in 1994. In Japan, the decline in the share of manufacturing employment began later still and was less precipitous than in other countries, the share falling from a high of 27 percent in 1973 to about 23 percent in 1994. On current trends, the share of employment in manufac-

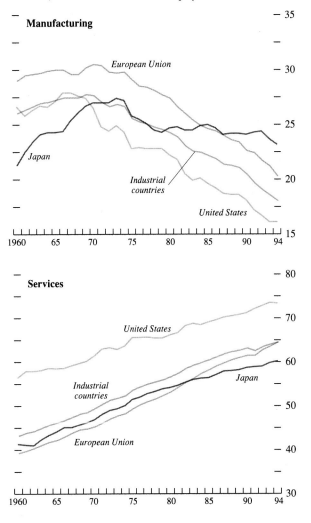

Chart 18. Selected Advanced Economies: Employment by Sector as a Share of Total Civilian Employment

(In percent)

The share of manufacturing employment has fallen in all industrial countries, while the share of services employment has risen.

Box 6. Global R&D Spillovers

National economies are interdependent. Each country depends on the supply of consumer goods, intermediate products, and capital goods from its trade partners, and each relies on its trade partners to provide markets for its own products. It is also becoming more and more apparent that countries rely on each other for transfers of technology, which also link their economic performance. This box summarizes some recent work evaluating the quantitative importance of research and development (R&D) and trade in influencing total factor productivity and output growth.[1]

In this work, existing estimates of international R&D spillovers—among industrial countries and from industrial to developing countries—were incorporated into an augmented version of MULTIMOD, the macroeconomic model of the international economy developed at the IMF. The estimates link productivity to business sector spending on R&D. More specifically, total factor productivity is assumed dependent on the domestic stock of R&D (for industrial countries), the trade-weighted average of foreign R&D stocks, and the openness of the economy (for developing countries).[2] The augmented version of MULTIMOD consists of linked econometric models for each of the seven largest industrial countries, the other industrial countries as a group, and four "regions" representing the newly industrialized economies, the net debtor developing countries of Africa and the Western Hemisphere, and other developing countries. The model

was used to simulate changes in R&D expenditures in the industrial countries, and in the exposure to trade of the developing countries, to obtain estimates of induced changes in total factor productivity, capital, output, and consumption.

The results illustrate several features of the gains from R&D (see chart).

- *Increases in R&D spending in an economy can significantly raise the long-run level of domestic output.* For instance, it is estimated that a sustained increase in R&D investment in the United States equivalent to ½ of 1 percent of GDP, which corresponds to a long-run increase in the stock of R&D of 10 percent of GDP, raises the level of U.S. real output by about 9 percent in the long run. About three-fourths of this gain comes though increases in total factor productivity and the remainder from higher investment in physical capital induced by higher total factor productivity. Half of the output gains occur during the first fifteen years. Over a period of a decade or two, therefore, sustained increases in R&D generate a significant boost to economic growth.

- *R&D spending can also generate significant spillovers, as R&D spending in one country raises output in other countries.* For example, when all industrial countries raise R&D spending by an amount equivalent to ½ of 1 percent of GDP, the long-run output gain in the United States is 70 percent higher than when only U.S. R&D spending rises. As the size of output spillovers among countries depends largely on their trade links, the spillovers tend to be particularly large among the European countries and between the United States and Canada. Nevertheless, output spillovers to developing countries tend to be larger than to industrial countries, reflecting the wider technology gap between industrial countries and developing countries.

- *Real consumption follows a similar pattern to output but with less variation across countries.* Consumption rises by less than output in the country carrying out the R&D, while it rises by more than output in

---

[1]For detailed results see Tamim Bayoumi, David T. Coe, and Elhanan Helpman, "R&D Spillovers and Global Growth," IMF Working Paper 96/47 (May 1996).

[2]The estimates of international R&D spillovers used in the simulations, which underline trade relations as the major transmission mechanism, are taken from David T. Coe and Elhanan Helpman, "International R&D Spillovers," *European Economic Review*, Vol. 39 (May 1995), pp. 859–87 and David T. Coe, Elhanan Helpman, and Alexander W. Hoffmaister, "North-South R&D Spillovers," *Economic Journal*, Vol. 107 (January 1997), pp. 134–49.

---

turing in the industrial countries is likely to continue to decline, and might fall to about 14 percent a decade from now.

The other side of this development has been a continuous increase in the share of employment in services (see Chart 18). This increase has been fairly uniform, with all industrial countries witnessing virtually continuous increases since around 1960. Among the major advanced economies, the share of employment in services is highest in the United States, at about 73 percent currently.

What accounts for deindustrialization? The declining share of manufacturing employment appears to mirror the decline in the current price share of manu-

facturing value added in GDP (Charts 18 and 19), suggesting that perhaps deindustrialization is the consequence of a shift in the pattern of expenditure away from manufactures toward services. When outputs in the two sectors are measured in constant prices, however, there does not appear to have been a shift in expenditure from manufacturing to services that corresponds to the magnitude of the shifts in employment between the two sectors. Relative to total output, the outputs of manufactures and services have remained fairly stable in the industrial countries as a whole (Chart 20). Hence, the growing current price share of services in value added primarily reflects rising relative prices of services in relation to manufactures,

Impact of Increased R&D on Output and Consumption

(Deviations from baseline, in percent)

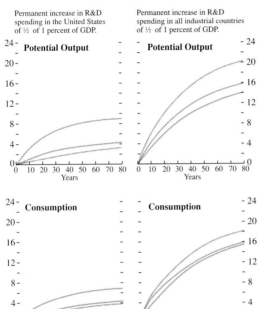

———— United States
———— Developing countries
———— Other industrial countries

Permanent increase in R&D spending in the United States of ½ of 1 percent of GDP.

Permanent increase in R&D spending in all industrial countries of ½ of 1 percent of GDP.

Potential Output

Potential Output

Consumption

Consumption

Years

an important mechanism through which the benefits of higher domestic R&D spending are disseminated abroad. Thus, for instance, the long-run rise in U.S. consumption from an increase in R&D spending in all industrial countries equivalent to ½ of 1 percent of GDP is more than double that when only U.S. R&D spending is increased (16 percent versus 7 percent). The size of these consumption spillovers increases with the openness of the economy, and particularly benefits close trading partners.

• *As demonstrated by the newly industrialized economies, developing countries can benefit from open trading policies because they facilitate technology transfer from industrial countries.* It is estimated that an increase in imports of manufactures by developing countries equivalent to 5 percentage points of their GDP—roughly equivalent to the increase that occurred in these countries between 1992 and 1995—raises output by about 9 percent in the long run and consumption by 6 percent. These results suggest that part of the success of the newly industrialized economies over the last twenty years can be attributed to productivity improvements stemming from foreign R&D spillovers through trade. Other factors that have boosted growth in these countries include rapid increases in labor and capital inputs.[3]

These results should be taken as illustrative only, since they depend on the specific model, mechanism, and parameters used in the simulations. Furthermore, it should not be inferred that the benefits from government-induced increases in R&D would match those largely generated by market mechanisms. They demonstrate clearly, however, that, based on reasonable parameter estimates, R&D links are an important element in the process of globalization.

other countries. This is because the country with higher R&D has to lower prices to sell its higher output. This deterioration in its terms of trade represents

[3]Alwyn Young, "The Tyranny of Numbers: Confronting the Statistical Realities of the East Asian Growth Experience," *Quarterly Journal of Economics*, Vol. 110 (August 1995), pp. 641–80.

which is attributable largely to relatively slower growth of productivity in services.[14]

[14]With unequal productivity growth in the two sectors tending to raise the relative price of services, there would be a tendency for substitution in demand away from services toward manufactures. The observed relative stability of the ratio of outputs of the two sectors suggests that any such substitution has been offset by other factors, such as shifts in demand toward services related to income growth. International trade also may have played a role. Since manufactured goods are generally more exposed to international competition than services, greater competitive pressures in manufacturing may have helped to compress unit labor costs and, hence, the relative price of manufactures. See Robert E. Rowthorn and John R. Wells, *Deindustrialization and Foreign Trade* (Cambridge, England: Cambridge University Press, 1987), and

Unlike the case for the industrial country average, the volume of manufacturing output as a share of total output does exhibit a trend for both Japan (until the early 1990s) and the United States (see Chart 20). For these countries, there thus appears to have been significant shifts in expenditures—from services to manufacturing in Japan, and from manufacturing to services in the United States—which offer a potential

William J. Baumol, Sue Anne Blackman, and Edward N. Wolff, *Productivity and American Leadership: The Long View* (Cambridge, Massachusetts: MIT Press, 1989) for a more detailed documentation and analysis of these trends in a historical perspective in the advanced economies.

Chart 19. Selected Advanced Economies: Value Added by Sector as a Share of GDP in Current Prices

(In percent)

Value added in manufacturing as a share of GDP in current prices has fallen in all industrial countries, while the share of value added in services has risen.

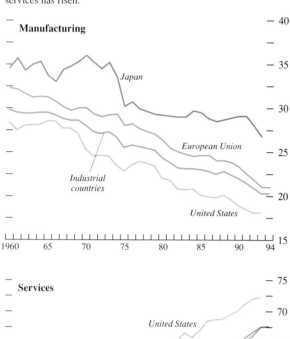

Manufacturing

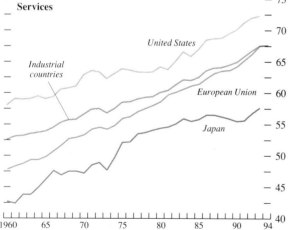

Services

explanation for the differences in the evolution in their shares of manufacturing employment. An examination of trade flows reveals, however, that the rise in the share in the volume of manufacturing output in Japan and the corresponding fall in the United States reflect to a large extent changes in net exports of manufactures in these countries, specifically the rising manufacturing trade surplus in Japan, and the growing manufacturing trade deficit in the United States (Charts 20 and 21).[15] Even in these cases, therefore, shifts in domestic expenditures do not seem to have been an important source of changes in the structure of employment. It should be noted that since the early 1990s, Japan appears to have started witnessing a decline in the share of employment in manufacturing, partly under the influence of a declining external surplus.

North-South trade could have adverse implications for manufacturing employment in the industrial countries if it involves high levels of imports of labor-intensive manufactures in exchange for capital-intensive exports. As discussed further below, under these conditions, even a balanced increase in North-South trade might lead to job losses in manufacturing in the advanced economies.[16] However, estimates of the impact of North-South trade on the share of manufacturing employment in the advanced economies indicate that such trade has at most had only a very small role.[17] Although industrial countries have become significant importers of manufactured products from developing countries, they remain net exporters of manufactures. This is especially the case for high value-added products, for which industrial countries maintain a significant comparative advantage.

Neither a shift in real expenditures from manufacturing to services nor North-South trade appears to have been a major determinant of the decline in the share of manufacturing employment in the industrial countries. Instead, deindustrialization appears to reflect mainly the impact of unequal rates of productivity growth in manufacturing and services. Clearly, if there is no systematic tendency for real expenditure on services to grow faster than that on manufactured goods, but productivity in manufacturing increases consistently faster than in services, then employment will

---

[15]The background paper to this *World Economic Outlook* by Robert Rowthorn and Ramana Ramaswamy, "Deindustrialization: Causes and Implications," *Staff Studies for the World Economic Outlook* (IMF, forthcoming) provides regression analysis in support of this hypothesis regarding Japan and the United States. A more general result of this study is that the pattern of trade specialization in manufacturing among the advanced countries is an important factor in accounting for the variation in the structure of employment from one advanced economy to another.

[16]This hypothesis has been put forward by Adrian Wood, *North-South Trade, Employment and Inequality: Changing Fortunes in a Skill-Driven World* (Oxford: Clarendon Press, 1994) and is discussed in more detail in the next section.

[17]See Rowthorn and Ramaswamy, "Deindustrialization: Causes and Implications."

tend to shift from manufacturing to services. The services sector will have to absorb an ever-greater proportion of total employment to keep its output rising in line with that of manufacturing. Table 12 shows that these long-term trends seem to hold broadly for the industrial countries as a whole between 1960 and 1994. The average annual growth rates of output have been roughly similar in services and manufacturing; however, labor productivity in manufacturing has consistently outpaced that of services. While the pattern varies among subperiods, the differentials in productivity growth have consistently been much larger than the differences in output growth between the two sectors, indicating the important role played by differential productivity growth in explaining deindustrialization.[18]

The decline in the share of employment in manufacturing in the industrial countries in the last two decades recalls the dramatic decline in the share of employment in agriculture throughout this century, which was made possible by the very rapid growth of productivity in agriculture. The typical pattern of changing sectoral shares of employment as economies develop and mature is illustrated in Chart 22. At the start of this century, more than a third of civilian employment in most industrial countries was in agriculture; today it is about 8 percent, and in the United States it is less than 3 percent.

Deindustrialization clearly cannot be regarded as a symptom of the failure of a country's manufacturing sector, or for that matter, of the economy as a whole. On the contrary, deindustrialization is a natural feature of the process of economic development in advanced economies, and in general is associated with rising living standards. This is not to deny that deindustrialization can, at times, be associated with adjustment difficulties in some branches of the manufacturing sector or in the economy as a whole. The service sector may be unable in the short term to absorb fully the labor released, because the overall growth of the economy is not fast enough, because of institutional rigidities in the labor market or regulatory constraints in the service sector, or because investment in the expanding services sector takes time. The adjustment difficulties may at times be exacerbated also by increased competition in domestic and foreign markets from "low-cost" producers or from foreign competitors that have adjusted more quickly or more efficiently. Deindustrialization

---

[18]It is well known that there are many data and conceptual problems in measuring output in services. It is possible that the slow growth of productivity in services could partly be a consequence of the undermeasurement of output growth in this sector. Some of these issues are discussed in Baumol, Blackman, and Wolff, *Productivity and American Leadership*, and at greater length in the collection of essays in Zvi Griliches, ed., *Output Measurement in the Service Sectors*, Studies in Income and Wealth, Vol. 56 (Chicago: Chicago University Press, 1992). These studies suggest that any measurement bias in this area is small in comparison with the large recorded difference in productivity growth between manufacturing and services.

Chart 20. Selected Advanced Economies: Value Added in Manufacturing as a Share of GDP in Constant Prices

(In percent; purchasing power parity weights)

Value added in manufacturing as a share of GDP in constant prices has shown no trend for industrial countries but has risen in Japan and declined in the United States.

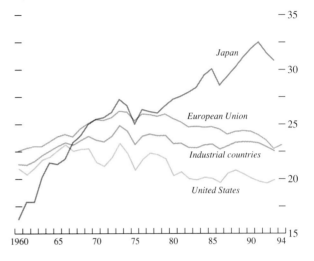

Chart 21. Selected Advanced Economies: Balance of Trade in Manufactured Goods

(In percent of GDP; purchasing power parity weights)

The rising constant price share of manufacturing value added in Japan and the falling share in the United States are reflected in corresponding movements in manufacturing trade balances.

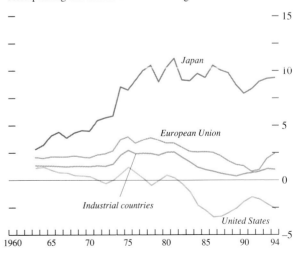

Table 12. Industrial Countries: Growth of Output and Employment

	1960–70	1971–94	1960–94
Output			
Manufacturing	6.3	2.5	3.6
Services	5.3	3.3	3.8
Output per person employed			
Manufacturing	4.6	3.1	3.6
Services	3.0	1.1	1.6
Employment			
Manufacturing	1.7	–0.6	0.0
Services	2.4	2.2	2.2

Chart 22. Changing Structure of Employment

The chart is a stylized depiction of the evolution of the sectoral distribution of employment during economic development. The share of employment in agriculture falls continuously, while in services it increases with the rise in per capita income. The share of industrial employment rises during the phase of industrialization and then falls as economies become more mature.

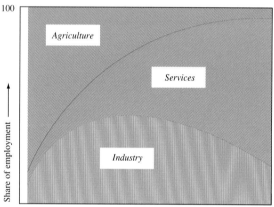

may be associated for a time, therefore, with rising unemployment or slower growth in living standards. Furthermore, a country can lose manufacturing jobs as a result of adverse shocks, policy mistakes, and temporary disturbances—for example, through a large real exchange rate appreciation. These considerations point to the importance of structural policies that maximize labor and product market flexibility and that facilitate the transfer of productive resources across sectors, as well as financial policies that promote macroeconomic stability at high levels of employment.

In this respect, the contrast between the United States and Europe is illustrative (Chart 23). Despite the very steep fall in the share of manufacturing employment in the United States, the absolute numbers employed in manufacturing have remained roughly constant since 1970, alongside a large increase in total civilian employment. The U.S. economy was thus able to absorb its relatively stronger labor force growth. Earnings have been stagnant, however, and income disparities have widened (see below). The experience of the European Union has been quite different. There, the falling share of manufacturing employment has been associated with a sharp decline in the absolute numbers employed in manufacturing. Moreover, unlike in the United States, there has been only a relatively small increase in total employment since 1970, which is reflected in the current high rates of unemployment in the European Union. Hence, while economic dynamism explains a large part of the decline in the share of manufacturing employment in both the United States and Europe, the process of deindustrialization has been associated with negative features—stagnant earnings and widening income disparities in one case, and high unemployment in the other. Even if more favorable cyclical conditions and supportive policies had facilitated the shift of resources from manufacturing to services, the transfer of resources associated with deindustrialization would still have occurred, though with more beneficial implications for employment during the adjustment period.

Among the advanced East Asian economies, both Korea and Taiwan Province of China began the process of deindustrialization around the latter half of the 1980s, as their real per capita incomes rose rapidly and reached the levels that had been achieved by many of the advanced economies in the early 1970s (Chart 24). There has, however, been a marked difference in recent decades between developments in these two economies on the one hand, and Hong Kong and Singapore on the other. While the share of manufacturing employment rose rapidly until the mid-1980s in both Korea and Taiwan Province of China, it has exhibited only a moderately declining trend in Singapore since 1981 and has been falling since the 1970s in Hong Kong. The difference appears to be primarily due to the fact that Singapore and Hong Kong are city-states, with no large agricultural sector. Consequently, they did not experience the shift in employment from agriculture to manufacturing associated with industrialization. The changes in the structure of employment in the deindustrialization phase, however, are likely to follow a similar pattern in all these economies.

An implication of continued deindustrialization is that the overall growth of productivity will be determined increasingly by what happens in the service sector. Over time, the ratio of employment in manufacturing to employment in services is likely to continue to decrease so that productivity growth in the manufacturing sector, even if high, will have a smaller impact on the overall growth of productivity in the economy. This points to the positive contribution to growth that could be made by deregulation and trade liberalization in the service sector and by increased investment in education and training to take full advantage of emerging technologies.

Deindustrialization is also likely to have implications for industrial relations in the advanced economies. In particular, the scope for centralized wage bargaining is likely to change over time. In dominantly service-based economies, it will be increasingly important to adopt remuneration arrangements that not only compensate for wide differences in skills and productivity but also offer incentives for human capital accumulation (Box 7).

Trade and Wages

Labor markets in the advanced economies have been characterized by marked increases in wage inequality in some countries between the more skilled and less skilled, and in other countries by rises in unemployment among the less skilled. This is the case however skill levels are defined, whether in terms of education, experience, or job classification. These labor market developments could have been caused by either an increase in the supply of less-skilled workers relative to the more skilled or an increase in the relative demand for more-skilled workers. In fact, however, the relative earnings and employment

Chart 23. Selected Advanced Economies: Employment

(In thousands)

The number of persons employed in manufacturing has fallen in the European Union since the early 1980s but has not declined in the United States or Japan.

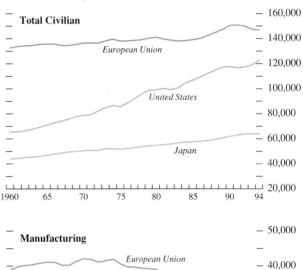

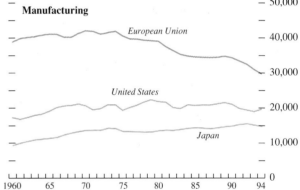

Chart 24. Selected East Asian Economies: Share of Manufacturing in Employment

(In percent)

The most dynamic East Asian economies have also started to deindustrialize in recent years.

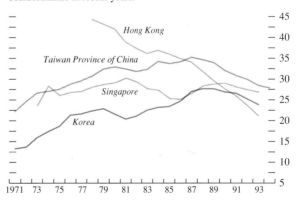

Box 7. Deindustrialization and the Labor Market in Sweden

Deindustrialization poses important institutional challenges in those advanced countries that have traditionally had centralized wage-bargaining arrangements. Industrial relations in these countries will have to adjust to the fact that there is likely to be a continuing shift in the structure of employment from manufacturing to services. The relationship between deindustrialization and wage-bargaining institutions and its implications for economic performance are well illustrated by the Swedish case.

The traditional "Swedish labor model" had two main elements. The first was the combination of centralized wage bargaining with an explicit policy of substantially narrowing wage differentials. The other was the leading role assigned to the traded goods sector in wage determination. In addition to the objective of reducing income inequality, the policy of compressing wage differentials during the 1960s and 1970s was motivated by the desire to promote shifts in the industrial structure from low-technology industries (where profits were squeezed by the wage policy) to high-technology industries (where profits were relatively high since workers were constrained in their ability to bargain for high wages). This policy proved successful in hastening structural change in Swedish industry and contributed to relatively high rates of growth during the 1960s and early 1970s. At the same time, in an attempt to maintain the international competitiveness of Swedish industry, wage increases in the traded goods sector were restricted by agreement between the social partners to be no higher than the sum of international price inflation and productivity increases in that sector. Wages in the nontraded goods sector were set with a view to maintaining broad parity with the traded goods sector. More recently, wage negotiations in Sweden have become less centralized than they used to be, the leading role assigned to the traded goods sector has weakened, and there has been some associated widening of wage differentials. Nevertheless, wage bargaining in Sweden continues to be more centralized, and wage differentials a lot more compressed, than in most other advanced economies.

Sweden's model of industrial relations did not prove conducive to maintaining high rates of growth in the period after the oil shock of the early 1970s. If anything, the growth slowdown was more pronounced in Sweden than

in most other advanced economies during the period. While the reasons for the relatively slow growth of productivity in Sweden from the mid-1970s are multidimensional (influences appear to have included the diminished prospects for "catching up," and the rapid growth of the public sector), the institutional structure of the labor market does appear to have played a role. One reason is that the potential for achieving rapid productivity growth by shifting production from low-tech to high-tech activities appears to have been largely exhausted. For instance, the data show that by the mid-1970s, the proportion of small firms had declined considerably.[1] Further gains in productivity therefore had to be achieved by increasing the efficiency with which existing enterprises operated. This, in turn, required the creation of appropriate incentive mechanisms for rewarding workers for effort, skill, and human capital accumulation. Implementing such incentive schemes would have resulted in a tendency for wage differentials to widen. But individual enterprises were constrained in their ability to introduce such incentives and, consequently, productivity growth suffered.[2]

To the extent that Sweden's problem of slow productivity growth is linked to the nature of its wage-bargaining institutions, it is likely to be compounded by the continuation of deindustrialization. As noted in this chapter, all advanced economies have experienced a secular decline in the share of manufacturing employment; however, this process has been particularly pronounced in Sweden (see

---

[1]It has been estimated that firms with at least 500 employees accounted for 60.5 percent of total employment in Sweden in 1986, in contrast to 30.4 percent of total employment in the European Union as a whole; at the other end of the spectrum, firms with fewer than 10 employees accounted for only 9.5 percent of total employment in Sweden—about half the corresponding share in the European Union. For a more detailed discussion of these trends, see Steven Davis and Magnus Henrekson, "Industrial Policy, Employer Size, and Economic Performance in Sweden," NBER Working Paper No. 5237 (Washington: National Bureau of Economic Research, August 1995).
[2]See Ramana Ramaswamy, "The Structural Crisis in the Swedish Economy: Role of Labor Markets," *Staff Papers*, IMF, Vol. 41 (June 1994), pp. 367–79, for a more detailed discussion of the relationship between labor market institutions and productivity growth in Sweden.

---

prospects of more-skilled workers have improved even though their relative supply has increased. If labor markets work freely, earnings can increase in the face of increased supply only if demand increases by more. In fact, labor demand has shifted toward skilled workers in two dimensions. First, demand for labor in the advanced economies has shifted *across* industries as the share of output produced by industries that intensively employ low-skilled workers has fallen and that produced by more skill-intensive industries has risen. The more important change, however, has been a change in skill demands *within* industries, as firms have shifted away from unskilled

toward skilled workers.[19] This shift in demand toward more-skilled workers has raised the relative wages of these workers.

---

[19]See Eli Berman, John Bound, and Zvi Griliches, "Changes in the Demand for Skilled Labor Within U.S. Manufacturing Industries: Evidence from the Annual Survey of Manufactures," *Quarterly Journal of Economics* (May 1994), pp. 367–97; Eli Berman, John Bound, and Steve Machin, "Implications of Skill Biased Technological Change: International Evidence" (unpublished; Boston: Boston University, 1997); and Dominique Goux and Eric Maurin, "The Decline in Demand for Unskilled Labor: An Empirical Analysis Method and Its Application to France" (unpublished; Paris: Institut National de la Statistique et des Études Économiques (INSEE), 1997).

Employment by Sector as a Share of Total Civilian Employment
(In percent)

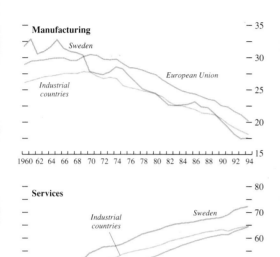

chart). The share of manufacturing employment in Sweden fell steeply from about 33 percent in the mid-1960s to about 17 percent in 1994. Over 70 percent of civilian employment in Sweden is now in the service sector, which includes a significant share of public sector employment. As in other advanced economies, the service sector in Sweden encompasses a wide variety of jobs. Some, as in financial services, require relatively high skills, while others, as in certain types of retailing, are likely to require lower skills. There are also wide varia-

tions of job security in the service sector. For instance, employment in public services is in general much more secure than employment in many retail services. While such differences, no doubt, also exist within the manufacturing sector, the diversity of jobs in the service sector is in all likelihood greater than in the manufacturing sector.

Given the diversity of skills, productivity levels, and value added associated with jobs in the service sector, it is particularly important that remuneration schemes reflect differences in the nature of work. Appropriate wage differentials are required not only to compensate for differences in the intensity of effort and skills, but also to offer incentives for human capital accumulation, and motivation, in order to enhance productivity and growth. As deindustrialization continues, the growth of productivity in the economy as a whole, and consequently the growth of living standards, will be determined to an increasing extent by productivity developments in the service sector. In this context, it becomes more important to provide the appropriate incentive structures for increasing productivity in services. A wage-bargaining system that is based on the competitiveness requirements of the traded goods sector, and which tends to impose relatively uniform wages across sectors, is unlikely to be an optimal labor market arrangement in an increasingly service-based economy, whatever may have been its justification in the past.

While all advanced economies may have to reform their industrial relations to varying degrees to cope with deindustrialization, the extent of adaptation may have to be more far reaching in countries, such as Sweden, that have had a tradition of centralized bargaining. Other countries, such as Austria, Denmark, Finland, France, Germany, and Norway, where trade union action has promoted social policy objectives have to deal with challenges of a similar nature, to varying degrees. This analysis does not imply that countries like Sweden with a strong tradition of promoting a relatively equal distribution of incomes will have to abandon egalitarian objectives altogether because of deindustrialization. These countries, and their social partners, will, however, have to rethink the appropriate policies for fostering those objectives while allowing the labor market to respond to the structural changes taking place in the economy.

In countries with relatively flexible wages set in decentralized labor markets, such as the United States and the United Kingdom, the decline in relative demand for less-skilled labor has translated into a widening gap between the wages of skilled and unskilled workers, with lower relative wages for unskilled workers. In the United States, inflation-adjusted wages of the less skilled have fallen in absolute terms since the early 1970s.[20]

[20]Including nonwage compensation, such as health care and pension plans, further widens the wage gap, since the share of fringe benefits received by skilled workers has also increased. See John Bound and George Johnson, "Changes in the Structure of Wages in the 1980s: An Evaluation of Alternative Explanations," *American Economic Review,*

This increased wage inequality can be seen in Chart 25, which shows that in the United States and the United Kingdom earnings of upper-income workers—those in the ninth decile of the earnings distribution—

Vol. 82 (June 1992), pp. 371–92, and Richard B. Freeman and Lawrence F. Katz, eds., *Differences and Changes in Wage Structure* (Chicago: University of Chicago Press, 1996), pp. 1–22. Richard Freeman, "When Earnings Diverge: Causes, Consequences, and Cures for the New Inequality in the U.S." (unpublished; Chicago: University of Chicago, 1996), estimates that real earnings of male high-school dropouts in the United States have fallen by 20 percent since the early 1970s. The consumer price index possibly overstates inflation and thus exaggerates the decline in real wages. See Box 4.

Chart 25. Selected Advanced Economies: Changes in Ratios of Earnings Deciles[1]

(Changes from 1980 to 1994, unless otherwise noted)

Wage inequality has risen significantly in some countries, especially the United Kingdom and the United States.

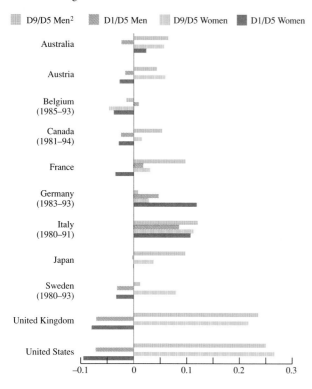

grew sharply in relation to the earnings of workers in the middle (fifth decile), while earnings of low-income workers (first decile) fell relative to those in the middle.

Other industrial countries have also experienced shifts in labor demand away from the less skilled toward the more skilled since the early 1980s, though with differing effects on the wage structure. Australia, Austria, Canada, Japan, and Sweden have experienced modest widenings in wage differentials, while Belgium has seen a narrowing. Countries with smaller increases in earnings inequality such as Germany and other European countries have suffered instead from higher rates of unemployment for less-skilled workers, as the combination of relatively rigid wages, frequently set in centralized labor markets, and explicit government policies have combined to put a floor under wages (Chart 26).[21]

Response of Wages to Import Competition

It is often asserted that globalization is a major cause of the declining relative wages and employment of less-skilled workers in the advanced economies. Perhaps the most visible aspect of this supposed link is the issue of whether increased international trade, particularly with low-wage developing countries, has contributed to declining wages and employment.

In principle, the channel through which international trade may affect wages is straightforward. Competition from low-cost imports alters the profit opportunities facing firms in the advanced economies. Firms respond by shifting resources toward industries in which profitability has risen and away from those where it has fallen. Trade flows thus give rise to countrywide shifts in factor demands. Thus, import competition from countries exporting unskilled-labor-intensive products will tend to lower the prices of such products and the profitability of their production relative to the prices and profitability of skilled-labor-intensive products, so that domestic firms will shift production toward skill-intensive goods. With fixed supplies of factors, this leads to changes in factor prices, and in particular to a relative decline in the

---

[1]Data are based on gross hourly earnings or gross earnings of full-time, full-year workers, except data from Austria, which include part-time workers.

[2]D9, D5, and D1 refer to the upper limits of the ninth, fifth, and first deciles, respectively. D5 is thus equal to the median of the distribution.

[21]The dispersion of individual earnings of full-time workers provides only one measure of inequality. From a societal point of view, other measures, which, for instance, consider the individual earnings of the entire working-age population or the earnings of households, rather than simply individuals in full-time work, may be just as important. On these measures, the degree of labor-income inequality in the United States is comparable with that in European countries (see OECD, *Economic Outlook*, Vol. 60 (December 1996)). The reason is that the adverse effect on labor-income inequality of the wider wage dispersion in the United States is offset by the favorable effect of higher employment. It should further be noted that the comparative dispersion of labor income differs from that of disposable income because of differences across countries in taxation and transfer payments.

earnings of unskilled labor.[22] What matters in this transmission channel from trade to wages is not the volume of goods flowing across countries, but rather the prices at which the goods trade.

The issue then is empirical: Have product prices in the advanced economies in fact changed in a way that is consistent with the notion that competition from imports has lowered the relative earnings of unskilled labor? That is, have prices of import-competing, low-skill-labor-intensive goods fallen relative to prices of high-skill-labor-intensive goods? If so, trade might have contributed to rising income inequality. But for trade to have been the main cause it must also be shown that the changes in product prices are primarily the result of trade rather than other influences.

There is in fact little evidence that product prices in the industrial countries have changed in a way that would confirm this relationship. For manufacturing industries in the industrial countries in the 1980s and 1990s, the prices of goods produced using relatively more skilled labor have for the most part fallen in relation to the prices of goods produced using relatively more unskilled labor.[23] And even after taking into account the effects of technological progress on relative prices, the change in relative prices attributable to international trade has favored goods produced by low-skilled, not high-skilled labor.[24]

Just as the empirical evidence indicates that imports have not lowered the relative prices of goods produced by unskilled labor, it also indicates that trade has had little effect on wages and employment in the industrial countries.[25] In the United States, changes in import

Chart 26. Selected Advanced Economies: Unemployment Rates
(In percent)

Unemployment rates in Europe and the United States have diverged sharply since the early 1980s.

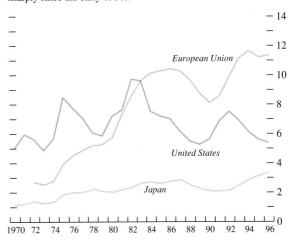

[22]This mechanism is the essence of the "Stolper-Samuelson Theorem," first expounded by Wolfgang F. Stolper and Paul A. Samuelson, "Protection and Real Wages," *Review of Economics Studies*, Vol. 9 (1941), pp. 58–73.

[23]This is documented for the United States by Robert Z. Lawrence and Matthew J. Slaughter, "International Trade and American Wages in the 1980s: Giant Sucking Sound or Small Hiccup?" *Brookings Papers on Economic Activity: Microeconomics 2* (1993), pp. 161–226; for the four largest countries of the European Union, by Damien Neven and Charles Wyplosz "Relative Prices, Trade and Restructuring in European Industry," Centre for Economic Policy Research, Working Paper No. 1451 (August 1996); and for a broad group of 13 OECD countries, by Steven S. Saeger, "Globalization and Economic Structure in the OECD" (unpublished Ph.D. dissertation; Cambridge, Massachusetts: Harvard University, May 1996). Jeffrey D. Sachs and Howard J. Shutz, "Trade and Jobs in U.S. Manufacturing," *Brookings Papers on Economic Activity: 1* (1994), pp. 1–84, suggest that falling prices of computers account for the declines in the prices of skill-intensive goods. For a review of the literature, see Matthew Slaughter and Phillip Swagel, "The Effect of Globalization on Wages in the Industrial Countries," *Staff Studies for the World Economic Outlook* (IMF, forthcoming).

[24]See Edward E. Leamer, "In Search of Stolper-Samuelson Effects on U.S. Wages," NBER Working Paper No. 5427 (Cambridge, Massachusetts: National Bureau for Economic Research, January 1996).

[25]See Ana L. Revenga, "Exporting Jobs? The Impact of Import Competition on Employment and Wages in U.S. Manufacturing," *Quarterly Journal of Economics* (February 1992), pp. 255–84, and Neven and Wyplosz, "Relative Prices, Trade and Restructuring."

prices have been found to have only small effects on wages and employment. For Germany, France, Italy, and the United Kingdom, there is no systematic pattern of effects of import competition on wages and employment. In Germany, wages and employment do appear to have been adversely affected by imports from developing countries but the magnitude of the effects has been small. In Italy and the United Kingdom, imports from developing countries have had no statistically significant effects on wages or employment, although imports from other industrial countries do seem to have had a significant influence.

The apparently small effects of developing country imports on industrial countries' domestic product and labor markets is not surprising given the relative magnitudes involved in terms of import shares. Despite the growing importance of developing countries in the world economy, merchandise imports from them range from around 20 percent to 40 percent of total merchandise imports in advanced economies, which corresponds to between 3 percent and 8 percent of total output. Low-wage imports are simply not that important for most advanced economies, in terms of either quantity or their impact on domestic prices. Increased trade with developing countries therefore most likely accounts for only a small part of the increase in wage dispersion and the shift in demand toward high-skilled workers.[26] Of course, for those workers affected, namely, those at the lower end of the income distribution, the effects may nonetheless be significant. And the overall effects of trade on wages and employment are not zero. But they are significantly less than other influences. Thus estimates of the proportion of the increased wage dispersion in the industrial countries in the 1980s and 1990s that can be accounted for by trade range approximately from zero to one-third, with the most convincing results in the range of 10 to 20 percent. Rather than by competition from low-priced imports, the increase of wage inequality in the 1980s and 1990s appears to have been driven principally by advances in technology that favor skilled labor.[27]

Capital Mobility and Labor Markets

Wages can also be affected by movements of capital and labor. Concerns have been expressed in a number of advanced economies that outflows of capital—particularly foreign direct investment, the related "exporting" of jobs, and outsourcing by domestic firms—have lowered domestic wages and employment. For example, the phenomenon of "*Standortwettbewerb*" (locational competition) under which German firms have been increasingly outsourcing production in recent years, especially to eastern European countries, has received much popular attention. Production and job creation abroad may clearly substitute for production at home, depending upon relative costs, competitiveness, market access, and other considerations. However, the limited evidence so far on the effects of outsourcing on labor markets in advanced economies indicates that workers in the home ("parent") country and workers employed in foreign subsidiaries either are only weak substitutes for one another in the production process or might even be complements, so that employment tends to rise or fall together in the parent and subsidiaries. In either case, although there may be some adverse effects in some industries, it does not appear that firms have substituted foreign for domestic workers on a large scale.[28]

Another effect might be that enhanced capital mobility might increase the degree to which workers bear the costs of adjustment to terms of trade shocks. Increased capital mobility narrows the range of variation of returns to capital within a country, because as a country integrates its capital market with the rest of the world, risk-adjusted rates of return increasingly match "world" rates. The effects of terms of trade movements cannot then be absorbed by all factors of production, so that labor, both more skilled and less skilled, must absorb more of the impact of any product price changes. Increased capital mobility may thus result in increased volatility of wages in response to external shocks. This would lead to greater wage dispersion if wages of low-skilled workers adjust downward more readily than those of high-skilled workers. In countries (such as in Europe) where variations in returns to capital are closely constrained by capital mobility and wages for low-skilled workers are downwardly inflexible in real terms owing to structural

---

[26]Import competition could play a larger role in affecting wages if it leads firms to adopt technologies that supplant low-skilled workers. However, it is not clear that trade has led to such changes in technology rather than technological advances affecting patterns of production and thus trade flows. Moreover, if trade makes unskilled-labor-intensive goods relatively cheaper and skilled-labor-intensive or capital-intensive goods more expensive, it would be expected to raise the relative prices of skilled labor and capital and thus increase incentives for the development of technologies that replaced these rather than unskilled workers. See Rowthorn and Ramaswamy, "Deindustrialization: Causes and Implications" for further discussion.

[27]For instance, the growth of information technology has significantly enhanced the productivity and earnings of workers able to utilize such technology. See in this context the discussions in Paul Krugman, "Technology's Revenge," *The Wilson Quarterly* (Autumn 1994), pp. 56–64, and Ramana Ramaswamy and Robert E. Rowthorn, "Efficiency Wages and Wage Dispersion," *Economica*, Vol. 58 (November 1991), pp. 501–14. Trade could increase the spread of new technology, and thus indirectly hasten the shift in favor of high-skilled workers.

[28]For evidence on the labor market effects of multinationals, see Matthew J. Slaughter, "Multinational Corporations, Outsourcing, and American Wage Divergence," NBER Working Paper No. 5253 (Cambridge, Massachusetts: National Bureau for Economic Research, September 1995); Robert C. Feenstra and Gordon Hanson, "Foreign Investment, Outsourcing, and Relative Wages," in *Political Economy of Trade Policy: Papers in Honor of Jagdish Bhagwati*, ed. by Robert C. Feenstra, Gene M. Grossman, and Douglas A. Irwin (Cambridge, Massachusetts: MIT Press, 1996); and Robert C. Feenstra and Gordon Hanson, "Globalization, Outsourcing, and Wage Inequality," *American Economic Review*, Vol. 86 (May 1996), pp. 240–45.

rigidities, the impact of terms of trade shocks will tend to fall on the number of workers employed rather than on wages. Increased capital mobility can thus potentially magnify the effect of external shocks on unemployment.

Immigration and Wages

In recent years, some advanced economies have experienced increased inflows of low-skilled workers, raising concern about the potential adverse effects of immigration on wages and the job prospects of low-skilled native workers. Empirical research, however, finds only very small effects of low-skilled immigration on wages and employment in the advanced economies in general, although effects in particular regions may be greater.[29] Mirroring the transatlantic difference in labor markets, immigration to European countries has typically led to some increased unemployment while immigration to the United States affects wages. Moreover, rigidities in European labor markets limit the speed of adjustment to changes such as migration and import competition, so that any adverse effects may tend to be longer lasting than in the United States. In both cases, the effect of low-skilled immigration falls most heavily on low-skilled workers, while wages and employment of high-skilled workers actually rise.

Immigration can also lead to increased growth, particularly if, as in the case of the recent influx of high-skilled migrants from the former Soviet Union to Israel, immigrants bring with them human capital that offsets the initial decrease in the per capita stock of physical capital that results from the immigration. In this case, the immigration potentially leads to increased investment as the higher levels of human capital raise the return to physical capital. The increase in investment would then be expected to lead to both higher wages and higher output. In recent years, however, immigrants to most advanced economies have had on average lower levels of skills than natives, suggesting that economy-wide growth effects from recent flows of immigration will be less immediate.

Public Policy Responses to Globalization

Globalization has been viewed with concern in many advanced economies, with the belief common that it harms the interests of workers, especially unskilled workers, either directly through immigration or indirectly through trade and capital outflows.

Particularly with respect to trade, these beliefs appear to be at odds with the evidence that import competition has generally had only modest effects on wages, employment, and income inequality in the advanced economies.

One explanation for this is that even though the advanced economies as a whole benefit from increased economic integration, the gains are typically distributed unevenly between groups within countries, with those adversely affected likely to experience adjustment costs and social dislocation. While policymakers might be tempted to allow their countries to forgo some gains from globalization in order to improve the welfare of particular constituents such as producers in certain sectors or less-skilled labor, restrictions on trade flows and capital movements are second-best policies compared with measures that directly compensate parties who do not share in the gains from globalization. Policies that seek to limit or delay the effects of globalization will dilute its benefits, which come in the form of lower prices for imports, as well as the increased flow of capital and technological innovations across countries. Rather than attempting to limit globalization, the appropriate policy response is instead to address the underlying structural rigidities that prevent labor markets from adjusting to technological change or external competition. In this respect, education and training are essential, since these are important means by which workers in advanced economies can upgrade their skills to match the demands of the changing global economy. It is also important to have in place well-targeted and cost-effective social safety nets that provide assistance to those displaced and ensure that they do not become marginalized.[30] Such safety nets, however, should not weaken incentives for workers and firms to make the adjustments to changes in the economic environment that form an essential and inevitable part of economic progress.

Capital Market Integration and Implications for Policy

The growing interdependence of national financial markets has significantly altered the environment in which monetary and fiscal policy are conducted. This section explores some of the implications for national policy autonomy, including the implementation and transmission of monetary policy, the conduct of fiscal policy, and the implications for tax competition and tax systems.

---

[29]See Rachel M. Friedberg and Jennifer Hunt, "The Impact of Immigrants on Host Country Wages, Employment and Growth," *Journal of Economic Perspectives*, Vol. 9 (Spring 1995), pp. 23–44, and Klaus F. Zimmerman, "Tackling the European Migration Problem," *Journal of Economic Perspectives*, Vol. 9 (Spring 1995), pp. 45–62.

---

[30]See Dani Rodrik, *Has Globalization Gone Too Far?* (Washington: Institute for International Economics, 1997) for a discussion of social dislocations that have accompanied changes in the global economy.

Table 13. Cross-Border Transactions in Bonds and Equities[1]

(In percent of GDP)

	1970	1975	1980	1985	1990	1995	1996[2]
United States	2.8	4.2	9.0	35.1	89.0	135.3	151.5
Japan[3]	. . .	1.5	7.7	63.0	120.0	65.1	82.8
Germany	3.3	5.1	7.5	33.4	57.3	169.4	196.8
France	. . .	. . .	8.4[4]	21.4	53.6	179.6	229.2
Italy	. . .	0.9	1.1	4.0	26.6	252.8	435.4
United Kingdom	. . .	. . .	. . .	367.5	690.1	. . .	. . .
Canada	5.7	3.3	9.6	26.7	64.4	194.5	234.8

Source: Bank for International Settlements (BIS).
[1]Gross purchases and sales of securities between residents and nonresidents.
[2]January to September.
[3]For 1996, data are based on settlement.
[4]The figure is for 1982.

Capital Flows and Interest Rates

Starting largely in the early 1970s, the relatively tight restrictions on international capital movements still in existence in many industrial countries began to be dismantled. The process of liberalization proved to be gradual, stretching well into the 1990s. The dismantling of capital and exchange controls coincided with an intense period of deregulation of domestic financial markets and of extensive financial innovations. The liberalization of financial markets together with the decline in transactions costs and the emergence of new financial instruments resulted in a dramatic growth in cross-border financial transactions.[31]

Gross capital flows have grown enormously since the early 1970s and especially in the past decade. For instance, cross-border transactions in bonds and equities in the major advanced countries were less than 10 percent of GDP in 1980 but were generally well over 100 percent of GDP in 1995 (Table 13). Gross flows of portfolio investment and foreign direct investment in the advanced countries more than tripled between the first half of the 1980s and the first half of the 1990s (Table 14). Foreign direct investment flows mainly represent the expansion of the international activities of multinational enterprises, so that the surge in foreign direct investment is a reflection of the globalization of business that has taken place in recent years. Worldwide flows of foreign direct investment began to surge in the mid-1980s, with the total flow of direct investment outward from the industrial countries more than quadrupling between 1984 and 1990 (Chart 27). In 1990–92, foreign direct investment fell as growth slowed in the industrial countries, but it subsequently recovered strongly. Three factors

[31]See Morris Goldstein and Michael Mussa, "The Integration of World Capital Markets," IMF Working Paper 93/95 (December 1993), also published in *Changing Capital Markets: Implications for Monetary Policy*, Federal Reserve Bank of Kansas City (August 1993), and Richard C. Marston, *International Financial Integration: A Study of Interest Differentials Between the Major Industrial Countries* (Cambridge, England; New York: Cambridge University Press, 1995).

Table 14. Gross Foreign Direct Investment plus Portfolio Investment[1]

(In percent of GDP)

	1970–74	1975–79	1980–84	1985–89	1990–95
Belgium-Luxembourg	. . .	3.4	5.1	14.3	41.5[2]
Canada	1.7	3.4	3.6	6.1	7.2
Denmark	. . .	0.6	0.9	3.5	7.2
France	. . .	1.3	2.1	4.1	7.2
Germany	1.2	1.3	1.7	5.2	6.3
Italy	0.9	0.3	0.6	1.7	5.7
Japan	. . .	0.6	2.6	5.9	3.7
Netherlands	7.3	4.7	6.0	10.9	11.1
Norway	. . .	5.6	0.4	6.6	2.1
Portugal	. . .	0.4	1.0	3.6	6.3
Spain	. . .	0.7	1.2	3.1	6.7
Sweden	1.0	1.2	1.7	5.0	7.0
Switzerland	. . .	4.5	9.4	14.7	12.8
United Kingdom	3.6	4.0	5.4	14.4	11.9
United States	1.0	1.5	1.4	2.9	3.3

[1]Sum of the absolute value of inward and outward foreign direct investment and portfolio investment.
[2]The figure is for 1990–94.

have been behind the recent rapid expansion: foreign direct investment is no longer confined to the largest firms, as an increasing number have become multinationals; the sectoral diversity of foreign direct investment has broadened, with the share of the service sector rising sharply; and the number of countries that are outward investors or hosts of foreign direct investment has risen considerably.[32] The benefits to the host country of foreign direct investment have in recent years been illustrated by the case of Ireland (Box 8).

By any measure, the volume of international financial transactions has been extraordinary. To single out one other measure, which is particularly relevant to the ability of monetary authorities to influence exchange rates through official intervention, average daily turnover in the foreign exchange market has grown from about $200 billion in the mid-1980s to around $1.2 trillion, equivalent to approximately 85 percent of all countries' foreign exchange reserves (Table 15).

The degree of capital market integration is much more limited, however, than gross flows would seem to suggest. First, it is interesting to note that net international capital flows do not show the explosive growth of gross flows. The current account imbalances of the advanced economies have remained rather small, both as a share of GDP and as compared with the levels experienced in the pre-1914 gold standard era (see Annex). In the 1990s, the absolute value of the advanced economies' current account imbalances relative to GDP has averaged around 2 percent. As regards foreign direct investment flows, although outward direct investment of the major advanced economies has increased more than twice as fast as output, it is still only a small proportion of domestic investment (see Chart 27). Furthermore, empirical evidence shows that domestic investment is financed mostly by domestic saving. This has been interpreted by some as implying that international capital mobility is low.[33] Others have argued, however, that the observed high correlation between domestic saving and investment rates need not be inconsistent with a high degree of capital mobility if, inter alia, goods markets are imperfectly integrated, if countries target current

---

[32]OECD, *Financial Market Trends*, No. 64 (Paris, June 1996), and Edward M. Graham, "Foreign Direct Investment in the World Economy," in *Staff Studies for the World Economic Outlook* (IMF, September 1995), pp. 120–35.

[33]Following Martin Feldstein and Charles Horioka, "Domestic Saving and International Capital Flows," *Economic Journal*, Vol. 90 (1980), pp. 314–29, a number of studies have found savings and investment rates highly correlated—for a review see Goldstein and Mussa, "The Integration of World Capital Markets," and Alan M. Taylor, "International Capital Mobility in History: The Saving-Investment Relationship," NBER Working Paper 5743 (Cambridge, Massachusetts: National Bureau for Economic Research, September 1996).

Chart 27. Selected Advanced Economies: Foreign Direct Investment Outflows[1]

Foreign direct investment flows have formed an important element in globalization.

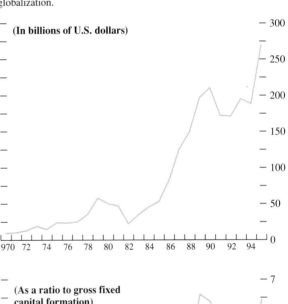

(In billions of U.S. dollars)

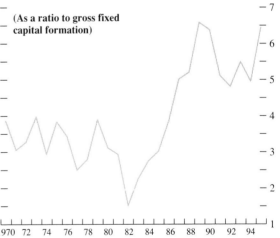

(As a ratio to gross fixed capital formation)

[1]Countries included are Belgium, Canada, France, Germany, Italy, Japan, the Netherlands, Sweden, Switzerland, the United Kingdom, and the United States. These countries account for over 80 percent of the total outward stock of foreign direct investment. Data prior to 1971 exclude Germany; 1975, France and Belgium; 1977, Japan; and 1983, Switzerland.

Box 8. Ireland Catches Up

During the 1990s, Ireland has ranked as the fastest growing economy in the European Union (EU). Growth peaked at about 10 percent in 1995, with inflation remaining well below the average for the EU. This strong growth performance—comparable with that of the newly industrialized countries of Asia—has accelerated Ireland's convergence toward the average level of per capita income in the EU (*see chart at right*). Financial discipline, improved international competitiveness, outward-looking policies, the successful attraction of inward investment in fast-growing activities, a skilled and growing labor force, and substantial EU transfers have been the underpinnings of Ireland's impressive economic performance.

In contrast to the recent period, the early 1980s were characterized by a rapid increase in government indebtedness, modest economic growth, and higher inflation. Double-digit budget deficits (in percent of GDP) raised the debt-to-GDP ratio to almost 120 percent by 1987 (*see chart below*). Real interest rates remained high, exacerbating the mounting debt burden. Recognizing that the economy was at the edge of a financial precipice, the authorities set targets for a sharp reduction in the deficit. Strict adherence to deficit targets—mainly achieved through expenditure restraint—combined with a monetary policy oriented toward price stability and the exchange rate anchor offered by the ERM, produced a solid foundation for economic recovery in the 1990s. The turnaround in economic performance has placed Ireland in a strong position to be one of the initial members of the planned Economic and Monetary Union (EMU).

Per Capita GDP
(In 1987 U.S. dollars; purchasing power parity terms)

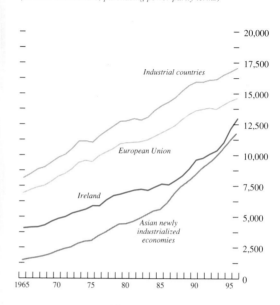

Ireland: General Government Budget Balance and General Government Debt
(In percent of GDP)

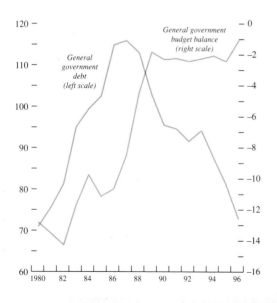

In the early 1990s, domestic demand was depressed owing to weak consumer demand and sharply declining investment. The main source of growth in the economy during this period was the largely foreign-owned, high-tech export sector, which expanded during 1990–93 at an annual rate of 9½ percent. Stronger gains in labor productivity in Ireland relative to trading partners steadily reduced unit labor costs. The resulting real effective depreciation of the Irish pound in turn provided a boost to the export sector (*see chart at right*). During 1994–96, however, overall growth rebounded, averaging about 8 percent. A number of factors contributed to this remarkable surge in economic activity. First, declines in interest rates and improved consumer confidence sparked a rebound in domestic demand from its depressed levels in the early 1990s. Second, fiscal policy did not restrain domestic demand. Third, and most important, the improved external environment combined with further improvements in competitiveness associated with growth in productivity contributed to an even better export performance. During 1994–96, export revenues for goods and services increased at an annual rate of about 15 percent, led by the high-tech manufacturing sectors.

Exports have played a significant role in supporting and boosting growth in Ireland, reflecting the substantial changes that have taken place in the manufacturing sector. Output and productivity in the sector have risen largely owing to the increasing importance of foreign direct investment in a number of dynamic high-tech sectors, which include office equipment, electrical engineer-

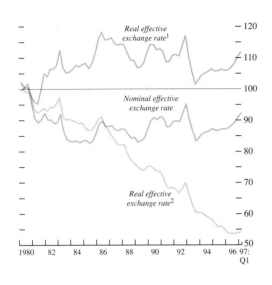

Ireland: Competitiveness Indicators
(1980 = 100)

Real effective exchange rate[1]

Nominal effective exchange rate

Real effective exchange rate[2]

1980 82 84 86 88 90 92 94 96 97: Q1

[1]Based on consumer price index.
[2]Based on normalized unit labor costs.

ing, instrument engineering, and pharmaceuticals. As a result, the Irish manufacturing sector has two fairly distinct parts: a modern sector, which is export oriented, efficient, and dominated by large foreign-owned firms, and a traditional sector, which tends to be less dynamic and more likely to produce for the local market. The increasing importance of the modern manufacturing sector is partly a result of policies designed to attract foreign direct investment. Domestic and foreign manufacturing firms and certain international financial services are subject to a preferential corporate tax rate. In addition, as elsewhere, many firms qualify for grants to defray start-up costs and research and development expenses. Ireland's increasingly skilled workforce and its membership in the

EU are also factors in attracting foreign investment—most notably from the United States and Japan—and enhancing the competitiveness of the modern manufacturing sector.

Net transfers from the EU—which declined from their peak in the early 1990s to about 4½ percent in 1996—have also contributed to Ireland's strong economic performance (*see table*). Structural fund transfers to Ireland, amounting to 2¼ percent of GNP in 1996, have supported public investment especially in infrastructure, training, and education. Eligibility for these funds is determined by how per capita income of Ireland compares with the EU average. With Ireland's progress in improving its per capita income position relative to the EU average, structural fund transfers may be reduced beginning in 1999 when the current program of transfers ends. An even larger source of EU transfers, however, has been subsidies received under the Common Agricultural Policy (CAP) through the Fonds Européen d'Orientation et Garantie Agricole (FEOGA). These payments are mainly based on agricultural prices and output in Ireland. In the longer term, further CAP reform, which is likely to be needed with the expansion of the EU, would result in cutbacks in such transfers.

Ireland's strong and broad-based growth performance during 1994–96 contributed to an unprecedented pace of job creation, with employment rising at an annual rate of nearly 4 percent, mainly in the service sector. Unemployment fell from 16½ percent in 1993 to 12 percent in 1996, still about 1 percentage point above the EU average. Long-term joblessness—which is concentrated among the unskilled and accounts for about half of total unemployment—remains a major problem, although recent employment programs to increase the attractiveness of hiring the long-term unemployed appear to hold some promise.

The scope for further increases in productivity arising from continued improvements in workforce skills, relatively rapid growth in the working age population (owing to demographics, rising female participation rates, and the return of Irish workers from abroad), and additional foreign direct investment point to annual growth in potential output of about 4 to 5 percent. This should allow Ireland to continue to catch up with average living standards in the rest of Europe, albeit probably at a more moderate pace than in recent years.

Net EU Transfers
(In percent of GNP)

	1990	1991	1992	1993	1994	1995	1996
FEOGA	5.3	5.3	4.2	4.6	3.8	3.4	3.7
Structural funds[1]	1.9	3.4	3.3	3.4	2.2	2.6	2.3
Contributions to EU	1.2	1.4	1.3	1.6	1.7	1.6	1.5
Net EU Transfers	6.0	7.3	6.2	6.4	4.4	4.4	4.6

Source: Ministry of Finance, *Budget,* various years.
[1]Includes payments under the FEOGA guidance fund, the European Social Fund, the European Regional Development Fund, the Cohesion Fund, and miscellaneous funds.

Table 15. Foreign Exchange Trading

(In billions of U.S. dollars and in percent)

	1986	1989	1992	1995
Global estimated turnover[1]	188	590	820	1190
As a ratio of:				
World exports of goods and services	7.4	15.8	17.4	19.1
Total reserves minus gold (all countries)	36.7	75.9	86.0	84.3

Sources: Bank for International Settlements; and International Monetary Fund.

[1]Daily average turnover, on spot, outright forward, and foreign exchange swap transactions, adjusted for local and cross-border double counting and for estimated gaps in reporting.

Figures are based on surveys of activities in the three largest exchange market centers (London, New York, and Tokyo) in 1986, and markets in 21 countries in 1989 and 26 countries in 1992 and 1995. The London, New York, and Tokyo markets accounted for 57 percent of global turnover in 1989, 54 percent in 1992, and 56 percent in 1995.

accounts, or if financial and real assets are not perfectly substitutable.[34]

In any event, the extent of financial market integration cannot be inferred from the volume of capital flows alone. In fact, international financial markets could be highly or even perfectly integrated, with asset prices adjusting in anticipation of capital flows, but with little or no arbitrage flows actually taking place. To assess the degree of financial market integration, it is also necessary to examine the extent to which asset prices are equalized.

This can be done at various levels. At one level, the integration of international financial markets requires that onshore and offshore yields on the same instruments, denominated in the same currency, are equalized. Since no currency risk is involved, yields can diverge only because of transaction and information costs and impediments to mobility, such as capital controls, political risk, and default risk. In keeping with the rapid decline in transactions costs and the dismantling of capital controls, onshore/offshore interest rate differentials have declined markedly during the past fifteen years and are now minuscule for most advanced economies, suggesting a very high degree of integration.

The trend toward closer integration is revealed also by the decline in deviations from covered interest parity (CIP).[35] With barriers between national markets greatly diminished, and not inhibiting potential arbitrage flows between national markets, and with currency risk eliminated by forward cover, departures from CIP have on average become much smaller.[36] Divergences from CIP for domestic short-term interest rates declined in the early 1980s in response to the financial deregulation and liberalization of capital movements undertaken by many countries (Chart 28). Since then the dispersion seems to have stabilized at a lower level, except for the temporary widenings associated with large disturbances, such as the 1992 European Monetary System (EMS) crisis.

Even with perfect capital mobility and no transaction costs, domestic nominal interest rates can of course still differ because of "currency premiums," comprising expected exchange rate changes and risk premiums. For countries maintaining fixed exchange rates, however, nominal interest rates can be expected to converge. Indeed, the dispersion of both short-term domestic interest rates and short-term Euromarket interest rates for European countries tended to decrease during the 1980s, a trend that was disrupted by the 1992 exchange market turbulence and the exit from the ERM of some major European currencies (Chart 29). Not surprisingly given the flexibility of their exchange rates, it is harder to detect a marked tendency for interest rates to converge among the three major industrial countries. Tests of uncovered interest parity (UIP) have generally concluded that UIP does not hold and that assets denominated in different currencies are imperfect substitutes.[37] Both time-varying, exchange rate risk premiums and systematic exchange rate forecast errors have been found to underlie deviations from UIP.[38]

[34]See, for instance, Michael Artis and Tamim Bayoumi, "Saving, Investment, Financial Integration, and the Balance of Payments," IMF Working Paper 89/102 (December 1989), and Jeffrey A. Frankel, "Quantifying International Capital Mobility in the 1980s," *On Exchange Rates* (Cambridge, Massachusetts: MIT Press, 1993), pp. 41–69.

[35]When CIP holds, the difference in interest rates on comparable instruments denominated in different currencies should equal the cost of cover in the forward exchange market.

[36]These departures, except for the wedge introduced by transactions costs, reflect "country premiums," that is, current capital controls or the expectation of future controls, and perceptions of default risk.

[37]UIP states that expected returns on investments in different currencies are equal when measured in a single currency. UIP is equivalent to the combination of CIP and the assumption that the forward exchange rate equals the expected future spot exchange rate.

[38]See Peter Isard, *Exchange Rate Economics* (Cambridge, England; New York: Cambridge University Press, 1995).

A deeper level of integration requires that capital flows equalize real interest rates between countries. Real interest rate parity is a more stringent condition than UIP because it requires in addition that expected changes in exchange rates equal anticipated inflation differentials. Thus, it also requires a close integration of goods markets. Nominal exchange rates have in fact departed considerably from the predictions of relative purchasing power parity (PPP), especially in the short run. It is only over long spans of years that there is more of a tendency for relative PPP to hold (Chart 30). The dispersion of real short-term interest rates declined in the 1980s but widened in the early 1990s in connection with various shocks, in particular, German unification and the EMS crises (Chart 31).[39]

In the case of long-term interest rates, lack of data prevents detailed analysis of parity conditions: no forward exchange rates or reasonable estimates of expected inflation are available for long horizons in most cases. The dispersion of nominal bond yields seems to parallel the dispersion of inflation rates. The supply shocks of the 1970s, combined with different policy responses, resulted in large cross-country differences in inflation rates and a corresponding increase in the dispersion of nominal bond yields. The decline in the dispersion during the 1980s was equally steep and is largely attributable to developments in Europe, where both inflation rates and policy fundamentals converged rapidly in preparation for EMU (Chart 32). For the three major advanced economies, there does not appear to have been any marked tendency for the dispersion of nominal bond yields to decline over time.

In summary, financial markets have become increasingly integrated, but they are far from forming a single global market. Still, the degree of integration is high enough to strongly affect the conduct and effects of macroeconomic, regulatory, and prudential policies.

Implications for Macroeconomic Policy

The issue of monetary policy autonomy arises mainly in the context of floating exchange rates. National monetary policy autonomy under fixed exchange rates is at best limited to the short run, when prices are sticky and exchange rates can move within relatively narrow bands; in the longer run, domestic monetary policy is determined by the anchor country. But the difference between fixed and floating exchange rate arrangements is in practice probably less sharp than may appear. The reason is that, irrespective of the exchange rate regime, reasonable price stability is now widely accepted to be the principal goal of

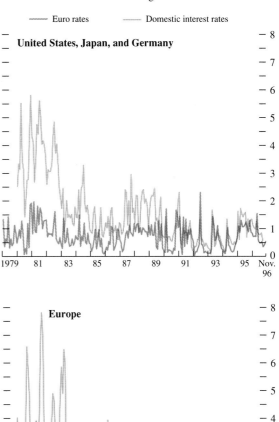

Chart 28. Selected Advanced Economies: Dispersion of Covered Interest Differentials[1]
(In percent a year; three-month rates)

Divergences from covered interest parity narrowed in the 1980s as financial markets became more integrated.

——— Euro rates   ——— Domestic interest rates

United States, Japan, and Germany

Europe

[1]Standard deviations of covered interest differentials between U.S. three-month rates and corresponding rates whose dollar returns are covered in the forward exchange market. In the bottom panel, the differential is with respect to German three-month rates. Europe comprises Germany, France, Italy, the United Kingdom, the Netherlands, and Switzerland. Data are monthly averages.

---

[39]Pravin Krishna and Bart Turtelboom, "The International Linkage of Real Interest Rates Revisited," IMF Working Paper (forthcoming) find that the comovement of real interest rates within Europe rose from the mid-1980s but find no evidence that the U.S.-Germany real interest rate link became stronger.

Chart 29. Selected Advanced Economies: Mean and Dispersion of Nominal Short-Term Interest Rates[1]

(In percent a year; three-month rates)

The dispersion of nominal interest rates declined in the European economies in the 1980s.

——— Euro rates   ——— Domestic interest rates

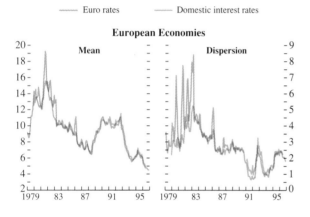

European Economies

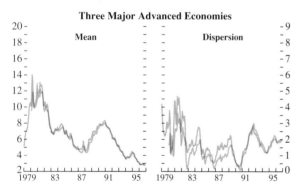

Three Major Advanced Economies

[1]Dispersion is defined as the standard deviation from the appropriate cross-country mean. European economies comprise Germany, France, Italy, the United Kingdom, the Netherlands, and Switzerland; the three major advanced economies consist of the United States, Japan, and Germany. Data are monthly averages.

monetary policy. The means chosen to achieve that goal, however, depend on the extent of capital market integration.

One of the main implications of high capital mobility is that it has made adjustable exchange rate pegs more difficult to sustain in the absence of strict policy convergence and appropriate economic fundamentals.[40] Also, asymmetric real shocks that require real exchange rate adjustments may cause difficulties, especially in countries with rigid labor and product markets. That is why it may be preferable for countries to adopt either permanently fixed (as in a monetary union or currency board arrangement) or fully flexible exchange rates. The vulnerability of fixed-but-adjustable exchange rate systems to changes in investor sentiment was most recently illustrated by the 1992 and 1993 ERM crises and the 1995 Mexican financial crisis.

With floating exchange rates, national monetary authorities have greater independence in choosing their inflation objective. Although monetary policy is strongly influenced by international financial markets, increased financial market integration does not appear to have diminished its effectiveness. Closely linked capital markets have, however, changed the monetary transmission mechanism by enhancing the role of the exchange rate. Domestic interest rates may have to adjust less to achieve the monetary policy objective because more adjustment comes through the exchange rate. The implications may be favorable for the distribution of demand across sectors, in that the burden of adjustment is not borne mainly by the domestic interest-sensitive components of expenditure. It may also have favorable fiscal effects as, in episodes that require monetary tightening, for instance, the burden of government debt service may be smaller when the adjustment in monetary conditions comes through both interest rates and the exchange rate, than when it comes mainly through interest rates.[41] The opposite can also occur, however, as market concerns about the appropriateness of domestic macroeconomic policies exert downward pressure on the exchange rate and may augment risk premiums in national interest rates. The experiences of Italy, Sweden, and some other European countries during 1993–95 demonstrate this latter point. But as those experiences also show, international financial markets can serve to "discipline" governments (either by raising default premiums or by forcing adjustments in exchange rates), encouraging the adoption of appropriate policies, and ultimately rewarding good policies.

[40]Lars E.O. Svensson, "Fixed Exchange Rates as a Means to Price Stability: What Have We Learned?" *European Economic Review,* Vol. 38 (April 1994), pp. 447–68.
[41]Any favorable fiscal effect would be muted in countries where a large proportion of the national debt is denominated in foreign currency.

Internationally integrated financial markets can pose challenges to policymakers if, as some believe, financial markets generate "excessive" volatility of assets prices. What constitutes excessive volatility is debatable. The evidence does not point to a rise in financial asset-price variability in recent decades.[42] Nor are there analytical grounds for believing that financial market integration increases volatility. However, the short-term volatility of asset prices, in particular exchange rates, can at times appear excessive, when compared with the volatility of their fundamental determinants. The crucial issue is whether or not the volatility of asset prices reflects the efficient functioning of financial markets. In this respect, it is not so much short-term volatility as significant and sustained misalignments of asset prices from values consistent with fundamentals that are of concern, because of the macroeconomic imbalances and economic distortions to which they can give rise.

Financial market prices can at times become misaligned, as exemplified by the overvaluation of the U.S. dollar in 1984–85, the rise in the stock market before the crash of 1987, and the appreciation of the yen in early 1995. Apart from the problems caused by the misalignments themselves, the eventual corrections can be disruptive and pose substantial risks for financial stability. Misalignments are often hard to identify because of the difficulty of assessing the level of asset prices consistent with macroeconomic fundamentals. And even when monetary authorities can identify a misalignment, say in the exchange market, the large volumes of private market flows may make it difficult for them to bring about a correction. Exchange market intervention by individual central banks may be insufficient for the task. Coordinated intervention may be more effective but may still be unable to match the resources of the private sector. Coordinated intervention may be far more effective, however, if it serves as a signal to markets of international macroeconomic policy cooperation and of a mutual commitment to the adoption of sustainable policies. The "quality" of intervention—in the sense of a signaling mechanism—may thus be even more important than the quantity of intervention. This was most recently illustrated in the summer of 1995, when coordinated intervention by the major central banks helped to bring about a correction of the yen/U.S. dollar rate from its excessively appreciated level.[43]

The opposite may also occur. Markets may become convinced that a particular exchange rate is unsustainable, making it impossible for official exchange mar-

___
[42]See Bank for International Settlements, *Financial Market Volatility: Measurement, Causes and Consequences,* BIS Conference Papers, Vol. 1 (Basle: Bank for International Settlements, Monetary and Economic Department, March 1996).

[43]For a discussion of this episode, see the October 1995 *World Economic Outlook,* pp. 32–37.

Chart 30. Advanced Economies: U.S. Dollar Exchange Rate Change and Inflation Differential

Deviations from relative purchasing power parity can be large in the short run and significant even in the longer run.

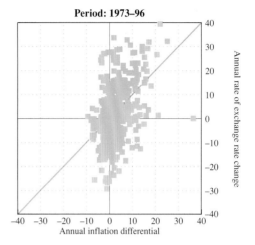

Period: 1973–96

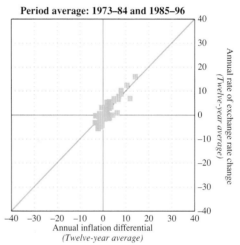

Period average: 1973–84 and 1985–96

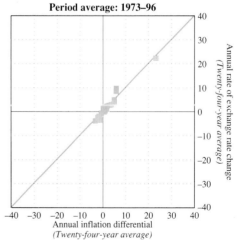

Period average: 1973–96

Chart 31. Selected Advanced Economies: Mean and Dispersion of Real Short-Term Interest Rates[1]
(In percent a year; three-month rates)

The dispersion of real short-term interest rates declined in the 1980s.

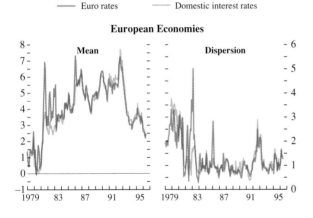

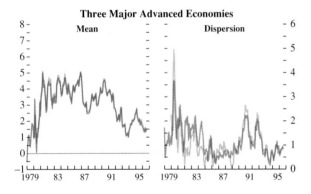

[1]Real interest rates are nominal rates deflated by the ex post 12-month change in the consumer price index. Dispersion is defined as the standard deviation from the appropriate cross-country mean. European economies comprise Germany, France, Italy, the United Kingdom, and the Netherlands; the three major advanced economies consist of the United States, Japan, and Germany.

ket intervention to support it effectively. The pressures against a parity may then be so intense that even extraordinarily large increases in interest rates may be ineffective, as experienced during the September 1992 ERM crisis.[44]

Another consequence of highly integrated financial markets is that shocks that occur in one market may be more easily transmitted to other markets. Shocks to asset prices in one country have at times spread quickly to similar assets in other countries, but generally they have not spilled over on a comparable scale into markets in other assets, so that the systemic consequences of disruptions in any one market have been limited. Nonetheless, the possibility cannot be dismissed that effects in different markets can interact to magnify shocks, thus increasing macroprudential or systemic risk. Increased integration also makes it possible, however, for disturbances to be absorbed by a bigger market, thus dampening the effects on any particular national market. In any event, the continuing globalization of financial markets will increasingly demand a broad multilateral approach to maintaining a sound and efficient international financial system.[45]

The enormous growth of financial markets has also increased the tendency for countries with open capital markets to experience large inflows of foreign capital. While not uncommon in the advanced economies, in recent years this has been most marked in some rapidly growing emerging market economies with developing financial markets. Capital inflows can ease a country's external financing constraint; but large inflows can also adversely affect macroeconomic stability by fueling inflation and raising real exchange rates to unsustainably high levels. The latter is more likely to be the case when the inflows are temporary, driven, for instance, by international interest rate movements or by shifts in market sentiment not supported by changes in the host country's fundamentals, rather than by improved longer-term investment opportunities. In some cases, the capital inflows may be attracted by high domestic interest rates required for domestic stabilization and may pose difficulties when the capital inflows are too large to be sterilized. Depending on the nature and the cause of the capital inflows, and depending also on institutional factors such as the structure of prudential regulations and supervision and the robustness of the domestic banking system, authorities have various instruments in addition to sterilized intervention for dealing with large

[44]The above discussion has focused on foreign exchange markets, the core of the international financial system, but similar considerations apply to other asset markets, in particular, equity and real estate markets. Recent examples include the run-up and subsequent collapse of equity and real estate prices in several countries in the latter half of the 1980s and the 1994 drop in bond prices.

[45]For a discussion of the issues involved, see *International Capital Markets: Developments, Prospects, and Key Policy Issues* (IMF, September 1996 and August 1995).

capital inflows. These include exchange rate, fiscal, and monetary adjustments, as well as financial regulatory measures and price-based capital controls (i.e., various types of financial transactions taxes, stamp duties, and fees).[46] The effectiveness of controls, though, is likely to be limited, and the inflows are likely to persist until policies are adjusted to address the factors providing the incentives for the inflows.

The increased integration of financial markets in recent years has made even more evident the well-known proposition that of the three objectives of independent monetary policy, fixed exchange rates, and open capital markets, policymakers can simultaneously adopt not more than two. Recognition of this constraint has induced some to advocate throwing "sand in the wheels" of the international financial market by taxing cross-border financial transactions.[47] The argument rests on the notion that a transactions tax will naturally tend to discourage short-term capital flows, which are assumed to be destabilizing and undesirable but not affect long-term capital flows, which are assumed to be desirable and based on fundamentals. On the whole, short-term capital flows are not socially undesirable, however, and, in any event, there is no clear way of discriminating between socially desirable and undesirable, or between stabilizing and destabilizing, short-term financial transactions. Nor is there any strong evidence that lower transaction costs are associated with higher asset-price volatility.[48] Moreover, from a practical perspective, unless the tax were implemented globally and across a broad range of financial instruments, its effect would simply be to shift the location of the trading and the instruments used. Governments have more and more come to recognize that the constraints imposed by financial market globalization are best addressed not by imposing restrictions on the free flow of capital, but rather by adopting sound, transparent, and sustainable macroeconomic policies that reduce the risk of sudden changes in market sentiment, and by engaging in international policy cooperation. At the "micro" level such cooperation can help to establish and to ensure the observance of a set of core regulatory and supervisory standards, and at the "macro" level it can help in the pursuit of policies that lead to the convergence of inflation at low

[46]For a discussion of the causes of large capital inflows to some developing and transition countries and the design of appropriate policy responses, see Annex IV in the October 1996 *World Economic Outlook*.

[47]For example, James Tobin, "A Proposal for International Monetary Reform," *Eastern Economic Journal,* Vol. 4 (1978), pp. 153–59.

[48]For instance, despite declining transactions costs, U.K. asset-price volatility (for treasury bills, ten-year gilts, equities, and sterling versus dollar exchange rate) has tended to decline since the late 1970s—see Nicola Anderson and Francis Breedon, "U.K. Asset Price Volatility Over the Last Fifty Years," in Bank for International Settlements, *Financial Market Volatility,* pp. 396–428.

Chart 32. Selected Advanced Economies: Mean and Dispersion of Nominal Bond Yields[1]
(In percent a year)

The dispersion of long-term interest rates declined steeply in the 1980s, especially in Europe.

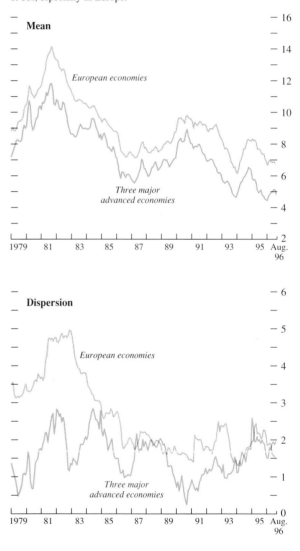

[1]Dispersion is defined as the standard deviation from the appropriate cross-country mean. European economies comprise Germany, France, Italy, the United Kingdom, Belgium, the Netherlands, and Switzerland; the three major advanced economies consist of the United States, Japan, and Germany.

rates and that avoid unwarranted fluctuations in exchange rates.

Implications for Tax Systems

In addition to the implications for the conduct of monetary and fiscal polices, globalization also has implications for countries' tax systems. The origins of national tax systems and the current structure of government spending can be traced back to a period with substantially less open economies and lower factor mobility. Correspondingly, taxation is largely based on the "territoriality principle," that is, the right to tax incomes and activities within the territory of the jurisdiction. In an increasingly global environment, this principle loses efficiency and can prove to be a potential source of conflict.[49]

Globalization may be expected increasingly to constrain governments' choice of tax structures and tax rates, especially in smaller countries. Internationally mobile factors of production—financial capital and some highly trained segments of the labor market—can more easily avoid taxes levied in particular countries. The scope for tax evasion by individuals and corporations has also been enhanced. Indeed, many countries have experienced an erosion of the capital income tax base. Some governments have responded to the erosion by establishing favorable tax regimes. This "tax competition" may affect the average tax level of some countries by obliging them to lower tax rates for certain taxes. To the extent that the allocation of capital will be driven by tax considerations rather than by pretax rates of return, the allocation of capital will be less efficient. In a similar vein, personal income taxes and expenditure policies related to social spending are likely to become a more important factor in labor migration. Presumably, globalization will increasingly tend to cause tax systems to converge either through tax harmonization or via tax competition across jurisdictions.

Implications for the Cycle and Inflation

Finally, the increased integration of national economies raises two other macroeconomic issues: Have output fluctuations become more synchronized across countries? And is globalization a force for lower inflation? Cyclical variations in output do not appear to have become more correlated internationally, as indicated by divergent movements in output gaps among the major advanced economies in recent years. The correlations were higher in the 1970s, because of the large supply shocks that affected all countries simultaneously. Also, although fluctuations in the growth of industrial production for the major advanced economies are strongly correlated with the "world business cycle" (i.e., the common component of international fluctuations), there have been no systematic differences in these correlations over time.[50] Country-specific shocks and common shocks account for most of the variability in output in the major advanced economies—from 75 percent to 95 percent according to one recent estimate.[51] The transmission of country-specific shocks through trade links is rather limited, except for those originating in the United States, which, because of that country's economic size, are felt more strongly abroad than those of other countries. Moreover, on the basis of correlations between trade and output, it does not appear that the international transmission of country-specific shocks through trade flows has increased in the past two decades or so.[52] Thus, apart from the influence of common disturbances, such as commodity price shocks or technology shocks, it is still mainly nonsynchronous domestic disturbances that drive business cycle fluctuations.

As for inflation, its decline in recent years is mainly the result of determined policy actions to bring it under control. But the increased openness to trade and capital flows may also have played a role in some cases. Foreign competition, outsourcing, and the increased internationalization of production may have served to suppress wage demands or raise productivity growth, thereby reducing cost pressures. These effects of globalization will tend, however, to result in one-time downward shifts in the price level rather than ongoing restraints on the rate of inflation. The aspect of globalization that is more likely to have a long-lasting influence on inflation is the discipline on domestic financial policies imposed by increased financial market integration.

* * *

Does globalization make it more difficult to achieve the legitimate and desirable aims of economic policy? On the whole, it would seem not, even though at times large short-term capital flows can adversely affect macroeconomic stability, and asset prices, including exchange rates, can as a result become misaligned. What globalization does, rather, is limit the scope for countries to pursue policies that are incompatible with medium-term financial stability. The disciplining effect of global financial and product markets applies

---

[49]For a detailed discussion of these issues see Vito Tanzi, "Globalization, Tax Competition and the Future of Tax Systems," IMF Working Paper 96/141 (December 1996), and *Taxation in an Integrating World* (Washington: Brookings Institution, 1995).

[50]Robin L. Lumsdaine and Eswar S. Prasad, "Identifying the Common Component in International Economic Fluctuations" (unpublished; IMF, December 1996).

[51]Stefania Fabrizio and J. Humberto Lopez, "Domestic, Foreign or Common Shocks?" IMF Working Paper 96/107 (September 1996).

[52]Manmohan Kumar and Eswar Prasad, "International Trade and the Business Cycle," IMF Working Paper (forthcoming).

not only to policymakers, via financial market pressures, but also to the private sector, by making it more difficult to sustain unwarranted wage increases and price markups. If markets adopt too sanguine a view of a country's economic policies and prospects, however, this could relax policy discipline for a time and result in a high adjustment cost when market perceptions change. Rather than acting as a constraint on the pursuit of appropriate policies, globalization can provide added leverage to such policies. It may also provide added flexibility. The greater international mobility of private capital, by easing financing constraints, can extend the time period over which countries can implement needed adjustments. Markets will be willing to provide this leeway, however, only if they perceive that countries really are making adjustments that fundamentally address existing and prospective imbalances. Otherwise, markets will eventually exert their own discipline, in such a way that the time period for adjustment may be brutally shortened.

IV

Globalization and the Opportunities for Developing Countries

Since the mid-1980s, the pace of globalization in the world economy has quickened considerably. World trade has increased nearly twice as fast as world GDP, financial markets in many countries have been liberalized rapidly, and capital flows to many developing countries have accelerated. Clearly, some economies have benefited from globalization enormously. With this *World Economic Outlook,* Hong Kong, Korea, Singapore, and Taiwan Province of China (together with Israel) are moved from the developing country group to the new advanced economy group; they vividly demonstrate the great successes that can be achieved when policies take advantage of these forces. But what do the pressures of globalization mean for economic performance and policy orientations in developing countries more generally? Do larger trade flows and more liberal financial markets benefit all countries equally, or are some economies better positioned to reap the gains than others? What do closer trade and financial linkages suggest for the cross-country income convergence process? Are there successive groups of developing countries following in the footsteps of the Asian success cases or not? Are there particular policies that can help countries enjoy the benefits of globalization, enhance economic performance, and reduce the danger of becoming marginalized? These issues are the focus of this chapter.

The chapter begins with a review of the key changes that are taking place in developing countries as the world becomes more integrated—in trade, in financial markets, and in the movement of people. Patterns of growth performance are then highlighted to examine the degree to which per capita incomes have been converging on those in the advanced economies. Many developing economies have shown substantial gains in living standards, and real per capita incomes on average have roughly doubled over the past thirty years. This average gain, however, is no greater than that achieved by the advanced economies, so that on average there has been no convergence of per capita income levels between the two groups of countries; in fact, in absolute terms there has been a widening. Moreover, evidence to be presented below suggests that there has been an increasing polarization among the developing countries. Highly successful developing countries, such as Chile, Malaysia, and Thailand, have been converging toward advanced economy per capita income levels quite rapidly, but many poor countries have been falling relatively farther behind. The reasons for this bipolar pattern and the factors that are associated with faster growth and convergence are then analyzed.

A key lesson seems to be that the pressures of globalization, especially in the past decade or so, have served to accentuate the benefits of good policies and the costs of bad policies. Countries that align themselves with the forces of globalization and embrace the reforms needed to do so, liberalizing markets and pursuing disciplined macroeconomic policies, are likely to put themselves on a path of convergence with the advanced economies, following the successful Asian newly industrialized economies (NIEs). These countries may expect to benefit from trade, gain global market share, and be increasingly rewarded with larger private capital flows. Countries that do not adopt such policies are likely to face declining shares of world trade and private capital flows, and to find themselves falling behind in relative terms.

The analysis then looks at what factors seem to be necessary and sufficient for faster per capita income growth. A main finding is that there are important policy complementarities. It is not just one type of policy that is needed, such as openness to trade, but rather a comprehensive set of policies and reforms that are mutually reinforcing. Finally the chapter looks at the problems of countries that seem in danger of being marginalized and suggests what policies might help put them on paths of higher growth and eventual convergence with more successful countries.

Forces of Integration

Changing Trade Linkages

A striking feature of the growth in world trade and capital flows over the past decade has been the heightened involvement of developing countries. Developing countries not only increased their share of world trade from 23 percent in 1985 to 29 percent in 1995, but they also deepened and diversified their trade linkages. Interdeveloping country trade increased from 31 percent of total developing country trade in 1985 to 37 percent in 1995. Between 1985 and 1995, the share of manufactured products in these countries' exports increased from 47 percent to 83 per-

Table 16. Advanced Economies Versus Developing Countries Including Newly Industrialized Economies: Diversification of Exports

(In percent of merchandise imports or exports)

	Advanced Economies (Excluding Newly Industrialized Economies)						Developing Countries Plus Newly Industrialized Economies					
	Imports			Exports			Imports			Exports		
	1975	1985	1995	1975	1985	1995	1975	1985	1995	1975	1985	1995
Nonfuel primary products	10.2	6.8	5.2	7.1	5.6	4.2	5.7	6.1	5.0	10.1	7.4	5.7
Fuel	26.0	22.4	8.4	5.9	8.9	3.8	15.9	19.9	7.2	61.4	45.4	11.2
Manufacturers	63.8	70.8	86.4	87.0	85.5	92.0	78.4	74.0	87.8	28.2	47.2	83.0

cent, which reflects the industrialization process they have been undergoing (Table 16). Despite these overall encouraging developments, there have been wide disparities among the developing countries (Chart 33). Except for countries in Asia and some in Latin America, integration with the world economy has been rather slow. Africa's share of world trade has continuously declined since the late 1960s, while for the major oil producing countries the share has fallen dramatically since oil prices and revenues peaked in the early 1980s.

The expansion, diversification, and deepening of developing countries' trade linkages have to a large extent been the result of significant changes in trade and exchange regimes. Statist and inward-looking policies of protectionism and import-substitution increasingly have been abandoned in favor of more outward-looking and open policies; trade and exchange regimes have been liberalized, with tariff and nontariff barriers lowered significantly. On the basis of a fairly restrictive definition of openness adopted in one study, 33 developing countries switched from relatively closed to open trade regimes between 1985 and 1995.[53] Moreover, many developing countries have committed themselves to further reductions of tariffs and nontariff barriers in the multilateral context of the Uruguay Round. The participation by developing countries in regional trading arrangements, which may entail risks of trade diversion as well as benefits of trade creation, has also increased in the last decade or so.[54]

---

[53]See Jeffrey D. Sachs and Andrew M. Warner, "Economic Convergence and Economic Policies," NBER Working Paper No. 5039 (Cambridge, Massachusetts: National Bureau of Economic Research, February 1995). They deem a country's trade regime to be closed if it has any *one* of the following characteristics: (1) nontariff barriers covering 40 percent or more of total trade, (2) average tariff rates of 40 percent or more, (3) a black market exchange rate in which the domestic currency is depreciated 20 percent or more relative to the official exchange rate, (4) a socialist economic system, or (5) a state monopoly on major exports.

[54]See Richard Harmsen and Michael Leidy, "Regional Trading Arrangements," in *International Trade Policies: The Uruguay Round and Beyond*, Vol. II, *Background Papers*, by Naheed Kirmani and others (IMF, 1994).

More Interconnected Capital Markets

Developing countries are also becoming increasingly integrated with the global financial system. Net private capital flows to developing countries (excluding the Asian NIEs) averaged about $150 billion a year over 1993–96 and almost hit $200 billion in 1996—nearly a sixfold increase from the average annual inflow over 1983–89. In fact, capital flows to one country, China, were larger in 1996 than they were to all developing countries as recently as 1989. These capital inflows roughly doubled in relation to developing country GDP between 1985 and 1996. Unlike in the 1970s and early 1980s when most capital flows represented bank lending, the largest flows in recent years have been in equity and portfolio investments (Chart 34). Such private capital flows rose from a low of ½ of 1 percent of developing country GDP in 1983–89 to 2–4 percent of GDP in each of the years 1994–96. Foreign direct investment has posted the largest rise. This has flowed overwhelmingly toward the emerging market countries that have been experiencing relatively fast economic growth. Asian developing countries received almost twice the net private capital inflows as a percentage of their GDP that African countries received over 1990–96 (Chart 35). Liberalization of financial markets in both recipient and source countries has helped to spur this growing capital market integration. Successful developing countries increasingly have lifted controls on cross-border flows, especially on capital inflows, and removed restrictions on payments for current account transactions. The number of developing countries accepting the obligations to maintain current account convertibility of their currencies under the IMF's Article VIII has increased from 41 in 1985 to 99 today. With China's acceptance of Article VIII in late 1996, the proportion of developing country trade carried out under current account convertibility has increased from around 30 percent in 1985 to nearly 70 percent in 1997 (Chart 36). Impressive growth performance and an improved track record in terms of macroeconomic stability by many developing countries, and emerging market countries in particular, also have promoted capital market integration by

Chart 33. Developing Countries and Asian Newly Industrialized Economies (NIEs): Trade[1]
(In percent of total world trade)

While the shares of world exports of the Asian newly industrialized economies and the rapidly industrializing economies have increased in the past decade, the shares of most other developing country regions have been roughly flat or have declined.

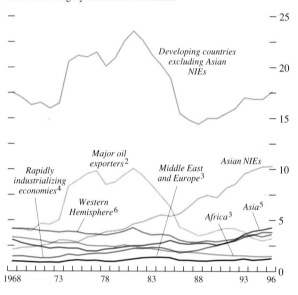

[1]Excluding Cyprus and Malta.
[2]Excluding Iraq.
[3]Excluding major oil exporters.
[4]Consists of Chile, Indonesia, Malaysia, and Thailand.
[5]Excluding Asian newly industrialized economies, Indonesia, Malaysia, and Thailand.
[6]Excluding major oil exporters and Chile.

making these markets more attractive to investors from advanced economies wishing to diversify their portfolios.

Changes in Employment and Relative Wages

As discussed in Chapter III, relative changes in employment and wages of skilled and unskilled labor in the advanced economies do not appear to have been closely related to increased trade or capital mobility. Instead, studies generally attribute the bulk of the decline in employment or relative wages of unskilled workers in advanced economies to a natural development progression as economies mature. Economic development has typically involved relative shifts of resources and output from agriculture to unskilled labor-intensive manufacturing, to high value-added manufacturing and services. Thus, the shift of employment away from manufacturing appears largely to reflect the forces of technological progress and capital deepening, rather than international trade pressures.[55] If advanced economies have flexible labor markets and good adjustment mechanisms, it can be viewed as natural and highly beneficial for them to shift their production to sectors with higher value added per unit of input than low value-added manufacturing.

Similar forces are at work in the developing countries themselves. Many of the developing countries that have integrated into the world economy have, for example, seen their highly skilled workers shift toward their tradable goods sectors, while their unskilled workers have shifted to nontradable sectors, such as construction and transportation.[56] This might imply temporary increases in unemployment as these economies adjust to the demands of closer integration into global markets. The rise in developing country incomes, in turn, helps to provide a growing market for some of the high-value-added output of the industrial countries. Increased North-South trade and integration may therefore be expected to lead to increasing prosperity in advanced and developing economies alike as both groups move up to the production of higher-value goods and services. Employment in the advanced economies can remain at high levels as the demand for services increases, provided labor markets are flexible, and employment in developing countries can increase as people shift out of the informal sector into the formal sector. However, the pressures of technology that tend to cause the relative incomes of certain groups of unskilled workers in both country groups todecline must be recognized and addressed by

---

[55]See, for example, Rowthorn and Ramaswamy, "Deindustrialization: Causes and Implications."
[56]See "Workers in an Integrated World," *World Development Report* (Washington: World Bank, 1995).

policies in such areas as social safety nets, and education and training.[57]

Changes in the Movement of People

The flow of people across national borders has also increased as the world economy has become more interconnected, although the flow remains relatively small. In 1990, roughly 120 million people were living in countries in which they were not born, up from 75 million in 1965. The share of the world's labor force that is foreign born increased by roughly half between 1965 and 1990. Although the largest portion of labor migration is from developing country to developing country, flows from developing countries to industrial countries have accelerated the most over the past two decades. As incomes in poor countries increase and as the wage differential between an advanced economy receiving immigrants and a poor country experiencing net emigration drops to less than about four to one, migration from the latter to the former tends to diminish.[58]

Labor flows almost certainly would have been greater without the surge in international trade already described. Some researchers have identified a hump-backed relationship between migration and trade, whereby trade helps to establish contacts, information networks, and channels that can lead to a temporary swelling of migration from poor countries to rich countries over the short and intermediate run.[59] Over the longer term, however, trade substitutes for the physical movement of capital and labor.

The free flow of factors, including labor, has many economic benefits—the main one being that it helps to maximize global output, promoting efficiency in both labor-supplying and labor-receiving countries. Countries receiving immigrant workers will find that certain production bottlenecks are opened up, which can reduce inflationary pressures, and that aggregate supply is boosted. Countries that receive foreign business managers or technical experts to help develop or manage enterprises are likely to find that the productivity in such facilities improves. Labor-exporting countries are likely to receive foreign resources in the form of worker remittances, which are estimated in one study to have totaled over $70 billion globally in 1995, or other flows.[60] These flows have been particularly im-

Chart 34. Developing Countries: Net Private Capital Flows[1]
(In percent of GDP)

Overall, capital flows to developing countries have rebounded sharply in the 1990s from the depressed levels of the 1980s. Direct investment has led the way.

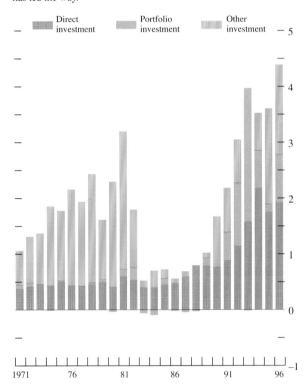

[1]Excludes major oil exporters. Because of data limitations, these data may include some official flows. Data for 1994 exclude Brazil.

---

[57]See Donald J. Robbins, "Evidence on Trade and Wages in the Developing World," OECD Development Centre Technical Paper No. 119 (December 1996). The author argues that contrary to the predictions of the factor price equalization theorem, the wages of unskilled workers in a number of developing countries have been falling in relative terms, probably because of the forces of technology.

[58]See Thomas Straubhaar, *On the Economics of International Labor Migration* (Bern; Stuttgart: Paul Haupt, 1988).

[59]See Phillip Martin, "Economic Aspects of International Migration" (unpublished: IMF, Research Department, December 1996).

[60]The estimate of worker remittances is from Martin, "Economic Aspects."

Chart 35. Developing Countries: Net Private Capital Flows, 1990–96[1]

(Annual average; in billions of U.S. dollars)

In proportion to GDP, capital flows to Asia have been running at twice the rate of flows to Africa,

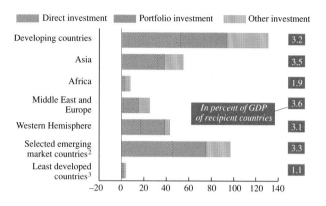

[1]Excludes Brazil in 1994.

[2]Comprises Argentina, Brazil, Chile, China, Colombia, India, Indonesia, Malaysia, Mexico, Pakistan, Peru, the Philippines, South Africa, Thailand, Turkey, and Venezuela.

[3]Comprises Afghanistan, Bangladesh, Benin, Bhutan, Botswana, Burkina Faso, Burundi, Cambodia, Cape Verde, Central African Republic, Chad, Comoros, Djibouti, Equatorial Guinea, Ethiopia, the Gambia, Guinea, Guinea-Bissau, Haiti, Kiribati, Lao People's Democratic Republic, Lesotho, Liberia, Madagascar, Malawi, Maldives, Mali, Mauritania, Mozambique, Myanmar, Nepal, Niger, Rwanda, São Tomé and Príncipe, Sierra Leone, Solomon Islands, Somalia, Sudan, Tanzania, Togo, Uganda, Vanuatu, Western Samoa, Republic of Yemen, Zaïre, and Zambia.

Chart 36. Advanced, Developing, and Transition Economies: Current Account Convertibility[1]

(In percent)

The pace of liberalization of exchange regimes in developing economies has quickened in recent years.

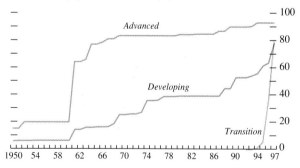

[1]Percent of advanced, developing, and transition economies that have accepted Article VIII of the IMF's Articles of Agreement; economies are weighted by their 1990–95 share of aggregate exports of all advanced, all developing, or all transition economies. As of March 31, 1997, a total of 138 countries had accepted Article VIII.

portant for certain countries, including Bangladesh, Pakistan, and the Philippines. Such countries may also find that their overseas workers acquire valuable skills that benefit the domestic economy when the workers return home.

Both groups of countries, however, have concerns about migration. Labor-receiving countries are concerned, for example, that an influx of unskilled workers will reduce wages or employment opportunities, or both, for native unskilled workers. As indicated, however, the forces of technological change are likely to play a bigger role, through deindustrialization and changes in the structure of demand for labor. Meanwhile, labor-exporting countries are often concerned that the loss of human capital, especially skilled labor—including the "brain drain"—may not be compensated by the flow of remittances from workers abroad, with a substantial portion of foreign labor earnings not repatriated or invested in unproductive domestic assets, such as real estate.[61]

With regard to likely future trends in migration, the economic forces that influence the desire of people to move, including the growing per capita income gaps between successful and unsuccessful countries, might seem to point to the likelihood of a substantial increase in the potential supply of migrants. On the other hand, the downward pressure on low-skilled wages in the advanced economies and the trend toward tighter immigration policies in many countries may tend to limit both legal and clandestine labor flows.

Implications for Relative Income Patterns and Convergence

How have these forces of integration affected cross-country growth and income patterns? In absolute terms, living standards as measured by real per capita incomes have risen substantially in most developing countries over the past thirty years. This is shown in Chart 37, where movements in absolute real per capita income are shown, measured in terms of average 1995 per capita GDP in the industrial countries. Even excluding the successful Asian NIEs, developing countries as a group more than doubled their real per capita income between 1965 and 1995, in line with the industrial countries. Most developing countries experienced substantial economic progress over the period. The gains have been nothing less than spectacular in some countries. Korea, for example, experienced almost a tenfold rise in per capita income

[61]For an analysis of the effects of human capital flight on growth, see Nadeem Ul Haque and Se-Jik Kim, "'Human Capital Flight': Impact of Migration on Income and Growth," *Staff Papers,* IMF, Vol. 42 (September 1995), pp. 577–607.

between 1965 and 1995, while Thailand saw a five-fold increase, and Malaysia a fourfold rise. In the developing countries of the Western Hemisphere average per capita incomes doubled between 1965 and 1980 before stagnating over the next 15 years, a period much of which was dominated by the debt crisis and its aftermath.

While the success stories illustrate that dramatic improvements in living standards are possible, many countries regrettably are not realizing their potential. In relative terms, most developing countries have failed to raise their per capita incomes toward those of the industrial countries (Chart 38). In fact, Asia is the only major region to have registered significant relative progress, in the sense of having achieved significant convergence toward industrial country living standards. The four Asian NIEs increased per capita incomes from 18 percent of the industrial country level in 1965 to 66 percent in 1995. For other Asian economies, the gap has also been reduced, with the fastest progress in the 1985–95 period. However, among the groups of countries in the Western Hemisphere, the Middle East and North Africa (MENA) region, and Africa, the gaps have widened since 1965 and especially since the mid-1970s. Western Hemisphere countries, for example, which had almost double the average NIE level of per capita income in 1965, saw the gap between their income level and that of the industrial countries gradually widen after the debt crisis of the 1980s. The average per capita income level of African countries fell in relative terms from 14 percent of the industrial country level in 1965 to just 7 percent in 1995. Africa and Asia roughly exchanged relative positions in this 30-year period. These regional developments in relative income performance seem to parallel the patterns of integration proxied, for example, by shares of world trade (Chart 33).

There has also been a sharp decline in upward mobility of developing countries within the international distribution of average per capita incomes and an increased tendency for countries to become polarized into high- and low-income clusters. Using the average per capita incomes of developing countries each year to define five income brackets—a lowest quintile for income levels from zero to 20 percent of the richest developing country level, a second quintile for income levels from 20 percent to 40 percent, and so forth—reveals an interesting profile. Of the 108 non-oil-producing developing countries for which data are available, 52 were in the lowest-income quintile in 1965, but the number had increased to 84 countries by 1995 (Table 17). Meanwhile, the number of developing countries in the middle-income categories fell rapidly. In 1965, 49 of these countries had incomes in the second and third income quintiles (between 20 percent and 60 percent of the richest developing country income level), but the number had dipped dramatically to just 21 countries by

Chart 37. Developing Countries and Asian Newly Industrialized Economies (NIEs): Real Per Capita Income[1]

(In percent of 1995 industrial country per capita GDP; purchasing power parity terms)

Per capita incomes in most developing country groups have increased since 1965, but progress has been far from uniform.

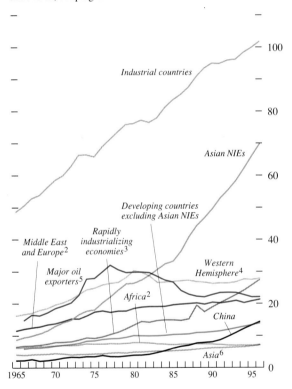

[1]Excluding Cyprus and Malta.
[2]Excluding major oil exporters.
[3]Consists of Chile, Indonesia, Malaysia, and Thailand.
[4]Excluding major oil exporters and Chile.
[5]Excluding Iraq.
[6]Excluding Asian newly industrialized economies, China, Indonesia, Malaysia, and Thailand.

Chart 38. Developing Countries and Asian Newly Industrialized Economies (NIEs): Relative Economic Performance[1]

(In percent of current industrial country per capita GDP; purchasing power parity terms)

With the exception of the Asian newly industrialized economies, China, and a group of four industrializing economies, most country groups have not experienced convergence toward per capita incomes in the industrial countries.

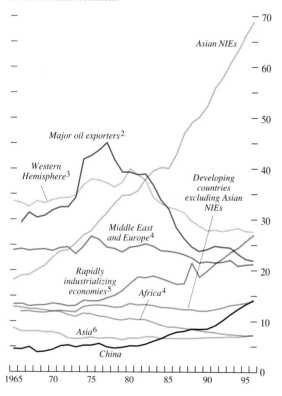

[1]Excluding Cyprus and Malta.
[2]Excluding Iraq.
[3]Excluding major oil exporters and Chile.
[4]Excluding major oil exporters.
[5]Consists of Chile, Indonesia, Malaysia, and Thailand.
[6]Excluding Asian newly industrialized economies, China, Indonesia, Malaysia, and Thailand.

1995.[62] Simply put, over the past thirty years the vast majority of developing countries—84 out of 108—have either stayed in the lowest-income quintile or fallen into that quintile from a relatively higher position. Moreover, there are now fewer middle-income developing countries, and upward mobility of countries seems to have fallen over time. While there was some tendency for countries to move to higher brackets and to progress relative to the advanced economies over the 1965–75 period, the forces of polarization seem to have become stronger since the early 1980s.

Income convergence requires that poor countries have faster per capita income growth than rich countries. Given the trends just discussed, it should not be surprising that there is little evidence of such income convergence between developing countries and advanced economies over recent decades. Chart 39 shows a scatter diagram of average per capita income growth rates over the period 1965–95 plotted against initial (1965) per capita income levels for both advanced and developing countries. If incomes in these countries were tending to converge toward some global average, there would be few data points in the northeast and southwest quadrants—the richest countries would not be growing faster than average, and the poorest countries would not be growing more slowly than average. However, as the diagram makes clear, there has been no such convergence trend. Even excluding the advanced economies from the diagram, to test whether there has been convergence just among the developing countries and newly industrialized economies themselves, suggests no such tendency (Chart 40).

This lack of cross-country income convergence may be surprising because there are many reasons to expect a converging pattern, especially in a more open and integrated world economy. First, there are wide technology gaps between advanced economies and developing countries, giving the latter great potential for technological catch-up. With open trade and liberal financial markets, poorer countries should be able to benefit from technology spillovers, such as through the stock of knowledge embedded in imported capital goods. Second, capital-to-labor ratios in developing countries are lower than in advanced economies, and other things equal this relative scarcity of capital might be expected to make the return from investment in the former higher than in the latter. In a world in which capital is free to flow in search of highest returns, there are therefore grounds for expecting that it might increasingly flow to developing countries where

[62]This thinning of the middle range of the developing country income distribution leads to a global income distribution that appears to be characterized by two large clusters at each end, which has been termed the "twin peaks" phenomenon. For example, see Danny T. Quah, "Twin Peaks: Growth and Convergence in Models of Distribution Dynamics," *Economic Journal,* Vol. 106 (July 1996), pp. 1045–55.

Table 17. Developing Countries and Asian Newly Industrialized Economies: Increased Polarization and Reduced Mobility in Cross-Country Relative Income[1]
(Per capita income in purchasing power parity terms; income distribution is in quintiles)

Countries that started out in the lowest income quintile have generally remained in the lowest quintile.

1965–75

		Final position in 1975 income distribution[2]					Number of Countries
		First	Second	Third	Fourth	Fifth	
Initial relative position in 1965 income distribution	First	46	6				52
	Second	4	23	7			34
	Third			7	6	2	15
	Fourth					2	2
	Fifth				1	4	5
	Number of countries	50	29	14	7	8	108

1975–85

		Final position in 1985 income distribution[2]					Number of Countries
		First	Second	Third	Fourth	Fifth	
Initial relative position in 1975 income distribution	First	50					50
	Second	20	9				29
	Third	1	11	2			14
	Fourth		5	2			7
	Fifth			6		2	8
	Number of countries	71	25	10	0	2	108

1985–95

		Final position in 1995 income distribution[2]					Number of Countries
		First	Second	Third	Fourth	Fifth	
Initial relative position in 1985 income distribution	First	71					71
	Second	13	11	1			25
	Third		6	3	1		10
	Fourth						0
	Fifth					2	2
	Number of countries	84	17	4	1	2	108

1965–95

		Final position in 1995 income distribution[2]					Number of Countries
		First	Second	Third	Fourth	Fifth	
Initial relative position in 1965 income distribution	First	50	1	1			52
	Second	27	6		1		34
	Third	7	6	1		1	15
	Fourth		1			1	2
	Fifth		3	2			5
	Number of countries	84	17	4	1	2	108

[1]Excluding major oil exporters, Malta, and Cyprus.

[2]The figure in each cell is the number of countries whose relative position in the initial and terminal year was in the income brackets corresponding to the row and column of that cell. For example, for the period 1965–95, the first row of numbers show that out of 52 countries that were in the bottom one-fifth of the income distribution in 1965, 50 remained in the bottom one-fifth, 1 country moved to the second quintile and 1 country to the third quintile in 1995. Similarly, the numbers in the first column show that out of the 84 countries in the bottom one-fifth of the income distribution in 1995, 50 were in the first quintile, and that 27 and 7 moved down from the second and third quintiles, respectively, of the 1965 income distribution. For a similar analysis, see V. V. Chari, Patrick J. Kehoe, and Ellen R. McGratten, *The Poverty of Nations: A Quantitative Exploration,* Staff Report No. 204, Federal Reserve Bank of Minneapolis (January 1996).

it can help boost income growth. These forces should work to promote productivity and income growth in developing countries and should therefore increase the likelihood of convergence.

So, given the empirical evidence, what remains of income convergence? The data appear to show that there is a tendency for countries to converge to long-term per capita income levels that are determined by

Chart 39. Advanced and Developing Economies: Convergence in Per Capita Income, 1965–95[1]

(In purchasing power parity terms)

The fact that many economies are in the southwest quadrant—lower than average per capita income in 1965 and slower than average growth over 1965–95—suggests a lack of convergence.

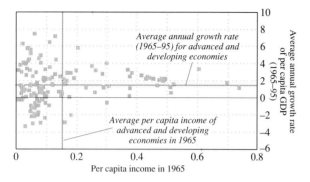

[1]Excluding Iraq, Kuwait, Lebanon, and Qatar; as a percent of industrial country per capita income in 1995. A necessary condition for convergence is that economies be concentrated in the upper left and lower right-hand quadrants.

Chart 40. Developing Countries and Asian Newly Industrialized Economies: Convergence in Absolute Income, 1965–95[1]

(In purchasing power parity terms)

Even among just the developing countries and the newly industrialized economies there is no evidence of convergence over 1965–95.

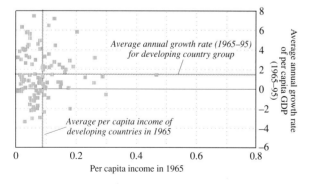

[1]Excluding Cyprus, Lebanon, Malta, and the oil exporting countries; as a percent of industrial country per capita income in 1995. A necessary condition for convergence is that countries are concentrated in the upper left and lower right-hand quandrants.

their own policies and resources. In cross-country analyses of growth, factors that have been found to be important in contributing positively to long-run potential per capita income include the skill level of the workforce, the absence of distortions affecting investment decisions, the degree of openness of the economy, macroeconomic stability, and freedom from political and civil unrest. A country's rate of convergence then depends upon these factors and the gap between its initial and potential income levels. The larger the gap, the faster the rate of growth, but the longer the time taken to converge.[63] China, for example, would take about 16 years to cut in half its current income gap with the advanced economies if it maintained its 10 percent a year real per capita growth rate of recent years (Table 18). Chile, even though it has been growing at less than half the rate of China, would halve its gap with the advanced economies in only ten years if it maintained its recent growth rate, because it has a higher current level of income. These two cases illustrate the point that although most developing countries are not converging toward advanced economy levels of income, there are some cases where growth conditions and policies are highly favorable, and where progress toward convergence can be achieved in a relatively short period of time.

Policies to Boost Growth and Promote Convergence

In the light of growth patterns that show many developing countries diverging away from advanced economy per capita income levels over recent decades, the question of how developing countries' growth performance could be improved gains urgency. What are the sources of economic growth and what policies could make a difference in whether a country converges toward high income levels? In simplest terms, economic growth springs from the accumulation of physical and human capital, labor, and advances in production technology (total factor productivity). Although views differ on the relative importance of these factors (see Box 9), for most developing countries conventional growth-accounting studies show that the accumulation of factors, especially physical capital, has accounted for the greater part of output growth. Recent estimates suggest that in the period 1960–92 roughly 60 to 70 percent of growth in per capita incomes was due to increases in physical capital per worker, while education con-

[63]After correcting for different long-run potential income levels resulting from differences in policies and resources, initially poorer countries do tend to grow faster than relatively richer countries. This tendency has been termed "conditional convergence" to signify the dependence on policies. For further details, see the box "Economic Convergence," in the October 1994 *World Economic Outlook*, pp. 94–95.

Table 18. Developing Countries: Convergence and Growth in Selected Countries[1]
(In percent)

	Relative Per Capita Income		Average Growth Rate of Relative Per Capita Income, 1985–95	Average Rate of Convergence, 1985–95[2]	Average Growth Rate of Relative Per Capita Income, 1990–95	Average Rate of Convergence, 1990–95[2]	Years to Close Half the Gap in 1995 at 1990–95 Growth Rate	Implied Rate of Convergence[2]	Implied Relative Per Capita Income After Halving of 1995 Gap
	1985	1995							
Chile	33.6	46.7	3.3	1.3	4.5	1.8	10	2.6	73.3
Indonesia	13.7	18.8	3.2	0.5	5.0	0.8	23	1.7	59.4
Malaysia	39.9	48.0	1.9	0.8	5.2	2.2	8	3.1	74.0
Thailand	20.5	36.1	5.8	1.6	6.0	1.8	11	3.0	68.0
Argentina	33.5	31.4	−0.6	−0.2	2.8	0.8	26	1.3	65.7
China	7.3	13.3	6.2	0.6	9.5	1.0	16	2.7	56.6
India[3]	5.8	6.9	1.7	0.1	1.9	0.1	112	0.4	53.4
Sri Lanka	14.5	15.8	0.9	0.1	2.8	0.4	46	0.9	57.9
Uganda	3.5	6.9	7.2	0.3	4.0	0.2	52	0.9	53.5
Uruguay	32.8	39.3	1.8	0.6	2.0	0.7	29	1.0	69.6
Bangladesh	6.6	6.9	0.4	0.03	1.5	0.1	141	0.3	53.4
Vietnam	0.7	0.9	2.7	0.02	4.8	0.04	87	0.6	50.4
Memorandum Asian newly industrialized economies[4]	56.4	86.7	4.7	2.9	4.6	3.4			

[1]All growth rates, rates of convergence, and relative per capita income levels are in relation to the average of advanced economies (excluding the newly industrialized economies). For example, the relative per capita income for any country (shown in the first two columns) is the ratio (in percent) of its per capita income to the average per capita income of advanced economies (excluding the newly industrialized economies). Income refers to GDP in U.S. dollars, based on purchasing power parity exchange rates. The simulations, summarized in the last three columns, assume that the industrial countries as a group maintain their current average rate of growth.

[2]The rate of convergence is defined as the percentage of the gap below the average per capita income of advanced economies (excluding the newly industrialized economies) that is reduced per year.

[3]For India, real per capita GDP growth in 1995 and 1996 has been significantly higher than the average for 1990–95. The average growth rate of relative per capita income in 1995–96 was 3 percent. If India maintains this growth rate then the number of years required to close half its gap with the advanced economies (excluding the newly industrialized economies) will be lowered to 69 years from 112 years as shown in the table.

[4]In 1995, Hong Kong's relative income was 114.6 percent, Korea's 54.6 percent, Singapore's 105.6 percent, and Taiwan Province of China's 72.1 percent of the average per capita GDP of advanced economies (excluding the newly industrialized economies).

tributed about 15 to 20 percent, and total factor productivity accounted for the remainder.[64] A comparison of fast- and slow-growing developing countries over the periods 1965–85 and 1985–95 shows that the shares of both investment and saving in GDP have been significantly higher for the first group (Table 19). It appears therefore that policies that raise the rates of investment and saving can play a crucial role in raising growth, if the investment is productive.[65] This section considers what role policies can play in boosting capital accumulation and total factor productivity.

---

[64]See Barry Bosworth, Susan M. Collins, and Yu-chin Chen, "Accounting for Differences in Economic Growth," *Brookings Institution Discussion Paper,* No. 115 (Washington: Brookings Institution, December 1995).

[65]Since the growth rate of output is necessarily equal to the investment-output ratio divided by the incremental capital-output ratio (ICOR), higher investment-output ratios will be associated with faster output growth unless the ICOR is at least commensurately higher (marginal productivity of capital lower). This relationship indicates also that raising the investment ratio may not boost growth if the capital stock added has a low productivity.

Ross Levine and David Renelt, "A Sensitivity Analysis of Cross-Country Growth Regressions," *American Economic Review,* Vol. 82

Macroeconomic Stability

By reducing uncertainty, macroeconomic stability allows investment and saving decisions to be made in a manner consistent with underlying economic fundamentals, thereby promoting an efficient allocation of resources. Macroeconomic stability also boosts confidence, which can encourage domestic investment and the inflow of foreign capital. Over 1985–95, median inflation was about 8 percent a year and fiscal deficits about 2 percent of GDP among the fastest-growing developing countries, while in the slowest-growing economies median inflation was about 14 percent a year and budget deficits averaged about 6 percent of GDP (Table 19). Empirical studies using large samples of country experiences suggest that the effect of inflation on growth becomes increasingly negative as inflation rises through some range, which some researchers put in the neighborhood of 8 percent a year,

---

(September 1992), pp. 942–63, find that among a variety of economic policy, political, and national indicators, only the share of investment in GDP turns out to have a positive and robust correlation with growth.

81

Box 9. Measuring Productivity Gains in East Asian Economies

In recent years, many economists have attempted to identify how much of the rapid economic growth in the East Asian region has been due to productivity growth and how much to the growth of factor inputs. These growth-accounting exercises have aimed to unearth the process underlying the impressive success stories of such economies as Hong Kong, Korea, Singapore, and Taiwan Province of China since the 1970s and Indonesia, Malaysia, and Thailand more recently. Identifying the growth process is important not only in evaluating the role played by policies but also in assessing the growth prospects of these economies and the lessons for others. However, largely as a result of the wide variety of accounting methodologies and empirical techniques, which are subject to a high degree of arbitrariness, little consensus has emerged regarding the relative importance of productivity growth vis-à-vis resource accumulation in accounting for the growth rates. While some studies find that almost all the growth in these countries can be attributed to unusually high rates of resource mobilization, leaving little to be explained by gains in productivity, others conclude that increases in productivity have been as high as 4 percent a year, thus accounting for a large proportion of output growth (*see table*).

To those who find little evidence of significant growth in factor productivity, the sustained high rates of output growth in the East Asian region are explained by the large increases in the use of inputs during the period.[1] They are more pessimistic about the prospects for continued growth in these countries at the high rates witnessed in the last two decades, since that would require continued high rates of resource mobilization, including the maintenance of domestic saving at over 30 percent of GDP and the availability of increasingly skilled labor. Others, however, are more optimistic about the future economic performance of these countries, given the evidence of productivity growth that they find, since if this continues, relatively high rates of output growth can be sustained even with lower rates of factor accumulation.

In general, a growth-accounting exercise deducts from output growth measured, for example, as the annual change in real GDP, a weighted average of the changes in aggregate physical and human capital and labor inputs and then interprets the residual as the growth of total factor productivity (TFP). There are two sets of problems associated with this approach that are at the root of the large variations in the estimates of productivity growth found in the various studies. Measures of the stock of aggregate physical capital are not only difficult to obtain but are also unreliable; they are generally constructed from his-

torical investment data, using simplifying and to some extent arbitrary assumptions about the quality and depreciation of capital. Proxies for human capital, such as the average number of years of schooling of the labor force, the proportion of the labor force with higher education, and so on, are not only largely arbitrary measures but they also fail fully to reflect cross-country differences in the quality of education. Similar data-related issues arise in measuring employment. Moreover, there is little uniformity in the classification and collection of such data across countries.

The second type of problem arises in determining the appropriate weight to attach to the growth of a factor in assessing its contribution to overall output growth. In principle, the weight should be the elasticity of output with respect to the factor concerned—that is, the proportionate increase in output when an additional unit of the particular factor is used in production. But this cannot be measured directly, and estimating it is not straightforward. For example, estimation using regression techniques generally suffers from the assumption that the weights are constant over the estimation period. In fact, however, the relative importance of different factors may well change over time, especially when an economy undergoes rapid transformation, as has been the case in the East Asian region. An alternative and more frequently used approach has been to approximate the output elasticity of a factor by its share in national income. This approximation is valid if factors are paid their marginal products; but this requires that there are no increasing returns to scale or externalities in the use of any factor, that technological progress is not embodied in factor inputs, and that all input and product markets are perfectly competitive. In fact, however, many industries are characterized by increasing returns, and factors such as human capital generate strong externalities. Furthermore, technological progress is often embodied in new inputs of capital and labor,[2] while the large profit markups[3] observed in some product markets do not support the assumption of perfect competition. In the presence of such markups in product markets, productivity growth, computed as the residual component of growth after the contributions of the different factors have been

---

[1]See Paul Krugman, "The Myth of Asia's Miracle," *Foreign Affairs,* Vol. 73 (November–December 1994), pp. 62–78.

[2]See Paul M. Romer, "Crazy Explanations for the Productivity Slowdown," *NBER Macroeconomics Annual,* 1987, ed. by Stanley Fischer (Cambridge, Massachusetts: MIT Press, 1987), pp. 163–203.

[3]There have been few studies that estimate markups for industries in the East Asian region. In industrial countries, which generally have a more competitive environment, in almost all industries markups are positive and large, for example, see Joaquim O. Martins, Stefano Scarpetta, and Dirk Pilat, "Mark-Up Ratios in Manufacturing Industries: Estimates for 14 OECD Countries," OECD Working Paper No. 162 (Paris: OECD, 1996).

Selected Developing Countries and Newly Industrialized Economies in Asia: Estimates of Total Factor Productivity Growth
(In percent a year)

	Young (1995)	Bosworth and Collins (1996)	Bosworth and Collins (1996)	Sarel (1995)	Sarel (1996)
	1966–90	1960–94	1984–94	1975–90	1979–96
Hong Kong	2.3	. . .	. . .	3.8	. . .
Korea	1.7	1.5	2.1	3.1	. . .
Singapore	0.2	1.5	3.1	1.9	2.5
Taiwan Province of China	2.6	2.0	2.8	3.5	. . .
Indonesia	. . .	0.8	0.9	. . .	0.9
Malaysia	. . .	0.9	1.4	. . .	2.0
Philippines	. . .	0.4	–0.9	. . .	–0.9
Thailand	. . .	1.8	3.3	. . .	2.0

Sources: Alwyn Young, "The Tyranny of Numbers: Confronting the Statistical Realities of the East Asian Growth Experience," *Quarterly Journal of Economics,* Vol. 110 (August 1995), pp. 641–80; Barry Bosworth and Susan M. Collins, "Economic Growth in East Asia: Accumulation Versus Assimilation," *Brookings Papers on Economic Activity: 2* (1996), pp. 135–203; Michael Sarel, "Growth in East Asia: What We Can and What We Cannot Infer From It," IMF Working Paper 95/98 (September 1995); and Michael Sarel, "Growth and Productivity in ASEAN Economies," paper presented at the Conference on "Macroeconomic Issues Facing ASEAN Countries," held in Jakarta, Indonesia on November 6–8, 1996.

accounted for, can be overestimated. Moreover, empirical evidence indicates that the residual component of growth is also correlated with demand-side variables, such as monetary and fiscal policies,[4] so that interpreting the residual as purely productivity growth may be misleading. Also crucial is the time period for which the analysis is conducted. During periods of rapid growth, the average rate of TFP increase has been disproportionately higher than during low growth periods.[5] In sum, given the large degree of arbitrariness in measuring inputs and their effect on output and given the differences in the time periods for which the accounting exercises have been performed, it is not surprising that estimates of TFP growth for countries in East Asia vary enormously (*see table*).

The low rates of TFP growth in the fast-growing East Asian economies found in some studies contrast with the finding that it has been the main contributor to the output growth of the industrial countries in recent decades.[6] However, it may not be surprising if the relative importance of the different sources of growth changes in the

process of economic development. Economic growth in the nineteenth century in the United States appears to have been largely due to increases in inputs rather than productivity growth[7] as was the growth of the Japanese economy between the Meiji Restoration and World War I. The experiences of the more advanced economies suggest that the accumulation of physical capital is an important source of growth in the early stages of economic development, but that once a relatively high level of capital intensity (capital-to-labor ratio) is reached, technological progress takes over as the principal source of growth.[8] Capital intensities in the economies of the East Asian region, including even the newly industrialized economies, are still significantly lower than they were in the industrial countries in the early 1960s. Given these relatively low capital-to-labor ratios, there is still plenty of room for input-based growth among fast-growing countries in the region. Consequently, even if productivity gains may not have contributed as much to growth as some studies suggest, the future growth prospects of the East Asian economies remain bright, and both their rapid rates of accumulation of capital and the high levels of efficiency with which it has been allocated remain impressive accomplishments.

[4]See, for example, Charles L. Evans, "Productivity Shocks and Real Business Cycles," *Journal of Monetary Economics,* Vol. 29 (April 1992), pp. 191–208.

[5]See Arnold C. Harberger, "Reflections on Economic Growth in Asia and the Pacific," *Journal of Asian Economies,* Vol. 7, No. 3 (1996), pp. 365–92.

[6]See Barry Bosworth, Susan M. Collins, and Yu-Chin Chen, "Accounting for Differences in Economic Growth," *Brookings Discussion Papers on International Economics,* No. 115 (October 1995), pp. 1–630.

[7]Moses Abramovitz and Paul A. David, "Reinterpreting Economic Growth: Parables and Realities," *American Economic Review,* Vol. 63 (1973), pp. 428–39.

[8]See Lawrence J. Lau, "The Sources of East Asian Economic Growth," Stanford University Working Paper (Palo Alto, California: Stanford University: November 1996).

Table 19. Developing Countries and Asian Newly Industrialized Economies: Policies and Economic Performance[1]

	Low Growth[2]		Medium Growth		High Growth	
	1970–84	1985–95	1970–84	1985–95	1970–84	1985–95
Initial conditions						
GDP per capita in initial year[3]	1,697	2,185	2,266	2,188	1,776	2,734
Human capital[4]	2.2	3.3	3.2	3.8	3.5	5.4
Macro conditions						
Saving[5]	17.8	16.5	18.5	19.2	26.0	31.4
Investment[5]	19.0	19.4	22.1	21.1	27.4	31.9
Inflation rate per year (median)	11.0	14.1	10.9	11.1	11.3	7.8
Fiscal conditions						
Fiscal balances[5]	–5.7	–5.6	–4.2	–3.3	–2.0	–2.4
Government expenditure[5]	19.9	25.0	19.6	20.0	19.5	18.9
Government revenue[5]	14.2	19.4	15.4	16.7	17.6	16.5
Monetary conditions						
Money + quasi-money[5]	33.0	38.4	28.7	36.4	25.6	64.9
Quasi-money[5]	16.5	24.3	13.8	22.9	10.0	36.6
Bank credit to the private sector[5]	20.4	25.4	18.5	31.0	21.0	63.1
International						
Net private capital flows[6]	20.2	11.8	12.9	19.9	66.9	68.3
Balance on current account[5]	–1.0	–2.6	–3.7	–1.4	–1.9	0.3
Exports[5]	11.3	17.2	14.9	17.2	18.2	33.0
Imports[5]	12.2	17.7	17.4	18.1	19.5	32.4

[1]Excludes major oil exporting countries, Cyprus, and Malta.

[2]Low growth is defined as per capita real income growth of less than one-half of 1 percent a year, which is roughly the mean growth rate minus one-half of the standard deviation of growth in the sample for the specified period. Correspondingly, high growth refers to rates above the mean plus one-half of the standard deviation (2.9 percent).

[3]Group average in U.S. dollar terms, using purchasing power parity weights.

[4]Average schooling years in population aged 15 and over. See Robert J. Barro and Jong-Wha Lee, "International Measures of Schooling Years and Schooling Quality," *American Economic Review, Papers and Proceedings,* Vol. 86 (May 1996), pp. 218–23.

[5]In percent of GDP.

[6]In percent of total private capital flow to developing countries. Excludes Asian newly industrialized economies.

and that the relationship may be nonlinear.[66] During episodes of low-to-moderate inflation, the effect of marginally higher or lower inflation on growth may be small, but high rates of inflation tend to have significant, negative growth effects. Large and persistent budget deficits also may slow growth, because they tend to reduce the supply of loanable funds for the private sector and crowd out private investment. Among many examples, an extreme case is Argentina, where growth rebounded from –6 percent in 1989 to nearly 9 percent in 1993 during a period when annual inflation was reduced from a rate close to 5,000 percent to 18 percent. Although it is difficult to establish from the data a close relationship between large fiscal deficits and low growth, many countries that have ex-

perienced low growth have also had large fiscal deficits. Countries such as Chile and Uganda, where strong fiscal adjustments were undertaken during the 1980s to promote macroeconomic stability, saw output shift to markedly steeper paths.[67]

Openness

Policies toward foreign trade are among the more important factors promoting economic growth and convergence in developing countries.[68] With open

---

[66]See, for example, the October 1996 *World Economic Outlook,* pp. 120–22, and Michael Sarel, "Nonlinear Effects of Inflation on Economic Growth," *Staff Papers,* IMF, Vol. 43 (March 1996), pp. 199–215. Also see Michael Bruno and William Easterly, "*Inflation Crises and Long-Run Growth,*" World Bank Working Paper No. 1517 (Washington: World Bank, September 1995).

[67]See May and October 1996 issues of the *World Economic Outlook* for a fuller discussion of the consequences of fiscal imbalances and inflation, respectively.

[68]Sachs and Warner, using their own openness indicator, claim that openness is the single most important factor in bringing about convergence. Dan Ben-David and Atiqur Rahman in "Technological Convergence and International Trade," Centre for Economic Policy Research Discussion Paper No. 1359 (London: CEPR, March 1996), find that among the richest 25 countries in the world there is significant evidence of absolute convergence within each country's main trading partners' group.

trade, domestic prices reflect world prices, thereby promoting the efficient allocation of resources. Open trade and capital account policies not only allow a country to exploit its comparative advantages in production, but they also promote the importation of lowest-cost products, often with embedded advanced technology. Trade also allows a country to employ a larger variety of intermediate goods and capital equipment that enhance the productivity of its own resources. Such spillovers of advanced technology into developing countries provide a key mechanism for productivity catch-up with advanced economies.[69] The strong correlation between policies fostering trade openness and fast economic growth is evident in Table 19. Over the period 1985–95, the developing countries that achieved the fastest economic growth were the countries that as a group had the highest ratios of imports and exports to GDP. Medium- and low-growth countries had import and export ratios that were roughly half as large as the fast-growing countries. Chart 41 shows that the group of countries that substantially liberalized their trade over the period 1988–92 experienced a sharp pickup in both exports and imports, and a noticeable increase in their absolute income levels.

Role of State-Owned Enterprises

Excessive state intervention in the economy limits the role of the private sector in economic activity, and administrative controls in product and financial markets distort resource allocation. The result is often low investment and growth, and poor investment quality. Among many developing countries, the direct involvement of the state in economic activity is large and widespread, with state-owned enterprises (SOEs) having monopoly rights in a large number of sectors, including manufacturing and the financial sector (see Box 10). While SOEs in developing countries generated 11 percent of GDP on average in the period 1978–91, in industrial countries their involvement was limited to about 5 percent. In countries such as Ethiopia, Somalia, Sri Lanka, and Tanzania, the SOE share of manufacturing has been in excess of 30 percent.

While the public sector's share of the economy has been large in many of the poorer developing countries, many of the more successful developing countries also have had large shares of manufacturing under state control. However, there has been a significant reduction in the involvement of state-owned enterprises over the years in the more successful cases. For example, in Taiwan Province of China, the share of such enterprises in manufacturing output fell from 56 percent in 1952 to about 21 percent in 1970, and by 1990 was

Chart 41. Selected Economies: Exports, Imports, and Per Capita Real Income[1]
(Simple group averages; in percent of GDP, unless otherwise noted)

A group of countries that liberalized trade over the period 1988–92 has experienced a sharp pickup in both exports and imports and an increase in per capita income levels.

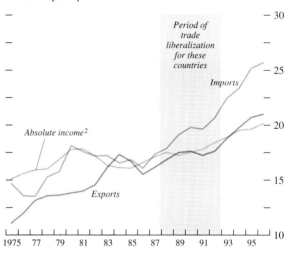

[1]Comprises Argentina, Brazil, China, India, Indonesia, Kenya, Mexico, the Philippines, Sri Lanka, Turkey, Uganda, and Uruguay. Among the countries that undertook major trade reforms in the period 1988–92, these were the 12 largest in terms of GDP.

[2]Percent of 1995 industrial country per capita GDP (in purchasing power parity terms).

---

[69]See David T. Coe, Elhanan Helpman, and Alexander W. Hoffmaister, "North-South R&D Spillovers," *Economic Journal*, Vol. 107 (January 1997), pp. 134–49.

Box 10.   Stabilization and Reform of Formerly Centrally Planned Developing Economies in East Asia

Several countries in East Asia, including Cambodia, China, the Lao People's Democratic Republic, and Vietnam, while undergoing development, are also in the process of moving from central planning toward economic systems based largely on market principles.[1] The experience of these countries differs substantially from that of the group of transition countries considered in Chapter V, reflecting both differences in the structures of their economies and in the nature of the process of transformation being undertaken.[2]

Though these countries differ greatly in size of population, they share many similarities in terms of economic structure, notably a population that remains largely rural and predominantly employed in agriculture. In Cambodia, the Lao People's Democratic Republic, and Vietnam, although the share of industry is increasing, the economies remain dominated by a family-based, rather than collectivized, agricultural sector (*see table*). The private sector remained active throughout the period of central planning in these three countries, and state-owned industries generally accounted for a relatively small part of the economy. This contrasts with the transition countries of eastern Europe and the former Soviet Union, where urban-based industries typically employed the majority of workers and accounted for the largest part of output, and where state-owned enterprises constituted a dominant share of the economy before the transition. This is true even for Mongolia, which as a result of tight economic alignment with the former Soviet Union is characterized by an urbanized population and an industrial structure more similar to the transition countries than to other newly emerging market economies in Asia. In China, although the economy until recently remained largely rural and the workforce concentrated in agriculture, central planning was more deeply embedded than in the other East Asian countries, with virtually no private enterprise before the initiation of reforms.

The particular structural characteristics of the East Asian economies have led to substantial differences in the evolution of their economies as compared with the countries in transition. Most striking has been the absence of sharp output drops of the kind suffered by the transition countries, although growth did slow at the start

of reforms in each country and briefly turned negative in the Lao People's Democratic Republic. Output is now growing at annual rates of 7–10 percent in all four countries. The absence of large output drops reflects, to some extent, the low initial level of output in the East Asian countries, partly as a result of war and civil conflict. But it is also attributable partly to the less pervasive nature of the initial economic distortions and hence of the transformation. In the East Asian economies, the transformation has consisted primarily of relatively narrowly focused economic reforms without accompanying political and social changes, and partly as a result there has been much less uncertainty and short-term instability than in many of the transition countries. The smaller share of industry, particularly in terms of the labor force, and the relative absence of a capital-intensive manufacturing base further meant that the East Asian countries did not face the challenge of replacing a massive amount of capital suddenly made obsolete by the end of central planning. Instead, the transformation has involved the establishment of conditions that would permit a shift from agriculture to industry.

These countries were also less closely integrated into the trading arrangements of the former Council for Mutual Economic Assistance (CMEA), and thus did not suffer to the same degree as the other members from its collapse, although Cambodia, the Lao People's Democratic Republic, and Vietnam all experienced both losses of financial assistance from the former Soviet bloc and declines in their terms of trade as prices of imports from the transition countries, such as energy and raw materials, adjusted upward to market levels. This limited degree of integration into the trading system of the other former centrally planned economies is another factor setting the East Asian countries apart from the transition economies of central Asia, which were far more severely disrupted by the breakdown of intraregional flows of raw materials with the collapse of central planning. The East Asian countries also benefited to some degree from their geographical proximity to the newly industrialized and other fast-growing economies of the region, which has led to investment in joint ventures and wholly owned subsidiaries formed to take advantage of expanding markets and low wages.

The process of reform began in China in 1978, in the Lao People's Democratic Republic in 1979 with comprehensive reforms starting in 1986, in Vietnam in 1985 with comprehensive reform starting in 1989, and in Cambodia in the early 1990s. At the start of their reforms, Cambodia, Vietnam, and the Lao People's Democratic Republic had only recently emerged from isolation or war. Initial reforms in the East Asian countries broadly followed the Chinese model in being principally aimed at boosting productivity, particularly in agriculture where reforms such as the undoing of collectivization proceeded most rapidly. At the same time, nonstate enterprises were allowed to expand by absorbing surplus labor from agriculture, while other reforms including the liberalization of regulations on joint ventures and foreign direct investment have been introduced more

---

[1]Myanmar has also taken some steps to reverse central planning; however, these reforms have so far been partial and have failed to achieve a fundamental transformation in the economic system.

[2]See John R. Dodsworth, Ajai Chopra, Chi D. Pham, and Hisanobu Shishido, "Macroeconomic Experiences of the Transition Economies in Indochina," IMF Working Paper 96/112 (October 1996) for an in-depth review of stabilizations in Vietnam, Cambodia, and the Lao People's Democratic Republic.; Eduardo Borensztein and Jonathan D. Ostry, "Accounting for China's Growth Performance," *American Economic Review,* Vol. 86 (May 1996), pp. 224–28 for a discussion of the effects of reforms on China; and Richard W.T. Pomfret, *Asian Economies in Transition: Reforming Centrally Planned Economies* (Cheltenham: Edward Elgar, 1996) for a broad overview of reforms across Asian countries.

Comparison Between Developing Countries in East Asia Moving Away from Central Planning and Selected Transition Countries in Eastern Europe and the Former Soviet Union

	1993 Share of GDP in		1990 Share of Labor Force in		1994 Percent Urban
	Agriculture	Industry	Agriculture	Industry	Population
Developing countries moving away from central planning					
Cambodia	51	...	74	7	20
China	20	48	72	15	29
Lao People's Democratic Republic	51	18	78	6	21
Vietnam	29	28	71	14	21
Selected transition countries					
Albania	40	13	55	23	37
Czech Republic	6	35	7	35	65
Moldova	35	48	33	30	51
Mongolia	21	46	32	22	60
Russia	9	51	14	42	73
Ukraine	35	47	20	40	70

Sources: World Bank, *World Development Report, 1996* and *Social Indicators of Development.*

gradually. Although productivity rose in agriculture as a result of the reforms, the striking difference between the share of the labor force in agriculture and the share of GDP produced by agriculture highlights the very low productivity levels in that sector, and thus the scope for continued industrialization. This remains particularly evident for China despite its head start in implementing reforms, possibly because its economy had been the most centralized, with the most distorted structure of production and prices.

A two-track system of prices has emerged in these countries, with controls on a narrow range of essential items, but prices of most goods (accounting for 80 to upward of 90 percent of prices at the retail level) now determined by market forces. In some countries, even before price liberalization, extensive informal markets fed by remittances from expatriates abroad and diverted export proceeds acted to reduce the price distortions of central planning.

In China, growth has risen significantly since the start of the reform progress, as increased productivity in agriculture and the employment of surplus rural labor in the nonstate manufacturing sector made possible fairly large increases in output. Reforms in agriculture that allowed farmers to benefit from harvests above specified levels met with an immediate supply response, though less progress has been made in boosting output in largely industrial state-owned enterprises, for which soft budget constraints and complex tax regulations continue to stifle incentives to raise productivity. Instead, the nonstate sector grew rapidly, particularly in coastal regions that benefited from foreign direct investment, which began in 1984 and surged in the early 1990s. Subsequent reforms have included trade liberalization, financial market reform including the establishment of offices by foreign banks, and exchange system liberalizations that culminated in convertibility for current account transactions in December 1996.

In Cambodia, the Lao People's Democratic Republic, and Vietnam, reforms were undertaken during periods in which monetization of large fiscal deficits led to sharp spikes in inflation, accompanied by extensive dollarization and widening gaps between official and informal exchange rates. Initial stabilization policies in all three countries comprised a mix of flexible exchange rates, trade liberalization, high interest rates, and reductions in government expenditures, particularly through cuts in subsidies to consumers and restrictions on soft credits to state-owned enterprises. Stabilizations from high inflation were largely money based, with steep expenditure cuts allowing reduced monetary expansion. Given the lack of resources, maintaining a stable exchange rate was not feasible at the start of the reforms; instead, official exchange rates were adjusted with increased frequency to track rates determined in parallel markets. Despite cuts in government expenditures, the boost in productivity that resulted from the reforms, particularly in the agricultural sector, served to maintain positive growth both before and throughout the macroeconomic stabilizations, while employment in the private industrial and service sectors rose rapidly during the early transition period and helped absorb workers released from the public sector.

Further market-oriented reforms are required to ensure continued growth that matches the potential of these countries. Following the success of their initial stabilizations, the newly emerging market economies of East Asia have each had to deal with the overheating problems that often accompany strong growth, including those associated with substantial inflows of foreign capital. Particularly important challenges for these countries are enhancing their infrastructure and developing modern banking systems, both of which will promote increased investment. Closer integration into the global economic and financial system will also promote further growth, including through increased trade.

down to 11 percent.[70] The SOE share of manufacturing output in China also has been dropping rapidly. However, the SOE share of financial resources remains large in China and could complicate macroeconomic policy and impede growth unless it is reduced quickly. Often state-owned enterprises are operated inefficiently, and despite their monopoly status they tend either to make low profits or to run persistent and large losses that burden government budgets. In India during 1989–94, for example, after-tax profits as a percent of total sales were roughly four times higher among private sector companies than in state-owned enterprises in comparable sectors.[71] Market-oriented structural reforms that limit state intervention to areas of genuine market failure (such as health, education, and infrastructure) and improve the efficiency of government may be expected to boost growth by reducing distortions and encouraging greater private sector participation.

Financial Liberalization

The mobilization of savings and their efficient allocation among competing investment projects require stable financial markets with well-designed instruments. Studies using long-run data have found a stable and positive correlation between growth and indicators of financial development, and also between the initial level of financial sector maturity and subsequent growth.[72] Countries that suffer from low growth have typically been characterized by a significantly lower level of financial development, as indicated by the ratio of broad money to GDP, than high-growth economies (Table 19). Although the positive relationship between financial development and economic growth is likely to be the result of two-way causation, and while there have been cases where countries have experienced rapid development with only modest degrees of financial openness, limited development of financial markets and institutions is likely to be a severe obstacle to overall economic development.[73] Also, it is becoming increasingly clear that financial liberalization needs to be accompanied by strengthened regulation and supervision of finan-

cial institutions for an economy to derive the greatest benefits.

Governance

How effective an economic reform package is in delivering higher growth and long-run prosperity often depends on the quality of governance in an economy. Definition of the concept of governance is far from straightforward, and judgments about its quality are subjective, but there are several facets on which there is some agreement. In many developing countries, a lack of transparency and accountability in public policymaking and excessive government intervention and regulation of economic activities have invited widespread rent-seeking behavior and corruption. Not only do weak governance and corruption tend to lower government tax revenue[74] and thereby both contribute to fiscal imbalances and reduce critical public investment in areas such as health and education, but they also deter both domestic and foreign direct investment. Inadequate protection of private property rights and a weak rule of law also have long been held to be critical obstacles to growth.[75] Reduced state intervention in economic affairs and greater transparency in regulatory policies can limit rent seeking and corruption and allow governments to focus on their essential tasks—of maintaining order and justice, of allocating public resources to priority uses, including investment in health and education, of helping to maintain macroeconomic stability, and of providing cost-effective and well-targeted social safety nets. While it is difficult to quantify the efficiency of governance and the extent of corruption, some studies based on rudimentary and somewhat subjective indicators suggest that weakness in these areas can have significant and lasting negative effects on growth.[76] Other studies using different proxies for the effectiveness of government, such as the quality of the bureaucracy (including its degree of autonomy from political pressure), expropriation risk, and so forth, have found little effect on growth.[77]

Human Resource Policies: Education and Population Growth

Investment in education and human capital leads to the acquisition of skills that raise efficiency and make

[70]See James A. Schmitz Jr., "The Role Played by Public Enterprises: How Much Does It Differ Across Countries?" *Quarterly Review,* Federal Reserve Bank of Minneapolis, Vol. 20 (Spring 1996), pp. 2–15.

[71]See Omkar Goswami, "Whither Corporate Sector Reforms in India?" paper presented at the seminar on "Putting India on a High-Growth Path: The Macroeconomic Strategy and Key Structural Reform" organized by the IMF, and held in Washington on March 6, 1996.

[72]See Ross Levine, "Financial Development and Economic Growth: Views and Agenda," World Bank Working Paper No. 1678 (Washington: World Bank, October 1996).

[73]Recent issues of the *World Economic Outlook,* especially the October 1996 *World Economic Outlook,* have discussed in detail the importance of financial development to the growth process.

[74]See Nadeem Ul Haque and Ratna Sahay, "Do Government Wage Cuts Close Budget Deficits? A Conceptual Framework for Developing Countries and Transition Economies," IMF Working Paper 96/19 (February 1996).

[75]This argument was made in 1776 by Adam Smith in *The Wealth of Nations* (New York: The Modern Library, 1937), p. 862, and was recently stressed by Sachs and Warner, "Economic Convergence."

[76]See Paolo Mauro, "The Effects of Corruption on Growth, Investment, and Government Expenditure," IMF Working Paper 96/98 (September 1996).

[77]For further details, see Robert J. Barro and Xavier Sala-i-Martin, *Economic Growth* (New York: McGraw Hill 1995), pp. 439–40.

more widespread the use of existing technology, and also promotes new technological development. Reflecting such investment, the level of initial human capital in high-growth countries has been significantly higher than in less-successful countries (Table 19). More formal analysis also finds that the initial level of education, especially at the primary level, is an important determinant of subsequent growth.[78] However, few studies have found evidence of a strong positive impact of changes in the level of education on growth.[79] Higher education has been found to have a relatively strong positive impact on growth, and public spending on education as a share of GDP has been found to be strongly and positively related to growth. These findings suggest that the quality of education is important. Also, social factors, such as the nature of institutions in society, affect the pace of economic development in a country. The initial level of social development, of which the level of human capital is an important component, is also significantly related to subsequent growth in per capita income and productivity.[80]

Among many of the poorer countries, high growth rates of population have undermined efforts to increase the average levels of education and health. Although rapid population growth increases the labor force and raises the output capacity of an economy, cross-country analyses of long-run data have shown that population growth has a negative effect on the growth of per capita income.[81] In many countries, despite attempts to contain the growth of population, which have varied according to national culture and values, progress has been slow. In these cases, long-run economic and social development and the alleviation of poverty hinge critically on greater success in slowing the rate of population growth.

Economic Convergence and the Importance of Policy Complementarities

While policies in all the areas discussed above can help promote the accumulation of physical and human capital and the development of technology, and thus help determine the growth performance of a country, a few key policy areas seem particularly important. To study the effects of some of these policies on growth outcomes, a data set for 110 developing countries was compiled for the period 1985–95—a time period when the global integration process described earlier was in full swing. Data were collected on trade openness; the degree of macroeconomic stability, proxied by the standard deviation of the rate of inflation; and the degree of government intervention in the economy, proxied by the share of government spending in GDP, which although not the best measure of government intervention suffers less than others from data-related problems. Countries were scored as "high," "medium," or "low" in each of these categories with cutoff points determined by statistical criteria, though necessarily with some degree of arbitrariness.[82] Developing countries with average 1985–95 real per capita GDP growth rates of 2.9 percent or higher were classified as high-growth countries (e.g., Chile, Thailand, Uganda), those with growth rates between 0.5 percent and 2.9 percent a year were classified as medium-growth countries (e.g., Colombia, Morocco, Pakistan), and those with growth rates lower than 0.5 percent a year were classified as low-growth countries (e.g., Cameroon, Ecuador, Zambia) (Table 20). Altogether 28 percent of all developing countries were classified as high-growth countries, while 44 percent fell into the low-growth category.

Three general policy combination clusters emerged. Approximately one-fifth of all developing countries in the data set had closed economies, poor macroeconomic stability, and a large government—all the presumed least favorable policies. Another fifth of the countries were moderately open, with moderate macroeconomic stability and a medium-sized government. Another fifth of the countries can be described as highly open with moderate to high macroeconomic stability and a small to medium-sized government— the presumed best policies. As expected, there was found to be a strong overall correlation between policies and income growth performance: countries with open trade positions, a stable macroeconomy, and a relatively small government tended to show better growth outcomes than countries that were less open, less stable, and had larger governments.

Perhaps the most interesting finding is that not one of these desirable policies by itself seems to have been sufficient to ensure that a country had high growth. That is, good performance in one category, but mediocre or poor performance in the other two categories, appears to have been a recipe for low growth. For example, among countries with the most open trade stances, but with only low or medium macro stability and large or medium-sized governments, only

---

[78]Barro and Sala-i-Martin, *Economic Growth,* pp. 436.

[79]See, for example, Lant Pritchett, "Where Has All the Education Gone?" World Bank Policy Research Working Paper No. 1581 (Washington: World Bank, March 1996).

[80]See Jonathan Temple and Paul Johnson, "Social Capability and Economic Development," Nuffield College Working Paper (Oxford, England: Nuffield College, July 1996). They use the Adelman-Morris index, which includes measures of the size of the agricultural sector, the extent of urbanization, social mobility, literacy, and mass communication to proxy the level of social development.

[81]For example, Levine and Renelt, "Sensitivity Analysis" report that a 1 percentage point increase in the growth rate of population reduces per capita GDP growth by roughly ½ of 1 percentage point. However, population growth and fertility may themselves be responsive to the rate of output growth.

[82]For all variables, the high category was defined as the mean value plus one-half of the standard deviation, or higher; the low category was the mean minus one-half of the standard deviation or lower; and the medium category included all values in between.

Table 20. Developing Countries Including Asian Newly Industrialized Economies: Relationship Between Policies and Growth, 1985–95, and Conditional Probabilities of Success[1]

(In percentage points)

	High Growth	Medium Growth	Low Growth	Number of Countries in Sample
	Percentage Distribution			
Percentage of countries	**28**	**28**	**44**	**110**
Conditioning policies				
High openness[2]	41	19	41	37
High macroeconomic stability[3]	41	32	27	41
Small government[4]	30	33	37	43
High openness with *at least* one other category being low and *at most* one other being medium	25	25	50	8
High macroeconomic stability with *at least* one other category being low and *at most* one other being medium	—	60	40	5
Small government with *at least* one other category being low and *at most* one other being medium	21	33	46	24
Low openness with *at least* one other category being high[2] and the other *at least* medium	19	43	38	21
Low macroeconomic stability with *at least* one other category being high and the other *at least* medium	—	—	100	1
Large government with *at least* one other category being high and the other *at least* medium	25	17	58	12
Policy combination with *at least* two categories being high[2] and the other medium	57	19	24	21

Source: Jahangir Aziz and Robert Wescott, "The Washington Consensus and Policy Complementarities in Developing Countries," IMF Working Paper (forthcoming).

[1]High-growth countries were the ones with average per capita real growth rates of 2.9 percent or higher over the period 1985–95, while the low-growth countries were the ones with average growth rates below ½ of 1 percent. For all variables, the high and low cutoff points were determined as mean plus one-half standard deviation and mean minus one-half standard deviation of the respective distributions.

[2]Openness is measured by the ratio of total foreign trade to GDP. A high degree of openness is defined as the case where the average of exports and imports as a percent of GDP is higher than 45 percent, while in the case of low openness it is lower than 27 percent.

[3]Macroeconomic stability is measured by the standard deviation of the rate of inflation in the period. Low macroeconomic stability was defined as having a standard deviation of inflation higher than 19 while high stability required a standard deviation of less than 5.

[4]Size of government is measured by the ratio of government expenditure to GDP. A large government is categorized as one with public expenditure of the central government above 38 percent of GDP, and a small government is one with less than 23 percent of GDP.

about one-fourth experienced high growth and about one-half low growth. Likewise, of the 24 countries that had the smallest size of government, but low or medium openness and stability, only about one-fifth achieved high growth, and about one-half posted low growth. Along a single policy dimension, the probability of failure in the case of high openness was just as high as in the case of a small government (Table 20).

The analysis also suggests that poor performance in one policy area can hold an economy back, even if other policies are favorable. To illustrate this necessity of comprehensively good policies, consider the countries that had medium or high macro stability and small or medium-sized governments, but low openness: only one in five had fast growth, and twice that fraction—two in five—had slow growth. Or, of countries with medium or high openness and stability, but an undesirably large government, fewer than one-third experienced fast growth, while nearly two out of three experienced low growth.

The key lesson that emerges is that no policy by itself is sufficient for fast growth, and that at least a moderate degree of policy success is necessary in several areas to support fast growth.[83] That is, good poli-

[83]This conclusion differs from that drawn by Sachs and Warner, "Economic Convergence." These authors test for the effectiveness of various policies in promoting higher-than-average economic growth and conclude that an open trade stance and protection of private property rights together are sufficient for fast growth.

cies tend to be mutually reinforcing and policy complementarities are important. For example, in a relatively open economy, financial markets may punish bad macroeconomic policies and reward good policies more vigorously than they would in a closed economy. To illustrate the importance of these complementarities, the developing countries with either medium or high degrees of success in all three policy areas had a three in five chance of achieving fast growth over 1985–95, and a better than three in four probability of either medium or fast growth (17 out of 21 such countries in the sample). Fewer than one out of four of these countries had low growth.

This simple analysis does not suggest an ironclad relationship between good policies and good growth outcomes, and certainly there are exceptions to the rule reflecting the influence of many other factors (social and institutional factors, resource endowments, and so forth) that also exert a strong influence on growth. Uruguay, for example, had low trade openness and only moderate macroeconomic stability over 1985–95, and yet experienced relatively fast economic growth. Other countries, such as Botswana, have experienced relatively fast growth despite having a large government sector. Rather this analysis suggests that for most of the 110 developing countries in the data set over 1985–95, the goal of fast income growth was most likely to be achieved by pursuing market-oriented policies (trade openness and small to medium-sized governments) in an environment of macroeconomic stability.

Reaping Gains from Globalization and Avoiding Marginalization

For countries with relatively strong fundamentals and the types of policies that the above analysis suggests are conducive to growth, openness has helped to speed up the convergence process. Malaysia and Thailand are examples of countries with these characteristics. The policy challenge for these countries is to safeguard their gains by maintaining a market-oriented policy stance, maintaining macroeconomic stability, and improving infrastructure and the supply of skilled labor so as to ease supply constraints in the economy. Overheating pressures often have been a consequence of strong capital inflows, and experience shows that although capital inflows can supplement domestic saving and contribute to strong economic performance, without appropriate policies or in the presence of large exogenous shocks such flows can raise a country's vulnerability to external and domestic financial disturbances. This was seen in the Mexican crisis, and it underscores again the importance of maintaining macroeconomic and financial stability, with a sustainable balance of payments. In addition, a scarcity of skilled labor can boost wage growth, erode external competi-

tiveness, and fuel inflationary pressures. This suggests that labor market reforms may also be necessary to ease such capacity constraints.

Countries should also aim to let domestic investors diversify their portfolios internationally, to reduce their risks and also to help prevent price bubbles in real estate and other domestic asset markets. In this respect, a gradual and cautious removal of capital controls within the framework of policies to promote a sound domestic banking system, along with an exchange rate policy that permits an appropriate degree of flexibility, will lessen the burden on fiscal adjustment and provide a better balance among policy instruments through a more developed financial sector. Additionally, many countries, such as China, Thailand, and Malaysia, are experiencing rapidly growing demands for transportation and other public facilities. Private sector participation in these areas, as employed in Malaysia (port facilities), the Philippines (power supply), and Chile (public utilities), can supplement government efforts to alleviate supply bottlenecks without burdening public finances excessively.

Policies for Avoiding Marginalization

Many of the countries near the bottom of the world's distribution of per capita incomes face difficult conditions, such as low stocks of human capital, poor resource bases, and political instability—including civil wars and regional conflicts that have acted to deter investment and growth. Many of these countries also suffer from high levels of public debt, including external debt, that was accumulated over years of poor fiscal management, commodity price shocks, macroeconomic instability, and poor governance. Still, a number of developing countries have overcome such obstacles, and there has been a resurgence of GDP growth in many countries where macroeconomic and structural reforms have been undertaken since the early 1990s. Between 1990 and 1995, the number of countries in sub-Saharan Africa with rates of real GDP growth greater than 4 percent increased steadily from 14 to 25, just as the number of countries with negative growth declined from 18 to 9. Uganda, which has implemented far-reaching reforms since the late 1980s, has been closing the gap with advanced economy income levels in the 1990s, and India has experienced average growth of 7 percent in 1995 and 1996, reflecting the effects of the liberalization program that started in 1992. Vietnam had an average real per capita income in 1990 of less than 1 percent of advanced economy levels but has been growing at more than 7 percent a year in real per capita terms aided by continued macroeconomic and structural reforms. Still, given the low levels of per capita income in such developing countries, relatively high growth rates will need to be sustained for many

91

years to close the gap with the advanced economies (see Table 18).

As the above analysis of policy complementarities suggests, a successful strategy for growth requires openness toward international trade, macroeconomic stability, and limited government intervention in the economy.[84] Protectionist trade policies, such as high tariffs and widespread nontariff barriers, clearly have obstructed the integration of many countries into the world economy. In sub-Saharan African countries, for example, tariffs average about 27 percent compared with 15 percent among the East Asian countries, and the average nontariff barrier coverage ratio is many times higher than in the world's fastest-growing developing country group. At least partly because of such policies, the sub-Saharan African share of world trade fell from roughly 3 percent in the mid-1950s to just over 1 percent in 1995. And in recent years, this region has been attracting only about 3 percent of the total foreign direct investment in developing countries. With the phased reductions in nontariff barriers under the Uruguay Round agreements, many of the low-income countries will also need to improve the competitiveness of their exports, which have enjoyed preferential treatment in the past.

In addition to becoming more open, poor countries also need to reform government operations. These countries have great needs in the areas of health, education, and infrastructure, but government spending has been channeled too heavily into defense (at least until recently), into subsidies for loss-making and in-efficient state enterprises, and into inefficient public administration. Spending needs to be rechanneled into more socially beneficial uses, and especially where international aid is available, project implementation needs to be improved. Governments in these countries also need to reform their revenue systems. In many countries, practices of arbitrary exemptions and weak enforcement have, in effect, led to the imposition of high tax rates on narrow tax bases. The result is that sectors that are subject to taxes have a strong incentive to evade them. To finance large fiscal deficits, many of these governments have resorted to financial repression, which has thwarted the development of financial markets, and to direct monetization, which has fueled inflation; and many have borrowed heavily in their small domestic capital markets, crowding out private investment and increasing public debt. These policies have fueled inflation and increased macroeconomic instability.

Many poor countries have accumulated large stocks of external debt, including debt owed to multilateral agencies. To address the debt problems of the heavily indebted poor countries, a joint initiative has been launched by the IMF and the World Bank that will provide special assistance to the countries that have followed sound policies but for whom traditional debt-relief mechanisms have failed to secure a sustainable external position (see Chapter II).[85] As many poor and formerly poor developing countries have demonstrated, the mutually reinforcing benefits of a return to external viability, greater international openness, domestic macroeconomic stability, and good governance with priority-based government spending can generate higher growth rates and rapid convergence.

---

[84]William Easterly and Ross Levine, "Africa's Growth Tragedy: A Retrospective, 1960–89," World Bank Working Paper No. 1503 (Washington: World Bank, August 1995), however, find that in addition to government intervention, political instability and spillovers between neighboring countries' economic performances are significant in explaining low growth.

[85]For further details on the Highly Indebted Poor Countries (HIPC) Initiative and the debt burden of these countries, see the October 1996 *World Economic Outlook,* pp. 74–76.

V

Integration of the Transition Countries into the Global Economy

The reintegration of the transition countries into the world economy is an essential element of their transformation process. For 50 years or more, these countries were engaged in an experiment in central planning that encompassed not only the domestic economy but also international economic relations. International trade and payments were largely directed by government rather than by market forces, and the group of countries involved limited their economic ties with the rest of the world as they sought to develop their cohesion and interdependence with each other. Trade and financial relations between the centrally planned economies and the market economies atrophied, while among the market economies they burgeoned. The failure of the experiment eventually became clear: before the shift to central planning, a number of countries in central Europe had per capita incomes equivalent to between one-half and two-thirds of those of the most advanced western European economies; by the end of the experiment they had fallen significantly further behind.

The countries in transition are now reversing the inward-looking legacy of central planning as they seek to catch up with a world economy whose performance has demonstrated the benefits of open international economic relations. This process of reintegration, through trade and financial flows, like other elements of the transformation process, is bound to take time, especially given that the dislocation created by central planning and by the isolation associated with it was so great. That dislocation, though not involving the physical destruction of capital, is comparable in some ways with that suffered by western Europe in World War II; in that case, substantial economic recovery may be considered to have taken a decade or more. Most of the countries in transition are now five to seven years into the transformation. How much has been achieved as far as reintegration is concerned? This question forms the main focus of this chapter.

The first part of the chapter examines the progress made in the liberalization of trade and payments arrangements—the policy area most closely connected with the reintegration objective. It is shown that there has been considerable variation across countries in the pace and extent of trade liberalization, that a majority of countries have fully removed exchange restrictions for current account transactions, and that several countries have taken steps to liberalize financial flows.

The second part looks at developments since the beginning of the transition in the growth and distribution of trade. It is shown that for many countries, there has been a massive reorientation of trade flows, as the concentration of trade with former partners in the Council for Mutual Economic Assistance (CMEA) has been replaced by a more balanced and market-determined distribution of exports and imports. In particular, the geographically proximate countries of the European Union now play a much more prominent role. The increasing reintegration into the global trading system has already been accompanied by some growth in productivity and wages in the transition countries, and these trade links represent an important channel through which these countries are gaining technological knowledge and managerial skills. Even though trade restrictions in the advanced economies do not in general appear to form a major impediment to the export of most manufactured goods, restrictions affecting certain "sensitive" industrial products and agriculture, where the transition economies have comparative advantage, have been, and remain, a significant obstacle to the full development of trade links.

The final part of the chapter examines the integration of the transition countries into the global financial system. Progress here is necessarily less far advanced than in trade. This is to be expected because the development of financial relationships and financial flows depends, in a way that trade does not, on such factors as an investor-friendly legal system and framework of property rights, taxation, and governance; macroeconomic stability; political stability; the soundness of the domestic financial system; and investor confidence. As experience in many contexts shows, these take time to build, even with the most sound and consistent policies of stabilization and reform.

The evidence presented in this chapter suggests that the reintegration of the transition economies into the global economy is still very much in progress. And the progress made differs widely among countries, as is indicated by Table 21. This shows that even though the relationship is not tight, partly because other factors are involved, the countries more advanced in transition, in terms of general progress with stabilization and reform policies, tend to be relatively advanced in the reintegration and also relatively advanced in eco-

Table 21. Countries in Transition: Progress in Integration and Economic Performance

	Transition Progress	Date of	Measures of Integration			Economic Performance in 1996	
	Transition Indicators[1]	Article VIII Acceptance[2]	Openness to trade[3]	Credit rating[4]	FDI per capita[5]	Yearly inflation (In percent)	Growth of real GDP (In percent)
Countries more advanced in transition[6]							
Czech Republic	3.4	10/95	60	IG	586	9	4.2
Hungary	3.4	1/96	33	IG	1,198	24	1.0
Estonia	3.3	8/94	80	...[7]	573	23	3.1
Poland	3.3	6/95	26	IG	121	20	5.5
Slovak Republic	3.2	10/95	63	IG	130	6	7.0
Croatia	3.1	5/95	49	IG	122	3	5.0
Latvia	3.1	6/94	50	IG	236	19	2.5
Slovenia	3.1	9/95	49	IG	325	10	3.5
Lithuania	2.9	5/94	30	SIG	66	25	3.5
Countries less advanced in transition[6]							
Russia	2.9	6/96	16	SIG	32	48	−2.8
Albania	2.7	...	26	...	77	13	8.2
Kyrgyz Republic	2.7	3/95	44	...	22	30	5.6
Moldova	2.7	6/95	53	SIG	44	24	−8.0
Bulgaria	2.6	...	32	SIG	70	123	−9.0
Kazakstan	2.6	7/96	31	SIG	166	39	1.0
Macedonia, former Yugoslav Republic of	2.6	...	45	...	33	2	1.1
Romania	2.6	...	30	SIG	66	39	4.1
Armenia	2.4	...	37	...	10	19	6.6
Georgia	2.4	12/96	15	...	3	40	10.5
Ukraine	2.4	...	44	...	21	80	−10.0
Uzbekistan	2.4	...	30	...	8	54	1.6
Azerbaijan	1.8	...	40	...	69	20	1.3
Belarus	1.8	...	39	...	5	52	2.0
Tajikistan	1.7	...	165	...	10	443	−7.0
Turkmenistan	1.1	...	177	...	84	992	−3.0
Memorandum							
Mongolia[8]	...	...	38	...	13	50	3.0

Sources: European Bank for Reconstruction and Development (EBRD); and IMF staff estimates.

[1]Simple average of the EBRD *Transition Report*'s nine indicators of progress in transition.

[2]Formal acceptance of the obligations of Article VIII of the IMF's Articles of Agreement generally represents the culmination of a process of liberalization of payments for current account transactions. Liberalization therefore usually preceded to a substantial extent the dates shown.

[3]Ratio of the average of exports and imports to GDP in 1996.

[4]IG denotes investment grade, SIG sub-investment grade; see Table 25.

[5]Cumulative 1991–96 per capita inflows in U.S. dollars; see Table 26.

[6]The allocation of transition countries to these two groups is an imperfect simplification, since the degrees of progress by different countries are closer to a continuum.

[7]The authorities in Estonia have deliberately not sought a credit rating.

[8]There are no transition indicators available for Mongolia.

nomic performance.[86] The countries that have made the most headway are in general significantly more advanced in trade than in financial flows. But many countries lag behind, and a few have made little progress at all.

---

[86]The measures used in the table are necessarily imperfect indicators. For example, ratios of trade to GDP reflect not only the degree of countries' integration with global markets but also country size, since large countries, being relatively self-sufficient, tend to have smaller trade flows, relative to the size of their economies, than small countries.

Liberalization of Trade and Payments

International trade played a smaller role under the system of central planning than in the market-based advanced and developing countries. To a large extent isolated from the world trading system and depending on a largely command-driven distribution of production responsibilities among the CMEA countries rather than on comparative advantage, these countries missed out on many of the benefits of trade. Under central planning, countries were also largely cut off from the international financial system. National currencies were not convertible, and domestic financial sectors and payments systems were not equipped to deal with international transactions. The planned economies had access to international loans, but foreign borrowing was undertaken by state banks on behalf of governments, and there was no direct linkage between this inflow of funds and internal economic activity and financial conditions.

Currency and Payments Arrangements

Orderly currency arrangements and a well-defined exchange rate policy, together with an effective payments and banking system and properly functioning foreign exchange markets, are prerequisites for international financial integration. Central and eastern European countries and the Baltic countries were able to make progress in these areas early in the transition because of the existence or introduction of independent national currencies and a rapid reorientation of trade and financial flows to the advanced economies, particularly in western Europe. Russia and most other countries of the former Soviet Union, on the other hand, were faced with a more prolonged period of uncertainty regarding monetary arrangements.

Most of the central and eastern European economies, which inherited national currencies, moved toward current account convertibility in the initial stages of the transition. Similarly, soon after gaining independence, the Baltic states took steps to introduce convertible currencies; Estonia and later on Lithuania also established currency boards. Estonia and Latvia in fact established fully convertible currencies, with no capital controls; and in practice Lithuania also has not applied such controls. Russia and other countries of the former Soviet Union continued to participate in a ruble area that, de facto, came into existence following the dissolution of the Union at the end of 1991. Attempts to sustain the ruble area failed, as member states could not agree on a workable institutional structure and rules for monetary coordination.[87]

By early 1994, all the countries in the region except Tajikistan had introduced separate currencies or coupons. Tajikistan introduced its own currency in May 1995, while Georgia and Ukraine replaced temporary national currencies with permanent ones in September 1995 and September 1996, respectively. Progress toward current account convertibility has been consolidated by the increasing number of countries accepting the obligations of Article VIII of the IMF's Articles of Agreement (see Table 21).

---

[87]The initial monetary uncertainty in the region is described in Thomas Wolf, Warren Coats, Daniel Citrin, and Adrienne Cheasty, *Financial Relations Among Countries of the Former Soviet Union*, IMF Economic Reviews, No. 1 (February 1994); and in Thomas Wolf, "Currency Arrangements in Countries of the Former Ruble Area and Conditions for Sound Monetary Policy," IMF Paper on Policy Analysis and Assessment 94/15 (July 1994).

Several transition countries have also taken steps toward capital account convertibility, the eventual realization of which will allow free movement of capital, and which is a requirement for membership in the EU. As mentioned above, the Baltic countries have not applied capital account restrictions since the outset of the transition. The countries that have become members of the OECD the Czech Republic, Hungary, and Poland—have taken measures to ease restrictions on capital flows, including inward real estate acquisitions and outward long-term portfolio investments. Substantial restrictions on capital flows remain in many of the countries less advanced in the transition—including surrender requirements on foreign currency earnings and prohibitions on ownership of foreign equity—but these restrictions are in practice often circumvented.

The transition countries inherited a settlement and banking system that was not designed to handle decentralized payments across countries. In particular, Russia and other countries of the former Soviet Union were confronted with severe payments problems following the dissolution of the Union, as they unsuccessfully attempted to sustain a ruble area. From the beginning of 1994 on, with the introduction of new currencies and the progressive elimination of controls on correspondent accounts, the opportunities for the decentralized financing of trade in the region improved. Problems remain, however, with clearances sometimes taking as long as two weeks. Trade finance facilities and mechanisms to deal with exchange rate fluctuations and with risks of nonpayment and nonperformance are still missing. Several countries—Belarus, Turkmenistan, and Uzbekistan in particular—continue to impose significant restrictions on their foreign exchange markets.

Trade Liberalization

The pace and extent of trade liberalization have varied greatly across the transition countries, with a number of countries, particularly the Baltics and the countries of central and eastern Europe, moving rapidly toward relatively liberal trade regimes. Contributing to the recovery of trade among these countries themselves following the initial collapse at the start of the transition, but also carrying risks of trade diversion from other partner countries, has been the formation of regional free trade areas. These include the Central Europe Free Trade Area (CEFTA), composed of the Czech Republic, Hungary, Poland, the Slovak Republic, and Slovenia, and the Baltic Free Trade Area (BFTA), which comprises the three Baltic countries. Attempts at free trade areas within the Commonwealth of Independent States (CIS), which would also carry risks of trade diversion, remain embryonic.

Despite the progress that has been made, barriers remain to trade among the transition countries, even for trade within the free trade areas, with restrictions concentrated in goods such as light manufactures and agricultural products, which make up an important part of transition country exports. These import restrictions have taken the form of both nontariff barriers and import surcharges. Although most restrictions on exports have been removed, these have been replaced in some instances by administrative procedures that impede trade. Moreover, protectionist sentiment has grown in countries where recovery has lagged. For transition countries to benefit from a continued expansion of trade, unilateral and multilateral steps will be needed to reduce trade barriers further.

Securing access to export markets in the advanced economies—the destination for the majority of exports from most non-CIS countries—is also of vital importance for the transition countries. A number of countries in the Baltics and central and eastern Europe received most-favored-nation status under the GATT early in the transition, and many of these enjoy preferential market access under bilateral arrangements such as the "Europe Agreements" concluded with the EU. Membership of the WTO has been extended to the transition countries in central and eastern Europe, with the exceptions of Albania, Croatia, and the former Yugoslav Republic of Macedonia, the applications of which are still being considered, and also to Mongolia. The Baltic countries, Russia, and most other countries of the former Soviet Union have also requested to join the organization. Nonetheless, substantial barriers, particularly import quotas, remain to transition country exports of "sensitive goods," such as agricultural products, iron and steel, textiles and apparel, and footwear, all of which are goods in which the transition countries would reasonably be expected to have comparative advantage vis-à-vis the advanced economies. Transition country exports also continue to be affected by antidumping actions, which often in effect penalize firms that are most successful at exporting.

Following the breakup of the Soviet Union, CIS countries attempted to maintain existing trading partnerships on the basis of government-negotiated, bilateral commodity delivery agreements. With the exception of Turkmenistan, direct state involvement has since been reduced. CIS countries continue, however, to negotiate delivery agreements, and the prices of some traded products remain below world levels, though movement toward market-based pricing continues. This state involvement in trade impedes industrial restructuring, distorts relative prices, and provides incentives for the accumulation of interstate arrears and the creation of fiscal burdens through price subsidies. It is important that it be reduced, with official procurement limited to satisfying government needs.

Revival and Reorientation of Trade

Since the start of the transformation, trade, particularly with the advanced economies, has become an increasingly important part of the transition country economies. In many countries in central and eastern Europe, the ratio of trade to output has risen from only 10 percent or less in 1990 to upward of 20 percent in 1995 (Chart 42). In the Baltics, Russia, and other countries of the former Soviet Union, the share of trade in GDP has fallen, but this reflects the collapse of trade within the former Soviet Union, while trade with the rest of the world has expanded, particularly in the Baltic countries. The average degree of openness to trade in the transition economies today compares favorably with both the advanced economies and developing countries. A word of caution is in order, however, since for a number of reasons output may be understated, so that the ratio of trade to output may be overstated. As discussed in Box 5, for example, there is evidence that official measures of output do not capture burgeoning informal and private sector activity, and thus tend to overstate the ratio of trade to GDP unless trade flows, for which there are typically more reliable data, are similarly understated.

A massive reorientation of trade followed the collapse of central planning, as import demand collapsed with the drop in output in most transition countries, and as the artificial patterns of trade within the former system were replaced by trade relations determined by market forces. This has led to increased trade with the advanced economies, particularly in Europe. This change in trade flows away from former centrally planned partner countries toward the advanced economies is evident in the central and eastern European countries (Chart 43). These countries benefited not only from their geographical proximity to western Europe, which now accounts for 60 percent of their trade, but also from better initial economic conditions, more rapid reform and macroeconomic stabilization, and more rapid improvements in market access granted by the advanced economies. However, this high degree of dependence on western European export markets makes the exports of the central and eastern European countries particularly sensitive to growth in the countries of the European Union, as was seen in the first half of 1996 when exports to western Europe fell as growth there slowed. Trade among the countries of central and eastern Europe has recently picked up, particularly among the CEFTA countries, where trade grew by 6–9 percent in the first half of 1996. Even so, aside from trade between the Czech and Slovak Republics, this trade accounts for only about 6–10 percent of total trade for each CEFTA member. Trade with developing countries has remained roughly constant at between 10 and 15 percent of total trade.

For the Baltics, Russia, and other countries of the former Soviet Union, trade with the advanced economies is also now far more important than during the period of central planning, with substantial changes evident as early as the 1989–91 period of perestroika. Payments difficulties led to a sharp initial fall in ruble-denominated trade among the newly independent states of the CIS. The fall in trade was magnified by the abandonment of the artificial production patterns of central planning, which depended on movements of raw materials and especially energy; the collapse of trade in energy and other commodities led to sharp declines in output and thus in trade of finished products. The removal of trade barriers, liberalization of payments arrangements, and establishment of convertible currencies in many countries of the CIS have led to a recovery of trade within the CIS, as well as between the CIS and the Baltic countries and the countries of central and eastern Europe. The value of intra-CIS trade grew by 25 percent between the first half of 1995 and the first half of 1996 following a 9 percent increase in 1995 from 1994, although much of the growth in the value of trade reflects increases in commodity prices rather than an expansion in the volume of trade.[88]

The Baltic countries rapidly liberalized trade, except for agriculture, which remains protected in Latvia and Lithuania, and have both removed state involvement and substantially reoriented trade toward the industrial countries. Although Russia remains the first or second largest trading partner for all three countries, they largely avoided or rapidly recovered from the collapse of trade between Russia and other countries of the former Soviet Union.

The commodity composition of trade has also changed during the transition. Exports from many central and eastern European countries have gradually changed from consisting predominantly of raw materials to including a significant proportion of light manufactures, such as textiles, footwear, and clothing. This success in manufactured exports reflects both unit labor costs that remain low relative to the industrial countries and country-specific quotas in export markets in both the EU and the United States, which have sheltered the transition countries to some extent from competition with exporters from developing countries. Foreign direct investment has also contributed to export success, with countries such as the Czech Republic, Hungary, the Slovak Republic, and Slovenia now exporting automobiles and other products to the EU from plants constructed with foreign capital and technology. Primary commodities and semimanufactures, however, still account for 40–50 percent of

Chart 42. Countries in Transition: Ratio of Trade to Output
(Average of exports and imports; in percent of GDP)

The transition countries have become increasingly integrated into the global system of trade, although the importance of trade among the countries of the former Soviet Union has fallen.

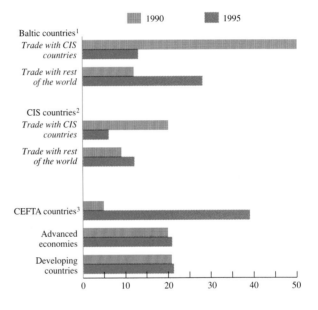

[1]Estonia, Latvia, and Lithuania.

[2]The Commonwealth of Independent States comprises Armenia, Azerbaijan, Belarus, Georgia, Kazakstan, Kyrgyz Republic, Moldova, Mongolia, Russia, Tajikistan, Turkmenistan, Ukraine, and Uzbekistan.

[3]The central European free trade area comprises Czech Republic, Hungary, Poland, Slovak Republic, and Slovenia.

---

[88]United Nations Economic Commission for Europe, *Economic Bulletin for Europe*, Vol. 48 (Geneva: United Nations, 1996) provides a detailed discussion of trade in the transition countries.

CEFTA countries' exports, and substantially more for the countries less advanced in the transition, such as Bulgaria and Romania. Exports of food and agricultural products to western Europe fell in 1996, but increased sharply to Russia and other CIS countries. Imports of machinery and equipment remained strong even as growth slowed in the countries of central and eastern Europe, a sign of buoyant investment that should bode well for these countries' future growth. Diversifying their production structure remains a challenge for the CIS countries, some of which are highly dependent on exports of a small number of commodities, such as cotton in Turkmenistan and Uzbekistan, and food and other agricultural products in Moldova.

Expansion of Trade: Prerequisites and Consequences

The experience of the transition countries, particularly those more advanced in the transition, points to a number of factors that are likely to have facilitated the expansion of trade. The countries that have enjoyed the most rapid integration into the global trading system have generally been those that early on pursued policies that achieved considerable success in macroeconomic stabilization. Although countries such as the Czech Republic and Poland generally enjoyed more favorable initial conditions than other transition countries, their early success at stabilization provided confidence to domestic and foreign investors that served to stimulate investment and an inflow of foreign capital, which in turn led to increased trade. The experience of the CIS countries highlights the importance of well-functioning multilateral clearing and payments mechanisms; the weakness of the mechanisms that existed often necessitated barter arrangements and stymied trade. Another important step in establishing conditions conducive to the expansion of trade has been the implementation of currency convertibility referred to earlier. This requires macroeconomic stabilization, since poor macroeconomic performance, particularly in terms of high or erratic inflation, leads to instability in open foreign exchange markets.

There is also evidence that the expansion of trade has been positively associated with the growth of productivity, though it is difficult to quantify the relationship meaningfully because the wholesale changes in the structure of the transition economies mean that it is often difficult to obtain reliable measures of productivity growth.[89] Structural reform of the domestic economy is particularly important to encourage the growth of exports, since measures that distort domestic prices are likely to affect productivity adversely

Chart 43. Central and Eastern European Countries: Composition of Trade by Partner
(In percent of total trade)

The transition countries have reoriented trade to the advanced economies.

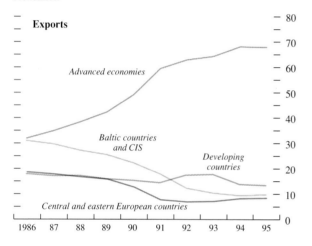

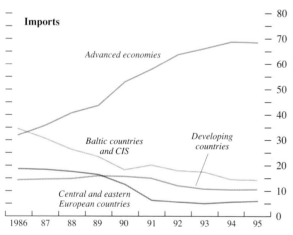

Note: CIS denotes Commonwealth of Independent States.

---

[89]Simeon Djankov and Bernard Hoekman, "Trade Reorientation and Post-Reform Productivity Growth in Bulgarian Enterprises," World Bank Policy Research Paper No. 1707 (Washington: World Bank, January 1997), find that trade is an important source of growth in total factor productivity at the firm level.

and reduce firms' competitiveness in export markets. Even within particular countries there is a substantial degree of dispersion in wage and productivity growth across industries, reflecting uneven progress in privatization and price and trade liberalization. Growth in imports can also lead to increased productivity and output, partly because imports provide a channel through which advanced technology is acquired by countries.[90]

Wages and Competitiveness

Nearly all the transition countries first experienced substantial currency depreciations with the collapse of central planning, and then real appreciations during their respective macroeconomic stabilizations. These real appreciations have occurred as prices have risen faster than in the industrial countries, while exchange rates vis-à-vis industrial country currencies have either remained roughly stable or depreciated more slowly than the inflation differential (Chart 44). Real appreciations are apparent in data both for bilateral real exchange rates vis-à-vis the dollar and deutsche mark and for multilateral real exchange rates based on trade weights. Much of the real appreciations that followed the initial phase of stabilization in most transition countries can be attributed to the undoing of substantial currency undervaluations that had developed earlier, reflecting both the low initial level of wages and adverse developments in the capital account reflecting uncertainty about the prospects for successful stabilization. Nonetheless, the unambiguous and substantial real appreciations that have occurred have raised concerns that transition country goods will lose their international competitiveness and have led to lobbying for import barriers and export subsidies, as well as for relaxation of monetary policies that have relied on a stable nominal exchange rate as an instrument in fighting inflation.

Much of the concern over the loss of competitiveness is focused on the rapid rise of wages measured in dollars, which have increased dramatically in most transition countries (Table 22). Part of the increase reflects the catch-up of undervalued transition country currencies, which translated into dollar wage gains. However, the more recent continuation of this process reflects not only catching up, but also productivity gains that have resulted from the industrial restructuring and deepening of the capital stock over the course of the transition, developments that would be expected to lead to increased wages. So long as the upward adjustment of dollar wages is matched by increased productivity in this way, it does not imply an increase in unit labor costs or a loss of competitiveness, but instead reflects progress made in the transition. While

Chart 44. Selected Countries in Transition: Real Exchange Rates vis-à-vis U.S. Dollar[1]
(1988 = 100)

Most transition countries have experienced real appreciations following macroeconomic stabilization.

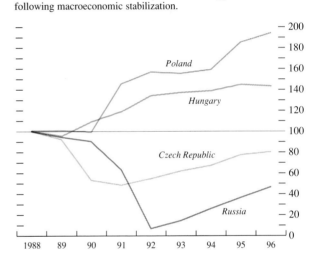

[1]In terms of relative consumer prices.

---

[90]Coe, Helpman, and Hoffmaister, "North-South R&D Spillovers."

Table 22. Countries in Transition: Dollar Wages in Manufacturing or Industry

(In U.S. dollars a month, net of social security taxes)

	1990	1991	1992	1993	1994	1995	1996[1]
Bulgaria	...	53	96	123	97	117	126
Czech Republic	...	132	162	196	231	296	316
Hungary	176	187	224	237	249	250	246
Poland	107	157	168	175	220	285	329
Romania	...	93	61	74	80	101	100
Slovak Republic	...	129	161	175	196	242	256
Estonia	...	...	46	78	137	211	255
Latvia	...	...	60	73	143	194	221
Lithuania	...	...	20	48	87	139	170
Belarus	...	...	27	23	33	74	95
Kazakstan	...	...	27	70	69	117	152
Kyrgyz Republic	...	...	14	16	34	53	56
Moldova	...	...	20	22	37	48	60
Russian Federation	...	...	32	63	96	115	185
Ukraine	...	...	28	14	26	47	55

Source: OECD, *Short-Term Economic Indicators: Transition Countries.*
[1]Based on data for the first half of 1996.

dollar wage growth in the more advanced economies of central and eastern Europe slowed somewhat in 1996, this may to some extent reflect the general appreciation of the dollar, particularly against the deutsche mark and other European currencies. (The deutsche mark is the currency of the most important trading partner of most transition countries.) When measured in deutsche mark rather than dollars, wages in most transition countries continued to grow substantially in 1996, pushing up unit labor costs in deutsche mark terms and substantiating concerns about competitiveness.[91]

It would clearly be cause for concern were wages to rise in relation to labor productivity in any transition country to such an extent that the rise in labor costs presaged a substantial deterioration in the trade balance. However, despite the growth of wages in terms of advanced economy currencies, it is not clear that wages have risen to unsustainable levels in any of the transition countries.[92] Given the scope for continued restructuring, capital deepening, and thus productivity growth, further gains in dollar wages are to be expected; they remain substantially lower than in the industrial countries.

---

[91]On the other hand, the fact that export prices in some transition countries, such as the Czech Republic and Estonia, have risen more rapidly than the prices of traded goods in western European trading partners may reflect quality upgrading in these countries' export industries, so that increases in unit labor costs may exaggerate the decline in competitiveness.

[92]Measures of "equilibrium wages" or "equilibrium real exchange rates" are especially difficult to calculate for the transition countries, since their production structures are continuing to undergo substantial changes. See László Halpern and Charles Wyplosz, "Equilibrium Exchange Rates in Transition Economies," IMF Working Paper 96/125 (November 1996), and Kornélia Krajnyák and Jeromin Zettelmeyer, "Competitiveness in Transition Economies: What Scope for Real Appreciation?" IMF Working Paper (forthcoming).

Progress with Financial Integration

The breakdown of central planning and the associated trading arrangements among centrally planned economies resulted in substantial external financing needs for several reasons. First, the move to world market prices generated severe terms of trade losses for many transition countries, energy importers in particular. Second, the introduction of currency convertibility on current account also required fairly large foreign exchange support. Third, the strong increase in external borrowing during the 1980s by a number of countries had resulted in unsustainable external debt positions; in several cases, debt-service moratoriums had to be declared. Finally, and more generally, the resources needed to modernize the industrial structure and infrastructure vastly exceeded domestic saving capacities.

The financing problems were particularly severe in Russia and other countries of the former Soviet Union. Within the Soviet Union, an elaborate system of fiscal transfers through the central budget, and of commodity (energy) deliveries at below world market prices had allowed most republics to consume more than they produced, with Russia the main donor.[93] Following the dissolution of the Soviet Union, explicit transfers were eliminated, and the major energy exporters, Russia and Turkmenistan, increased prices for interstate deliveries of oil and gas to near world levels. The result was a severe adverse terms of trade shock for the Baltic countries and the energy-importing countries of the former Soviet Union. The countries benefiting from the highest implicit transfers per capita before the transition, Georgia and Moldova, were the biggest losers, with estimated terms of trade losses of

---

[93]Other countries that were hit by severe financing problems following the breakdown of old transfer systems include the former Yugoslav Republic of Macedonia and Mongolia.

more than 35 percent and more than 43 percent, respectively, in interstate trade between 1990 and 1994.[94]

From the outset of the transformation process, it was recognized that the financing needs of the transition economies could not be met solely by private financial markets. The IMF and the World Bank Group assumed central roles in organizing the efforts to mobilize official financial support, including arrangements for debt relief. In addition to their own financial support, the application of conditionality by the Bretton Woods institutions was the catalytic element for other official financial assistance, including balance of payments support by the EU and other advanced economies.[95] At the same time, it was understood that official financial support would not be available on a large scale and over an extended period. The main purposes of the official assistance were to help transition countries adjust to the external shocks they had suffered, achieve macroeconomic stabilization, and undertake structural reform, thereby creating the conditions that would attract private foreign financing.[96]

By early 1997, almost all transition economies had received financial assistance from the Bretton Woods institutions and other official assistance.[97] Official net medium- to long-term flows into the transition economies during 1990–96 amounted to around $80 billion, including $17 billion from the IMF. Official loans have paved the way for increasing private financial flows, the share of which in total financing has increased from 15 percent in 1991 to 65 percent in 1996, accounted for mostly by an increase in foreign direct investment flows (Chart 45 and Table 23). The share of official financing flows into central and eastern

Chart 45. Countries in Transition: Medium- to Long-Term Net Financial Flows
(In billions of U.S. dollars)

The share of private financing is increasing.

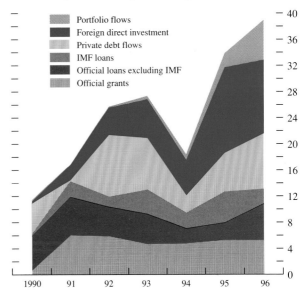

---

[94]Yuri Dikhanov, "Measuring the Terms of Trade in the Countries of the Former Soviet Union," in *Foreign Trade Statistics in the USSR and Successor States,* Studies of Economies in Transition No. 18, ed. by Misha Belkindas and Olga V. Ivanova (Washington: World Bank, 1995), pp. 55–73; and Wolf, Coats, Citrin, and Cheasty, *Financial Relations.*

[95]The EU organized balance of payments financing for a number of central and eastern European countries. This assistance, which was provided by the 24 OECD countries and the EU as such, was closely coordinated with the IMF. It was put in place to help augment official reserves and thereby facilitate the liberalization of foreign exchange payments and the introduction of convertible currencies. For the rationale behind this initiative, see the contribution by Flemming Larsen to the panel discussion in *Currency Convertibility in Eastern Europe,* ed. by John Williamson (Washington: Institute for International Economics, 1991), pp. 349–53.

[96]For a number of low-income transition countries, however, official assistance will continue to be needed on a longer-term basis; these countries qualify for official development assistance according to the OECD criteria. In addition, substantial official financing will be needed for the reconstruction program in Bosnia and Herzegovina.

[97]Only one member, Turkmenistan, has not received any financial support from the IMF, reflecting both its relatively strong external position and its lack of a comprehensive reform program, while the Federal Republic of Yugoslavia has yet to be admitted to membership.

101

Table 23. Countries in Transition: Net Medium- to Long-Term Financial Flows

(In billions of U.S. dollars)

	1991	1992	1993	1994	1995	1996
Total flows	16.8	25.7	27.3	18.3	33.8	38.9
Official flows	14.3	11.9	13.0	9.4	12.7	13.1
Grants	6.0	5.8	4.6	4.7	5.2	5.2
Loans	8.3	6.1	8.4	4.7	7.4	7.9
Bilateral	4.1	2.5	1.6	1.0	0.6	2.9
Multilateral, excluding IMF	1.8	2.1	3.1	1.3	2.1	2.7
IMF	2.4	1.6	3.7	2.4	4.7	2.2
Private flows	2.6	13.8	14.3	8.9	21.1	25.9
Debt flows	0.2	9.5	7.9	2.7	6.0	8.5
Guaranteed	0.1	9.1	7.0	1.0	2.1	6.9
Commercial bank loans	−3.7	−0.3	−1.1	−1.8	0.3	...
Bonds	1.4	1.0	4.2	2.6	1.6	...
Other	3.0	8.5	3.5	0.3	0.2	...
Nonguaranteed	0.1	0.4	0.9	1.7	3.9	1.7
Foreign direct investment	2.4	4.2	6.0	5.4	13.1	11.3
Portfolio flows	—	0.1	0.5	0.8	2.1	6.1
Share of private flows (in percent)	15	54	53	49	63	66
Of which: central and eastern European and Baltic countries						
Total flows	8.8	16.1	16.2	10.7	21.1	...
Official flows	6.3	3.4	3.7	4.3	1.7	...
Grants	3.4	2.1	1.5	2.3	3.7	...
Loans	2.9	1.3	2.2	2.0	−1.9	...
Bilateral	0.3	0.6	0.2	0.4	0.4	...
Multilateral, excluding IMF	0.2	0.2	0.2	1.5	0.4	...
IMF	2.4	0.5	1.8	0.1	−2.7	...
Private flows	2.6	12.7	12.6	6.4	19.4	...
Debt flows	0.2	9.5	7.9	1.8	8.0	...
Guaranteed	0.1	9.1	7.0	0.1	4.2	...
Commercial bank loans	−0.6	−1.7	−0.8	−2.2	1.7	...
Bonds	1.4	1.0	4.2	2.3	2.4	...
Other	−0.2	−0.5	0.1	0.1	—	...
Nonguaranteed	0.1	0.4	0.9	1.7	3.8	...
Foreign direct investment	2.4	3.2	4.2	3.8	9.5	...
Portfolio flows	—	0.1	0.5	0.9	2.0	...
Share of private flows (in percent)	29	79	77	60	92	...

Sources: European Bank for Reconstruction and Development; IMF; and World Bank.

Europe has declined sharply. The countries most advanced in the transition process have full access to private financing and no longer rely on official assistance. A number of countries at intermediate stages of transition, such as Kazakstan, Moldova, Romania, and Russia have raised medium- and long-term funds on the international financial markets while continuing to draw upon official assistance. The increasing role of private financial flows to both groups of countries is discussed in more detail in the next section.

The Increasing Role of Private Financing

Many transition economies have gained substantial access to private financing. As macroeconomic stabilization has typically involved a combination of high domestic interest rates and broadly stable nominal exchange rates, private financing initially took mainly the form of short-term flows, including repatriated flight capital. Such inflows were often substantial compared with the size of the economy, posing considerable challenges for monetary policy.[98] The

---

[98]For recent discussions of this issue see Guillermo Calvo, Ratna Sahay, and Carlos Végh, "Capital Flows in Central and Eastern Europe: Evidence and Policy Options" in *Private Capital Flows to Emerging Markets After the Mexican Crisis,* ed. by Guillermo Calvo, Morris Goldstein, and Eduard Hochreiter (Washington: Institute for International Economics, 1996), pp. 57–90; Jang-Yung Lee, "Implications of a Surge in Capital Inflows: Available Tools and Consequences for the Conduct of Monetary Policy," IMF Working Paper 96/53 (May 1996); and Pierre Siklos, "Capital Flows in a Transitional Economy and the Sterilization Dilemma: The Hungarian Case," IMF Working Paper 96/86 (August 1996); data on the short-term flows can be found in the 1995 and 1996 *Economic Bulletin for Europe.*

next stage in the development of private financing to these countries has involved an increase in the importance of more stable medium- and long-term flows. This section reviews the transition countries' experience in attracting the three main forms of medium- and long-term private financing: international bonds and syndicated loans, foreign direct investment, and investment from abroad in domestic debt securities and equities.

International Lending and Bond Markets

A number of transition countries have made considerable progress in gaining access to the international lending and bond markets. Access to these markets can help creditworthy borrowers meet financing needs that exceed the capacities of the domestic market, and can act as a valuable source of expertise and financial discipline. The basic economic conditions needed for a transition country to gain access to international financial markets are, in addition to reasonable macroeconomic stability and progress with structural reform, a normalization of relations with creditors in cases of previous debt-service problems and a sustainable external debt position.

For those transition countries that experienced debt-servicing problems before or at the outset of the transformation, agreements with official creditors at the Paris Club and commercial creditors at the London Club have been indispensable for regaining access to the international financial markets. Many centrally planned economies, including the Soviet Union, rapidly increased their external borrowing in the 1980s and eventually were unable to service their debt. Poland already faced difficulties servicing its external debt before the end of the decade, while Bulgaria declared a unilateral moratorium on its external debt in early 1990. The breakup of two relatively indebted countries, the Soviet Union and Yugoslavia, further complicated the external debt problem.

Substantial progress was made in the early years of the transformation process in normalizing relations with Paris and London Club creditors, and this process is now nearly completed. A number of issues remain to be resolved regarding inherited Soviet claims on developing countries, unsettled interstate claims and liabilities among the CIS states, and claims of former CMEA members on Russia. Settlement of developing countries' debt to Russia and of the interstate liabilities incurred by low-income CIS countries will require further negotiations on debt reduction and rescheduling agreements; however, these discussions should not impede the further integration of Russia and other CIS states into international financial markets (Box 11).

The agreements with the London and Paris Clubs and other creditors, together with growth in export revenues, have put most transition economies in a po-

sition to service their outstanding external debt with room for prudent additional borrowing. Debt burdens, as measured by the ratio of gross external debt to exports, have improved considerably for Albania, Bulgaria, and Poland, mainly as a result of debt agreements. By this criterion, the debt burden of Hungary, which entered the transformation process as a relatively indebted country but did not seek a rescheduling agreement, has also been eased significantly, while countries such as Croatia, the Czech Republic, Slovakia, and Slovenia have maintained relatively light debt burdens inherited from the pretransition period. Following the agreements whereby Russia assumed all the Soviet external liabilities, the other CIS states started the transition in a favorable position, while Russia itself benefited from a series of agreements with external creditors. On the basis of the gross debt-export ratio and in line with the World Bank's classification criteria, in 1996 four transition countries—Armenia, Bulgaria, Hungary, and the Kyrgyz Republic—were moderately indebted, while Albania and Georgia were severely indebted (Table 24).[99]

Recent progress in gaining access to international financial markets is reflected in the growing number of countries receiving international credit ratings from the major rating agencies and in their upgrading of some countries. In the past two years, the countries more advanced in the transition process also have made the largest gains in semiannual surveys of country risk rankings and accounted for most of the place gainers (Table 25). Seven transition countries—the Visegrád countries (the Czech Republic, Hungary, Poland, and Slovakia), Croatia, Latvia, and Slovenia—are now rated as investment grade. An increasing number of countries and a broadening range of borrowers are raising funds on the international financial markets.[100] At the end of 1994, only three countries—the Czech Republic, Hungary, and Slovakia—had raised substantial amounts in these markets. The number of transition countries borrowing on international markets increased sharply in 1995, as Poland and Romania reentered the market after long absences, and, for the first time, Latvia and Lithuania issued international bonds, while the Kyrgyz Republic obtained its first international loan. The number of borrowers continued to expand in 1996 and early 1997; Croatia, Kazakstan, Russia, and Slovenia launched debut Eurobond issues, and Croatia received its first medium-term syndicated loan. Borrowers were until recently almost exclusively governments and central

---

[99]According to the World Bank's *World Debt Tables*, a country is moderately indebted when its debt-export ratio exceeds 132 percent, and severely indebted when the ratio is higher than 220 percent.

[100]See United Nations Economic Commission for Europe, *Economic Bulletin for Europe* and *Economic Survey of Europe*; and World Bank, *Financial Flows and the Developing Countries: A World Bank Quarterly.*

Box 11. Normalizing the Transition Countries' Creditor Relations

The transition countries that experienced debt-servicing problems before or at the outset of the transformation have made substantial progress in normalizing relations with Paris and London Club creditors.

A number of *central and eastern European countries* reached agreement on debt-rescheduling arrangements during 1991–95. Between 1991 and 1994, *Bulgaria* obtained three successive arrangements with Paris Club creditors on its official debt, and in 1994, a debt and debt-service-reduction agreement was reached with the London Club of commercial creditors, within the framework of the Brady plan. The Paris Club agreed in 1994 to implement the second stage of a 1991 debt-reduction agreement with *Poland,* and a Brady-style deal with commercial creditors was concluded in October 1994. In mid-1995, *Albania* and its foreign commercial bank creditors signed an agreement that involved a deeply discounted restructuring of the country's bank debt.

Resolution of the debt problem of the *former Yugoslavia* continues to be complicated by unresolved issues relating to the division among the successor states of the so-called unallocated debt.[1] In spite of these unresolved issues, three successor states have successfully normalized their relations with official and commercial creditors. By the end of 1996, *Croatia, the former Yugoslav Republic of Macedonia,* and *Slovenia* had reached understandings with the creditors of both the London and Paris Clubs, each assuming responsibility for a share of the unallocated debt. As far as Paris Club indebtedness is concerned, Slovenia has been negotiating bilateral arrangements with creditor governments following a mid-1993 understanding, while Croatia and the former Yugoslav Republic of Macedonia obtained debt reschedulings in their 1995 arrangements with the Club.

Relations with the official creditors of *Russia and other countries of the former Soviet Union* were clarified in a rescheduling agreement in April 1993, in which *Russia,* under an agreement in principle with other successor states, declared itself solely responsible for the entire debt of the former Soviet Union. Russia has signed three further agreements with the Paris Club on the long-term restructuring of its official debt, the most recent in April 1996, and reached an agreement in principle with the London Club in November 1995, to be finalized in mid-1997. Russia completed the normalization of its financial relations with all the main advanced economies in the fall of 1996, by reaching understandings on unsettled claims by French creditors, including holders of bonds issued under the czarist regime, and by concluding

an agreement on the rescheduling of uninsured commercial debt owed by the former Soviet Union.[2]

While substantial progress has been achieved in normalizing relations with commercial and official creditors in the advanced economies, a number of issues remain regarding inherited Soviet claims on developing countries; unsettled interstate claims and liabilities among members of the Commonwealth of Independent States (CIS); and claims of former Council for Mutual Economic Assistance (CMEA) members on Russia and vice versa. Claims on developing countries result from substantial credits extended by the Soviet Union. The exact amount of such claims is yet to be determined, in part because the parties have not agreed on the ruble exchange rate to be used for valuation. All these claims were inherited by Russia following its assumption of sole responsibility for the Soviet external debt in exchange for its external assets. Unsettled interstate claims and liabilities reflect three major types of transactions: official credits, including the balances on bilateral correspondent accounts from the 1992–93 period; arrears on payments for deliveries under officially sponsored bilateral trade contracts, mainly for oil and gas and with Russia and Turkmenistan as the principal creditors; and cross-border interenterprise arrears assumed by governments to provide financial support for particular sectors or industries.[3] Finally, some central and eastern European countries have claims on Russia and vice versa, originating in transferable ruble balances outstanding when the CMEA was dissolved.

Settlement of the developing country debt to Russia and of the interstate liabilities incurred by low-income CIS countries will require further negotiations. During 1996, Russia reached agreements with Nicaragua and Peru, which involved deep discounts on the face value of its claims, and continued negotiations with the other CIS countries and with the Czech Republic and Hungary. Russia is discussing with the Paris Club possible participation in the Club as part of the efforts to normalize its creditor relations with developing countries.

---

[1]The unallocated debt refers to obligations incurred by the former Yugoslavia and its national bank and which could not be traced to funding of specific projects located in any of the successor republics.

[2]A number of countries of the Commonwealth of Independent States (CIS), which on independence had modest debt obligations, having signed the agreement with Russia on the debt of the former Soviet Union, accumulated sizable obligations toward non-CIS countries during 1991–94, in addition to liabilities toward other CIS countries. From 1994 on, Georgia incurred payments arrears on its external debt service, and during 1995–96 the country concluded a number of bilateral rescheduling agreements, including arrangements with Austria and the Islamic Republic of Iran.

[3]Amer Bisat, "Ukraine's Gas Arrears: Issues and Recommendations," IMF Paper on Policy Analysis and Assessment 96/3 (April 1996) presents an analysis of Ukraine's external gas arrears to Russia.

---

banks, but have started to include municipalities and regional authorities and private and partially privatized companies.

Improvements in the terms and conditions on which funds have been made available to some transition countries are a further indication of progress with in-

Table 24. Countries in Transition: Ratios of Gross External Debt to Export

(In percent)

	1991	1992	1993	1994	1995	1996
Albania	602	986	1,810	657	268	242
Armenia	0	0	76	131	195	158
Azerbaijan	0	0	6	29	50	47
Belarus	1	15	34	41	38	52
Bulgaria	387	247	262	208	172	160
Croatia	345	43	46	53	71	70
Czech Republic	71	59	54	65	61	60
Estonia	0	4	7	6	6	11
Georgia	0	35	147	204	259	253
Hungary	219	186	267	320	206	201
Kazakstan	0	32	36	75	62	56
Kyrgyz Republic	0	1	80	113	133	164
Latvia	0	3	15	24	20	23
Lithuania	2	8	14	20	29	32
Macedonia, former Yugoslav Republic of	0	0	0	86	102	129
Moldova	0	2	65	102	105	128
Mongolia	65	79	109	130	115	133
Poland	308	277	276	184	123	112
Romania	51	63	76	77	73	98
Russia	155	183	168	152	128	126
Slovak Republic	81	35	46	44	39	49
Slovenia	0	21	23	25	27	30
Ukraine	0	59	27	49	50	43
Uzbekistan	0	18	34	33	27	38

ternational financial market integration. The interest margin for U.S. dollar-denominated syndicated loans negotiated by Hungary dropped from 180 basis points in the summer of 1995 to 50 basis points in the summer of 1996, and to less than 30 basis points by the end of 1996. Similar margins have been offered on sovereign syndicated loans for Slovenia and to large Czech companies, which now borrow at terms approaching those for corporate borrowers in western European countries. Poland's first Eurobond issue in June 1995 was at a spread of more than 180 basis points; in the fall of 1996, the bonds traded at around 70 basis points. Croatia's early 1997 and Slovenia's mid-1996 debut Eurobonds were issued at similar spreads. The countries at intermediate stages of transition are still facing substantial spreads, however, as indicated by the launch spread of 365 basis points in the case of Russia's first Eurobond.

Role of Foreign Direct Investment

Foreign direct investment (FDI) can potentially play a vital role in the transformation process. The countries in transition need substantial fixed investment, as they inherited an obsolete fixed capital stock and an inadequate infrastructure. From a macroeconomic point of view, foreign direct investment complements domestic saving and contributes to total investment in the economy without adding to the external debt burden. Moreover, it has the advantage of usually bringing with it advanced technology, management, and

marketing skills, as well as access to export markets.[101] However, uncertainties regarding property rights and the legal and fiscal environment in which businesses can operate naturally tend to deter foreign direct investment. Reflecting such uncertainties, FDI flows into many transition economies have remained relatively small and often directed at local markets. As the economic transition progresses, foreign direct investment may be expected to gain in prominence and to become more diversified and export oriented.

Although foreign direct investment into transition economies has increased since 1991, the flows have been relatively small compared with other regions and with initial expectations. The annual flow to central and eastern Europe, the Baltics, and the CIS rose from around $2.5 billion in 1991 to about $13 billion in 1995.[102] Partly owing to a slowdown in privatizations, foreign direct investment into these countries is esti-

---

[101]On the role of foreign direct investment in transition countries see also the May 1995 *World Economic Outlook*, pp. 60–65. Recent surveys include Klaus-Dieter Schmidt, "Foreign Direct Investment in Eastern Europe: State-of-the-Art and Prospects," in *Transforming Economies and European Integration,* ed. by Rumen Dobrinsky and Michael Landesmann (Aldershot: Edward Elgar, 1996), pp. 268–89, and Richard Stern, "Putting Foreign Direct Investment in Eastern Europe into Perspective: Turning a Macroeconomic Failure Into a Microeconomic Success Story," in the same volume, pp. 297–310.

[102]The main data sources for information on the aggregate flow of FDI into transition economies are the yearly issues of EBRD, *Transition Report,* United Nations Economic Commission for Europe, *Economic Bulletin for Europe,* and World Bank, *World Debt Tables—External Finance for Developing Countries.*

Table 25. Countries in Transition: Credit Ratings and Country Risk Rankings

	1993	1994	1995	1996[1]
Credit ratings[2]				
Bulgaria				SIG
Croatia				IG
Czech Republic	IG	IG*	IG*	IG*
Hungary	SIG	SIG	SIG	IG
Kazakstan				SIG
Latvia				IG
Lithuania				SIG
Moldova				SIG
Poland			IG	IG
Romania				SIG
Russia				SIG
Slovak Republic		SIG	SIG*	IG
Slovenia				IG
Country risk rankings[3]				
Czech Republic	43	39	41	35
Estonia	122	102	76	71
Hungary	46	44	44	44
Latvia	132	125	116	75
Lithuania	130	121	118	59
Poland	72	73	72	55
Romania	75	77	64	61
Slovak Republic	63	66	51	49
Slovenia	61	53	50	34

Sources: Moody's and Standard & Poor's press releases; and, for the rankings, *Euromoney* (September 1996).

[1]January–March 1997.

[2]Foreign currency, long-term, sovereign debt ratings. IG denotes investment grade, SIG sub-investment grade, * an upgrade. A sub-investment grade is reported as long as at least one agency assigned such a grade. Transition countries not included in the list did not receive a rating.

[3]The country risk rankings are based upon weighted scores of analytical, credit, and market access indicators in nine categories.

mated to have declined to about $11 billion in 1996, contributing to an FDI-based capital stock of around $42 billion. Transition economies still attract substantially less foreign direct investment than other regions; the cumulative inflow during 1991–96 is estimated to have equaled around 4 percent of the transition countries' GDP, compared with around 6 percent for Latin America and around 13 percent for the East Asian developing countries.

The geographical and sectoral distribution of foreign direct investment in the early years of the transformation has been uneven. In terms of destination, the central and eastern European and Baltic countries attracted more than 70 percent of the cumulative foreign direct investment inflows into the transition economies during the 1991–96 period, with Hungary and the Czech Republic alone accounting for close to 50 percent of total inflows. On average, per capita FDI received by the CIS countries was less than 15 percent of the inflows into the central and eastern European and Baltic countries (Table 26). In terms of countries of origin, Austria, Germany, and the United States have been the main investors, accounting for more

than two-thirds of the investment into the transition economies in 1994 and for almost two-thirds of the cumulative investment inflow in 1988–94. Austria and Germany are also the advanced economies with the highest shares of foreign direct investment in transition countries relative to other destinations. In terms of sectoral composition, finally, data through 1994 indicate that a large share of foreign direct investment in the early years of the transition was placed in sectors mainly oriented toward supplying the domestic market, such as the trade and distribution sectors, and, within manufacturing, the food-, beverage-, and tobacco-processing industries.[103]

The uneven geographical and sectoral pattern of foreign direct investment is related to a number of factors that partly reflect the characteristics of the transformation process.[104] First, FDI inflows have tended to be highest in the countries most advanced in the transition process. Second, they have been influenced by the form and timing of the privatization process: countries such as Estonia and Hungary that chose a privatization policy that included major sales to foreign investors, rather than voucher-based mass privatization schemes or management and employee buyouts, have been particularly successful in attracting foreign direct investment. Third, a considerable proportion of direct investment has come from neighboring countries or from countries with historical and cultural ties or existing business and trade linkages. Fourth, early foreign direct investment has often been motivated by opportunities to gain a first-mover advantage in new markets; these incentives have been important for inward-looking foreign direct investment in the larger transition countries and for investment in the trade and distribution sectors and the vehicle-building and food-processing industries.[105]

The Czech Republic, Estonia, and Hungary, have attracted inflows of foreign direct investment comparable with those received by prominent emerging market

[103]Gábor Hunya and Jan Stankovsky, "Foreign Direct Investment in Central and East European Countries and the Former Soviet Union" (Vienna: The Vienna Institute for Comparative Economic Studies, 1996), include data on the sectoral breakdown of FDI for a number of eastern European and Baltic countries. Stefano Manzocchi, "Sectoral Patterns of FDI in Central and Eastern Europe: A Note" (unpublished; Department of Economics, University of Ancona, December 1996), offers a preliminary analysis of the further sectoral breakdown within the manufacturing sector.

[104]For recent studies on this topic see Melanie Lansbury, Nigel Pain, and Katerina Smidkova, "Foreign Direct Investment in Central Europe Since 1990: An Econometric Study," *National Institute Economic Review,* No. 156 (May 1996), pp. 104–14, and Hans Peter Lankes and Anthony Venables, "Foreign Direct Investment in Economic Transition: The Changing Pattern of Investments," *Economics of Transition,* Vol. 4 (1996), pp. 331–47, a study based upon a survey of companies that have planned or undertaken FDI projects in the region.

[105]Most studies based on survey data conclude that market seeking was the prime motive and that factor cost advantages were of less importance for the majority of early investments. See Lankes and Venables, "Foreign Direct Investment," for an overview.

Table 26. Countries in Transition: Net Foreign Direct Investment
(In millions of U.S. dollars)

	Yearly Inflows						Cumulative Inflows	Cumulative Per Capita Inflows[1]
	1991	1992	1993	1994	1995	1996		
Total	**2,374**	**4,195**	**5,950**	**5,412**	**13,082**	**11,250**	**42,263**	**100**
Albania	—	10	45	53	70	70	248	71
Armenia	—	—	—	3	10	23	36	10
Azerbaijan	—	—	—	22	275	601	898	120
Belarus	—	7	18	10	7	12	54	5
Bulgaria	56	42	40	105	165	180	588	65
Croatia	100	13	74	100	100	200	587	123
Czech Republic	393	983	552	749	2,526	1,165	6,368	617
Estonia	—	80	154	212	202	210	859	558
Georgia	—	—	—	8	6	20	34	6
Hungary	1,474	1,471	2,329	1,097	4,410	1,986	12,767	1,256
Kazakstan	—	100	473	635	859	930	2,997	180
Kyrgyz Republic	—	—	10	45	61	31	146	31
Latvia	—	43	51	155	165	200	614	239
Lithuania	—	10	23	60	55	96	244	65
Macedonia, former Yugoslav Republic of	—	—	—	24	12	35	70	32
Moldova	25	16	14	18	72	46	191	43
Mongolia	—	2	8	7	7	7	31	13
Poland	117	284	580	542	1,134	2,205	4,862	126
Romania	37	73	95	347	417	410	1,379	61
Russia	–25	700	900	630	2,000	2,000	6,205	42
Slovak Republic	197	50	134	170	70	66	687	128
Slovenia	—	113	112	140	140	145	650	325
Tajikistan	—	9	12	12	13	13	59	10
Turkmenistan	—	11	79	103	64	80	337	81
Ukraine	—	170	200	91	266	436	1,163	23
Uzbekistan	—	9	48	73	–24	84	190	8

[1]Cumulative 1991–96 per capita inflows in U.S. dollars.

economies in other regions, and since the four influences referred to above are partly temporary, foreign direct investment into other transition countries may be expected at least to some degree to imitate these examples. It may also be expected that foreign direct investment will become more outward looking and generate increased trade flows, as foreign firms take advantage of the transition countries' relatively highly educated and skilled workers and low labor costs. Steps that have been taken in a number of transition countries to allow foreign access to the infrastructure, public utilities, and financial intermediation sectors will offer an additional stimulus to foreign direct investment (Box 12).[106]

Foreign Investment in Domestic Securities and Equity Placements

Foreign investment in domestic securities and international equity placements in the form of depository

receipts are an increasingly important source of external finance for some of the transition economies and the fastest growing segment in overall private financing. Progress in the establishment of well-functioning markets for private and government debt securities and for equities, together with initially high yields, have attracted a growing number of foreign investors, specialized investment funds in particular. Demand from investors should in turn help lower interest rates on domestic debt instruments and improve the efficiency and liquidity of domestic stock markets, while encouraging accountability among local firms; foreign investors can provide valuable expertise and exert pressure to bring domestic financial institutions and markets up to international standards.

Local markets for government securities are among the most advanced financial markets in a number of transition economies and have attracted considerable interest among foreign investors. High yields in foreign currency terms motivated sizable foreign purchases of domestic government securities in the Czech Republic in 1994–95, Poland in 1995, and, following a partial liberalization of foreign access to the treasury bill market, Russia in 1996. Foreigners invested around $4 billion in the Russian treasury bill market in 1996, and a continuing increase in nonresident purchases is expected as the Russian govern-

---

[106]The growing importance of infrastructural investment in the transition countries is highlighted in Laurence Carter, Frank Sader, and Pernille Holtedahl, "Foreign Direct Investment in Central and Eastern European Infrastructure," World Bank Foreign Investment Advisory Service Occasional Paper No. 7 (Washington: The World Bank, 1996).

Box 12. Foreign Direct Investment Strategies in Hungary and Kazakstan

Hungary and Kazakstan rank among the transition economies that were most successful in attracting foreign direct investment (FDI) during 1991–96. Of all transition economies, Hungary received the highest FDI inflows in both absolute and per capita terms, with its cumulative per capita inflow of $1250 among the highest in the world. Kazakstan was the leading recipient of per capita FDI among the CIS countries, though the cumulative inflow of less than $200 is small compared with most central and eastern European countries and Estonia. A better understanding of the FDI flows into these two countries also sheds light on patterns of FDI into the transition economies in general, including the significant differences between eastern European and CIS countries. In general, the experiences of Hungary and Kazakstan illustrate both how stabilization and reform are essential for attracting FDI and how country-specific factors can play an important role too.

Hungary's leading position among transition countries in attracting FDI is rooted in the early start and strong outward orientation of its transformation process. The country liberalized prices, foreign trade, and foreign participation in companies ahead of other transition economies and created a stable and transparent legal framework for FDI early in the transition, following the adoption of a new investment law in 1988. Having already developed strong business relationships with western companies and enhanced its creditworthiness by meeting its debt-service obligations, Hungary adopted a general policy of promoting greater foreign participation in the domestic economy. The 1989 privatization program, which involved selling medium- and large-sized state enterprises to foreign investors, was a central element of this outward-looking policy and acted as a major stimulus for FDI inflows, which surged from $300 million in 1990 to $2.3 billion in 1993.[1] Following a slow-down of privatization and FDI inflows in 1994, a revised privatization program was adopted in May 1995 aimed at selling large enterprises in the energy, financial, and infrastructure sectors to foreign investors; as a result, about 95 percent of 1995 privatization revenues were

in foreign currency, and FDI peaked at more than $4 billion compared with little more than $1 billion in the previous year. Companies with foreign participation have begun to play a role in the Hungarian economy similar to that in smaller western European countries. Such enterprises now form a very dynamic part of the economy in terms of investment and output performance and account for well over half of the country's exports. According to the Hungarian Privatization Research Institute, at the end of 1996 more than two-thirds of the country's 200 largest companies had foreign participation; foreign investors hold majority stakes in the utilities and banking sectors.

The Hungarian experience also illustrates the shift in the sectoral composition and orientation of FDI as the process of transformation and international integration advances. Initially, FDI was mostly channeled into industry and mainly driven by the motive of securing presence in a new and expanding market.[2] From 1994 on, FDI inflows into sectors other than industry gained in importance, reducing industry's share in cumulative FDI from around two-thirds in mid-1993 to less than one-half by the end of 1996. The move toward sectoral diversification was reinforced following the adoption of the revised privatization program in 1995, as a result of which the private sector share and foreign participation in energy, infrastructure, telecommunications, and banking are now higher than in several western European countries. Foreign direct investment into industry is being reoriented from projects directed at the domestic market to projects involving intrafirm specialization and trade. With the privatization process nearing completion, there has been a growing importance of reinvested profits and investment projects not related to privatization.

Kazakstan followed Hungary's example in creating a legal framework for FDI early in the transition and in targeting its privatization program for major companies toward foreign investors, in particular by seeking foreign participation in the exploitation of the country's vast nat-

---

[1]For an analysis of FDI during 1990–95, see Gábor Hunya, "Foreign Direct Investment in Hungary: A Key Element of Economic Modernization," Vienna Institute for Comparative Economic Studies Research Report No. 226 (February 1996).

[2]The importance of market access among the factors determining initial FDI into Hungary is reflected in the answers to an investor survey. See Miklós Szanyi, "Experiences with Foreign Direct Investment in Hungary," *Russian and East European Finance and Trade,* Vol. 31 (May–June 1995), pp. 6–30.

---

ment has announced a further liberalization of foreign access.

Foreign investment in equities, which remained modest until 1995, surged in a number of countries in 1996. Nonresident investors now account for substantial shares of stock market holdings and turnover in the Czech Republic, Hungary, Poland, and Russia and have contributed to very sharp increases in stock market prices in 1996; stock market indices, computed in U.S. dollar terms, rose by almost 100 percent in

Budapest, by more than 70 percent in Warsaw, and by more than 150 percent in Moscow. The Hungarian and Polish markets have been included in the International Finance Corporation's investable country indices for emerging markets since 1993, the Czech market since 1995, and the Russian and Slovak markets since February 1997. By the end of 1996, eight more transition economies had functioning stock markets; most of them, however, are still small and fairly illiquid and have not yet attracted strong foreign interest.

ural resources. The first laws on FDI were introduced while the country was still gaining independence, and the first major privatization program, adopted in March 1993, included ambitious plans to sell to foreign investors up to 180 large enterprises, mainly in the raw materials and heavy industry sectors. In the following two years, however, the expected strong increase in FDI inflows did not materialize, and the government made little progress in selling large enterprises to foreign investors.

A number of factors explain why foreigners were hesitant to invest in Kazakstan in the early years of the transition. Macroeconomic instability and frequent changes in the government caused economic and political uncertainty. Additional uncertainty resulted from bureaucratic practices, complicated and erratically administered tax and investment regulations, and ad hoc changes in laws and contractual arrangements. Finally, the procedures for selling large companies to foreign investors were complex and the valuation of such companies complicated by the absence of internationally accepted accounting standards.[3] In these circumstances, foreign investors were unwilling to commit substantial financial resources, with the exception of a limited number of projects in the oil and gas sectors, characterized by long investment horizons, and in the food-processing and tobacco industries, where first-mover advantages are important.

In an attempt to bring in the management and technological expertise of foreign investors while limiting their financial risk, in late 1994 the Kazak government introduced a management contract scheme for large state-owned enterprises, whereby foreign firms were given the right to manage enterprises for a limited period of time. In exchange for bonuses or shares in profits, or both, and, in most cases, a priority right to purchase the majority of the firm's shares at the end of the contract, management companies were obliged to redeem, up-front, outstanding arrears of the enterprise, implement preprivatization restructuring, or carry out specified investment projects. Starting at the end of 1994, about 60 of the country's largest enterprises, including most of the heavy industry plants, were put under management contracts. In 1995,

around 40 percent of FDI was absorbed by enterprises managed by foreign companies, and the share of these enterprises in total exports may have been similar to that in Hungary.

The Kazak experience with management contracts has been a mixed success. Management contracts were often awarded without competitive procedures, on the basis of incomplete and vague legal contracts and with insufficient safeguards against short-term opportunistic behavior; a number of contracts were canceled because of poor performance. On the other hand, in a number of cases these contracts have facilitated more efficient operations and restructuring in preparation for privatization. The contracts should therefore be seen as a temporary solution for the period until uncertainty has been reduced to a degree where foreign investors are willing to commit financial resources. During 1996, the monitoring of contracts was reinforced and direct sales of large enterprises were accelerated; at the end of 1996, the government ceased awarding new contracts. By early 1997, most of Kazakstan's large metal mines and smelters, a number of coal mines, oil producers and power plants, and the country's giant steel factory had been sold off, mainly to foreign investors. The government also initiated the partial sale of the infrastructure, telecommunications, and utilities sectors to foreign investors, thereby imitating the switch in privatization focus in Hungary after 1995. However, geography probably makes Kazakstan less attractive as an FDI destination for small businesses, which typically account for most of the number of FDI projects. By the end of 1996, less than 3,000 companies with foreign participation were operating in the country compared with around 30,000 in Hungary.

A comparison of the patterns of FDI into Hungary and Kazakstan illustrates the fact that a legal framework and an outward-looking economic policy, while necessary, are not sufficient to generate large FDI inflows. Such inflows are impeded if there is a climate of general financial uncertainty and poor implementation of laws and regulations. Once the appropriate legal and economic environment is created, transition countries have the prospect of steadily increasing FDI inflows into broad sectors of the economy. At the same time, the size and composition of FDI will continue to reflect differences in factors such as geography, proximity to major markets, human capital, and natural resources endowment.

[3]In a June 1996 survey conducted by the International Tax and Investment Centre among 46 foreign investors, bureaucratic practices and a nontransparent fiscal and regulatory framework were regarded as major barriers for FDI into Kazakstan.

In light of the practical problems and risks involved in investing directly in the stock markets of the transition countries, corporations in these economies have started to organize international equity placements in the form of American or global depository receipts.[107]

[107]Depository receipts are negotiable equity-based certificates that represent underlying shares listed on the stock markets of the transition countries and are held in custody with a depository bank; they are listed and traded on the stock exchanges of advanced economies.

Corporations from four transition economies made depository receipt placements of around $300 million in 1994, with Hungarian companies accounting for the bulk of this activity. This amount was doubled in 1995, and the issuer base was broadened to three more countries. Mainly because of activity by Russian companies, which were authorized to place American depository receipts in September 1995, placements again doubled in 1996, including issues by major Russian energy producers Gazprom and Lukoil.

The integration of the transition countries into international financial markets in many respects is still in its initial stages, notwithstanding the impressive progress of the more advanced countries in gaining and improving access. Private financial flows into these countries remain relatively small. In 1996, foreign direct investment into the transition countries was equivalent to only 14 percent of the inflow into the East Asian and Latin American countries, while international bond issues by transition countries were less than 5 percent of the issues by the other two country groups, and medium- and long-term syndicated loan commitments amounted to less than 15 percent.

Moreover, financial integration has to advance in a number of more qualitative dimensions. First, while some countries can expect to gain access to private financing once delays in macroeconomic stabilization and structural reform have been overcome, some of the smaller economies in southeast Europe, the Caucasus, and central Asia with low incomes and limited natural resources are likely to remain dependent on official financing for years to come. Second, the transition countries need to make further progress toward eliminating capital flight and restoring order to the process of capital outflows, which as such—as legitimate investment abroad by residents of these countries—could bring additional gains from international financial integration. Most transition countries experienced substantial capital flight during the first years of the transformation. In Russia, for instance, substantial current account surpluses were only partially reflected in corresponding reported increases in financial or equity claims on foreign countries. Recently, orderly outflows have started to pick up. Foreign direct investment from the transition economies, Czech and Russian investments in neighboring countries in particular, have been increasing, and the Czech koruna, Slovak koruna, and Croatian kuna have been selected as currencies of denomination for Eurobonds. Third, structural weaknesses in the transition economies' domestic financial sectors have to be overcome to increase the scope for further integration. Factors that inhibit the growth of foreign activity include banking technology below international standards, nonperforming loans, weak regulation, and illiquid and untransparent equity markets.[108]

Regional Integration Initiatives

While making efforts to integrate further into the world economy, most transition economies have at the same time opted for new forms of regional coopera-

tion. In addition to a number of new regional arrangements and institutions, two major integration initiatives are under way: 10 central and eastern European and Baltic countries are making efforts to gain admission to the EU, while 12 newly independent countries of the former Soviet Union have been trying to promote economic and financial cooperation within the framework of the CIS.

The EU has taken a number of steps to prepare the ground for eventual enlargement toward central and eastern Europe. Starting in 1991, the EU signed ten Europe Agreements with transition countries.[109] Under these agreements, the associated countries have committed themselves to adapting their economic legislation to that of the EU, and both parties have introduced free trade, albeit with substantial exceptions in certain sectors such as steel, textiles, and agriculture. The Essen European Council of December 1994 agreed that countries that signed the Europe Agreements would become eligible for membership and outlined the so-called preaccession strategy. To assist the associated countries in preparing for integration into the single market, a white paper setting out guidelines was issued and the Phare support program, initially developed to assist the central and eastern European countries with structural reform challenges, was refocused on integration. Negotiations for membership could start within six months following the current intergovernmental conference, which is discussing reform of the EU decision-making process and is scheduled to complete its work in mid-1997.

Enlargement of the EU to the East raises a number of major issues.[110] First, enlargement could involve significant and unevenly distributed economic and budgetary costs for both the existing members and the associated countries; the agricultural and structural funds transfer programs would probably have to be reformed if they were to be maintained with full participation of the newcomers. Second, enlargement poses a challenge for the proper functioning of the single market as new members may not be able to fully implement the core legislation, the "*acquis communautaire*," in this area or to face full-fledged competition across all sectors. Third, admitting up to ten more countries may complicate the decision-making process in the Union and may eventually require additional institutional reform beyond what is being considered at the current intergovernmental conference. Fourth, countries wanting to join the Union may also

[108]For a discussion of these issues, see Michael S. Borish, Wei Ding, and Michel Noël, *On the Road to EU Accession: Financial Sector Development in Central Europe,* World Bank Discussion Paper No. 345 (Washington: World Bank, September 1996).

[109]Such agreements were signed with Poland and Hungary in 1991, the Czech Republic, Slovakia, Romania, and Bulgaria in 1993, the Baltic countries in 1995, and Slovenia in 1996.

[110]See Lóránd Ambrus-Lakatos and Mark Schaffer, eds., *Coming to Terms with Accession,* Forum Report of the Economic Policy Initiative No. 2 (London: CEPR and Institute for East-West Studies, 1996), and Chapter 1 of United Nations Economic Commission for Europe, *Economic Bulletin for Europe* (Geneva: United Nations, 1996).

want to participate in the planned monetary union; the permanent fixing of exchange rates may, however, be particularly difficult for these countries as long as they are continuing to undergo rapid and extensive structural change.

Uncertainties surrounding the conditions and timetable for EU admission notwithstanding, the associated countries' best strategy is to strive for progressive reintegration with the world economy, including western Europe. Policies required for further progress in transition to a market economy and international integration in general will at the same time help to satisfy the conditions for accession to the EU.

* * *

After decades of central planning, the transition economies were left with highly distorted trade patterns and inadequate financial systems largely cut off from international capital flows. Since the beginning of the transformation, they have made substantial progress in reorienting trade and have started the process of reintegration with international financial markets. This process, which requires investor confidence and an appropriate financial infrastructure to be built, will be prolonged. While the most advanced transition countries in central and eastern Europe have become emerging market economies, a number of countries less advanced in transition have only begun to gain access to international financial markets.

Countries that have delayed stabilization and reform efforts still have little prospect of receiving significant private financing in the near future.

The record of the early years shows that progress in transition policies generally is clearly associated with increasing integration with the world economy and that both are associated with economic performance, as reflected in growth and inflation rates. The question remains as to where further progress in the transformation process will take these countries, and what their role in the global economy eventually will be. The primary aspiration of the transition countries is to enhance their long-term prospects for growth and prosperity, while more particular aspirations include integration with, and eventually achieving, the living standards of western Europe for the central and eastern European economies, establishing itself as a major player on the world economic scene for Russia, and exploiting the opportunities offered by vast energy resources for countries in the Caucasian and Caspian region. As was discussed in the October 1996 *World Economic Outlook,* transition countries face the prospect of achieving quite high growth rates in the medium term, provided they persevere with policies of macroeconomic stabilization and structural reforms, including opening up to the world economy. Increasing trade and international financial flows will be essential to bring about the growth that will allow these countries to realize their aspirations.

Annex

Globalization in Historical Perspective

The post–World War II phenomenon of globalization—the increasingly close international integration of markets both for goods and services, and for capital—may in many ways be viewed as a resumption of a trend observed in the world economy a century ago. By some measures, international economic integration increased just as much in the 50 years before World War I as in recent decades, and reached comparable levels. Then, as now, integration was driven in large part by the proliferation of markets and rapid technological change. The process was interrupted and reversed from 1914 to after World War II.

The process observed before 1914 could hardly be called "globalization," however, since large parts of the world did not participate and also because the speed of transport and communication was such that it was much less feasible than it is today to organize markets, or to operate firms, at the global level. Furthermore, international financial markets today are characterized by much larger gross flows, with a much larger variety of financial instruments being traded across borders. Nevertheless, the trends we have been observing in recent decades are in a sense taking us back to the future.

International Trade

The period from the mid-nineteenth century to World War I exhibited relatively rapid growth in world trade, as the expansion of exports (3.5 percent a year) significantly outpaced that of real output (2.7 percent a year). The share of exports in world output reached a peak in 1913 not surpassed until 1970.[1] Growth in trade occurred partly as a consequence of reduced tariffs (Chart 46) and greatly reduced transportation costs, reflecting the proliferation of railroads and

Chart 46. Advanced Economies: Effective Tariff Rates
(In percent)

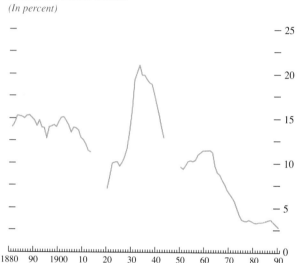

Sources: Brian Mitchell, *International Historical Statistics: Europe, 1750–1988* (Houndmills, Basingstoke, England: Macmillan, 3rd ed., 1992); Angus Maddison, *Dynamic Forces in Capitalist Development: A Long-Run Comparative View* (Oxford: Oxford University Press, 1991).

Notes: Effective tarriff rates are calculated as the ratio of customs revenues to the value of total imports. Data are GDP-weighted averages for the following countries: Belgium, Canada, Denmark, France, Germany, Italy, the Netherlands, Portugal, Spain, Sweden, the United Kingdom, and the United States.

This Annex was prepared by Professor Michael Bordo, Rutgers University, and Kornélia Krajnyák, World Economic Studies Division, Research Department.

[1]Paul Bairoch and Richard Kozul-Wright, "Globalization Myths: Some Historical Reflections on Integration, Industrialization, and Growth in the World Economy," United Nations Conference on Trade and Development Discussion Paper No. 113 (March 1996), p. 5.

steamships.[2] The period also witnessed a marked convergence of commodity prices across countries.[3]

The process of trade liberalization in Europe began with Britain's unilateral movement to free trade with the Abolition of the Corn Laws in 1846.[4] It spread to other countries with the Cobden Chevalier Treaty of 1860 between Britain and France. This Treaty, in addition to reducing French tariff rates, incorporated a most-favored-nation (MFN) clause in which each contracting party agreed to extend to the other any reduction in tariff rates it introduced vis-à-vis a third party. Because France reduced its tariff rates only with Britain, this gave other trading partners an incentive to sign similar treaties with it. Within the next two decades virtually all of Europe reduced tariffs (to the 10–15 percent range from above 35 percent) in a series of bilateral agreements with MFN clauses.[5]

Combined with the fact that nontariff barriers were of secondary importance and foreign exchange transactions were not controlled under the classical gold standard that prevailed before 1914, the network of bilateral commercial treaties constituted, de facto, a liberal multilateral trade regime. However, the system suffered from two drawbacks: it did not guarantee tariff reductions, and the treaties were subject to renegotiation upon expiry. These two defects were rectified in the multilateral arrangements instituted after World War II.[6] Although the liberalization process was reversed after 1879 with the institution of tariffs by Germany and then other countries, the level of effective protection (with the principal exception of the United States) remained low by twentieth century standards until 1914.[7]

The outbreak of World War I led to a series of quantitative restrictions on trade by the belligerents. After the war, many countries reduced their restrictions but substituted tariffs instead. A renewed movement toward liberalization under the Gold Exchange Standard (1925–31) ended with the Great Depression. In the face of plummeting agricultural prices a number of countries raised tariffs in 1929. In June 1930, the United States passed the Smoot-Hawley tariff, which raised duties on imports by 23 percent; most countries retaliated. In addition to tariffs, countries instituted quantitative restrictions and other trade barriers in an attempt to stimulate their economies.

In the face of deflation, some countries—the United Kingdom and the sterling area and the United States—left the gold standard, devalued their currencies, and pursued expansionary policies; others (the gold bloc—France, Italy, Belgium, the Netherlands, and Switzerland) stayed on gold but raised tariffs. A third group—Germany, Austria, and other central European countries—used exchange controls to create a series of bilateral (barter) trade agreements. As a result of these obstacles, world trade plummeted even faster than real output. By the mid-1930s, tariff protection was reduced somewhat following the U.S. Reciprocal Trade Agreement Act of 1934, under which the United States negotiated a series of bilateral agreements.

After World War II, the General Agreement on Tariffs and Trade (GATT) was created by the international community, along with the IMF, the World Bank, and other international organizations. Based on the principles of multilateral cooperation, the GATT had a mandate to roll back tariffs from their prewar peaks and to continue reducing them in the future. The GATT was extremely successful in 1947 in the first Geneva Round in reducing tariffs by 35 percent. Successive rounds in the 1950s, 1960s (the Kennedy Round), and the 1970s (Tokyo Round) and the recent Uruguay Round have virtually eliminated tariffs on manufactured goods. The World Trade Organization (WTO), which succeeded GATT in 1994, is currently engaged in reducing nontariff barriers and protection, including in areas not covered by the GATT.[8]

Capital Market Integration

In the 50 years before World War I, there was a massive flow of capital from the core countries of western Europe to the rapidly developing economies of the Americas, Australia, and elsewhere. At its peak, the net capital outflow from Britain represented 9 percent of GNP and was almost as high from France, Germany, and the Netherlands.[9] This compares with the peaks in Japan's and Germany's current account surpluses in the mid- and late 1980s of 4–5 percent of GDP. Before

[2]Douglas A. Irwin, "Multilateral and Bilateral Trade Policies in the World Trading System: An Historical Perspective," in *New Dimensions in Regional Integration,* ed. by J. De Melo and A. Panagariya (Cambridge, England; New York: Cambridge University Press, 1993), pp. 90–119.

[3]Douglas A. Irwin, "The United States in a New Global Economy? A Century's Perspective," *American Economic Review, Papers and Proceedings* (May 1996), pp. 41–46.

[4]The British reduction in tariffs reflected a shift in political and economic power as a consequence of the Industrial Revolution, which began around 1750. An emerging coalition between manufacturers and industrial workers who would benefit from low tariffs on grain in the years after the Napoleonic wars wrested control over Parliament from the large landowners who had earlier benefited from protection. See Douglas A. Irwin, *Against the Tide: An Intellectual History of Free Trade* (Princeton: Princeton University Press, 1996).

[5]See Irwin, "Multilateral and Bilateral Trade Policies."

[6]Ibid.

[7]Forrest Capie, "Tariff Protection and Economic Performance in the Nineteenth Century," in *Policy and Performance in International Trade,* ed. by J. Black and L.A. Winters (New York: St. Martin's Press, 1983).

[8]Douglas A. Irwin, "The GATT in Historical Perspective," *American Economic Review, Papers and Proceedings,* Vol. 85 (May 1995), pp. 323–28.

[9]See Bairoch and Kozul-Wright, "Globalization Myths."

World War I, private capital moved without restrictions. Much of it flowed into bonds financing railroads and other infrastructure in the new world and into long-term government debt, although there also was substantial foreign direct investment. The extent of net capital flows is illustrated in Chart 47, which shows a five-year moving average of the mean absolute value of the ratio of the current account balance to GDP for 12 countries, and Chart 48, which shows the current account balances for one large capital exporter (the United Kingdom), one large capital importer (Canada), and a country with smaller imbalances (the United States).[10] Evidence of tight capital market integration from 1850 to 1913 is also provided by low and declining onshore and offshore interest differentials between the United Kingdom and the United States, and by the low dispersion of real rates of interest (Chart 49).[11]

Free capital mobility before 1914 was closely related to the fact that much of the world was on the gold standard, the key role of which was to maintain convertibility of national currencies into gold. A credible commitment to gold in turn meant that monetary policy could not be used extensively to stabilize the domestic economy in the event of either internal or external shocks.[12] The credibility of the commitment to gold by the core countries was reinforced by stabilizing flows of short-term capital, and, in turn, long-term capital flowed from the core to peripheral countries adhering to gold because adherence to gold served as "a good-housekeeping seal of approval"—as evidence that countries followed standards of financial probity.[13]

Chart 47. Selected Countries: External Capital Flows[1]

(In percent of GDP; five-year moving average)

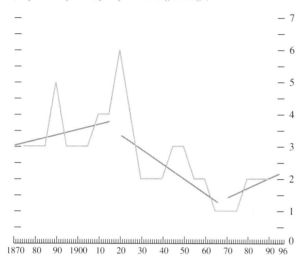

[1]Five-year moving average of the mean absolute value of the ratio of the current account balance to GDP for Argentina, Australia, Canada, Denmark, France, Germany, Italy, Japan, Norway, Sweden, the United Kingdom, and the United States.

[10]Maurice Obstfeld and Alan Taylor, "The Great Depression as a Watershed: International Capital Mobility over the Long Run," in *The Defining Moment: The Great Depression and the American Economy in the Twentieth Century,* ed. by M. D. Bordo, C. Goldin, and E. White (Chicago: University of Chicago Press, forthcoming).

[11]Obstfeld and Taylor, "The Great Depression." Other evidence includes low correlations between investment and savings ratios, Alan Taylor, "International Capital Mobility in History: The Saving-Investment Relationship," NBER Working Paper No. 5743 (Cambridge, Massachusetts: National Bureau of Economic Research, September 1996); purchasing power parity tests, Alan Taylor, "International Capital Mobility in History: Purchasing Power Parity in the Long Run," NBER Working Paper No. 5742 (Cambridge, Massachusetts: National Bureau of Economic Research, September 1996); and uncovered interest parity, Charles Calomiris and Glenn R. Hubbard, "International Adjustment Under the Classical Gold Standard: Evidence for the U.S. and Britain, 1879–1914," in *Modern Perspectives on the Gold Standard,* ed. by Tamim Bayoumi, Barry Eichengreen, and Mark P. Taylor (Cambridge, England; New York: Cambridge University Press, 1996).

[12]A commonly referred to proposition in international macroeconomics is that only two of the following three objectives can be met simultaneously: capital mobility, monetary policy independence, and fixed exchange rates. The gold standard encompassed the first and third.

[13]See Barry Eichengreen, *Globalizing Capital: History of the International Monetary System* (Princeton, New Jersey: Princeton University Press, 1996); and Michael D. Bordo and Hugh Rockoff, "The Gold Standard as a Good Housekeeping Seal of Approval," *Journal of Economic History,* Vol. 56 (June 1996), pp. 389–428.

International capital markets disintegrated from the outset of World War I until the mid-1960s, as can be seen in Charts 47 and 49. With the outbreak of World War I, the gold standard was suspended by the belligerents, and capital and exchange controls were imposed. After the war, controls were removed and the reinstated gold standard was characterized by virtually free capital mobility. However, the Gold Exchange Standard was not as credible or viable as the prewar standard, and countries following macroeconomic policies inconsistent with maintaining gold convertibility became subject to destabilizing capital flows. With the onset of the Great Depression, many countries imposed extensive and increasingly binding capital controls in an attempt to use monetary and fiscal policy to insulate themselves from deflation and depression. By the eve of World War II, capital flows had dried up.

After the war, the international monetary system created at Bretton Woods in 1944 attached the highest importance to restoring multilateral payments and current account convertibility, but enshrined restrictions on capital movements as a key element of the adjustable peg system. Based on the perception that floating exchange rates in the interwar period had been excessively volatile and subject to destabilizing speculation,[14] and on their own experience of those years, it was the view of the principal architects of the Bretton Woods system, John Maynard Keynes and Harry Dexter White, that resort to capital controls had to be allowed if, with fixed (though adjustable) parities, domestic stabilization policy was to be used to maintain full employment.

Once current account convertibility was achieved by the major European countries by 1959 (even though the obligations of the IMF's Article VIII were not formally accepted until early 1961), the currencies of countries following policies inconsistent with the maintenance of their parities were subject to speculative attacks as private agents devised ways to circumvent capital controls.[15] As the Bretton Woods system became more fragile and U.S. gold reserves were threatened, the United States began imposing restrictions on capital outflows in 1965. Despite the attempt to quell speculation, the Bretton Woods system collapsed in August 1971 and the world shifted to a floating exchange rate regime among the major currencies in 1973.[16]

---

[14]This perception was strongly influenced by Ragnar Nurkse's study for the League of Nations, *International Currency Experience* (Princeton, New Jersey: League of Nations, 1944).

[15]The method often used was referred to as "leads and lags"—the practice of accelerating payments in domestic currency and delaying foreign currency receipts in the expectation of a devaluation of the domestic currency (see Obstfeld and Taylor, "The Great Depression").

[16]See Michael D. Bordo, "The Bretton Woods International Monetary System: A Historical Overview," in *A Retrospective on the Bretton Woods System: Issues for International Monetary Reforms,* ed. by M.D. Bordo and B. Eichengreen (Chicago: University of Chicago Press, 1993), and Margaret Garritsen de Vries, *The IMF in a Changing World, 1945–85* (Washington: IMF, 1986).

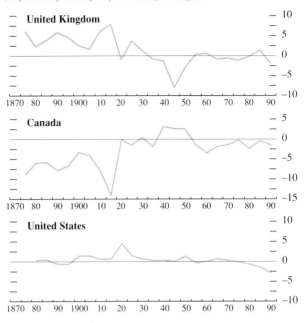

Chart 48. Selected Major Industrial Countries: Current Account Balances
(In percent of GDP; five-year moving averages)

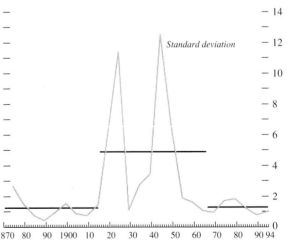

Chart 49. Selected Countries: Dispersion of Real Interest Rates[1]
(In percent)

[1]Five-year averages for the United States, Germany, France, Italy, the United Kingdom, Canada, and Sweden. Data prior to 1955 exclude Germany and prior to 1911 exclude France, Italy, and Sweden.

Within a decade, major countries dismantled their capital controls—the United States and Germany by 1974–75, the United Kingdom by 1979, Japan largely by 1980, and the rest of Europe by the end of the 1980s. Policymakers came to appreciate that with floating exchange rates, capital mobility was not incompatible with independent monetary policy conducted to stabilize domestic economic activity. Also in the past decade or so a number of developing countries have also opened up their capital accounts, extending the geographical limits of capital market integration beyond those prevailing in the pre-1914 period. The decline in the dispersion of real interest rates for select countries also suggests (Chart 49) that the world has been moving back to a regime of more tightly linked capital markets. This time, however, capital market integration is characterized by much larger gross flows, though not by larger net flows, than in the pre-1914 era.

Goods and capital market integration before 1914, combined with a high degree of labor mobility, led to considerable convergence in living standards among the industrial countries.[17] Not all segments of society, however, gained from greater integration and openness. Thus, trade liberalization in the nineteenth century induced a political reaction by those harmed by reduced protection, leading to calls to raise tariffs. At the same time, reductions in the rate of growth of real wages in countries with massive immigration before 1914 led to sharp restrictions on the movement of people.

Free capital mobility was incompatible with monetary policy independence under the interwar gold standard and was jettisoned in the face of depression. Even today under floating rates, capital mobility can create difficulties, not only for countries following inconsistent policies, but also for countries with sound fundamentals that may experience large-scale capital inflows and associated overheating pressures as witnessed in many emerging market countries in recent years. Such difficulties have led some to call for restrictions on the free movement of capital. For developing countries and economies in transition, fully opening the capital account is likely to take some time and will need to be preceded by adequate progress in liberalizing the domestic economy and establishing a sound banking system. However, for advanced economies whose capital markets are already highly integrated, the costs of retreating from integration would today be considerably higher than in the past. In capital markets, new technologies have created a vast network of interlocking arrangements within and between firms as well as new international financial instruments and new markets. Also, international deregulation has occurred hand in hand with deregulation in domestic financial markets. Attempts to restrict international capital mobility would not only increase the costs of financial intermediation but would likely prove futile. In goods markets, extensive integration at the firm level of multinational sources of supply and production processes, as well as the spread of multinational corporations, makes it more difficult to erect trade barriers. These factors are recognized by policymakers across the world. The lessons from history suggest that globalization, although driven in large part by technological advances, is not simply a product of technical forces. Policies too have a major role to play by fostering and maintaining open trade and payments arrangements.

---

[17]See Jeffrey G. Williamson, "Globalization, Convergence, and History," *Journal of Economic History,* Vol. 56 (June 1996), pp. 277–306.

Statistical Appendix

The statistical appendix presents historical data, as well as projections. It comprises four sections: Assumptions, Data and Conventions, Classification of Countries, and Statistical Tables.

The assumptions underlying the estimates and projections for 1997–98 and the medium-term scenario for 1999–2002 are summarized in the first section. The following section provides a general description of the data, and the conventions used for calculating country group composites. The classification of countries in the various groups presented in the *World Economic Outlook* is summarized in the third section. With this issue of the *World Economic Outlook*, Israel and four newly industrialized Asian economies have been added to the industrial country group, which in its expanded form appears with the new label "advanced economies."

The last, and main, section comprises the statistical tables. Data in these tables have been compiled on the basis of information available at the end of March 1997. The figures for 1997 and beyond are shown with the same degree of precision as the historical figures, solely for convenience; since they are projections, the same degree of accuracy is not to be inferred.

Assumptions

Real effective *exchange rates* for the advanced economies are assumed to remain constant at their average levels during March 1–18, 1997, except that the bilateral exchange rates among the ERM currencies are assumed to remain constant in nominal terms. For 1997 and 1998, these assumptions imply average U.S. dollar/SDR conversion rates of 1.380 and 1.374, respectively.

Established *policies* of national authorities are assumed to be maintained. The more specific policy assumptions underlying the projections for selected advanced economies are described in Box 2.

It is assumed that the *price of oil* will average $19.69 a barrel in 1997 and $18.36 a barrel in 1998. In the medium term, the oil price is assumed to remain unchanged in real terms.

With regard to *interest rates,* it is assumed that the London interbank offered rate (LIBOR) on six-month U.S. dollar deposits will average 6.0 percent in 1997 and 6.1 percent in 1998; that the three-month certificate of deposit rate in Japan will average 0.6 percent in

1997 and 2.0 percent in 1998; and that the three-month interbank deposit rate in Germany will average 3.3 percent in 1997 and 3.9 percent in 1998.

Data and Conventions

Data and projections for 181 countries form the statistical basis for the *World Economic Outlook* (the World Economic Outlook database). The data are maintained jointly by the IMF's Research Department and area departments, with the latter regularly updating country projections based on consistent global assumptions.

Although national statistical agencies are the ultimate providers of historical data and definitions, international organizations are also involved in statistical issues, with the objective of harmonizing methodologies for the national compilation of statistics, including the analytical frameworks, concepts, definitions, classifications, and valuation procedures used in the production of economic statistics. The World Economic Outlook database reflects information from both national source agencies and international organizations.

The completion in 1993 of the comprehensive revision of the standardized *System of National Accounts 1993 (SNA)* and the IMF's *Balance of Payments Manual (BPM)* represented important improvements in the standards of economic statistics and analysis.[1] The IMF was actively involved in both projects, particularly the new *Balance of Payments Manual*, which reflects the IMF's special interest in countries' external positions. Key changes introduced with the new *Manual* were summarized in Box 13 of the May 1994 *World Economic Outlook*. The process of adapting country balance of payments data to the definitions of the new *Balance of Payments Manual* began with the May 1995 *World Economic Outlook*. However, full concordance with the *BPM* is ultimately dependent on the provision by national statistical compilers of revised country data, and hence the *World Economic Outlook* estimates are still only partly adapted to the *BPM*.

---

[1]Commission of the European Communities, IMF, OECD, UN, and World Bank, *System of National Accounts 1993* (Brussels/ Luxembourg, New York, Paris, and Washington, 1993); and IMF, *Balance of Payments Manual, Fifth Edition* (1993).

Composite data for country groups in the *World Economic Outlook* are either sums or weighted averages of data for individual countries. Arithmetically weighted averages are used for all data except inflation and money growth for the developing and transition country groups, for which geometric averages are used. The following conventions apply.

- Country group composites for exchange rates, interest rates, and the growth rates of monetary aggregates are weighted by GDP converted to U.S. dollars at market exchange rates (averaged over the preceding three years) as a share of world or group GDP.

- Composites for other data relating to the domestic economy, whether growth rates or ratios, are weighted by GDP valued at purchasing power parities (PPPs) as a share of total world or group GDP.[2]

- Composite unemployment rates and employment growth are weighted by labor force as a share of group labor force.

- Composites relating to the external economy are sums of individual country data after conversion to U.S. dollars at the average market exchange rates in the years indicated for balance of payments data, and at end-of-year market exchange rates for debt denominated in currencies other than U.S. dollars. Composites of changes in foreign trade volumes and prices, however, are arithmetic averages of percentage changes for individual countries weighted by the U.S. dollar value of exports or imports as a share of total world or group exports or imports (in the preceding year).

For central and eastern European countries, external transactions in nonconvertible currencies (through 1990) are converted to U.S. dollars at the implicit U.S. dollar/ruble conversion rates obtained from each country's national currency exchange rate for the U.S. dollar and for the ruble.

Unless otherwise indicated, multiyear averages of growth rates are expressed as compound annual rates of change.

Classification of Countries

Advanced Economies: An Expanded Industrial Country Group

Beginning with this *World Economic Outlook*, Israel and four newly industrialized economies in Asia—

Hong Kong, Korea, Singapore, and Taiwan Province of China—are added to the group of countries traditionally known as industrial countries. The expanded group is referred to as "advanced economies." To preserve a degree of continuity, the industrial country group, as previously defined, is, where relevant, shown as a memorandum item to the group of advanced economies.

This reclassification of five economies, previously classified among the developing countries, reflects their rapid economic development and the fact that they all now share a number of important characteristics with the industrial countries, including relatively high income levels (comfortably within the range of those in the industrial country group), well-developed financial markets and high degrees of financial intermediation, and diversified economic structures with rapidly growing service sectors. The expanded group is labeled advanced economies in recognition of the declining share of employment in manufacturing common to all members of the group.

Summary of the Country Classification

As before, the country classification in the *World Economic Outlook* divides the world into three major groups: advanced economies, developing countries, and countries in transition.[3] Rather than being based on strict criteria, economic or otherwise, this classification has evolved over time with the objective of facilitating analysis by providing a reasonably meaningful organization of data. A few countries are presently not included in these groups, either because they are not IMF members, and their economies are not monitored by the IMF, or because databases have not yet been compiled. Cuba and the Democratic People's Republic of Korea are examples of countries that are not IMF members, whereas San Marino, among the advanced economies, and Brunei Darussalam and Eritrea, among the developing countries, are examples of economies for which databases have not been completed. It should also be noted that, owing to lack of data, only three of the former republics of the dissolved Socialist Federal Republic of Yugoslavia (Croatia, the former Yugoslav Republic of Macedonia, and Slovenia) are included in the group composites for countries in transition.

Each of the three main country groups is further divided into a number of subgroups. Among the advanced economies, the seven largest in terms of GDP, collectively referred to as the major industrial countries, are distinguished as a subgroup, and so are the 15

---

[2]See Annex IV of the May 1993 *World Economic Outlook*. See also Anne-Marie Gulde and Marianne Schulze-Ghattas, "Purchasing Power Parity Based Weights for the *World Economic Outlook*," in *Staff Studies for the World Economic Outlook* (IMF, December 1993), pp. 106–23.

[3]As used here, the term "country" does not in all cases refer to a territorial entity that is a state as understood by international law and practice. It also covers some territorial entities that are not states, but for which economic policies are formulated, and statistical data are maintained, on a separate and independent basis.

current members of the European Union and the four newly industrialized Asian economies. The developing countries are classified by region, as well as into a number of analytical and other groups. A regional breakdown is also used for the classification of the countries in transition. Table A provides an overview of these standard groups in the *World Economic Outlook*, showing the number of countries in each group and the average 1996 shares of groups in aggregate PPP-valued GDP, total exports of goods and services, and total external debt.

General Features and Compositions of Groups in the *World Economic Outlook* Classification

Advanced Economies

The composition of advanced economies (28 countries) is shown in Table B. The seven largest countries in this group in terms of GDP—the United States, Japan, Germany, France, Italy, the United Kingdom, and Canada—constitute the subgroup of *major industrial countries*, often referred to as the G-7 countries. The current members of the *European Union* (15 countries) and the *newly industrialized Asian economies* are also distinguished as subgroups. Composite data shown in the tables under the heading "European Union" cover the current 15 members of the European Union for all years, even though the membership has increased over time.

In 1991 and subsequent years, data for *Germany* refer to west Germany *and* the eastern Länder (i.e., the former German Democratic Republic). Before 1991, economic data are not available on a unified basis or in a consistent manner. Hence, in tables featuring data expressed as annual percent change, these apply to west Germany in years up to and including 1991, but to unified Germany from 1992 onward. In general, data on national accounts and domestic economic and financial activity through 1990 cover west Germany only, whereas data for the central government and balance of payments apply to west Germany through June 1990 and to unified Germany thereafter.

Developing Countries

The group of developing countries (127 countries) includes all countries that are not classified as advanced economies or as countries in transition, together with a few dependent territories for which adequate statistics are available.

The *regional breakdowns* of developing countries in the *World Economic Outlook* conform to the IMF's *International Financial Statistics (IFS)* classification—*Africa, Asia, Europe, Middle East,* and *Western Hemisphere*—with one important exception. Because all of the developing countries in Europe except Cyprus, Malta, and Turkey are included in the group

of countries in transition, the *World Economic Outlook* classification places these three countries in a combined *Middle East and Europe* region. It should also be noted that in both classifications, Egypt and the Libyan Arab Jamahiriya are included in this region, not in Africa. Three additional regional groupings—two of them constituting part of Africa and one a subgroup of Asia—are included in the *World Economic Outlook* because of their analytical significance. These are *Sub-Sahara, Sub-Sahara excluding Nigeria and South Africa,* and *Asia excluding China and India.*

The developing countries are also classified according to *analytical criteria* and into *other groups.* The analytical criteria reflect countries' composition of export earnings and other income from abroad, a distinction between net creditor and net debtor countries, and, for the net debtor countries, financial criteria based on external financing source and experience with external debt servicing. Included as "other groups" are currently the heavily indebted poor countries, the least developed countries, and Middle East and north Africa. The detailed composition of developing countries in the regional, analytical, and other groups is shown in Tables C through E.

The first analytical criterion, by *source of export earnings*, distinguishes among five categories: *fuel* (Standard International Trade Classification—SITC 3); *manufactures* (SITC 5 to 9, less 68); *nonfuel primary products* (SITC 0, 1, 2, 4, and 68); *services, factor income, and private transfers* (exporters of services and recipients of income from abroad, including workers' remittances); and *diversified export earnings.* Countries whose 1990–93 export earnings in any of the first four of these categories accounted for more than half of total export earnings are allocated to that group, while countries whose export earnings were not dominated by any one of these categories are classified as countries with diversified export earnings (see Table C for listing of countries).

The financial criteria first distinguish between *net creditor* and *net debtor countries.* Net creditor countries are defined as developing countries with positive net external assets at the end of 1995.[4] Countries in the much larger net debtor group are differentiated on the basis of two additional financial criteria: by *main source of external financing* and by *experience with debt servicing* during the 1991–95 period.[5]

---

[4]If information on the net external asset position is unavailable, the inclusion of countries in this group is based on whether they have cumulated a substantial current account surplus over the past 25 years to 1995.

[5]Within the classification experience with debt servicing, a distinction is made between countries with and without debt-servicing difficulties. During the 1991–95 period, 65 countries incurred external payments arrears or entered into official or commercial bank debt-rescheduling agreements. This group of countries is referred to as *countries with recent debt-servicing difficulties.* All other net debtor countries are included in the group referred to as *countries without recent debt-servicing difficulties.*

Table A. Classification by Standard *World Economic Outlook* Groups and Their 1996 Shares in Aggregate GDP, Exports of Goods and Services, and Total External Debt[1]

(In percent of total for group or world)

	Number of Countries	GDP		Exports of Goods and Services		External Debt
		←		*Share of total for*		→
		Advanced economies	World	Advanced economies	World	
Advanced economies	**28**	**100.0**	**56.6**	**100.0**	**78.6**	
Major industrial countries	**7**	80.2	45.4	62.0	48.7	
United States		36.5	20.7	16.3	12.8	
Japan		14.2	8.0	9.1	7.2	
Germany		8.3	4.7	12.0	9.4	
France		6.3	3.5	7.3	5.7	
Italy		5.8	3.3	6.4	5.0	
United Kingdom		5.8	3.3	6.5	5.1	
Canada		3.3	1.9	4.4	3.4	
Other advanced economies	**21**	19.8	11.2	38.0	29.9	
Memorandum						
Industrial countries *(former definition)*	**23**	93.6	53.0	86.5	67.9	
European Union	**15**	36.0	20.4	51.4	40.4	
Newly industrialized Asian economies	**4**	5.9	3.4	13.0	10.2	
		Developing countries	World	Developing countries	World	Developing countries
Developing countries	**127**	**100.0**	**39.2**	**100.0**	**17.3**	**100.0**
Regional groups						
Africa	**50**	8.6	3.4	11.3	1.9	16.1
Sub-Sahara	**47**	6.2	2.4	8.5	1.5	12.5
Excluding Nigeria and South Africa	**45**	3.7	1.5	4.2	0.7	9.4
Asia	**26**	57.3	22.5	42.7	7.3	31.6
Excluding China and India	**24**	18.5	7.3	25.3	4.3	20.3
Middle East and Europe	**17**	11.7	4.6	21.7	3.7	15.4
Western Hemisphere	**34**	22.4	8.8	24.3	4.2	36.9
Analytical groups						
By source of export earnings						
Fuel	**16**	10.0	3.9	20.8	3.6	13.0
Nonfuel	**111**	90.0	35.2	79.2	13.6	87.0
Manufactures	**6**	54.3	21.3	37.2	6.4	31.9
Primary products	**40**	5.1	2.0	6.4	1.1	11.7
Services, income, and private transfers	**39**	3.8	1.5	4.7	0.8	5.4
Diversified	**26**	26.8	10.5	30.9	5.3	37.9
By external financing source						
Net creditor countries	**6**	2.9	1.1	12.4	2.1	0.9
Net debtor countries	**121**	97.1	38.0	87.6	15.0	99.1
Official financing	**63**	9.6	3.8	8.5	1.5	15.5
Private financing	**34**	63.8	25.0	61.5	10.6	57.4
Diversified financing	**24**	23.7	9.3	17.9	3.0	26.1
Net debtor countries by debt-servicing experience						
Countries with recent difficulties	**65**	27.4	10.7	26.8	4.6	49.8
Countries without recent difficulties	**56**	69.7	27.3	60.8	10.4	49.3
Other groups						
Heavily indebted poor countries	**40**	4.2	1.6	4.3	0.7	11.4
Least developed countries	**46**	4.5	1.7	2.7	0.5	7.9
Middle East and north Africa (MENA)	**21**	11.7	4.6	20.3	3.5	15.7
		Countries in transition	World	Countries in transition	World	Countries in transition
Countries in transition	**28**	**100.0**	**4.2**	**100.0**	**4.2**	**100.0**
Central and eastern Europe	**18**	57.1	2.4	58.0	2.5	50.5
Excluding Belarus and Ukraine	**16**	46.4	1.9	49.3	2.1	46.5
Russia		33.8	1.4	35.5	1.5	45.7
Transcaucasus and central Asia	**9**	9.1	0.4	6.5	0.3	3.9

[1]The GDP shares are based on the purchasing power parity (PPP) valuation of country GDPs.

Table C *(concluded)*

	Fuel	Manufactures	Primary Products	Services, Factor Income, and Private Transfers	Diversified Source of Export Earnings
Western Hemisphere	Trinidad and Tobago Venezuela	Brazil	Bolivia Chile Guyana Honduras Nicaragua Peru Suriname	Antigua and Barbuda Aruba Bahamas, The Barbados Belize Dominican Republic El Salvador Grenada Haiti Jamaica Panama Paraguay St. Kitts and Nevis St. Lucia St. Vincent and the Grenadines	Argentina Colombia Costa Rica Dominica Ecuador Guatemala Mexico Netherlands Antilles Uruguay

Table D. Developing Countries by Region and Main External Financing Source

	Net Creditor Countries	Net Debtor Countries		
		By main external financing source		
		Official financing	Private financing	Diversified financing
Africa				
Sub-Sahara				
Angola				•
Benin		•		
Botswana				•
Burkina Faso		•		
Burundi		•		
Cameroon		•		
Cape Verde		•		
Central African Republic		•		
Chad		•		
Comoros		•		
Congo		•		
Côte d'Ivoire				•
Djibouti		•		
Equatorial Guinea		•		
Ethiopia		•		
Gabon		•		
Gambia, The		•		
Ghana				•
Guinea				•
Guinea-Bissau		•		
Kenya		•		
Lesotho		•		
Liberia		•		
Madagascar		•		
Malawi		•		
Mali				•
Mauritania		•		
Mauritius				•
Mozambique, Republic of		•		
Namibia		•		
Niger		•		
Nigeria		•		
Rwanda		•		
São Tomé and Príncipe		•		
Senegal		•		
Seychelles			•	
Sierra Leone			•	
Somalia		•		
South Africa			•	
Sudan		•		
Swaziland				•
Tanzania		•		
Togo				•
Uganda		•		
Zaïre		•		
Zambia		•		
Zimbabwe		•		
North Africa				
Algeria			•	
Morocco		•		
Tunisia				•

Table D (*continued*)

	Net Creditor Countries	Net Debtor Countries By main external financing source		
		Official financing	Private financing	Diversified financing
Asia				
Afghanistan, Islamic State of				●
Bangladesh		●		
Bhutan		●		
Cambodia		●		
China			●	
Fiji			●	
India				●
Indonesia				●
Kiribati		●		
Lao People's Democratic Republic		●		
Malaysia			●	
Maldives		●		
Marshall Islands		●		
Micronesia, Federated States of		●		
Myanmar			●	
Nepal		●		
Pakistan		●		
Papua New Guinea				●
Philippines				●
Solomon Islands		●		
Sri Lanka				●
Thailand			●	
Tonga		●		
Vanuatu		●		
Vietnam		●		
Western Samoa		●		
Middle East and Europe				
Bahrain			●	
Cyprus			●	
Egypt				●
Iran, Islamic Republic of			●	
Iraq				●
Jordan		●		
Kuwait	●			
Lebanon				●
Libya	●			
Malta			●	
Oman	●			
Qatar	●			
Saudi Arabia	●			
Syrian Arab Republic				●
Turkey			●	
United Arab Emirates	●			
Yemen, Republic of			●	
Western Hemisphere				
Antigua and Barbuda			●	
Argentina			●	
Aruba		●		
Bahamas, The			●	
Barbados				●
Belize		●		

Table D (concluded)

	Net Creditor Countries	Net Debtor Countries		
		By main external financing source		
		Official financing	Private financing	Diversified financing
Bolivia		•		
Brazil			•	
Chile			•	
Colombia			•	
Costa Rica				
Dominica		•		
Dominican Republic				•
Ecuador			•	
El Salvador		•		
Grenada				•
Guatemala			•	
Guyana		•		
Haiti		•		
Honduras		•		
Jamaica				•
Mexico			•	
Netherlands Antilles		•		
Nicaragua		•		
Panama			•	
Paraguay		•		
Peru			•	
St. Kitts and Nevis			•	
St. Lucia			•	
St. Vincent and the Grenadines			•	
Suriname			•	
Trinidad and Tobago			•	
Uruguay			•	
Venezuela			•	

Table E Other Developing Country Groups

	Heavily Indebted Poor Countries	Least Developed Countries	Middle East and North Africa
Africa			
Sub-Sahara			
Angola	•		
Benin	•	•	
Botswana		•	
Burkina Faso	•	•	
Burundi	•	•	
Cameroon	•		
Cape Verde		•	
Central African Republic	•	•	
Chad	•	•	
Comoros		•	
Congo	•		
Côte d'Ivoire	•		
Djibouti		•	•
Equatorial Guinea	•	•	
Ethiopia	•	•	
Gambia, The		•	
Ghana	•		
Guinea	•	•	
Guinea-Bissau	•	•	
Kenya	•		
Lesotho		•	
Liberia	•	•	
Madagascar	•	•	
Malawi		•	
Mali	•	•	
Mauritania	•	•	•
Mozambique, Republic of	•	•	
Niger	•	•	
Rwanda	•	•	
São Tomé and Príncipe	•	•	
Senegal	•		
Sierra Leone	•	•	
Somalia	•	•	•
Sudan	•	•	•
Tanzania	•	•	
Togo	•	•	
Uganda	•	•	
Zaïre	•	•	
Zambia	•	•	
North Africa			
Algeria			•
Morocco			•
Tunisia			•
Asia			
Afghanistan, Islamic State of		•	
Bangladesh		•	
Bhutan		•	
Cambodia		•	
Kiribati		•	
Lao People's Democratic Republic	•	•	
Maldives		•	
Myanmar	•	•	
Nepal		•	

Table E *(concluded)*

	Heavily Indebted Poor Countries	Least Developed Countries	Middle East and North Africa
Solomon Islands		•	
Vanuatu		•	
Vietnam	•		
Western Samoa		•	
Middle East and Europe			
Bahrain			•
Egypt			•
Iran, Islamic Republic of			•
Iraq			•
Jordan			•
Kuwait			•
Lebanon			•
Libya			•
Oman			•
Qatar			•
Saudi Arabia			•
Syrian Arab Republic			•
United Arab Emirates			•
Yemen, Republic of	•	•	•
Western Hemisphere			
Bolivia	•		
Guyana	•		
Haiti		•	
Honduras	•		
Nicaragua	•		

Table F. Countries in Transition by Region

Central and Eastern Europe		Russia	Transcaucasus and Central Asia
Albania	Lithuania	Russia	Armenia
Belarus	Macedonia, former Yugoslav Republic of		Azerbaijan
Bosnia and Herzegovina	Moldova		Georgia
Bulgaria	Poland		Kazakstan
Croatia	Romania		Kyrgyz Republic
Czech Republic	Slovak Republic		Mongolia
Estonia	Slovenia		Tajikistan
Hungary	Ukraine		Turkmenistan
Latvia	Yugoslavia, Federal Republic of		Uzbekistan

List of Tables

		Page
Output		
A1.	Summary of World Output	131
A2.	Advanced Economies: Real GDP and Total Domestic Demand	132
A3.	Advanced Economies: Components of Real GDP	133
A4.	Advanced Economies: Unemployment, Employment, and Real Per Capita GDP	135
A5.	Developing Countries: Real GDP	137
A6.	Developing Countries—by Country: Real GDP	138
A7.	Countries in Transition: Real GDP	141
Inflation		
A8.	Summary of Inflation	142
A9.	Advanced Economies: GDP Deflators and Consumer Prices	143
A10.	Advanced Economies: Hourly Earnings, Productivity, and Unit Labor Costs in Manufacturing	144
A11.	Developing Countries: Consumer Prices	145
A12.	Developing Countries—by Country: Consumer Prices	146
A13.	Countries in Transition: Consumer Prices	149
Financial Policies		
A14.	Summary Financial Indicators	150
A15.	Advanced Economies: General and Central Government Fiscal Balances and Balances Excluding Social Security Transactions	151
A16.	Advanced Economies: General Government Structural Balances	153
A17.	Advanced Economies: Monetary Aggregates	154
A18.	Advanced Economies: Interest Rates	155
A19.	Advanced Economies: Exchange Rates	156
A20.	Developing Countries: Central Government Fiscal Balances	157
A21.	Developing Countries: Broad Money Aggregates	158
Foreign Trade		
A22.	Summary of World Trade Volumes and Prices	159
A23.	Nonfuel Commodity Prices	161
A24.	Advanced Economies: Export Volumes, Import Volumes, and Terms of Trade	162
A25.	Developing Countries—by Region: Total Trade in Goods	163
A26.	Developing Countries—by Source of Export Earnings: Total Trade in Goods	165
Current Account Transactions		
A27.	Summary of Payments Balances on Current Account	167
A28.	Advanced Economies: Balance of Payments on Current Account	168
A29.	Advanced Economies: Current Account Transactions	169
A30.	Developing Countries: Payments Balances on Current Account	170
A31.	Developing Countries—by Region: Current Account Transactions	172
A32.	Developing Countries—by Analytical Criteria: Current Account Transactions	174

Table A1. Summary of World Output[1]

(Annual percent change)

	Average 1979–88	1989	1990	1991	1992	1993	1994	1995	1996	1997	1998
World	**3.4**	**3.7**	**2.7**	**1.8**	**2.8**	**2.7**	**4.1**	**3.7**	**4.0**	**4.4**	**4.4**
Advanced economies	**2.9**	**3.7**	**2.7**	**1.2**	**1.9**	**1.2**	**3.1**	**2.5**	**2.5**	**2.9**	**2.9**
United States	2.7	3.4	1.3	−1.0	2.7	2.3	3.5	2.0	2.4	3.0	2.2
European Union	2.2	3.5	3.0	1.6	1.0	−0.5	2.9	2.5	1.6	2.4	2.9
Japan	3.8	4.8	5.1	4.0	1.1	0.1	0.6	1.4	3.6	2.2	2.9
Other advanced economies	4.6	4.2	3.4	2.8	3.3	4.0	5.7	4.8	4.1	4.4	4.7
Developing countries	**4.3**	**4.2**	**4.0**	**4.9**	**6.5**	**6.5**	**6.8**	**6.0**	**6.5**	**6.6**	**6.5**
Regional groups											
Africa	2.4	3.4	2.0	1.8	0.7	0.9	2.9	2.9	5.0	4.7	4.8
Asia	6.7	6.1	5.7	6.7	9.4	9.3	9.6	8.9	8.2	8.3	7.7
Middle East and Europe	2.2	2.8	5.3	3.1	6.1	4.3	0.3	3.8	4.5	3.9	3.9
Western Hemisphere	2.7	1.8	1.1	3.6	3.1	3.7	5.0	1.3	3.5	4.4	5.1
Analytical groups											
By source of export earnings											
Fuel	0.6	3.5	4.5	4.4	5.9	2.1	0.2	2.6	3.0	3.8	3.9
Nonfuel	5.0	4.3	4.0	5.0	6.6	7.1	7.6	6.4	6.8	6.9	6.7
By external financing source											
Net creditor countries	0.4	4.0	6.2	5.8	7.9	5.8	0.5	1.0	3.6	1.7	2.1
Net debtor countries	4.5	4.2	3.9	4.9	6.5	6.5	7.0	6.2	6.5	6.8	6.6
Official financing	3.4	3.6	4.0	4.3	2.7	2.5	3.9	3.5	5.4	5.1	5.2
Private financing	4.8	3.4	3.6	5.8	7.9	7.9	7.7	6.3	6.7	7.0	6.9
Diversified financing	4.3	6.4	4.7	2.9	4.4	4.6	6.2	6.9	6.6	6.8	6.3
Net debtor countries by debt-servicing experience											
Countries with recent difficulties	2.3	1.9	0.8	2.5	2.5	2.6	4.0	3.2	3.8	4.8	5.2
Countries without recent difficulties	5.9	5.4	5.5	6.0	8.3	8.2	8.2	7.4	7.6	7.5	7.1
Countries in transition	**2.9**	**2.1**	**−3.6**	**−8.0**	**−11.7**	**−6.3**	**−6.7**	**−0.8**	**0.1**	**3.0**	**4.8**
Central and eastern Europe	...	...	...	−10.8	−8.8	−4.0	−1.8	1.6	1.6	3.0	4.7
Excluding Belarus and Ukraine	...	...	...	−11.5	−5.8	0.5	3.7	5.0	3.4	3.3	4.7
Russia, Transcaucasus, and central Asia	...	...	...	−5.4	−14.6	−8.8	−12.8	−4.0	−1.9	3.0	4.9
Memorandum											
Median growth rate											
Advanced economies	3.0	3.8	3.0	2.2	1.7	1.2	3.7	2.7	2.7	3.1	3.1
Developing countries	3.2	3.6	3.1	2.9	3.6	3.4	3.8	4.1	4.3	4.7	4.8
Countries in transition	3.4	3.0	−2.3	−11.9	−13.9	−8.4	0.4	1.5	2.7	4.0	5.1
Output per capita											
Advanced economies	2.2	3.0	1.9	0.4	1.2	0.5	2.5	1.8	1.9	2.3	2.3
Developing countries	2.0	0.6	2.1	2.9	4.2	4.4	4.5	4.4	4.7	4.9	4.7
Countries in transition	2.3	1.6	−4.2	−8.1	−11.9	−6.4	−6.8	−0.8	0.1	3.0	4.7
Value of world output in billions of U.S. dollars											
At market exchange rates	12,695	20,445	23,024	24,733	23,547	24,100	26,141	29,063	29,935	30,595	32,530
At purchasing power parities	15,032	23,804	25,432	26,764	28,103	29,503	31,271	33,153	35,113	37,427	40,035

[1]Real GDP.

Table A2. Advanced Economies: Real GDP and Total Domestic Demand

(Annual percent change)

	Average 1979–88	1989	1990	1991	1992	1993	1994	1995	1996	1997	1998	Fourth Quarter[1] 1996	1997	1998
Real GDP														
Advanced economies	**2.9**	**3.7**	**2.7**	**1.2**	**1.9**	**1.2**	**3.1**	**2.5**	**2.5**	**2.9**	**2.9**	...	...	...
Major industrial countries	2.8	3.6	2.5	0.8	1.8	1.0	2.8	2.0	2.2	2.6	2.6	2.7	2.6	2.6
United States	2.7	3.4	1.3	−1.0	2.7	2.3	3.5	2.0	2.4	3.0	2.2	3.1	2.6	2.2
Japan	3.8	4.8	5.1	4.0	1.1	0.1	0.6	1.4	3.6	2.2	2.9	3.1	2.1	3.5
Germany[2]	1.8	3.6	5.7	5.0	2.2	−1.1	2.9	1.9	1.4	2.3	3.0	2.2	2.9	2.7
France	2.2	4.3	2.5	0.8	1.2	−1.3	2.8	2.2	1.3	2.4	3.0	2.0	3.1	2.8
Italy	2.7	2.9	2.2	1.1	0.6	−1.2	2.1	3.0	0.7	1.0	2.4	0.2	0.8	2.9
United Kingdom[3]	2.5	2.2	0.4	−2.0	−0.5	2.1	3.8	2.5	2.1	3.3	2.8	2.6	3.7	2.0
Canada	3.2	2.4	−0.2	−1.8	0.8	2.2	4.1	2.3	1.5	3.5	3.4	2.3	3.9	3.2
Other advanced economies	3.5	4.5	3.9	2.9	2.4	2.0	4.5	4.2	3.7	3.8	4.1	...	...	...
Spain	2.3	4.7	3.7	2.3	0.7	−1.2	2.1	2.8	2.2	2.8	3.4	...	...	...
Netherlands	1.6	4.7	4.1	2.3	2.0	0.8	3.4	2.1	2.7	3.0	2.9	...	...	...
Belgium	1.5	3.4	3.7	1.6	1.7	−1.3	2.3	1.9	1.4	2.3	2.2	...	...	...
Sweden	2.2	2.4	1.4	−1.1	−1.4	−2.2	3.3	3.6	1.1	2.0	2.5	...	...	...
Austria	2.1	3.8	4.3	2.8	2.0	0.4	3.0	1.8	1.1	1.7	2.8	...	...	...
Denmark	2.1	0.6	1.6	1.2	0.2	1.5	4.2	2.7	2.4	2.7	2.5	...	...	...
Finland	3.8	5.7	—	−7.1	−3.6	−1.2	4.5	4.5	3.2	4.4	3.4	...	...	...
Greece[4]	1.8	3.8	—	3.1	0.4	−1.0	1.5	2.0	2.6	3.0	3.1	...	...	...
Portugal	2.8	5.7	4.0	2.2	1.7	−1.2	0.7	2.3	3.2	3.3	3.5	...	...	...
Ireland	3.1	6.1	8.0	2.1	4.0	3.1	6.5	10.3	7.0	6.3	5.6	...	...	...
Luxembourg	4.2	9.9	3.4	5.4	5.8	8.5	4.1	3.5	3.7	3.7	3.5	...	...	...
Switzerland	2.2	3.9	2.3	—	−0.3	−0.8	1.0	0.1	−0.7	0.7	2.3	...	...	...
Norway	3.2	0.9	1.9	3.1	3.3	2.8	5.0	3.3	4.8	4.2	3.2	...	...	...
Israel	3.6	1.2	6.1	6.3	6.6	3.5	6.8	7.1	4.4	4.8	4.8	...	...	...
Iceland	4.0	0.2	1.2	1.3	−3.4	0.9	3.5	2.1	5.5	3.0	2.4	...	...	...
Korea	7.8	6.4	9.5	9.1	5.1	5.8	8.6	8.9	7.1	5.6	6.3	...	...	...
Australia	3.3	4.4	1.4	−1.1	2.3	3.4	5.2	3.2	4.0	3.2	3.7	...	...	...
Taiwan Province of China	8.1	8.2	5.4	7.6	6.8	6.3	6.5	6.0	5.6	6.0	6.3	...	...	...
Hong Kong	8.2	2.6	3.4	5.1	6.3	6.1	5.3	4.8	4.5	5.0	5.0	...	...	...
Singapore	7.3	9.6	9.0	7.3	6.2	10.4	10.1	8.8	7.0	6.6	6.1	...	...	...
New Zealand	1.9	0.8	−0.2	−1.7	0.9	5.0	5.9	3.4	2.7	3.7	3.0	...	...	...
Memorandum														
Industrial countries	2.7	3.6	2.5	0.8	1.7	0.9	2.9	2.1	2.3	2.7	2.7	...	...	...
European Union	2.2	3.5	3.0	1.6	1.0	−0.5	2.9	2.5	1.6	2.4	2.9	...	...	...
Newly industrialized Asian economies	8.0	6.6	7.3	8.0	5.8	6.3	7.6	7.4	6.3	5.7	6.1	...	...	...
Real total domestic demand														
Advanced economies	**2.9**	**3.9**	**2.7**	**0.8**	**1.9**	**0.9**	**3.3**	**2.4**	**2.6**	**2.7**	**2.8**	...	...	...
Major industrial countries	2.8	3.4	2.2	0.2	1.7	0.9	2.9	2.0	2.3	2.6	2.5	2.6	2.5	2.5
United States	2.7	2.7	0.9	−1.6	2.8	2.9	3.9	2.0	2.5	3.3	2.3	3.3	3.1	2.2
Japan	3.7	5.6	5.2	2.9	0.4	0.1	1.0	2.2	4.5	1.5	2.2	3.0	1.5	2.7
Germany	1.6	2.9	5.2	4.8	2.8	−1.3	2.8	2.1	0.8	1.6	2.8	1.3	1.7	2.8
France	2.3	3.9	2.8	0.6	0.2	−2.2	3.0	2.0	0.9	1.8	2.5	1.6	2.2	2.5
Italy	2.9	2.9	2.5	1.8	0.5	−4.5	1.6	2.3	0.3	0.8	3.0	−0.6	0.2	2.7
United Kingdom	3.0	2.9	−0.6	−3.1	0.2	2.0	2.9	1.5	2.0	4.3	3.1	2.2	4.9	2.4
Canada	3.4	4.3	−0.5	−1.2	0.4	2.0	3.1	1.0	1.6	4.2	3.4	4.5	2.8	3.4
Other advanced economies	3.2	6.1	4.7	3.1	2.5	0.7	4.8	4.2	3.5	3.1	3.8	...	...	...
Memorandum														
Industrial countries	2.7	3.6	2.3	0.3	1.6	0.6	3.0	2.1	2.3	2.6	2.6	...	...	...
European Union	2.3	3.7	2.9	1.4	1.0	−1.8	2.6	2.2	1.3	2.2	2.9	...	...	...
Newly industrialized Asian economies	7.1	10.3	10.5	9.6	6.6	5.7	8.5	6.9	6.5	4.0	5.0	...	...	...

[1]From fourth quarter of preceding year.
[2]Data through 1991 apply to west Germany only.
[3]Average of expenditure, income, and output estimates of GDP at market prices.
[4]Based on revised national accounts for 1988 onward.

Table A3. Advanced Economies: Components of Real GDP

(Annual percent change)

	Average 1979–88	1989	1990	1991	1992	1993	1994	1995	1996	1997	1998
Private consumer expenditure											
Advanced economies	**3.0**	**3.4**	**2.9**	**1.4**	**2.4**	**1.7**	**2.7**	**2.3**	**2.6**	**2.4**	**2.6**
Major industrial countries	3.0	3.0	2.6	0.9	2.1	1.6	2.4	2.1	2.3	2.2	2.4
United States	3.0	2.3	1.7	−0.6	2.8	2.8	3.1	2.3	2.5	2.8	2.4
Japan	3.6	4.8	4.4	2.5	2.1	1.2	1.9	2.0	2.8	1.4	2.0
Germany[1]	1.7	2.8	5.4	5.6	2.8	0.3	1.0	1.8	1.3	0.8	2.7
France	2.4	3.0	2.7	1.4	1.4	0.2	1.4	1.8	2.3	1.3	2.9
Italy	3.3	3.3	2.4	2.7	1.0	−2.4	1.5	1.7	0.6	1.0	2.2
United Kingdom	3.5	3.2	0.6	−2.2	−0.1	2.5	2.6	1.9	3.0	3.9	2.5
Canada	3.1	3.4	1.0	−1.6	1.3	1.6	2.9	1.4	2.4	2.9	2.7
Other advanced economies	3.1	5.2	4.2	3.8	3.5	2.0	3.9	3.5	3.6	3.2	3.5
Memorandum											
Industrial countries	2.9	3.1	2.6	1.0	2.1	1.3	2.4	2.1	2.3	2.2	2.4
European Union	2.4	3.3	3.0	2.3	1.5	−0.1	1.7	1.8	1.9	1.8	2.6
Newly industrialized Asian economies	7.2	10.3	8.9	8.5	7.5	7.0	7.6	6.2	6.0	4.9	5.4
Public consumption											
Advanced economies	**2.5**	**2.2**	**2.6**	**2.0**	**1.5**	**0.9**	**0.9**	**0.9**	**1.3**	**0.7**	**1.2**
Major industrial countries	2.3	1.8	2.1	1.5	1.1	0.7	0.8	0.8	1.0	0.5	1.0
United States	2.3	2.7	2.3	1.0	−0.1	—	0.2	−0.3	0.5	−0.3	0.7
Japan	2.9	2.0	1.5	2.0	2.0	2.4	2.4	3.5	2.3	2.2	1.6
Germany[1]	1.8	−1.6	2.2	0.5	4.3	—	1.3	2.0	2.4	0.8	1.5
France	2.6	0.4	2.1	2.8	3.4	3.4	1.1	0.9	1.6	1.2	1.0
Italy	2.7	0.9	1.3	1.7	1.1	0.5	—	−0.5	0.2	−1.1	−0.2
United Kingdom	1.1	1.4	2.5	2.6	−0.1	−0.1	1.7	1.5	0.8	2.5	1.7
Canada	2.1	4.0	3.2	2.7	1.0	0.5	−1.7	−0.7	−1.8	−1.2	0.8
Other advanced economies	3.3	4.2	4.8	4.1	3.1	1.5	1.6	1.5	2.6	1.4	2.2
Memorandum											
Industrial countries	2.4	2.0	2.3	1.7	1.2	0.8	0.8	0.9	1.0	0.6	1.1
European Union	2.2	1.1	2.3	2.1	2.2	1.0	0.9	1.1	1.2	0.8	1.2
Newly industrialized Asian economies	5.7	8.4	8.8	8.1	7.1	2.7	2.2	2.3	6.0	2.4	3.5
Gross fixed capital formation											
Advanced economies	**3.0**	**5.5**	**2.7**	**−1.6**	**1.5**	**−0.3**	**4.8**	**4.0**	**4.8**	**4.5**	**4.5**
Major industrial countries	2.8	4.6	1.9	−2.4	1.9	—	4.5	3.3	4.7	4.5	4.2
United States	2.5	2.0	−1.4	−6.6	5.2	5.1	7.9	5.2	6.1	5.8	3.9
Japan	4.0	8.2	8.5	3.3	−1.5	−2.0	−0.8	1.1	8.7	1.7	2.6
Germany[1]	1.0	6.3	8.5	6.0	3.5	−5.6	4.2	1.5	−0.8	3.6	4.0
France	1.8	7.9	2.8	—	−2.8	−6.7	1.3	2.6	−0.5	1.3	2.5
Italy	2.5	4.4	3.6	0.8	−1.8	−12.8	0.2	5.9	1.8	1.6	7.5
United Kingdom	3.6	6.0	−3.5	−9.5	−1.5	0.6	2.9	−0.1	1.0	8.2	7.0
Canada	5.5	6.1	−3.5	−2.9	−1.5	0.6	5.9	−0.1	6.4	9.8	7.1
Other advanced economies	3.6	9.5	6.2	1.8	0.1	−1.6	6.1	6.9	5.4	4.4	5.6
Memorandum											
Industrialized countries	2.8	5.2	1.9	−2.5	1.3	−0.7	4.4	3.7	4.5	4.6	4.4
European Union	2.2	7.1	3.8	−0.3	−0.9	−6.5	2.2	3.6	1.2	3.9	5.2
Newly industrialized Asian economies	7.5	13.5	16.7	11.0	6.1	6.5	10.2	9.2	8.9	3.5	5.6

133

Table A3 *(concluded)*

	Average 1979–88	1989	1990	1991	1992	1993	1994	1995	1996	1997	1998
Final domestic demand											
Advanced economies	**2.9**	**3.8**	**3.0**	**1.0**	**1.9**	**1.0**	**2.7**	**2.4**	**2.9**	**2.5**	**2.8**
Major industrial countries	2.8	3.2	2.5	0.4	1.8	1.0	2.4	2.0	2.6	2.4	2.5
United States	2.8	2.4	1.3	−1.4	2.7	2.7	3.3	2.4	2.8	2.9	2.4
Japan	3.6	5.5	5.4	2.7	0.9	0.3	1.1	1.9	4.5	1.6	2.2
Germany[1]	1.6	2.6	5.4	4.7	3.3	−1.2	1.8	1.8	1.1	1.4	2.8
France	2.3	3.6	2.6	1.3	0.8	−0.7	1.3	1.8	1.6	1.3	2.4
Italy	3.0	3.1	2.4	2.1	0.5	−4.0	1.0	2.0	0.7	0.7	2.8
United Kingdom	3.0	3.4	0.2	−2.6	−0.3	1.6	2.4	1.5	2.2	4.3	3.1
Canada	3.4	4.1	0.4	−1.0	0.6	1.1	2.6	0.6	2.5	3.7	3.4
Other advanced economies	3.2	6.0	5.0	3.4	2.5	1.2	4.1	4.0	3.8	3.1	3.8
Memorandum											
Industrial countries	2.8	3.5	2.5	0.5	1.7	0.7	2.4	2.1	2.6	2.4	2.6
European Union	2.3	3.7	3.0	1.7	1.2	−1.3	1.6	2.0	1.6	2.0	2.8
Newly industrialized Asian economies	7.1	11.0	11.6	9.3	6.5	6.2	7.8	6.8	6.8	4.1	5.2
Stock building[2]											
Advanced economies	**—**	**0.2**	**−0.3**	**−0.2**	**−0.1**	**−0.1**	**0.6**	**—**	**−0.3**	**0.2**	**—**
Major industrial countries	—	0.2	−0.3	−0.2	−0.1	−0.1	0.6	—	−0.3	0.3	—
United States	−0.1	0.4	−0.4	−0.2	0.2	0.2	0.6	−0.4	−0.3	0.4	−0.1
Japan	—	0.1	−0.2	0.2	−0.4	−0.1	−0.2	0.3	—	−0.1	—
Germany[1]	—	0.3	−0.1	0.1	−0.5	−0.2	1.0	0.3	−0.3	0.3	—
France	—	0.4	0.2	−0.7	−0.6	−1.5	1.7	0.2	−0.6	0.5	0.1
Italy	—	−0.2	0.1	−0.3	0.1	−0.6	0.6	0.3	−0.4	0.1	0.2
United Kingdom	—	−0.4	−0.8	−0.5	0.5	0.4	0.5	0.1	−0.2	—	—
Canada	—	0.2	−1.0	−0.1	−0.2	0.9	0.5	0.3	−0.8	0.5	—
Other advanced economies	0.1	0.1	−0.2	−0.3	—	−0.4	0.7	0.3	−0.2	—	—
Memorandum											
Industrial countries	—	0.2	−0.3	−0.2	−0.1	−0.1	0.6	—	−0.3	0.2	—
European Union	—	0.1	−0.1	−0.3	−0.1	−0.5	0.9	0.2	−0.3	0.2	0.1
Newly industrialized Asian economies	0.1	−0.5	−0.9	0.3	0.1	−0.5	0.7	0.2	−0.2	−0.2	−0.1
Foreign balance[2]											
Advanced economies	**—**	**−0.2**	**0.1**	**0.4**	**—**	**0.3**	**−0.2**	**—**	**−0.1**	**0.2**	**0.1**
Major industrial countries	−0.1	—	0.2	0.5	—	—	−0.2	—	−0.1	0.1	0.1
United States	−0.1	0.5	0.3	0.6	−0.1	−0.7	−0.5	—	−0.1	−0.2	−0.1
Japan	0.2	−0.7	—	1.0	0.6	—	−0.3	−0.8	−0.9	0.7	0.8
Germany[1]	0.3	0.9	0.8	0.5	−0.6	0.2	0.1	−0.1	0.6	0.6	0.3
France	−0.2	0.3	−0.3	0.2	0.9	0.9	−0.2	0.2	0.4	0.6	0.5
Italy	−0.2	—	−0.4	−0.7	—	3.4	0.5	0.7	0.4	0.2	−0.5
United Kingdom	−0.6	−0.8	1.0	1.2	−0.7	—	0.9	0.9	−0.4	−0.4	−0.4
Canada	−0.3	−1.6	0.6	−0.6	0.5	0.3	0.9	1.2	−0.2	−0.6	—
Other advanced economies	0.3	−1.6	−0.6	−0.2	—	1.2	−0.3	−0.1	0.2	0.7	0.4
Memorandum											
Industrial countries	−0.1	−0.1	0.2	0.5	0.1	0.3	−0.1	—	−0.1	0.1	0.1
European Union	−0.1	−0.4	—	0.1	−0.1	1.3	0.3	0.3	0.3	0.3	—
Newly industrialized Asian economies	1.3	−3.0	−2.5	−1.4	−0.4	0.7	−0.8	0.6	0.2	1.8	1.2

[1]Data through 1991 apply to west Germany only.
[2]Changes expressed as percent of GDP in the preceding period.

Table A4. Advanced Economies: Unemployment, Employment, and Real Per Capita GDP

(In percent)

	Average[1] 1979–88	1989	1990	1991	1992	1993	1994	1995	1996	1997	1998
Unemployment rate											
Advanced economies	**6.8**	**6.0**	**5.9**	**6.6**	**7.3**	**7.7**	**7.6**	**7.3**	**7.3**	**7.2**	**7.0**
Major industrial countries	6.8	5.9	5.8	6.5	7.2	7.3	7.2	6.9	6.9	7.0	6.7
United States[2]	7.3	5.3	5.6	6.9	7.5	6.9	6.1	5.6	5.4	5.5	5.5
Japan	2.5	2.3	2.1	2.1	2.2	2.5	2.9	3.1	3.3	3.1	3.0
Germany[3]	6.6	6.8	6.2	5.5	7.7	8.9	9.6	9.4	10.3	11.3	10.6
France	8.7	9.4	8.9	9.4	10.3	11.6	12.3	11.6	12.4	12.8	12.3
Italy[4]	9.3	12.0	11.0	10.9	10.7	10.2	11.3	12.0	12.1	12.3	12.0
United Kingdom	8.8	6.2	5.8	8.0	9.7	10.3	9.3	8.2	7.5	6.2	6.0
Canada	9.3	7.5	8.1	10.4	11.3	11.2	10.4	9.5	9.7	9.4	8.8
Other advanced economies	7.1	6.5	6.3	6.8	7.7	9.0	9.1	8.5	8.4	8.2	7.9
Spain	17.0	17.3	16.2	16.3	18.4	22.7	24.2	22.9	22.1	21.4	20.7
Netherlands	7.4	7.7	7.0	6.6	6.6	7.7	8.7	8.3	7.6	7.1	6.3
Belgium	10.9	9.3	8.7	9.3	10.3	12.0	12.9	12.9	12.6	12.8	12.6
Sweden	2.5	1.4	1.5	2.9	5.3	8.2	8.0	7.7	8.1	7.2	6.7
Austria	3.0	3.1	3.2	3.5	3.6	4.2	4.4	4.6	4.7	4.8	4.8
Denmark	8.6	9.3	9.6	10.5	11.2	12.3	12.2	10.3	8.8	8.2	8.1
Finland	5.2	3.5	3.5	7.6	13.1	17.9	18.4	17.2	16.3	15.1	14.0
Greece	7.1	7.5	7.0	7.7	8.7	9.7	9.6	10.0	9.8	9.6	9.3
Portugal	8.2	5.8	4.7	4.1	4.1	5.5	6.8	7.2	7.3	7.4	7.5
Ireland	13.4	15.7	13.5	15.4	16.2	16.6	15.5	13.4	12.4	11.6	11.0
Luxembourg	1.3	1.4	1.3	1.4	1.6	2.1	2.7	2.8	2.8	2.8	2.8
Switzerland	0.6	0.5	0.5	1.1	2.5	4.5	4.7	4.2	4.7	5.5	5.5
Norway	2.5	4.9	5.2	5.5	5.9	6.0	5.4	4.9	4.8	4.0	3.8
Israel	5.4	8.9	9.6	10.6	11.2	10.0	7.8	6.3	6.7	6.8	6.5
Iceland	0.7	1.7	1.8	1.5	3.0	4.4	4.8	5.0	4.3	4.1	4.0
Korea	3.9	2.6	2.5	2.3	2.4	2.8	2.4	2.0	2.1	2.2	2.2
Australia	7.6	6.2	7.0	9.6	10.8	10.9	9.7	8.5	8.6	8.4	8.0
Taiwan Province of China	2.0	1.6	1.7	1.5	1.5	1.5	1.6	1.8	2.6	2.5	2.4
Hong Kong	3.1	1.1	1.3	1.8	2.0	2.0	2.0	3.2	2.9	2.9	2.8
Singapore	3.7	2.2	1.7	1.9	2.7	2.7	2.6	2.7	3.0	3.0	3.0
New Zealand	4.7	7.1	7.8	10.3	10.3	9.5	8.1	6.3	6.2	6.0	5.9
Memorandum											
Industrial countries	7.1	6.3	6.2	6.9	7.8	8.2	8.1	7.7	7.7	7.7	7.4
European Union	8.7	8.7	8.1	8.5	9.9	11.1	11.6	11.2	11.3	11.3	10.8
Newly industrialized Asian economies	3.3	2.2	2.1	2.0	2.1	2.4	2.2	2.1	2.3	2.4	2.3
Growth in employment											
Advanced economies	**1.2**	**2.0**	**1.6**	**0.2**	**−0.1**	**−0.1**	**1.0**	**1.1**	**0.9**	**1.2**	**1.1**
Major industrial countries	1.1	1.8	1.5	—	−0.1	—	0.9	0.8	0.7	1.0	0.9
United States	1.8	2.0	1.3	−0.9	0.7	1.5	2.3	1.5	1.4	1.9	1.1
Japan	1.1	1.9	2.0	1.9	1.1	0.2	0.1	0.1	0.5	0.8	0.8
Germany[3]	0.4	1.5	3.0	1.7	−1.9	−1.8	−0.7	−0.1	−1.0	−0.9	0.2
France	—	1.5	1.1	0.2	−0.6	−1.1	−0.2	1.4	0.1	0.2	1.1
Italy	0.4	0.1	1.4	1.4	−1.1	−4.1	−1.7	−0.5	0.1	—	0.5
United Kingdom	0.5	2.7	0.4	−3.1	−2.5	−0.8	0.8	0.8	0.7	0.8	0.4
Canada	2.2	2.1	0.6	−1.9	−0.6	1.4	2.1	1.6	1.3	1.6	2.0
Other advanced economies	1.2	2.5	1.9	0.7	0.1	−0.5	1.3	2.1	1.7	1.6	1.7
Memorandum											
Industrial countries	1.1	1.9	1.5	−0.1	−0.2	−0.3	0.8	1.0	0.8	1.1	1.0
European Union	0.3	1.7	1.7	0.1	−1.4	−2.0	−0.4	0.7	0.4	0.4	0.8
Newly industrialized Asian economies	2.3	3.1	2.3	2.4	1.9	1.5	2.8	2.2	1.8	2.1	2.1

135

Table A4 *(concluded)*

	Average[1] 1979–88	1989	1990	1991	1992	1993	1994	1995	1996	1997	1998
Growth in real per capita GDP											
Advanced economies	**2.2**	**3.0**	**1.9**	**0.4**	**1.2**	**0.5**	**2.5**	**1.8**	**1.9**	**2.3**	**2.3**
Major industrial countries	2.1	2.8	1.6	—	1.1	0.4	2.2	1.5	1.6	2.1	2.1
United States	1.7	2.4	0.3	−2.0	1.6	1.2	2.5	1.1	1.5	2.1	1.3
Japan	3.2	4.4	4.7	3.6	0.7	−0.2	0.4	1.2	3.3	2.0	2.7
Germany[3]	1.8	2.6	3.8	4.2	1.4	−1.8	2.6	1.6	1.1	2.2	3.1
France	1.7	3.8	2.0	0.4	0.8	−1.7	2.4	2.0	0.9	2.0	2.6
Italy	2.6	2.7	2.0	0.8	0.9	0.2	1.9	3.0	0.6	0.9	2.4
United Kingdom	2.3	1.9	0.1	−2.6	−0.9	1.8	3.5	2.7	1.8	3.0	2.5
Canada	2.1	0.7	−1.7	−3.0	−0.4	1.1	3.0	1.1	0.4	2.4	2.4
Other advanced economies	2.8	3.8	3.1	2.0	1.8	1.3	3.7	3.2	2.9	3.1	3.4
Memorandum											
Industrial countries	2.1	2.9	1.7	—	1.0	0.3	2.2	1.6	1.7	2.1	2.1
European Union	2.0	3.1	2.3	1.0	0.7	−0.6	2.5	2.2	1.4	2.2	2.7
Newly industrialized Asian economies	6.4	5.5	6.0	6.9	4.8	5.4	6.3	6.2	5.3	4.7	5.1

[1]Compound annual rate of change for employment and per capita GDP; arithmetic average for unemployment rate.
[2]The projections for unemployment have been adjusted to reflect the new survey techniques adopted by the U.S. Bureau of Labor Statistics in January 1994.
[3]Data through 1991 apply to west Germany only.
[4]New series starting in 1993, reflecting revisions in the labor force surveys and the definition of unemployment to bring data in line with those of other advanced economies.

Table A5. Developing Countries: Real GDP

(Annual percent change)

	Average 1979–88	1989	1990	1991	1992	1993	1994	1995	1996	1997	1998
Developing countries	**4.3**	**4.2**	**4.0**	**4.9**	**6.5**	**6.5**	**6.8**	**6.0**	**6.5**	**6.6**	**6.5**
Regional groups											
Africa	2.4	3.4	2.0	1.8	0.7	0.9	2.9	2.9	5.0	4.7	4.8
Sub-Sahara	2.4	3.3	2.2	1.4	0.5	1.7	2.6	4.0	4.4	4.4	5.0
Excluding Nigeria and South Africa	2.9	2.5	1.3	1.2	0.8	1.6	2.9	4.7	5.6	5.1	5.6
Asia	6.7	6.1	5.7	6.7	9.4	9.3	9.6	8.9	8.2	8.3	7.7
Excluding China and India	4.9	7.8	7.7	6.9	6.2	5.9	6.8	7.4	6.9	7.0	6.7
Middle East and Europe	2.2	2.8	5.3	3.1	6.1	4.3	0.3	3.8	4.5	3.9	3.9
Western Hemisphere	2.7	1.8	1.1	3.6	3.1	3.7	5.0	1.3	3.5	4.4	5.1
Analytical groups											
By source of export earnings											
Fuel	0.6	3.5	4.5	4.4	5.9	2.1	0.2	2.6	3.0	3.8	3.9
Manufactures	6.6	5.3	3.8	5.7	8.5	9.2	9.7	8.5	7.7	7.9	7.6
Nonfuel primary products	2.3	1.9	1.1	3.0	3.8	4.6	5.1	6.1	5.6	5.4	5.8
Services, factor income, and private transfers	4.6	2.1	2.1	2.5	2.5	2.9	3.1	3.8	4.3	5.0	5.1
Diversified	3.4	3.4	5.1	4.5	4.5	4.4	4.7	2.6	5.7	5.4	5.3
By external financing source											
Net creditor countries	0.4	4.0	6.2	5.8	7.9	5.8	0.5	1.0	3.6	1.7	2.1
Net debtor countries	4.5	4.2	3.9	4.9	6.5	6.5	7.0	6.2	6.5	6.8	6.6
Official financing	3.4	3.6	4.0	4.3	2.7	2.5	3.9	3.5	5.4	5.1	5.2
Private financing	4.8	3.4	3.6	5.8	7.9	7.9	7.7	6.3	6.7	7.0	6.9
Diversified financing	4.3	6.4	4.7	2.9	4.4	4.6	6.2	6.9	6.6	6.8	6.3
Net debtor countries by debt-servicing experience											
Countries with recent difficulties	2.3	1.9	0.8	2.5	2.5	2.6	4.0	3.2	3.8	4.8	5.2
Countries without recent difficulties	5.9	5.4	5.5	6.0	8.3	8.2	8.2	7.4	7.6	7.5	7.1
Other groups											
Heavily indebted poor countries	2.6	2.4	1.3	0.8	2.1	2.2	3.1	5.0	5.4	5.4	5.7
Least developed countries	2.8	3.0	2.7	2.0	3.2	4.1	3.4	5.7	5.4	5.4	5.3
Middle East and north Africa	1.8	3.4	3.5	3.6	5.3	2.5	2.2	2.2	4.5	4.2	3.9
Memorandum											
Real per capita GDP											
Developing countries	2.0	0.6	2.1	2.9	4.2	4.4	4.5	4.4	4.7	4.9	4.7
Regional groups											
Africa	−0.5	0.6	−0.8	−1.1	−1.8	−1.9	0.3	0.3	2.5	2.1	2.2
Asia	5.0	1.2	4.0	4.9	7.6	7.5	7.6	7.3	6.7	6.7	6.2
Middle East and Europe	−1.3	0.5	3.2	1.2	1.6	1.1	−3.6	0.9	2.2	1.5	1.4
Western Hemisphere	0.5	−0.6	−0.8	1.6	1.1	1.8	3.2	0.7	1.8	2.7	3.4

137

Table A6. Developing Countries—by Country: Real GDP[1]

(Annual percent change)

	Average 1979–88	1989	1990	1991	1992	1993	1994	1995	1996
Africa	**2.4**	**3.4**	**2.0**	**1.8**	**0.7**	**0.9**	**2.9**	**2.9**	**5.0**
Algeria	0.6	4.8	−1.4	0.2	2.3	−2.2	−0.9	3.9	4.0
Angola	2.5	0.1	−0.5	−2.2	−3.4	−25.0	9.0	12.0	8.6
Benin	3.1	−2.5	3.1	4.7	4.1	3.2	4.3	4.8	5.5
Botswana	11.0	9.2	7.3	7.6	3.0	1.9	3.0	4.9	6.1
Burkina Faso	3.3	0.9	−1.5	10.0	2.5	−0.8	1.2	3.9	5.5
Burundi	3.4	1.3	3.5	5.0	2.7	−5.8	−6.7	−3.7	−3.6
Cameroon	5.8	−1.8	−6.2	−3.8	−3.1	−3.2	−2.5	3.3	5.0
Cape Verde	5.5	6.2	−0.8	1.4	3.3	4.2	3.8	4.7	4.0
Central African Republic	1.6	3.4	−1.7	−0.8	−2.8	−2.3	7.7	2.4	−0.9
Chad	1.9	5.8	1.9	8.5	8.0	−15.7	10.2	2.8	6.0
Comoros	4.2	−3.2	2.5	−3.0	7.7	3.8	−2.3	−2.3	1.9
Congo	7.3	2.9	0.9	2.4	2.6	−1.0	−5.5	2.2	4.8
Côte d'Ivoire	1.5	2.9	−1.1	—	−0.2	−0.2	1.8	7.0	6.5
Djibouti	1.4	−2.6	−0.6	0.4	−0.2	−3.9	−2.9	−3.1	−0.2
Equatorial Guinea	2.0	−1.2	3.3	−1.1	14.0	7.1	6.8	14.9	37.3
Ethiopia	2.8	0.2	3.4	−6.7	−6.5	12.0	1.7	5.4	12.4
Gabon	−0.4	7.0	13.5	6.1	−3.3	2.3	3.6	3.7	3.2
Gambia, The	4.3	4.3	5.7	2.2	4.4	1.8	1.3	−4.0	3.2
Ghana	1.1	5.1	3.4	5.3	3.9	5.0	3.8	4.5	5.0
Guinea	2.4	4.0	4.3	2.4	3.0	4.7	4.0	4.4	4.5
Guinea-Bissau	3.0	2.9	4.6	5.1	1.1	2.1	3.2	4.4	6.2
Kenya	4.3	5.8	4.5	1.4	−0.8	0.3	3.1	4.9	4.2
Lesotho	2.7	10.4	3.7	1.7	2.6	8.0	11.5	9.3	13.1
Liberia	0.6	−10.8	0.3	2.9	1.9	2.2	2.2	2.7	2.7
Madagascar	0.8	4.1	3.1	−6.3	1.2	2.1	—	1.8	2.0
Malawi	2.0	1.3	5.7	8.7	−7.3	9.7	−10.2	9.6	10.4
Mali	1.3	11.8	0.4	−0.9	8.4	−2.4	2.3	6.4	4.0
Mauritania	5.7	2.2	−1.8	2.6	1.7	4.9	4.2	4.3	4.4
Mauritius	4.6	5.7	4.7	6.4	4.8	6.7	4.2	3.3	4.4
Morocco	4.0	2.5	3.9	6.9	−4.1	−1.0	11.6	−7.6	10.3
Mozambique, Rep. of	0.2	6.5	0.9	4.9	−0.8	19.3	5.0	1.5	5.7
Namibia	1.7	2.2	0.3	7.4	8.2	−1.9	6.5	2.6	2.0
Niger	1.8	1.0	−1.3	2.4	−6.5	1.4	4.0	3.0	3.6
Nigeria	1.0	7.2	8.2	4.8	2.9	2.3	1.3	2.5	2.1
Rwanda	3.4	−5.7	0.4	−4.3	6.6	−6.8	−49.0	24.6	13.3
São Tomé and Príncipe	−0.2	3.1	−2.2	1.2	0.7	1.1	2.2	2.0	2.2
Senegal	3.5	−1.4	4.5	−0.7	2.8	−2.1	2.0	4.8	5.2
Seychelles	3.1	10.3	7.5	2.7	6.9	5.1	−1.6	−1.8	3.2
Sierra Leone	0.5	5.0	1.6	−8.0	−9.6	0.1	3.5	−10.0	4.9
Somalia	0.8	2.4	...	...	...	...	...	...	...
South Africa	2.3	2.4	−0.3	−1.0	−2.2	1.3	2.7	3.4	3.1
Sudan	1.6	1.5	—	6.1	8.6	5.0	4.3	4.5	4.0
Swaziland	4.1	8.3	9.7	2.5	1.3	3.4	3.4	2.5	2.5
Tanzania	2.8	3.9	4.6	6.4	4.7	3.9	3.5	3.8	4.5
Togo	1.4	4.1	−0.4	−0.9	−6.3	−18.5	15.2	8.1	5.9
Tunisia	4.0	2.6	7.1	3.9	7.8	2.0	3.3	2.5	7.5
Uganda	2.1	6.5	5.6	3.4	8.3	6.3	11.5	9.8	7.0
Zaïre	1.8	−1.3	−6.6	−8.4	−10.5	−13.5	−3.9	−0.6	1.3
Zambia	1.5	−3.7	−0.5	—	−2.5	6.4	−3.0	−3.9	5.0
Zimbabwe	4.8	5.7	−0.8	4.6	−8.4	3.0	6.3	2.3	8.1

Table A6 (continued)

	Average 1979–88	1989	1990	1991	1992	1993	1994	1995	1996
Asia	**6.7**	**6.1**	**5.7**	**6.7**	**9.4**	**9.3**	**9.6**	**8.9**	**8.2**
Afghanistan, Islamic State of	−1.4	−7.1	−2.6	0.8	1.0	−3.1	−3.0	26.2	6.0
Bangladesh	3.8	5.0	5.1	4.1	4.8	4.8	4.7	4.9	5.0
Bhutan	7.6	4.5	5.9	3.9	4.4	5.0	5.1	6.9	6.0
Cambodia	. . .	3.5	1.2	7.6	7.0	4.1	4.0	7.6	7.5
China	9.8	4.1	3.8	9.2	14.3	13.5	12.6	10.5	9.7
Fiji	1.9	13.9	3.2	1.5	4.8	3.5	4.2	2.4	3.3
India	4.7	7.4	5.9	1.7	4.1	5.0	7.0	7.4	6.9
Indonesia	4.9	9.1	9.0	8.9	7.2	7.3	7.5	8.2	7.8
Kiribati	−4.8	−2.2	−3.2	2.8	−1.6	0.9	1.8	2.5	2.6
Lao P.D. Republic	4.7	9.9	6.7	4.0	7.0	5.9	8.1	7.1	7.5
Malaysia	5.8	9.2	9.6	8.6	7.8	8.3	9.2	9.5	8.4
Maldives	10.3	9.3	16.2	7.6	6.3	6.2	6.6	7.2	6.5
Marshall Islands	. . .	−1.7	3.2	0.1	0.1	4.1	2.8	3.7	−2.5
Micronesia, Fed. States of	. . .	−1.7	−2.7	4.3	−1.2	5.7	1.4	1.0	1.0
Myanmar	1.9	3.7	2.8	−0.7	9.7	5.9	6.8	7.2	7.0
Nepal	3.6	4.6	6.4	4.1	3.4	7.1	3.0	5.8	4.2
Pakistan	6.4	4.7	5.6	8.2	5.0	0.8	3.9	4.4	6.0
Papua New Guinea	1.9	−1.4	−3.0	9.5	11.8	16.6	5.2	−2.9	2.3
Philippines	1.9	6.2	3.0	−0.6	0.3	2.1	4.4	4.8	5.5
Solomon Islands	2.1	4.3	1.0	2.0	12.3	4.0	5.8	6.9	4.4
Sri Lanka	4.6	2.3	6.2	4.6	4.3	6.9	5.6	5.4	3.5
Thailand	6.7	12.2	11.6	8.1	8.1	8.3	8.8	8.7	6.7
Vanuatu	2.1	4.5	5.2	4.5	−0.7	4.4	2.6	3.2	3.0
Vietnam	4.9	7.8	4.9	6.0	8.6	8.1	8.8	9.5	9.5
Western Samoa	1.1	1.9	−9.4	−2.3	−0.2	4.1	−6.5	9.6	5.8
Middle East and Europe	**2.2**	**2.8**	**5.3**	**3.1**	**6.1**	**4.3**	**0.3**	**3.8**	**4.5**
Bahrain	2.1	2.4	4.6	4.6	7.8	8.2	2.3	1.2	1.6
Cyprus	6.3	8.0	7.3	0.4	9.7	1.5	6.1	5.3	2.4
Egypt	5.9	3.0	2.4	1.2	0.3	0.5	2.7	3.2	4.3
Iran, Islamic Republic of	−2.0	4.5	11.2	8.6	8.1	2.1	0.9	3.1	4.2
Iraq	0.7	12.0	−26.0	−61.3	—	—	1.0	2.0	2.0
Jordan	5.0	−13.4	1.0	1.8	16.1	5.6	8.1	6.9	5.2
Kuwait	−3.4	25.9	−26.2	−41.0	69.9	48.6	0.2	1.6	1.6
Lebanon	1.3	−42.2	−13.4	38.2	4.5	7.0	8.0	6.5	7.0
Libya	−0.8	−7.8	8.2	12.0	−4.2	0.1	−0.9	−1.1	2.0
Malta	4.2	8.2	6.2	6.3	4.7	4.5	5.0	6.2	3.5
Oman	8.5	3.0	8.4	6.0	8.5	6.2	3.8	4.6	3.8
Qatar	−0.4	5.3	−14.8	−0.4	5.9	2.8	—	−2.7	3.6
Saudi Arabia	1.7	−0.2	8.9	9.7	3.1	−0.5	0.3	—	2.5
Syrian Arab Republic	3.9	−9.0	7.6	7.1	10.5	3.9	5.5	5.0	5.0
Turkey	4.0	0.3	9.2	0.8	5.0	7.7	−4.7	7.5	6.4
United Arab Emirates	−2.0	13.3	17.5	0.2	2.7	−0.9	1.9	5.8	9.9
Yemen Arab Republic, former	7.7	3.4	1.7	. . .	. . .	. . .	. . .	. . .	. . .
Yemen, former P.D. Republic of	0.2	2.5	3.0	. . .	. . .	. . .	. . .	. . .	. . .
Yemen, Republic of	. . .	. . .	. . .	—	4.2	5.9	—	3.6	2.5

Table A6 *(concluded)*

	Average 1979–88	1989	1990	1991	1992	1993	1994	1995	1996
Western Hemisphere	**2.7**	**1.8**	**1.1**	**3.6**	**3.1**	**3.7**	**5.0**	**1.3**	**3.5**
Antigua and Barbuda	7.1	6.3	3.5	4.4	1.1	3.5	4.8	−4.2	5.0
Argentina	0.4	−7.0	−1.3	10.5	10.3	6.3	8.5	−4.6	4.4
Aruba	...	9.1	11.7	3.8	3.8	3.8	3.8	3.8	3.8
Bahamas, The	4.3	2.3	1.2	−2.7	−2.0	1.7	0.9	0.3	3.0
Barbados	2.1	3.6	−3.3	−3.9	−5.7	0.8	4.0	2.9	4.5
Belize	3.5	13.0	11.0	3.0	9.3	3.4	1.6	3.8	3.0
Bolivia	−0.4	3.6	4.4	4.6	2.8	4.1	4.2	3.8	5.0
Brazil	3.2	3.3	−3.1	0.3	−0.8	4.2	5.7	4.2	3.0
Chile	3.3	9.9	3.3	7.3	11.0	6.3	4.2	8.5	7.2
Colombia	3.6	3.4	4.3	2.0	4.0	5.4	5.8	5.4	3.0
Costa Rica	2.4	5.6	3.6	2.2	7.3	6.0	4.5	2.5	−1.2
Dominica	3.5	−1.1	6.3	2.2	2.7	1.9	2.1	1.8	3.2
Dominican Republic	3.6	4.8	−5.8	1.0	8.0	3.0	4.3	4.8	7.3
Ecuador	2.8	0.3	3.0	5.0	3.6	2.0	4.3	2.3	1.8
El Salvador	−1.5	0.9	4.9	3.6	7.4	7.4	6.0	6.3	2.0
Grenada	4.6	5.8	5.2	3.6	1.2	−1.2	2.3	2.7	3.0
Guatemala	1.0	3.9	3.1	3.7	4.8	3.9	4.0	4.9	3.1
Guyana	−2.0	−3.3	−2.5	6.1	7.8	8.2	8.6	5.0	7.9
Haiti	0.9	1.1	−0.1	−3.0	−14.8	−2.6	−10.6	4.5	2.0
Honduras	2.7	4.3	0.1	3.3	5.6	6.0	−1.5	4.5	4.5
Jamaica	1.8	4.7	4.1	0.8	1.8	1.0	0.5	0.5	—
Mexico	3.0	4.2	5.1	4.2	3.6	2.0	4.5	−6.2	5.1
Netherlands Antilles	0.3	7.8	1.5	1.8	3.7	0.3	2.4	—	−2.4
Nicaragua	−3.7	−1.7	−0.1	−0.2	0.4	−0.2	3.3	4.2	4.5
Panama	1.8	1.6	8.1	9.4	8.2	5.5	2.9	2.3	2.0
Paraguay	3.8	5.8	3.1	2.5	1.8	4.1	3.1	4.2	1.6
Peru	1.8	−11.7	−3.3	2.9	−1.8	6.4	13.1	7.0	2.8
St. Kitts and Nevis	5.7	6.7	3.0	3.9	3.5	5.0	4.1	4.8	6.7
St. Lucia	6.0	9.1	4.1	2.3	7.1	2.1	2.2	4.1	3.7
St. Vincent and the Grenadines	6.0	6.5	5.4	3.1	4.9	2.1	−0.4	6.7	3.3
Suriname	−2.0	4.0	0.1	2.9	4.0	−2.2	−7.0	4.0	4.0
Trinidad and Tobago	−2.1	−0.7	1.5	2.7	−1.7	−1.6	3.8	2.4	3.2
Uruguay	1.5	1.3	0.9	3.2	7.9	3.0	6.8	−2.4	4.8
Venezuela	1.1	−8.6	6.5	9.7	6.1	0.3	−2.9	3.4	−1.2

[1]For many countries, figures for recent years are IMF staff estimates. Data for some countries are for fiscal years.

Table A7. Countries in Transition: Real GDP[1]

(Annual percent change)

	Average 1979–88	1989	1990	1991	1992	1993	1994	1995	1996
Central and eastern Europe	...	...	...	**−10.8**	**−8.8**	**−4.0**	**−1.8**	**1.6**	**1.6**
Albania	1.8	9.8	−10.0	−28.0	−7.2	9.6	9.4	8.9	8.2
Belarus	...	...	...	−1.2	−9.7	−10.6	−12.2	−10.2	2.0
Bulgaria	4.3	−0.5	−9.1	−11.7	−7.3	−1.5	1.8	2.6	−9.0
Croatia	...	...	...	...	...	−3.7	0.8	1.5	5.0
Czech Republic	...	...	...	...	...	−0.9	2.6	4.8	4.2
Czechoslovakia, former	2.4	4.5	−0.4	−15.9	−8.5	...	...	...	...
Estonia	...	...	...	−7.9	−21.6	−8.4	−0.1	3.2	3.1
Hungary	1.7	0.7	−3.5	−11.9	−3.1	−0.6	2.9	1.5	1.0
Latvia	...	...	...	−11.1	−35.2	−16.1	2.2	0.4	2.5
Lithuania	...	...	...	−13.1	−51.9	−24.2	1.0	3.1	3.5
Macedonia, former Yugoslav Rep. of	...	...	...	...	...	−8.4	−4.0	−1.4	1.1
Moldova	...	...	...	−17.5	−29.1	−1.2	−31.2	−3.0	−8.0
Poland	0.8	0.2	−11.6	−7.0	2.6	3.8	6.0	6.5	5.5
Romania	2.8	−5.8	−5.6	−12.9	−8.8	1.5	3.9	7.1	4.1
Slovak Republic	...	...	...	...	...	−3.7	4.6	6.8	7.0
Slovenia	...	...	...	...	...	2.8	5.3	3.9	3.5
Ukraine	...	...	...	−11.9	−17.0	−16.8	−23.0	−12.0	−10.0
Yugoslavia, former	1.3	0.8	−7.5	−17.0	−34.0	...	...	...	...
Russia	...	...	...	**−5.0**	**−14.5**	**−8.7**	**−12.6**	**−4.0**	**−2.8**
Transcaucasus and central Asia	...	...	...	**−7.2**	**−15.1**	**−9.4**	**−13.4**	**−3.9**	**1.6**
Armenia	...	...	...	−12.4	−52.6	−14.1	5.4	6.9	6.6
Azerbaijan	...	...	...	−0.7	−22.1	−23.1	−18.1	−11.0	1.3
Georgia	...	...	...	−20.6	−44.8	−25.4	−11.4	2.4	10.5
Kazakstan	...	...	...	−13.0	−14.0	−12.0	−25.0	−8.9	1.0
Kyrgyz Republic	...	...	...	−7.9	−13.9	−15.5	−20.1	1.3	5.6
Mongolia	6.6	4.2	−5.6	−9.2	−9.5	−3.0	2.3	6.3	3.0
Tajikistan	...	...	...	−7.1	−28.9	−11.1	−21.4	−12.5	−7.0
Turkmenistan	...	...	...	−4.7	−5.3	−10.0	−18.8	−8.2	−3.0
Uzbekistan	...	...	...	−0.5	−11.1	−2.3	−4.2	−0.9	1.6

[1]Data for some countries refer to real net material product (NMP) or are estimates based on NMP. For many countries, figures for recent years are IMF staff estimates. The figures should be interpreted only as indicative of broad orders of magnitude because reliable, comparable data are not generally available. In particular, the growth of output of new private enterprises or of the informal economy is not fully reflected in the recent figures.

Table A8. Summary of Inflation

(In percent)

	Average 1979–88	1989	1990	1991	1992	1993	1994	1995	1996	1997	1998
GDP deflators											
Advanced economies	**6.6**	**4.4**	**4.5**	**4.5**	**3.3**	**2.8**	**2.2**	**2.3**	**2.0**	**2.0**	**2.2**
United States	5.4	4.2	4.3	4.0	2.7	2.6	2.3	2.5	2.0	2.1	2.7
European Union	7.8	4.9	5.2	5.5	4.5	3.6	2.6	2.9	2.6	2.2	2.1
Japan	2.3	2.0	2.3	2.5	1.7	0.8	0.2	−0.6	—	0.3	0.3
Other advanced economies	11.9	6.1	5.7	5.4	3.5	3.3	2.9	3.2	3.0	2.9	2.9
Consumer prices											
Advanced economies	**6.8**	**4.5**	**5.2**	**4.7**	**3.5**	**3.1**	**2.6**	**2.6**	**2.4**	**2.5**	**2.5**
United States	6.1	4.8	5.4	4.2	3.0	3.0	2.6	2.8	2.9	2.9	3.0
European Union	7.5	4.7	5.4	5.1	4.5	3.8	2.9	3.0	2.5	2.2	2.1
Japan	2.7	2.3	3.1	3.3	1.7	1.2	0.7	−0.1	0.1	1.3	1.2
Other advanced economies	11.8	5.9	6.3	6.5	4.1	3.5	3.4	3.6	3.3	3.2	3.2
Developing countries	**31.8**	**64.9**	**68.1**	**35.9**	**38.8**	**46.9**	**51.3**	**21.3**	**13.1**	**9.7**	**8.5**
Regional groups											
Africa	15.5	18.8	15.5	24.6	32.1	29.5	38.6	32.1	24.8	12.0	6.9
Asia	8.3	11.8	6.6	7.8	7.0	10.4	14.7	11.8	6.6	6.2	6.5
Middle East and Europe	19.0	21.4	22.1	25.3	26.6	24.7	32.4	33.8	24.5	21.0	19.1
Western Hemisphere	93.6	340.0	442.9	129.8	153.2	212.6	213.7	36.0	20.4	12.9	9.3
Analytical groups											
By source of export earnings											
Fuel	12.4	20.9	14.1	18.9	23.9	25.5	33.9	38.8	30.3	14.5	7.8
Nonfuel	35.8	72.3	77.6	38.4	40.9	49.9	53.6	19.4	11.3	9.2	8.5
By external financing source											
Net creditor countries	3.4	1.7	3.2	6.4	3.8	4.2	3.4	4.7	2.1	1.8	1.8
Net debtor countries	33.1	67.8	71.1	37.1	40.2	48.7	53.2	21.8	13.4	9.9	8.7
Official financing	17.8	22.6	18.0	25.5	23.5	22.0	27.3	21.4	14.9	10.1	6.7
Private financing	46.1	111.2	117.0	49.5	56.2	70.8	77.3	25.5	14.3	10.8	9.3
Diversified financing	12.7	9.8	13.2	14.8	12.0	11.6	11.6	12.6	10.5	7.7	7.8
Net debtor countries by debt-servicing experience											
Countries with recent difficulties	60.7	238.2	293.7	106.2	132.0	179.2	191.8	36.3	19.0	11.3	7.5
Countries without recent difficulties	17.9	15.5	12.1	12.5	11.2	12.8	16.8	16.4	11.3	9.4	9.1
Countries in transition	**6.4**	**26.8**	**35.6**	**95.9**	**597.1**	**486.1**	**246.0**	**119.2**	**40.4**	**30.7**	**11.6**
Central and eastern Europe	...	...	...	95.0	263.7	307.0	141.0	70.5	32.1	38.2	13.4
Excluding Belarus and Ukraine	...	...	...	98.0	103.5	74.4	44.6	25.4	24.5	41.0	12.9
Russia	...	...	...	92.7	1,353.0	699.8	302.0	190.1	47.8	14.2	7.8
Transcaucasus and central Asia	...	...	...	114.0	880.2	1,096.1	1,532.6	260.2	70.0	51.9	14.5
Memorandum											
Median inflation rate											
Advanced economies	7.2	4.9	5.4	4.0	3.2	3.0	2.4	2.4	2.1	2.4	2.2
Developing countries	10.1	9.0	10.4	12.1	9.8	9.5	11.1	10.0	7.0	5.4	5.0
Countries in transition	1.1	2.0	6.7	101.4	871.0	472.2	131.6	36.2	24.2	16.5	10.0

Table A9. Advanced Economies: GDP Deflators and Consumer Prices

(Annual percent change)

	Average 1979–88	1989	1990	1991	1992	1993	1994	1995	1996	1997	1998	Fourth Quarter[1] 1996	1997	1998
GDP deflators														
Advanced economies	6.6	4.4	4.5	4.5	3.3	2.8	2.2	2.3	2.0	2.0	2.2	...	...	...
Major industrial countries	5.7	4.0	4.1	4.1	3.0	2.5	1.8	2.0	1.8	1.8	2.0	1.6	1.9	2.0
United States	5.4	4.2	4.3	4.0	2.7	2.6	2.3	2.5	2.0	2.1	2.7	1.8	2.5	2.7
Japan	2.3	2.0	2.3	2.5	1.7	0.8	0.2	−0.6	—	0.3	0.3	−0.1	0.9	0.1
Germany[2]	3.1	2.4	3.2	3.9	5.5	3.9	2.2	2.2	1.0	1.5	1.8	0.5	2.1	1.7
France	7.8	3.0	3.1	3.3	2.1	2.5	1.5	1.7	1.6	1.7	1.8	1.4	1.9	1.8
Italy	12.7	6.3	7.6	7.7	4.7	4.4	3.5	5.0	5.0	2.7	2.1	5.7	0.7	1.6
United Kingdom	8.2	7.1	6.4	6.5	4.6	3.2	1.9	2.3	3.1	2.8	2.3	3.3	2.1	3.2
Canada	6.2	4.8	3.1	2.9	1.2	1.1	0.7	1.5	1.3	2.0	1.7	1.7	1.8	1.7
Other advanced economies	11.0	6.3	6.4	6.3	4.8	4.1	3.5	3.6	3.1	2.8	2.9	...	...	...
Spain	11.0	7.1	7.3	7.1	6.9	4.3	4.0	4.9	3.3	2.6	2.5	...	...	...
Netherlands	2.6	1.2	2.3	2.7	2.3	1.9	2.0	1.5	2.3	2.0	2.3	...	...	...
Belgium	4.6	4.6	2.9	3.1	3.6	3.8	2.5	1.4	1.8	2.0	2.0	...	...	...
Sweden	7.9	8.0	8.8	7.6	1.0	2.6	2.5	3.7	0.9	2.3	2.6	...	...	...
Austria	4.2	2.9	3.3	4.0	4.2	3.4	3.3	2.1	1.9	1.9	1.9	...	...	...
Denmark	6.6	4.2	2.5	2.4	3.2	0.6	1.6	1.8	2.0	2.3	2.3	...	...	...
Finland	7.6	6.1	5.7	2.6	0.7	2.4	1.3	2.2	1.0	1.1	1.6	...	...	...
Greece	18.3	14.5	20.6	19.8	14.6	14.1	10.9	9.3	8.8	7.2	5.9	...	...	...
Portugal	19.3	12.0	12.1	14.8	13.0	6.9	5.1	5.0	3.4	2.9	2.7	...	...	...
Ireland	9.4	5.4	−0.8	1.8	2.2	4.2	1.2	0.5	2.0	2.1	2.4	...	...	...
Luxembourg	4.6	−0.3	1.7	2.8	3.3	—	8.0	0.3	1.8	1.2	2.0	...	...	...
Switzerland	3.6	4.2	5.7	5.5	2.6	2.0	1.9	2.5	0.3	0.1	1.5	...	...	...
Norway	8.2	5.7	3.8	2.5	−0.5	2.1	0.6	3.1	4.2	2.5	2.5	...	...	...
Israel	113.3	20.2	16.1	20.6	12.1	11.5	12.3	9.2	11.2	8.0	6.8	...	...	...
Iceland	38.6	19.8	16.7	7.6	3.8	2.3	2.1	2.7	3.1	2.8	2.6	...	...	...
Korea	9.9	5.3	9.9	10.1	6.1	5.1	5.5	5.4	3.8	3.6	4.0	...	...	...
Australia	8.7	7.6	4.6	2.1	1.4	1.5	1.1	2.8	2.0	2.6	2.2	...	...	...
Taiwan Province of China	5.0	3.3	3.8	3.8	3.9	3.5	1.9	1.9	3.5	2.1	2.6	...	...	...
Hong Kong	9.5	12.3	7.5	9.2	9.7	8.5	7.2	4.4	5.6	6.5	5.8	...	...	...
Singapore	3.6	4.8	5.0	3.4	1.2	5.4	4.3	2.5	1.8	1.8	2.0	...	...	...
New Zealand	13.1	5.5	4.0	0.4	1.3	2.7	0.8	2.2	2.1	1.9	1.6	...	...	...
Memorandum														
Industrial countries	6.1	4.3	4.3	4.3	3.2	2.6	2.0	2.2	1.9	1.9	2.0	...	...	...
European Union	7.8	4.9	5.2	5.5	4.5	3.6	2.6	2.9	2.6	2.2	2.1	...	...	...
Newly industrialized Asian economies	7.9	5.7	7.3	7.6	5.6	5.1	4.5	4.0	3.8	3.4	3.7	...	...	...
Consumer prices														
Advanced economies	6.8	4.5	5.2	4.7	3.5	3.1	2.6	2.6	2.4	2.5	2.5	...	...	...
Major industrial countries	6.0	4.3	4.8	4.3	3.2	2.8	2.2	2.3	2.2	2.3	2.3	2.3	2.3	2.3
United States	6.1	4.8	5.4	4.2	3.0	3.0	2.6	2.8	2.9	2.9	3.0	3.2	2.9	3.0
Japan	2.7	2.3	3.1	3.3	1.7	1.2	0.7	−0.1	0.1	1.3	1.2	0.4	1.7	1.0
Germany[2,3]	3.0	2.8	2.7	3.5	5.1	4.5	2.7	1.8	1.5	1.8	2.0	1.5	1.9	2.0
France	8.0	3.5	3.4	3.2	2.4	2.1	1.7	1.8	2.0	1.6	1.8	1.7	1.9	1.8
Italy	12.1	6.3	6.5	6.3	5.2	4.5	4.0	5.4	3.9	2.4	2.0	2.8	1.9	1.9
United Kingdom[4]	7.6	5.9	8.1	6.8	4.7	3.0	2.4	2.8	2.9	2.6	2.5	3.2	2.5	2.5
Canada	6.6	5.0	4.8	5.6	1.5	1.8	0.2	2.2	1.7	1.7	1.8	1.9	2.0	1.7
Other advanced economies	10.6	5.8	6.7	6.3	4.9	4.1	4.1	3.7	3.3	3.1	3.0	...	...	...
Memorandum														
Industrial countries	6.3	4.4	5.0	4.5	3.3	2.9	2.3	2.4	2.3	2.3	2.3	...	...	...
European Union	7.5	4.7	5.4	5.1	4.5	3.8	2.9	3.0	2.5	2.2	2.1	...	...	...
Newly industrialized Asian economies	7.4	5.8	7.1	7.5	5.9	4.6	5.7	4.7	4.3	4.3	4.0	...	...	...

[1]From fourth quarter of preceding year.
[2]Data through 1991 apply to west Germany only.
[3]Based on the revised consumer price index for united Germany introduced in September 1995.
[4]Retail price index excluding mortgage interest.

Table A10. Advanced Economies: Hourly Earnings, Productivity, and Unit Labor Costs in Manufacturing
(*Annual percent change*)

	Average 1979–88	1989	1990	1991	1992	1993	1994	1995	1996	1997	1998
Hourly earnings											
Advanced economies	**8.1**	**6.4**	**6.2**	**6.2**	**5.5**	**3.1**	**3.1**	**3.7**	**3.7**	**3.2**	**3.7**
Major industrial countries	7.2	5.1	5.8	6.1	5.2	3.3	2.8	3.6	3.3	2.8	3.4
United States	6.4	3.3	4.7	5.3	4.4	2.4	2.8	3.6	3.6	2.9	3.5
Japan	3.9	6.7	6.5	5.9	4.6	2.6	2.7	2.5	1.7	1.3	3.1
Germany[1]	5.3	4.2	5.7	7.3	9.6	6.8	2.0	4.2	3.2	2.3	3.0
France	9.8	4.8	4.8	5.4	4.6	3.3	3.7	2.5	2.6	2.9	3.2
Italy	14.6	9.7	8.5	9.7	7.2	5.0	2.1	6.3	5.3	4.3	4.0
United Kingdom	11.0	9.0	9.0	8.0	5.1	4.3	4.4	5.1	3.7	4.3	4.9
Canada	6.5	5.3	5.2	4.7	3.5	2.1	1.6	1.4	3.2	3.0	1.9
Other advanced economies	12.5	12.7	8.3	6.4	6.8	2.1	4.4	4.4	5.8	4.9	4.9
Memorandum											
Industrial countries	7.5	5.5	6.1	6.3	5.4	3.4	2.9	3.6	3.4	2.9	3.4
European Union	9.6	7.2	7.2	7.6	7.0	5.0	3.2	4.3	3.7	3.5	3.7
Newly industrialized Asian economies	11.8	29.7	9.4	2.1	8.0	−5.4	6.2	4.7	8.6	6.9	7.5
Productivity											
Advanced economies	**3.2**	**3.5**	**1.9**	**1.8**	**2.4**	**1.5**	**4.6**	**3.6**	**3.0**	**2.5**	**2.5**
Major industrial countries	3.0	2.9	2.2	2.1	2.4	1.6	4.6	3.6	3.0	2.5	2.5
United States	2.5	1.8	1.8	2.5	3.4	2.1	3.2	3.3	4.0	2.6	2.3
Japan	3.2	4.5	2.8	1.5	−3.7	−1.6	3.5	4.9	3.9	2.7	3.4
Germany[1]	2.8	3.1	3.5	2.9	4.0	3.3	8.7	4.0	4.2	3.0	3.0
France	4.2	5.1	1.5	1.3	4.2	−0.2	8.9	3.0	2.0	3.4	2.4
Italy	4.5	3.0	1.4	1.3	3.9	1.9	5.6	6.9	−1.1	1.7	1.8
United Kingdom	3.7	4.4	2.2	2.1	4.3	4.7	4.4	1.9	−0.3	0.9	2.4
Canada	1.4	0.5	3.3	1.0	4.3	3.1	3.8	−0.9	0.9	1.0	1.1
Other advanced economies	3.8	6.2	0.6	0.4	2.3	1.1	4.9	3.8	2.9	2.8	2.5
Memorandum											
Industrial countries	3.1	3.1	1.9	2.0	2.4	1.9	4.8	3.6	2.9	2.5	2.4
European Union	3.8	4.3	1.9	2.0	3.7	3.0	7.1	3.9	1.5	2.4	2.3
Newly industrialized Asian economies	6.2	13.1	—	−4.4	1.3	−6.9	2.4	5.3	5.1	3.7	4.0
Unit labor costs											
Advanced economies	**4.8**	**2.9**	**4.3**	**4.3**	**3.1**	**1.5**	**−1.5**	**0.1**	**0.7**	**0.6**	**1.1**
Major industrial countries	4.1	2.1	3.5	4.0	2.8	1.7	−1.7	—	0.3	0.3	0.9
United States	3.8	1.5	2.9	2.7	0.9	0.3	−0.4	0.3	−0.3	0.3	1.2
Japan	0.7	2.0	3.5	4.3	8.6	4.3	−0.7	−2.3	−2.1	−1.4	−0.4
Germany[1]	2.5	1.0	2.1	4.2	5.4	3.4	−6.2	0.2	−1.0	−0.7	—
France	5.3	−0.3	3.3	4.0	0.3	3.6	−4.8	−0.5	0.6	−0.5	0.7
Italy	9.6	6.5	7.1	8.3	3.2	3.0	−3.3	−0.6	6.4	2.5	2.1
United Kingdom	7.0	4.4	6.7	5.7	0.7	−0.4	—	3.1	4.0	3.4	2.4
Canada	5.0	4.8	1.8	3.7	−0.8	−1.0	−2.1	2.4	2.3	2.0	0.8
Other advanced economies	8.1	6.1	7.5	5.6	4.1	1.0	−0.6	0.3	2.5	1.8	2.0
Memorandum											
Industrial countries	4.3	2.3	4.0	4.2	3.0	1.5	−1.7	0.1	0.6	0.5	1.0
European Union	5.6	2.8	5.3	5.6	3.2	2.0	−3.5	0.5	2.2	1.1	1.4
Newly industrialized Asian economies	4.3	13.6	8.4	5.1	4.8	1.3	2.2	−1.5	2.2	2.2	2.4

[1]Data through 1991 apply to west Germany only.

Table A11. Developing Countries: Consumer Prices
(Annual percent change)

	Average 1979–88	1989	1990	1991	1992	1993	1994	1995	1996	1997	1998
Developing countries	**31.8**	**64.9**	**68.1**	**35.9**	**38.8**	**46.9**	**51.3**	**21.3**	**13.1**	**9.7**	**8.5**
Regional groups											
Africa	15.5	18.8	15.5	24.6	32.1	29.5	38.6	32.1	24.8	12.0	6.9
Sub-Sahara	18.1	23.7	16.9	27.6	37.7	37.6	46.4	39.6	31.5	14.8	8.0
Excluding Nigeria and South Africa	20.3	20.6	20.9	37.9	45.4	43.3	59.6	43.9	42.1	16.7	9.1
Asia	8.3	11.8	6.6	7.8	7.0	10.4	14.7	11.8	6.6	6.2	6.5
Excluding China and India	9.9	8.3	9.8	11.0	7.6	7.8	7.9	8.5	7.4	5.9	6.6
Middle East and Europe	19.0	21.4	22.1	25.3	26.6	24.7	32.4	33.8	24.5	21.0	19.1
Western Hemisphere	93.6	340.0	442.9	129.8	153.2	212.6	213.7	36.0	20.4	12.9	9.3
Analytical groups											
By source of export earnings											
Fuel	12.4	20.9	14.1	18.9	23.9	25.5	33.9	38.8	30.3	14.5	7.8
Manufactures	33.7	89.3	98.4	41.7	57.6	78.9	83.9	18.5	7.0	6.4	6.5
Nonfuel primary products	44.2	120.1	144.0	82.4	42.7	33.4	37.0	23.7	20.2	13.4	7.9
Services, factor income, and private transfers	15.9	19.4	22.0	21.5	19.6	13.6	14.2	12.3	9.2	6.6	5.8
Diversified	40.1	49.1	48.0	29.1	18.9	16.1	16.6	21.4	19.3	14.8	13.5
By external financing source											
Net creditor countries	3.4	1.7	3.2	6.4	3.8	4.2	3.4	4.7	2.1	1.8	1.8
Net debtor countries	33.1	67.8	71.1	37.1	40.2	48.7	53.2	21.8	13.4	9.9	8.7
Official financing	17.8	22.6	18.0	25.5	23.5	22.0	27.3	21.4	14.9	10.1	6.7
Private financing	46.1	111.2	117.0	49.5	56.2	70.8	77.3	25.5	14.3	10.8	9.3
Diversified financing	12.7	9.8	13.2	14.8	12.0	11.6	11.6	12.6	10.5	7.7	7.8
Net debtor countries by debt-servicing experience											
Countries with recent difficulties	60.7	238.2	293.7	106.2	132.0	179.2	191.8	36.3	19.0	11.3	7.5
Countries without recent difficulties	17.9	15.5	12.1	12.5	11.2	12.8	16.8	16.4	11.3	9.4	9.1
Other groups											
Heavily indebted poor countries	28.6	30.9	31.8	51.8	44.4	43.1	57.0	42.6	39.0	15.9	8.9
Least developed countries	18.4	24.9	25.5	39.7	36.0	29.0	38.4	23.5	19.3	12.4	8.2
Middle East and north Africa	13.2	12.7	14.6	17.9	19.0	15.6	19.9	19.9	12.5	9.0	6.9
Memorandum											
Median											
Developing countries	10.1	9.0	10.4	12.1	9.8	9.5	11.1	10.0	7.0	5.4	5.0
Regional groups											
Africa	10.7	9.0	10.1	10.5	10.1	9.3	24.6	12.3	8.3	6.0	4.8
Asia	8.7	8.0	9.6	12.0	8.9	8.8	7.9	8.1	6.1	5.4	5.1
Middle East and Europe	7.0	3.8	9.0	9.0	6.9	5.0	4.7	5.0	6.5	4.0	4.0
Western Hemisphere	13.0	15.2	21.8	22.7	12.1	10.7	8.3	10.2	7.1	5.5	5.0

Table A12. Developing Countries—by Country: Consumer Prices[1]

(Annual percent change)

	Average 1979–88	1989	1990	1991	1992	1993	1994	1995	1996
Africa	**15.5**	**18.8**	**15.5**	**24.6**	**32.1**	**29.5**	**38.6**	**32.1**	**24.8**
Algeria	9.2	9.2	16.7	25.9	31.7	16.1	38.4	21.9	15.1
Angola	13.1	1.8	1.8	83.6	299.1	1,379.5	949.8	2,672.0	4,182.0
Benin	3.3	−0.2	1.1	2.1	5.9	0.5	38.6	15.1	4.7
Botswana	11.8	11.6	11.3	11.8	16.1	14.3	10.6	10.5	8.6
Burkina Faso	6.4	−0.5	−0.5	2.2	−2.0	1.0	24.7	7.8	6.0
Burundi	8.2	11.7	7.0	9.0	4.5	9.7	14.7	19.4	12.0
Cameroon	8.4	1.6	1.5	−0.6	1.9	−3.7	12.7	26.9	6.4
Cape Verde	12.6	5.3	10.6	8.0	7.0	5.9	3.4	8.4	5.0
Central African Republic	7.1	0.6	−0.2	−2.8	−0.8	−2.9	24.5	19.2	3.5
Chad	6.0	−4.9	0.5	4.2	−3.8	−7.0	41.3	9.5	10.0
Comoros	6.1	5.7	1.6	1.7	−1.4	2.0	21.7	7.1	5.0
Congo	7.5	4.0	2.6	−1.6	−3.9	4.9	42.9	8.6	10.6
Côte d'Ivoire	8.5	1.0	−0.7	1.6	4.2	2.1	25.8	14.3	6.6
Djibouti	5.7	3.0	7.8	6.8	3.4	4.4	6.5	4.9	4.0
Equatorial Guinea	18.8	7.2	0.7	4.9	−3.2	0.3	38.9	11.4	6.0
Ethiopia	6.3	2.2	9.6	20.8	23.0	10.1	1.2	13.4	0.9
Gabon	6.3	6.6	6.0	3.3	−10.8	0.6	36.1	10.0	5.1
Gambia, The	16.2	10.8	10.2	9.1	12.0	5.9	4.0	4.0	4.8
Ghana	47.3	25.3	37.2	18.0	10.1	24.9	24.9	59.5	45.6
Guinea	31.4	28.3	19.4	19.6	16.6	7.1	4.2	5.6	5.0
Guinea-Bissau	52.1	80.8	33.0	57.6	69.4	48.2	15.2	45.4	50.7
Kenya	11.5	7.6	11.2	19.6	27.3	46.0	28.8	1.7	9.0
Lesotho	14.7	14.7	11.6	17.7	17.2	13.1	8.2	9.3	8.9
Liberia	6.1	25.3	10.0	10.0	10.0	10.0	10.0	10.0	10.0
Madagascar	18.8	9.0	11.8	8.5	15.3	9.2	39.1	49.0	19.7
Malawi	16.9	12.5	11.9	8.2	23.2	22.8	34.7	83.1	37.7
Mali	3.7	−0.2	1.6	1.5	−5.9	−0.6	24.8	12.4	7.0
Mauritania	8.7	9.0	6.4	5.6	10.1	9.3	4.1	6.5	3.0
Mauritius	10.4	16.0	10.7	12.8	2.9	8.9	9.4	6.1	5.8
Morocco	8.1	3.1	7.0	8.0	5.7	5.2	5.1	6.1	3.0
Mozambique, Rep. of	32.2	42.1	43.7	33.3	45.1	42.3	63.1	54.4	44.6
Namibia	12.9	15.5	12.0	11.9	17.7	8.5	10.8	10.0	8.0
Niger	4.8	−0.8	−2.0	−1.9	−1.7	−0.4	35.6	10.9	4.7
Nigeria	16.6	50.5	7.4	13.0	44.6	57.2	57.0	70.0	29.3
Rwanda	6.1	1.0	4.2	19.6	9.5	12.4	64.0	22.0	8.9
São Tomé and Príncipe	10.4	42.9	42.2	46.5	33.7	31.8	48.0	64.5	25.3
Senegal	7.6	0.4	0.3	−1.8	−0.1	−0.7	32.1	8.1	3.0
Seychelles	5.0	1.5	3.9	2.0	3.2	1.3	1.8	0.2	−1.0
Sierra Leone	53.4	60.8	110.9	102.7	65.5	17.6	18.4	29.8	28.8
Somalia	44.5	110.4	...	...	...	...	...	...	...
South Africa	14.5	14.8	14.4	15.2	13.9	9.7	9.0	8.6	7.4
Sudan	32.3	65.3	56.0	111.0	110.0	103.0	118.0	57.0	85.0
Swaziland	14.3	6.3	13.6	11.0	8.2	11.3	13.8	12.3	11.0
Tanzania	28.6	31.2	30.4	31.7	24.8	23.8	30.2	34.0	25.7
Togo	5.6	−1.2	1.1	0.3	1.6	−0.1	35.3	15.7	5.0
Tunisia	8.7	7.7	6.5	8.2	5.8	4.0	4.7	6.3	5.0
Uganda	106.7	45.4	24.5	42.2	30.0	6.5	6.1	7.4	5.0
Zaïre	57.3	104.1	81.3	2,154.4	4,129.2	1,893.1	23,760.5	541.8	610.6
Zambia	26.7	123.3	107.0	97.7	165.7	183.3	54.6	34.9	43.1
Zimbabwe	12.9	12.8	17.4	23.3	42.1	27.6	22.3	22.6	21.4

146

Table A12 *(continued)*

	Average 1979–88	1989	1990	1991	1992	1993	1994	1995	1996
Asia	**8.3**	**11.8**	**6.6**	**7.8**	**7.0**	**10.4**	**14.7**	**11.8**	**6.6**
Afghanistan, Islamic State of	15.1	89.8	157.8	166.0	58.2	34.0	20.0	14.0	14.0
Bangladesh	11.7	8.7	6.0	6.3	3.5	3.1	6.3	6.3	3.5
Bhutan	9.2	8.5	9.4	13.3	16.0	8.9	8.1	10.7	7.0
Cambodia	...	55.3	141.8	197.0	75.0	114.5	−0.5	7.8	6.0
China	5.6	17.8	2.1	2.7	5.4	13.0	21.7	14.8	6.0
Fiji	7.5	5.7	11.9	6.1	8.2	6.5	4.9	5.2	0.6
India	9.1	6.5	9.9	13.0	9.8	8.8	9.8	10.2	7.0
Indonesia	11.1	6.4	7.8	9.4	7.5	9.7	8.5	9.4	7.9
Kiribati	6.9	5.3	3.8	5.7	4.0	6.1	5.1	6.5	4.0
Lao P.D. Republic	47.7	59.7	35.7	13.4	9.8	6.3	6.8	25.7	7.5
Malaysia	2.2	2.6	2.8	2.6	4.7	3.5	3.7	3.4	3.5
Maldives	11.1	7.2	3.6	14.7	16.8	20.2	16.5	5.4	3.5
Marshall Islands	...	2.2	0.7	4.0	10.3	5.0	5.6	7.3	4.0
Micronesia, Fed. States of	...	4.5	3.5	4.0	5.0	6.0	4.0	4.0	4.0
Myanmar	8.4	23.8	21.9	29.1	22.3	33.6	22.4	28.9	20.0
Nepal	7.7	11.5	9.8	21.0	8.9	8.9	7.6	7.0	7.0
Pakistan	6.8	7.2	9.7	11.8	9.5	9.6	11.8	12.1	10.3
Papua New Guinea	6.4	4.5	7.0	7.0	4.3	5.0	2.9	17.3	11.6
Philippines	15.0	10.6	12.7	18.7	8.9	7.6	9.0	8.1	8.4
Solomon Islands	11.0	14.9	8.6	10.8	9.2	10.4	17.1	9.8	7.2
Sri Lanka	12.6	11.6	21.5	12.2	11.4	11.7	8.4	7.7	14.0
Thailand	6.1	5.5	6.0	5.7	4.1	3.3	5.0	5.8	5.8
Vanuatu	8.3	7.5	5.0	5.6	4.1	1.7	2.7	1.7	2.5
Vietnam	118.4	35.0	67.0	68.1	17.5	5.2	14.5	12.8	6.0
Western Samoa	13.7	6.4	15.2	8.5	1.7	18.4	1.0	7.0	3.5
Middle East and Europe	**19.0**	**21.4**	**22.1**	**25.3**	**26.6**	**24.7**	**32.4**	**33.8**	**24.5**
Bahrain	2.2	1.2	1.3	1.0	—	2.1	0.4	3.1	1.2
Cyprus	6.3	3.8	4.5	5.0	6.5	4.9	4.7	3.1	3.0
Egypt	16.3	20.2	21.2	19.5	21.1	11.2	9.0	9.4	7.2
Iran, Islamic Republic of	18.9	17.4	9.0	20.7	24.4	22.9	35.2	49.4	23.0
Iraq	18.0	15.0	50.0	50.0	50.0	75.0	60.0	50.0	30.0
Jordan	5.8	25.7	16.1	8.2	4.0	3.3	3.5	2.4	6.5
Kuwait	3.4	3.3	1.8	16.9	5.7	0.4	2.5	0.7	0.9
Lebanon	63.4	72.2	68.8	51.5	120.0	24.7	8.0	10.6	9.5
Libya	9.8	1.3	8.6	11.7	18.0	23.0	17.0	10.0	7.0
Malta	4.1	0.8	3.0	2.5	1.6	4.1	4.1	4.0	3.8
Oman	2.5	1.6	10.0	4.6	1.0	1.2	−0.7	−1.3	2.0
Qatar	4.3	3.3	3.0	4.4	3.1	−0.9	1.3	1.2	3.0
Saudi Arabia	0.4	1.0	2.1	4.6	−0.4	0.8	0.6	5.0	1.0
Syrian Arab Republic	20.9	10.0	11.1	9.0	11.0	13.2	15.0	8.0	8.0
Turkey	49.5	63.3	60.3	66.0	70.1	66.1	106.3	93.6	82.3
United Arab Emirates	5.9	3.3	0.6	5.5	6.9	5.0	3.9	4.8	3.3
Yemen Arab Republic, former	13.8	19.4	14.0	...	...	...	...	...	...
Yemen, former P.D. Republic of	5.7	—	2.1	...	...	...	...	...	...
Yemen, Republic of	...	...	...	44.9	50.6	62.3	71.8	48.0	29.0

Table A12 *(concluded)*

	Average 1979–88	1989	1990	1991	1992	1993	1994	1995	1996
Western Hemisphere	**93.6**	**340.0**	**442.9**	**129.8**	**153.2**	**212.6**	**213.7**	**36.0**	**20.4**
Antigua and Barbuda	6.7	3.7	7.0	5.7	3.0	3.1	3.5	2.9	1.7
Argentina	226.0	3,080.5	2,314.7	171.7	24.9	10.6	4.2	3.4	0.1
Aruba	. . .	4.0	5.8	5.6	3.9	5.2	5.2	5.2	5.2
Bahamas, The	6.6	5.4	4.6	7.1	5.7	2.7	1.3	2.2	1.5
Barbados	7.9	6.3	3.0	6.3	6.1	1.1	0.1	1.9	2.4
Belize	3.0	2.1	3.0	5.6	2.8	1.6	2.3	2.9	2.4
Bolivia	231.5	15.2	17.1	21.4	12.1	8.5	7.9	10.2	10.4
Brazil[2]	33.3	1,319.9	2,740.0	413.3	991.4	2,103.3	2,124.0	. . .	11.1
Chile	22.8	17.0	26.0	21.8	15.4	12.7	11.4	8.2	7.4
Colombia	23.6	25.9	29.1	30.4	27.0	22.4	22.8	20.9	20.8
Costa Rica	24.7	16.5	19.0	28.7	21.8	9.8	13.5	23.2	17.6
Dominica	8.6	6.9	−30.3	5.5	5.5	1.6	—	1.3	1.7
Dominican Republic	16.9	40.7	50.5	47.1	4.3	5.2	8.3	12.5	5.4
Ecuador	26.3	75.7	48.4	48.8	54.6	45.0	27.3	23.0	24.4
El Salvador	17.8	17.6	24.0	14.4	11.2	18.5	10.6	10.1	9.8
Grenada	8.4	5.6	2.8	2.6	3.8	2.8	2.6	2.2	2.8
Guatemala	12.4	13.0	41.0	35.1	10.2	13.4	12.5	8.4	10.6
Guyana	20.4	89.7	63.6	101.5	28.2	11.7	13.6	12.3	7.1
Haiti	7.5	11.0	20.4	19.0	21.3	18.8	37.4	30.2	21.9
Honduras	7.7	7.0	21.2	26.0	9.1	10.7	22.5	18.5	8.3
Jamaica	18.1	16.1	24.8	68.6	57.5	24.5	31.7	21.7	21.5
Mexico	64.8	20.0	26.7	22.7	15.5	9.8	7.0	35.0	34.1
Netherlands Antilles	5.5	3.8	3.7	3.8	1.5	1.9	1.9	2.7	3.5
Nicaragua	244.8	4,709.3	3,127.5	7,755.3	40.5	20.4	7.7	11.2	6.8
Panama	3.6	0.2	1.9	1.4	1.8	0.5	1.3	0.9	2.0
Paraguay	20.5	26.0	38.2	24.3	15.1	18.3	20.6	13.4	8.2
Peru	116.6	3,398.7	7,481.6	409.5	73.5	48.6	23.7	11.2	11.5
St. Kitts and Nevis	4.6	5.1	4.2	4.2	2.8	1.8	2.6	1.7	1.0
St. Lucia	5.9	4.4	3.8	6.2	5.6	0.8	2.6	5.9	3.3
St. Vincent and the Grenadines	7.3	2.7	7.3	5.9	3.8	4.3	0.4	2.4	4.5
Suriname	13.6	0.8	21.8	26.0	43.7	143.4	368.5	235.9	3.0
Trinidad and Tobago	12.8	4.6	11.0	3.8	6.5	11.1	5.6	5.3	3.6
Uruguay	55.2	80.4	112.5	101.8	68.5	54.1	44.7	42.3	28.3
Venezuela	15.6	84.5	40.7	34.2	31.4	38.1	60.8	59.9	99.9

[1]For many countries, figures for recent years are IMF staff estimates. Data for some countries are for fiscal years.

[2]Data are based on a price index of domestic demand, which is a weighted average of the consumer price index, the wholesale price index, and a price index for construction activity. The year-on-year increase in 1995 in this price index was 59.6 percent, which largely was the result of carryover effects from the high inflation rate prevailing prior to the introduction of the real on July 1, 1994. Consequently, the inflation rate from December 1994 to December 1995, which was 14.8 percent, better reflects the underlying inflation rate during 1995.

Table A13. Countries in Transition: Consumer Prices[1]
(Annual percent change)

	Average 1979–88	1989	1990	1991	1992	1993	1994	1995	1996
Central and eastern Europe	...	...	...	**95.0**	**263.7**	**307.0**	**141.0**	**70.5**	**33.1**
Albania	—	—	—	35.8	225.2	85.0	22.6	7.8	12.7
Belarus	...	...	...	83.5	969.0	1,188.0	2,220.0	709.0	52.0
Bulgaria	1.9	6.4	23.9	333.5	82.0	72.8	96.0	62.1	123.0
Croatia	...	...	...	...	...	1,516.0	97.5	1.6	3.5
Czech Republic	...	...	...	...	...	20.8	10.0	9.1	9.0
Czechoslovakia, former	1.8	1.4	10.8	59.0	11.0	...	...	...	...
Estonia	...	...	...	210.6	1,069.0	89.0	39.8	28.9	23.1
Hungary	8.1	16.9	29.0	34.2	23.0	22.5	18.8	28.2	23.6
Latvia	...	...	...	124.4	951.3	109.1	35.9	25.1	18.8
Lithuania	...	...	...	224.7	1,020.5	410.4	72.1	39.5	24.7
Macedonia, former Yugoslav Rep. of	...	...	...	...	...	334.5	126.5	16.1	2.5
Moldova	...	...	...	162.0	1,276.0	788.5	329.6	30.2	23.5
Poland	27.2	251.1	585.8	70.3	43.0	35.3	32.2	27.8	19.9
Romania	3.6	—	5.1	161.1	210.4	256.1	136.7	32.3	38.8
Slovak Republic	...	...	...	...	...	23.0	13.4	9.9	6.0
Slovenia	...	...	...	...	...	32.3	19.8	12.6	9.7
Ukraine	...	...	...	91.2	1,209.7	4,734.9	891.0	376.0	80.0
Yugoslavia, former	63.2	1,239.9	583.1	117.4	6,146.6	...	...	...	...
Russia	...	...	...	**92.7**	**1,353.0**	**699.8**	**302.0**	**190.1**	**47.8**
Transcaucasus and central Asia	...	...	...	**114.0**	**880.2**	**1,096.1**	**1,532.6**	**260.2**	**70.0**
Armenia	...	...	...	100.3	824.5	3,731.8	5,273.4	176.7	18.6
Azerbaijan	...	...	...	105.6	912.6	1,129.7	1,664.4	411.7	19.8
Georgia	...	...	...	78.5	887.4	3,125.4	15,606.5	162.6	40.2
Kazakstan	...	...	...	91.0	1,381.0	1,662.3	1,879.9	176.3	39.1
Kyrgyz Republic	...	...	...	85.0	854.6	772.4	228.7	52.5	30.4
Mongolia	0.2	—	—	20.2	202.6	268.4	87.6	56.8	50.0
Tajikistan	...	...	...	111.6	1,156.7	2,194.9	350.4	610.0	443.0
Turkmenistan	...	...	...	102.5	492.9	3,102.4	1,748.0	1,005.0	992.0
Uzbekistan	...	...	...	169.0	645.2	534.0	1,568.0	304.6	54.0

[1]For many countries, inflation for the earlier years is measured based on a retail price index. Consumer price indices with a broader and more up-to-date coverage are typically used for more recent years.

Table A14. Summary Financial Indicators

(In percent)

	1989	1990	1991	1992	1993	1994	1995	1996	1997	1998
Advanced economies										
Central government fiscal balance[1]										
Advanced economies	−2.1	−2.5	−3.0	−4.0	−4.2	−3.6	−3.1	−2.6	−2.0	−1.8
United States	−2.4	−3.0	−3.5	−4.7	−3.9	−2.7	−2.1	−1.4	−1.5	−1.3
European Union	−2.9	−3.5	−3.8	−4.9	−5.9	−5.3	−4.4	−3.9	−2.7	−2.5
Japan	−1.2	−0.5	−0.2	−1.7	−2.7	−3.5	−4.2	−4.3	−3.5	−3.3
Other advanced economies	−0.2	−0.6	−1.9	−2.2	−2.1	−1.3	−0.9	−0.8	—	0.3
General government fiscal balance[1]										
Advanced economies	−1.1	−2.0	−2.7	−3.7	−4.2	−3.4	−3.2	−2.7	−2.0	−1.8
United States	−1.7	−2.7	−3.3	−4.4	−3.6	−2.3	−2.0	−1.4	−1.5	−1.3
European Union	−2.4	−3.6	−4.4	−5.3	−6.5	−5.8	−5.2	−4.4	−3.1	−2.9
Japan	2.5	2.9	2.9	1.5	−1.6	−2.3	−3.7	−4.6	−2.9	−2.7
Other advanced economies	0.1	−0.9	−2.3	−3.3	−2.6	−0.9	−0.3	−0.1	0.4	0.7
General government structural balance[1]										
Advanced economies	−2.6	−3.5	−3.3	−3.7	−3.4	−2.9	−2.7	−2.2	−1.5	−1.5
Growth of broad money										
Advanced economies	9.4	8.2	5.8	3.2	3.9	2.5	4.4	5.0	...	...
United States	5.2	4.1	3.1	1.8	1.3	0.6	4.0	4.6	...	...
European Union	10.3	11.6	9.5	4.7	6.0	2.2	4.4	5.6	...	...
Japan	12.0	7.4	2.3	−0.2	2.2	2.8	3.3	3.2	...	...
Other advanced economies	17.3	11.9	8.7	8.2	8.0	9.3	8.2	7.6	...	...
Short-term interest rates[2]										
United States	8.1	7.5	5.4	3.4	3.0	4.2	5.5	5.1	5.5	5.6
Japan	4.7	6.9	7.0	4.1	2.7	1.9	1.0	0.3	0.6	2.0
Germany	7.1	8.4	9.2	9.5	7.2	5.3	4.5	3.3	3.3	3.9
LIBOR	9.3	8.4	6.1	3.9	3.4	5.1	6.1	5.6	6.0	6.1
Developing countries										
Central government fiscal balance[1]										
Weighted average	−4.6	−3.2	−3.6	−2.9	−3.3	−2.6	−2.4	−2.2	−1.5	−1.3
Median	−4.5	−3.9	−4.0	−3.7	−4.2	−4.0	−3.7	−2.9	−2.0	−1.6
General government fiscal balance[1]										
Weighted average	−5.5	−3.9	−3.9	−3.6	−3.8	−3.0	−3.0	−2.9	−2.0	−2.0
Median	−4.8	−3.9	−3.8	−3.9	−4.2	−3.9	−3.5	−2.3	−1.7	−1.3
Growth of broad money										
Weighted average	101.3	96.6	77.2	84.3	83.6	69.7	25.7	22.8	18.6	16.4
Median	16.5	17.9	18.8	17.6	16.3	18.8	16.1	13.4	11.8	10.2
Countries in transition										
Central government fiscal balance[1]	−2.6	−4.4	−9.1	−10.4	−6.2	−7.2	−3.8	−3.4	−3.4	−2.5
General government fiscal balance[1]	−2.4	−4.0	−9.2	−13.6	−6.4	−6.9	−3.9	−4.0	−3.8	−2.6
Growth of broad money	99.1	23.6	117.9	939.2	267.3	142.5	65.4	24.6	23.9	17.3

[1]In percent of GDP.
[2]For the United States, three-month treasury bills; for Japan, three-month certificates of deposit; for Germany, three-month interbank deposits; for LIBOR, London interbank offered rate on six-month U.S. dollar deposits.

Table A15. Advanced Economies: General and Central Government Fiscal Balances and Balances Excluding Social Security Transactions[1]

(In percent of GDP)

	1989	1990	1991	1992	1993	1994	1995	1996	1997	1998
General government fiscal balance										
Advanced economies	**−1.1**	**−2.0**	**−2.7**	**−3.7**	**−4.2**	**−3.4**	**−3.2**	**−2.7**	**−2.0**	**−1.8**
Major industrial countries	−1.2	−2.1	−2.7	−3.8	−4.3	−3.5	−3.4	−3.0	−2.3	−2.1
United States	−1.7	−2.7	−3.3	−4.4	−3.6	−2.3	−2.0	−1.4	−1.5	−1.3
Japan	2.5	2.9	2.9	1.5	−1.6	−2.3	−3.7	−4.6	−2.9	−2.7
Germany[2]	0.1	−2.0	−3.3	−2.8	−3.5	−2.4	−3.5	−3.8	−3.3	−2.9
France[3]	−1.1	−1.4	−2.0	−4.0	−5.8	−5.8	−5.0	−4.1	−3.3	−3.4
Italy[4]	−9.9	−11.0	−10.2	−9.5	−9.6	−9.0	−7.1	−6.8	−3.3	−4.1
United Kingdom[5]	0.9	−1.2	−2.5	−6.3	−7.8	−6.8	−5.6	−4.4	−3.1	−2.1
Canada	−2.9	−4.1	−6.6	−7.4	−7.3	−5.3	−4.1	−1.8	−0.3	0.3
Other advanced economies	−0.8	−1.7	−2.6	−3.5	−4.0	−2.8	−2.3	−1.6	−0.9	−0.6
Spain	−2.8	−3.9	−5.0	−4.1	−7.5	−6.2	−6.6	−4.4	−3.2	−3.0
Netherlands	−4.7	−5.1	−2.9	−3.9	−3.2	−3.4	−4.0	−2.3	−2.2	−1.8
Belgium	−6.4	−5.6	−6.6	−7.2	−7.4	−5.1	−4.1	−3.4	−2.9	−2.6
Sweden	5.4	4.2	−1.1	−7.8	−12.3	−10.3	−7.9	−2.5	−0.8	0.3
Austria	−2.8	−2.2	−2.7	−1.9	−4.2	−4.8	−5.3	−3.9	−2.5	−2.8
Denmark	−0.5	−1.5	−2.1	−2.9	−3.9	−3.4	−1.9	−1.6	−0.1	—
Finland	6.3	5.3	−1.5	−5.9	−8.0	−6.2	−5.2	−2.6	−1.9	−0.7
Greece	−14.4	−16.1	−11.5	−12.3	−14.2	−12.1	−9.2	−7.6	−5.1	−3.5
Portugal	−2.3	−5.5	−6.6	−3.5	−6.8	−5.7	−4.9	−4.0	−2.9	−2.5
Ireland	−1.8	−2.3	−2.2	−2.4	−2.2	−2.0	−2.4	−1.0	−1.6	−1.6
Luxembourg	4.6	5.0	−0.4	−0.8	0.5	0.9	0.4	−0.1	−0.1	−0.1
Switzerland	0.8	—	−2.1	−3.5	−3.7	−2.8	−1.8	−2.2	−2.9	−2.5
Norway	3.6	4.2	2.1	−1.7	−1.4	0.4	3.3	6.3	6.3	7.3
Israel	−5.8	−4.5	−4.4	−3.1	−2.3	−1.2	−3.1	−4.2	−3.2	−2.5
Iceland	−4.6	−3.3	−2.9	−2.8	−4.5	−4.7	−3.1	−1.7	−1.0	−0.7
Korea[6]	0.2	−0.6	−1.6	−2.6	−1.0	3.3	3.0	1.0	1.0	1.0
Australia[7]	1.5	0.5	−2.2	−4.4	−4.5	−3.4	−2.1	−1.5	−0.9	−0.1
Taiwan Province of China	3.6	0.8	0.5	0.3	0.6	0.2	0.4	0.2	0.2	0.2
Hong Kong	2.1	0.7	3.2	2.5	2.3	1.3	−0.3	0.3	1.8	1.5
Singapore	9.9	11.4	10.3	11.3	14.3	14.2	12.7	8.6	8.9	7.8
New Zealand[8]	−1.8	−2.3	−2.3	−4.6	−0.7	2.2	3.7	3.2	2.7	3.2
Memorandum										
Industrial countries	−1.3	−2.2	−2.8	−3.9	−4.5	−3.8	−3.5	−3.0	−2.2	−2.0
European Union	−2.4	−3.6	−4.4	−5.3	−6.5	−5.8	−5.2	−4.4	−3.1	−2.9
Newly industrialized Asian economies	2.2	0.7	0.4	−0.2	0.9	2.7	2.3	1.1	1.4	1.2
Fiscal balance excluding social security transactions										
United States	−4.3	−5.2	−5.5	−6.3	−5.3	−4.1	−4.0	−3.7	−3.7	−3.6
Japan	−0.7	−0.6	−0.7	−2.0	−4.8	−5.4	−6.5	−7.3	−5.5	−4.9
Germany[2]	−0.6	−2.9	−4.0	−2.8	−3.7	−2.6	−3.2	−3.5	−3.3	−2.9
France	−1.4	−1.5	−1.8	−3.2	−4.3	−4.8	−4.1	−3.5	−2.8	−2.9
Italy[4]	−4.7	−5.6	−5.1	−3.9	−5.0	−4.2	−2.7	−2.3	1.0	0.4
Canada	−1.3	−2.4	−4.8	−5.3	−5.0	−3.0	−1.9	0.5	1.9	2.4

Table A15 *(concluded)*

	1989	1990	1991	1992	1993	1994	1995	1996	1997	1998
Central government fiscal balance										
Advanced economies	**−2.1**	**−2.5**	**−3.0**	**−4.0**	**−4.2**	**−3.6**	**−3.1**	**−2.6**	**−2.0**	**−1.8**
Major industrial countries	−2.3	−2.8	−3.0	−4.2	−4.3	−3.7	−3.2	−2.8	−2.2	−2.0
United States[9]	−2.4	−3.0	−3.5	−4.7	−3.9	−2.7	−2.1	−1.4	−1.5	−1.3
Japan[10]	−1.2	−0.5	−0.2	−1.7	−2.7	−3.5	−4.2	−4.3	−3.5	−3.3
Germany[2,11]	−0.9	−2.0	−1.9	−1.3	−2.1	−1.5	−1.5	−2.2	−1.7	−1.5
France[11]	−1.3	−1.4	−1.6	−2.9	−4.2	−4.6	−3.9	−3.5	−2.7	−3.0
Italy[4]	−10.7	−10.2	−10.3	−10.4	−10.0	−9.5	−7.4	−7.0	−3.3	−3.9
United Kingdom	1.2	−1.1	−2.3	−7.0	−8.0	−6.6	−5.2	−4.5	−3.2	−2.3
Canada	−3.2	−3.9	−4.5	−4.2	−4.9	−3.8	−3.4	−2.0	−0.7	−0.1
Other advanced economies	−1.2	−1.6	−2.6	−3.2	−3.9	−3.1	−2.5	−1.9	−1.2	−0.9
Memorandum										
Industrial countries	−2.3	−2.7	−3.1	−4.2	−4.5	−3.8	−3.3	−2.8	−2.2	−1.9
European Union	−2.9	−3.5	−3.8	−4.9	−5.9	−5.3	−4.4	−3.9	−2.7	−2.5
Newly industrialized Asian economies	1.5	1.2	−0.3	−0.3	0.4	0.9	0.8	—	0.7	0.6

[1]On a national income accounts basis except as indicated in footnotes. See Box 1 for a summary of the policy assumptions underlying the projections.
[2]Data through 1990 apply to west Germany only.
[3]Adjusted for valuation changes of the foreign exchange stabilization fund.
[4]Data from 1996 onward reflect a new accounting methodology.
[5]Excludes asset sales.
[6]Data include social security transactions, i.e., the operations of the public pension plan.
[7]Data exclude net advances, primarily privatization receipts and net policy-related lending.
[8]Data from 1992 onward are on an accrual basis and not strictly comparable with previous cash-based data.
[9]Data are on a budget basis.
[10]Data are on a national income basis and exclude social security transactions.
[11]Data are on an administrative basis and exclude social security transactions.

Table A16. Advanced Economies: General Government Structural Balances[1]

(In percent of potential GDP)

	1989	1990	1991	1992	1993	1994	1995	1996	1997	1998
Structural balance[2]										
Advanced economies	**−2.6**	**−3.5**	**−3.3**	**−3.7**	**−3.4**	**−2.9**	**−2.7**	**−2.2**	**−1.6**	**−1.5**
Major industrial countries	−2.6	−3.4	−3.1	−3.5	−3.3	−2.7	−2.6	−2.2	−1.6	−1.6
United States	−3.0	−3.8	−3.1	−4.1	−3.4	−2.5	−2.1	−1.6	−1.9	−1.7
Japan	1.4	1.4	1.5	0.9	−1.1	−1.1	−2.0	−3.3	−1.7	−1.6
Germany[3]	—	−3.2	−5.2	−3.8	−2.3	−1.2	−2.2	−1.8	−1.1	−1.2
France	−2.3	−2.7	−2.4	−3.5	−3.3	−3.7	−3.2	−1.9	−1.4	−1.8
Italy[4]	−11.4	−12.4	−11.2	−9.6	−8.1	−7.6	−6.2	−5.4	−1.7	−2.7
United Kingdom	−2.0	−3.7	−2.7	−3.8	−4.3	−3.9	−3.6	−2.9	−2.1	−1.5
Canada	−5.1	−4.9	−4.9	−4.8	−4.6	−3.6	−2.7	—	0.9	1.0
Other advanced economies	−3.0	−4.2	−4.7	−4.6	−4.3	−3.8	−3.6	−1.9	−1.2	−1.0
Spain	−5.0	−7.0	−8.0	−5.9	−5.7	−4.9	−5.3	−3.2	−2.0	−2.4
Netherlands	−4.3	−5.8	−3.6	−4.3	−2.6	−3.1	−3.6	−2.2	−2.5	−2.4
Belgium	−7.1	−7.2	−7.9	−8.2	−6.3	−4.2	−3.3	−2.4	−2.1	−2.0
Sweden	1.5	0.3	−2.8	−6.5	−7.0	−7.1	−6.7	−0.7	0.6	1.3
Austria	−3.9	−3.6	−3.9	−2.5	−3.8	−4.8	−5.1	−3.3	−1.7	−2.3
Denmark	0.1	−0.6	−1.3	−0.8	−0.9	−1.6	−1.6	−1.0	0.3	0.3
Finland	3.3	2.3	0.1	−1.1	−1.4	−1.3	−2.3	−0.6	−0.8	−0.1
Greece	−15.4	−16.2	−12.0	−12.4	−13.1	−10.9	−8.1	−6.7	−4.6	−3.3
Portugal	−3.4	−7.1	−8.1	−4.8	−6.4	−4.5	−3.7	−3.0	−2.2	−2.1
Ireland	−1.8	−3.8	−2.0	−1.3	0.1	—	−2.3	−1.0	−1.6	−1.5
Norway	4.4	5.7	3.9	0.2	0.2	1.0	3.5	6.2	5.8	6.5
Australia[5]	0.5	—	−1.1	−2.6	−2.8	−2.6	−1.6	−1.2	−0.8	−0.1
New Zealand[6]	−4.3	−6.9	−4.8	−2.2	0.6	2.2	3.3	3.2	2.5	3.2
Memorandum										
European Union[7]	−3.7	−5.3	−5.4	−5.1	−4.5	−4.0	−3.9	−2.8	−1.6	−1.8

[1]On a national income accounts basis.

[2]The structural budget position is defined as the actual budget deficit (or surplus) less the effects of cyclical deviations of output from potential output. Because of the margin of uncertainty that attaches to estimates of cyclical gaps and to tax and expenditure elasticities with respect to national income, indicators of structural budget positions should be interpreted as broad orders of magnitude. Moreover, it is important to note that changes in structural budget balances are not necessarily attributable to policy changes but may reflect the built-in momentum of existing expenditure programs. In the period beyond that for which specific consolidation programs exist, it is assumed that the structural deficit remains unchanged.

[3]Data through 1990 apply to west Germany only. The estimate of the fiscal impulse for 1995 is affected by the assumption by the federal government of the debt of the Treuhandanstalt and various other agencies, which were formerly held outside the general government sector. At the public sector level, there would be an estimated withdrawal of fiscal impulse amounting to just over 1 percent of GDP.

[4]Data from 1996 onward reflect a new accounting methodology.

[5]Excludes commonwealth government privatization receipts.

[6]Excludes privatization proceeds.

[7]Excludes Luxembourg.

Table A17. Advanced Economies: Monetary Aggregates

(Annual percent change)[1]

	1989	1990	1991	1992	1993	1994	1995	1996
Narrow money[2]								
Advanced economies	**4.0**	**6.8**	**7.1**	**8.2**	**8.8**	**4.2**	**5.3**	**3.9**
Major industrial countries	3.1	6.5	6.6	8.3	8.4	3.7	4.7	3.4
United States	0.5	4.1	7.9	14.4	10.6	2.5	−1.6	−4.6
Japan	2.4	4.5	9.5	3.9	7.0	4.2	13.1	9.7
Germany[3]	5.6	29.6	3.4	10.8	8.5	5.2	6.8	12.4
France	7.7	3.9	−4.7	−0.2	1.4	2.8	7.7	0.4
Italy	10.3	6.6	10.5	0.7	7.6	3.3	1.3	3.6
United Kingdom	5.7	2.7	3.0	2.8	6.0	6.8	5.6	7.0
Canada	3.3	−0.9	5.5	5.7	14.6	6.9	5.9	17.2
Other advanced economies	9.9	8.1	10.2	7.2	11.2	6.9	8.6	6.7
Memorandum								
Industrial countries	3.6	6.7	6.6	8.0	8.5	4.0	5.0	4.1
European Union	7.5	11.7	4.0	3.7	6.5	4.5	6.2	7.1
Newly industrialized Asian economies	13.2	4.4	25.5	12.8	17.6	11.2	11.7	−1.5
Broad money[4]								
Advanced economies	**9.4**	**8.2**	**5.8**	**3.2**	**3.9**	**2.5**	**4.4**	**5.0**
Major industrial countries	8.5	7.6	3.6	2.2	2.8	1.7	3.8	4.3
United States	5.2	4.1	3.1	1.8	1.3	0.6	4.0	4.6
Japan	12.0	7.4	2.3	−0.2	2.2	2.8	3.3	3.2
Germany[3]	5.5	19.7	6.3	7.6	10.9	1.6	3.6	8.7
France	9.9	9.0	2.0	5.1	−2.9	1.8	4.5	−2.4
Italy	7.3	6.1	5.8	0.1	3.8	1.0	−2.0	3.2
United Kingdom	18.9	12.2	5.6	2.7	4.9	4.0	9.9	9.4
Canada	14.5	8.2	4.5	3.1	3.2	2.7	4.0	2.2
Other advanced economies	14.6	11.3	17.4	7.8	9.6	6.7	7.6	8.3
Memorandum								
Industrial countries	9.2	8.0	5.4	2.7	3.5	2.0	4.1	4.8
European Union	10.3	11.6	9.5	4.7	6.0	2.2	4.4	5.6
Newly industrialized Asian economies	18.6	14.9	20.3	16.1	15.5	17.1	12.8	8.7

[1]Based on end-of-period data.

[2]M1 except for the United Kingdom, where M0 is used here as a measure of narrow money; it comprises notes in circulation plus bankers' operational deposits. M1 is generally currency in circulation plus private demand deposits. In addition, the United States includes traveler's checks of nonbank issues and other checkable deposits and excludes private sector float and demand deposits of banks. Japan includes government demand deposits and excludes float. Germany includes demand deposits at fixed interest rates. Canada excludes private sector float.

[3]Data through 1989 apply to west Germany only. The growth rates for the monetary aggregates in 1990 are affected by the extension of the currency area.

[4]M2, defined as M1 plus quasi-money, except for Japan, Germany, and the United Kingdom, for which the data are based on M2 plus certificates of deposit (CDs), M3, and M4, respectively. Quasi-money is essentially private term deposits and other notice deposits. The United States also includes money market mutual fund balances, money market deposit accounts, overnight repurchase agreements, and overnight Eurodollars issued to U.S. residents by foreign branches of U.S. banks. For Japan, M2 plus CDs is currency in circulation plus total private and public sector deposits and installments of Sogo Banks plus CDs. For Germany, M3 is M1 plus private time deposits with maturities of less than four years plus savings deposits at statutory notice. For Italy, M2 comprises M1 plus term deposits, passbooks from the Postal Office, and CDs with maturities of less than 18 months. For the United Kingdom, M4 is composed of non-interest-bearing M1, private sector interest-bearing sterling sight bank deposits, private sector sterling time bank deposits, private sector holdings of sterling bank CDs, private sector holdings of building society shares and deposits, and sterling CDs less building society holdings of bank deposits and bank CDs and notes and coins.

Table A18. Advanced Economies: Interest Rates

(In percent a year)

	1989	1990	1991	1992	1993	1994	1995	1996	March 1997
Policy-related interest rate[1]									
Major industrial countries	9.2	9.0	7.1	5.6	4.1	5.2	4.9	4.3	4.2
United States	8.4	7.3	4.4	2.8	3.0	5.5	5.7	5.6	5.4
Japan	6.3	8.2	6.2	3.8	2.4	2.2	0.4	0.4	0.4
Germany	7.6	8.6	9.3	8.8	6.1	4.8	3.9	3.0	3.0
France	11.2	10.1	10.8	11.0	6.5	5.3	4.7	3.3	3.2
Italy	12.6	12.3	12.7	14.5	10.5	8.8	10.7	8.3	7.1
United Kingdom	15.0	14.0	10.5	7.0	5.5	6.2	6.5	6.0	6.0
Canada	12.1	11.6	7.4	6.8	3.8	5.5	5.7	3.0	3.0
Short-term interest rate[2]									
Advanced economies	**8.6**	**9.1**	**8.2**	**6.9**	**5.4**	**4.9**	**5.2**	**4.2**	**4.7**
Major industrial countries	8.2	8.7	7.5	6.2	4.7	4.4	4.8	3.7	4.3
United States	8.1	7.5	5.4	3.4	3.0	4.2	5.5	5.1	5.5
Japan	4.7	6.9	7.0	4.1	2.7	1.9	1.0	0.3	0.4
Germany	7.1	8.4	9.2	9.5	7.2	5.3	4.5	3.3	3.2
France	9.3	10.2	9.7	10.5	8.4	5.8	6.6	3.9	3.2
Italy	12.6	12.3	12.7	14.5	10.5	8.8	10.7	8.3	7.1
United Kingdom	13.9	14.8	11.5	9.5	5.9	5.5	6.7	6.0	6.3
Canada	12.0	12.8	8.8	6.6	4.8	5.5	7.0	4.2	3.2
Other advanced economies	10.6	11.4	11.2	10.6	8.6	7.2	7.3	6.3	6.3
Memorandum									
Industrial countries	8.5	9.1	8.1	6.8	5.3	4.7	5.1	4.0	4.3
European Union	10.2	11.1	10.9	11.2	8.5	6.5	6.7	5.0	4.7
Newly industrialized Asian economies	9.9	10.9	11.4	9.7	8.4	8.8	9.0	8.5	10.9
Long-term interest rate[3]									
Advanced economies	**8.5**	**9.4**	**8.7**	**7.9**	**6.6**	**7.1**	**6.8**	**6.1**	**6.2**
Major industrial countries	8.1	9.0	8.3	7.4	6.2	6.8	6.4	5.8	5.8
United States	8.5	8.6	7.9	7.0	5.9	7.1	6.6	6.4	6.7
Japan	5.1	7.0	6.3	5.1	4.0	4.2	3.3	3.0	2.3
Germany	7.1	8.9	8.5	7.8	6.4	7.1	6.9	6.3	5.8
France	8.8	10.0	9.0	8.6	6.9	7.4	7.6	6.3	5.7
Italy[4]	13.2	13.6	13.1	13.1	11.3	10.3	11.9	9.2	7.6
United Kingdom	10.2	11.8	10.1	9.1	7.5	8.2	8.2	7.8	7.5
Canada	9.8	10.8	9.4	8.1	7.2	8.4	8.1	7.2	6.5
Other advanced economies	10.8	11.8	10.8	10.3	8.5	8.8	8.9	7.8	7.6
Memorandum									
Industrial countries	8.5	9.4	8.6	7.8	6.5	7.0	6.7	6.0	5.9
European Union	9.9	11.2	10.3	9.8	8.1	8.3	8.6	7.2	6.6
Newly industrialized Asian economies	13.5	13.8	15.0	13.6	10.9	11.1	11.0	10.8	11.2

[1]For the United States, federal funds rate; for Japan, overnight call rate; for Germany, repurchase rate; for France, day-to-day money rate; for Italy, three-month treasury bill gross rate; for the United Kingdom, base lending rate; and for Canada, overnight money market financing rate.

[2]For the United States, three-month certificates of deposit (CDs) in secondary markets; for Japan, three-month CDs; for Germany, France, and the United Kingdom, three-month interbank deposits; for Italy, three-month treasury bills gross rate; and for Canada, three-month prime corporate paper.

[3]For the United States, yield on ten-year treasury bonds; for Japan, over-the-counter sales yield on ten-year government bonds with longest residual maturity; for Germany, yield on government bonds with maturities of nine to ten years; for France, long-term (seven- to ten-year) government bond yield (Emprunts d'Etat à long terme TME); for Italy, secondary market yield on fixed-coupon (BTP) government bonds with two to four years' residual maturity; for the United Kingdom, yield on medium-dated (ten-year) government stock; and for Canada, average yield on government bonds with residual maturities of over ten years.

[4]March 1997 data refer to yield on ten-year government bonds.

Table A19. Advanced Economies: Exchange Rates

	1989	1990	1991	1992	1993	1994	1995	1996	March[1] 1997
	National currency units per U.S. dollar								
U.S. dollar nominal exchange rates									
Japanese yen	138.0	144.8	134.7	126.7	111.2	102.2	94.1	108.8	122.1
Deutsche mark	1.88	1.62	1.66	1.56	1.65	1.62	1.43	1.50	1.70
French franc	6.38	5.45	5.64	5.29	5.66	5.55	4.99	5.12	5.75
Italian lira	1,372.09	1,198.10	1,240.61	1,232.41	1,573.67	1,612.44	1,628.93	1,542.95	1,698.28
Pound sterling[2]	1.64	1.78	1.76	1.76	1.50	1.53	1.58	1.56	1.60
Canadian dollar	1.18	1.17	1.15	1.21	1.29	1.37	1.37	1.36	1.37
Spanish peseta	118.4	101.9	103.9	102.4	127.3	134.0	124.7	126.7	144.4
Dutch guilder	2.12	1.82	1.87	1.76	1.86	1.82	1.61	1.69	1.92
Belgian franc	39.4	33.4	34.1	32.1	34.6	33.5	29.5	31.0	35.1
Swedish krona	6.45	5.92	6.05	5.82	7.78	7.72	7.13	6.71	7.65
Austrian schilling	13.2	11.4	11.7	11.0	11.6	11.4	10.1	10.6	12.0
Danish krone	7.31	6.19	6.40	6.04	6.48	6.36	5.60	5.80	6.50
Finnish markka	4.29	3.82	4.04	4.48	5.71	5.22	4.37	4.59	5.09
Greek drachma	162.4	158.5	182.3	190.6	229.2	242.6	231.7	240.7	267.7
Portuguese escudo	157.5	142.6	144.5	135.0	160.8	166.0	151.1	154.2	171.1
Irish pound	0.71	0.60	0.62	0.59	0.68	0.67	0.62	0.63	0.64
Swiss franc	1.64	1.39	1.43	1.41	1.48	1.37	1.18	1.24	1.47
Norwegian krone	6.90	6.26	6.48	6.21	7.09	7.06	6.34	6.45	6.86
Israeli new sheqel	1.9	2.0	2.3	2.5	2.8	3.0	3.0	3.2	3.4
Icelandic krona	57.0	58.3	59.0	57.5	67.6	69.9	64.7	66.5	71.3
Korean won	671.5	707.8	733.4	780.7	802.7	803.4	771.3	804.5	872.6
Australian dollar	1.26	1.28	1.28	1.36	1.47	1.37	1.35	1.28	1.27
New Taiwan dollar	26.41	26.85	26.81	25.16	26.39	26.46	26.49	27.46	27.52
Hong Kong dollar	7.80	7.79	7.77	7.74	7.74	7.73	7.74	7.73	7.74
Singapore dollar	1.95	1.81	1.73	1.63	1.62	1.53	1.42	1.41	1.43
New Zealand dollar	1.67	1.68	1.73	1.86	1.85	1.69	1.52	1.45	1.43
	Annual percent change								
Real effective exchange rates[3]									
United States	3.1	−5.9	−2.4	−1.4	2.6	−1.1	−5.5	5.9	...
Japan	−4.7	−10.1	6.7	4.1	22.0	7.6	5.7	−14.7	...
Germany	−1.3	4.7	−1.0	3.6	6.7	2.3	8.1	−0.6	...
France	−1.7	2.3	−4.0	1.4	2.2	—	0.4	−2.1	...
United Kingdom	−5.3	−0.3	3.5	−3.7	−8.2	−0.8	−4.3	3.3	...
Italy	4.6	3.0	0.9	−1.4	−16.3	−6.2	−7.8	10.1	...
Canada	6.7	1.5	3.1	−7.2	−8.3	−6.7	−3.7	2.1	...
Spain	9.2	6.3	3.9	3.3	−8.2	−7.5	−3.4	0.9	...
Netherlands	−4.4	0.2	−2.2	2.6	2.8	−2.1	0.3	−5.0	...
Belgium	−0.3	3.5	−0.5	1.4	1.4	2.0	1.8	−4.2	...
Sweden	7.7	−0.1	−0.6	0.5	−24.0	−2.7	−1.8	9.9	...
Austria	−3.2	−1.9	−3.4	0.5	0.3	−2.0	−4.0	−6.4	...
Denmark	−1.2	5.4	−3.9	1.2	3.1	1.1	4.9	−0.4	...
Finland	4.4	1.3	−8.5	−18.0	−15.3	4.9	11.0	−7.0	...
Ireland	−5.3	−0.3	−6.7	−1.7	−8.1	−5.4	−5.5	−4.0	...
Switzerland	−3.9	6.4	2.6	−4.4	1.0	9.1	5.9	−0.9	...
Norway	−0.4	−0.4	−0.6	−0.2	−1.4	0.8	4.9	0.2	...

[1]March 1997 data refer to the average for March 1–18, 1997, the reference period for the exchange rate assumptions. See "Assumptions" in the introduction to this Statistical Appendix.

[2]Expressed in U.S. dollars per pound.

[3]Defined as the ratio, in common currency, of the normalized unit labor costs in the manufacturing sector to the weighted average of those of its industrial country trading partners, using 1989–91 trade weights.

Table A20. Developing Countries: Central Government Fiscal Balances
(In percent of GDP)

	1989	1990	1991	1992	1993	1994	1995	1996	1997	1998
Developing countries	**−4.6**	**−3.2**	**−3.6**	**−2.9**	**−3.3**	**−2.6**	**−2.4**	**−2.2**	**−1.5**	**−1.3**
Regional groups										
Africa	−5.4	−3.4	−4.5	−5.5	−8.7	−6.1	−4.4	−3.5	−1.5	−1.1
Sub-Sahara	−6.2	−5.2	−6.2	−7.0	−9.7	−7.0	−4.8	−4.6	−1.8	−1.2
Excluding Nigeria and South Africa	−6.8	−6.8	−6.6	−8.8	−8.2	−6.8	−5.0	−5.3	−3.6	−2.3
Asia	−3.6	−3.2	−3.0	−2.9	−2.9	−2.4	−2.1	−2.1	−1.6	−1.5
Excluding China and India	−2.4	−1.6	−1.8	−2.1	−1.9	−1.2	−0.9	−0.8	−0.5	−0.5
Middle East and Europe	−8.7	−8.4	−11.5	−5.9	−7.1	−5.8	−4.6	−4.2	−2.8	−2.8
Western Hemisphere	−3.9	−0.2	−0.2	−0.3	−0.2	−0.3	−1.3	−1.1	−0.6	−0.2
Analytical groups										
By source of export earnings										
Fuel	−6.9	−5.9	−8.3	−5.7	−8.7	−7.3	−4.8	−1.6	0.1	−0.1
Manufactures	−3.7	−2.4	−2.6	−2.7	−2.6	−1.9	−2.2	−2.3	−1.6	−1.4
Nonfuel primary products	−4.6	−4.7	−4.1	−5.0	−5.4	−4.0	−2.9	−3.3	−1.9	−1.1
Services, factor income, and private transfers	−10.4	−9.9	−12.7	−4.4	−3.9	−3.4	−2.1	−2.1	−1.3	−1.1
Diversified	−4.1	−2.0	−1.8	−1.5	−1.9	−1.9	−1.8	−2.2	−1.8	−1.6
By external financing source										
Net creditor countries	−4.6	−11.2	−19.7	−11.6	−9.1	−8.2	−5.3	−1.6	0.6	−1.9
Net debtor countries	−4.6	−2.9	−3.0	−2.6	−3.1	−2.4	−2.3	−2.3	−1.6	−1.3
Official financing	−6.6	−5.7	−6.2	−5.5	−8.1	−6.0	−4.9	−4.6	−2.5	−2.2
Private financing	−3.0	−0.9	−1.2	−1.5	−1.7	−1.3	−1.5	−1.6	−1.0	−0.7
Diversified financing	−7.5	−6.5	−6.0	−4.3	−4.7	−4.1	−3.5	−3.1	−2.6	−2.5
Net debtor countries by debt-servicing experience										
Countries with recent difficulties	−6.5	−2.7	−3.6	−2.7	−4.0	−2.9	−3.0	−2.1	−1.0	−0.4
Countries without recent difficulties	−3.5	−3.0	−2.7	−2.6	−2.7	−2.3	−2.1	−2.3	−1.8	−1.6
Other groups										
Heavily indebted poor countries	−8.6	−8.6	−7.6	−9.6	−9.0	−7.4	−5.2	−5.1	−3.5	−2.4
Least developed countries	−8.0	−7.8	−6.7	−7.4	−7.3	−7.0	−5.5	−5.7	−4.4	−3.7
Middle East and north Africa	−8.9	−7.6	−10.4	−5.8	−7.3	−6.1	−4.7	−3.1	−1.9	−2.0
Memorandum										
Median										
Developing countries	−4.5	−3.9	−4.0	−3.7	−4.2	−4.0	−3.7	−2.9	−2.0	−1.6
Regional groups										
Africa	−4.9	−4.0	−4.9	−4.8	−6.5	−5.8	−4.3	−3.4	−2.2	−1.7
Asia	−4.8	−6.9	−5.5	−5.0	−3.8	−3.4	−3.4	−2.4	−2.8	−2.5
Middle East and Europe	−6.0	−5.5	−6.9	−4.3	−6.3	−6.4	−4.2	−3.0	−3.0	−2.7
Western Hemisphere	−3.6	−1.7	−1.3	−1.6	−1.6	−1.8	−2.3	−1.7	−1.1	−0.8

Table A21. Developing Countries: Broad Money Aggregates

(Annual percent change)

	1989	1990	1991	1992	1993	1994	1995	1996	1997	1998
Developing countries	**101.3**	**96.6**	**77.2**	**84.3**	**83.6**	**69.7**	**25.7**	**22.8**	**18.6**	**16.4**
Regional groups										
Africa	15.5	18.9	27.8	34.2	27.4	40.8	24.6	19.8	15.1	12.0
Sub-Sahara	18.8	21.3	31.3	40.2	31.5	50.8	29.9	22.7	16.7	13.2
Asia	24.7	23.5	22.9	22.9	23.3	24.0	23.1	21.8	19.3	16.5
Excluding China and India	37.3	25.1	23.0	20.4	21.3	18.5	22.2	20.2	20.0	18.2
Middle East and Europe	21.4	19.3	27.2	26.0	26.2	38.3	34.6	31.1	22.9	22.1
Western Hemisphere	504.7	436.1	253.1	281.3	280.7	174.0	24.0	20.3	16.3	13.9
Analytical groups										
By source of export earnings										
Fuel	14.3	18.0	17.8	20.1	21.6	25.9	24.8	22.1	15.4	13.8
Manufactures	159.5	162.8	134.8	208.5	234.1	164.9	25.9	18.9	16.0	14.4
Nonfuel primary products	154.8	185.8	132.9	56.0	44.3	50.2	30.4	27.5	21.3	16.7
Services, factor income, and private transfers	17.5	22.7	26.1	21.0	21.2	18.9	17.0	15.3	15.4	14.2
Diversified	115.9	77.1	51.5	31.9	27.8	32.2	26.1	27.7	23.5	21.1
By external financing source										
Net creditor countries	3.7	4.2	8.1	3.0	1.9	3.5	5.8	6.2	4.8	3.9
Net debtor countries	110.5	105.1	83.3	92.1	91.5	75.7	27.2	23.9	19.4	17.1
Official financing	46.5	48.5	37.6	38.5	30.6	36.7	19.9	17.0	16.2	13.6
Private financing	180.4	167.7	122.8	134.1	133.5	102.0	28.2	24.8	20.1	17.4
Diversified financing	22.0	18.0	20.4	22.2	22.3	26.4	26.7	23.6	18.6	17.5
Net debtor countries by debt-servicing experience										
Countries with recent difficulties	265.5	256.3	178.6	232.2	243.7	162.7	24.9	21.0	16.2	14.6
Countries without recent difficulties	27.6	27.4	30.7	26.6	24.6	31.1	28.9	26.3	22.2	19.3
Other groups										
Heavily indebted poor countries	69.6	63.2	52.3	64.6	48.8	71.2	44.6	33.2	23.3	17.0
Least developed countries	26.2	34.1	54.0	54.3	43.9	43.0	28.8	23.6	20.9	17.0
Middle East and north Africa	13.5	13.6	16.7	15.2	16.5	15.7	19.4	16.9	13.8	13.9
Memorandum										
Median										
Developing countries	16.5	17.9	18.8	17.6	16.3	18.8	16.1	13.4	11.8	10.2
Regional groups										
Africa	14.7	14.8	16.0	13.5	13.2	30.1	16.8	12.4	11.8	10.1
Asia	17.9	18.4	20.5	18.7	18.7	19.8	16.2	14.9	15.1	14.9
Middle East and Europe	12.4	11.4	14.9	12.0	10.3	9.1	10.2	10.0	10.0	9.4
Western Hemisphere	18.6	27.5	33.7	24.5	17.0	18.3	20.3	12.2	11.4	10.2

Table A22. Summary of World Trade Volumes and Prices

(Annual percent change)

	Average 1979–88	1989	1990	1991	1992	1993	1994	1995	1996	1997	1998
Trade in goods and services											
World trade[1]											
Volume	4.3	7.4	5.5	3.9	5.0	4.1	9.2	9.2	5.6	7.3	6.8
Price deflator											
In U.S. dollars	4.1	1.1	9.0	−0.7	2.1	−4.2	2.3	8.4	−0.7	−3.5	0.2
In SDRs	3.4	6.0	3.0	−1.5	−0.8	−3.4	−0.2	2.3	3.7	1.5	0.6
Volume of trade											
Exports											
Advanced economies	5.0	7.8	6.7	5.7	5.2	3.4	8.9	8.4	5.0	6.9	6.7
Developing countries	2.1	6.9	6.7	4.0	10.2	7.1	12.4	11.2	7.0	11.0	8.0
Imports											
Advanced economies	5.0	8.5	5.7	3.1	4.7	1.8	9.7	8.7	5.3	5.9	6.1
Developing countries	2.7	5.3	5.9	7.9	9.2	8.8	7.2	11.6	8.3	10.7	8.4
Terms of trade											
Advanced economies	—	−0.3	−0.4	0.5	0.6	1.1	—	—	−0.1	−1.0	−0.4
Developing countries	1.0	2.2	1.8	−5.2	−2.3	−1.7	0.4	2.0	0.4	−0.9	−0.3
Trade in goods											
World trade[1]											
Volume	4.6	7.1	5.1	4.2	5.5	4.1	9.9	9.7	5.4	7.3	7.2
Price deflator											
In U.S. dollars	3.8	1.5	8.3	−1.3	1.3	−4.5	2.6	8.9	−0.7	−3.2	0.1
In SDRs	3.1	6.5	2.4	−2.1	−1.6	−3.6	0.1	2.8	3.7	1.9	0.5
World trade prices in U.S. dollars[2]											
Manufactures	4.7	−0.6	9.9	−0.4	3.6	−5.7	3.1	11.2	−2.8	−2.1	1.4
Oil	...	21.2	28.7	−15.8	−1.6	−11.6	−5.5	8.0	18.9	−3.6	−6.7
Nonfuel primary commodities	2.7	−1.6	−6.4	−5.7	0.1	1.8	13.6	8.2	−1.3	—	−0.3
World trade prices in SDRs[2]											
Manufactures	3.9	4.2	3.8	−1.2	0.6	−4.9	0.6	5.0	1.6	3.0	1.8
Oil	...	27.1	21.6	−16.5	−4.4	−10.9	−7.8	1.9	24.3	1.4	−6.4
Nonfuel primary commodities	1.9	3.2	−11.6	−6.5	−2.8	2.7	10.8	2.1	3.1	5.2	0.1

Table A22 *(concluded)*

	Average 1979–88	1989	1990	1991	1992	1993	1994	1995	1996	1997	1998
Trade in goods											
Volume of trade											
Exports											
Advanced economies	5.5	7.7	6.3	5.6	5.0	2.8	9.5	8.8	5.1	6.6	7.3
Developing countries	1.4	8.2	7.3	3.6	10.1	7.1	12.4	11.7	6.0	11.3	8.0
Fuel exporters	−3.8	14.9	6.7	−4.1	11.0	−1.3	6.0	3.8	9.2	14.6	0.6
Nonfuel exporters	6.4	5.7	7.5	7.5	9.7	10.4	14.6	14.1	5.2	10.5	9.8
Imports											
Advanced economies	5.4	7.8	5.2	4.1	5.2	2.1	10.8	9.1	4.8	6.2	6.2
Developing countries	3.0	6.5	5.5	6.5	14.3	10.5	7.7	12.1	7.2	11.3	9.1
Fuel exporters	−0.7	2.4	0.9	−1.4	25.2	−6.3	−8.6	1.7	2.3	21.8	5.6
Nonfuel exporters	4.5	7.9	6.9	8.7	11.2	15.2	11.5	14.0	8.0	9.8	9.6
Price deflators in SDRs											
Exports											
Advanced economies	3.0	4.7	2.4	−1.7	−0.7	−3.4	0.4	3.3	2.6	0.5	−0.1
Developing countries	3.2	15.7	3.3	−2.8	−2.4	−2.0	−0.3	0.7	6.6	4.5	0.9
Fuel exporters	1.9	16.7	14.8	−7.2	−4.0	−4.5	−6.1	0.4	11.3	3.6	2.5
Nonfuel exporters	2.3	15.4	−1.8	−0.6	−1.7	−1.1	1.7	0.8	5.4	4.8	0.5
Imports											
Advanced economies	3.0	6.0	3.1	−3.1	−2.2	−5.2	—	2.9	3.6	1.3	0.8
Developing countries	2.4	10.8	1.5	1.7	−1.8	0.2	−1.1	—	5.7	5.6	1.0
Fuel exporters	1.5	5.8	1.9	8.4	−8.3	2.0	−5.2	6.0	7.0	5.2	1.2
Nonfuel exporters	3.0	12.4	1.3	−0.2	0.1	−0.3	−0.1	−1.1	5.5	5.7	0.9
Terms of trade											
Advanced economies	—	−1.2	−0.7	1.5	1.5	1.9	0.4	0.4	−1.0	−0.7	−0.9
Developing countries	0.8	4.4	1.8	−4.5	−0.6	−2.2	0.8	0.7	0.9	−1.0	—
Fuel exporters	0.4	10.2	12.6	−14.4	4.7	−6.3	−0.9	−5.3	4.1	−1.5	1.3
Nonfuel exporters	−0.7	2.6	−3.1	−0.4	−1.8	−0.7	1.9	1.8	−0.1	−0.8	−0.4
Memorandum											
World exports in billions of U.S. dollars											
Goods and services	2,141	3,727	4,273	4,391	4,717	4,724	5,283	6,247	6,535	6,747	7,214
Goods	1,721	3,000	3,404	3,484	3,720	3,708	4,178	4,986	5,196	5,371	5,744

[1]Average of annual percent change for world exports and imports. The estimates of world trade comprise, in addition to trade of advanced economies and developing countries (which is summarized in the table), trade of countries in transition.

[2]As represented, respectively, by the export unit value index for the manufactures of the advanced economies; the average of U.K. Brent, Dubai, and West Texas Intermediate crude oil spot prices; and the average of world market prices for nonfuel primary commodities weighted by their 1987–89 shares in world commodity exports.

Table A23. Nonfuel Commodity Prices[1]

(Annual percent change; U.S. dollar terms)

	Average 1979–88	1989	1990	1991	1992	1993	1994	1995	1996	1997	1998
Nonfuel primary commodities	**2.7**	**−1.6**	**−6.4**	**−5.7**	**0.1**	**1.8**	**13.6**	**8.2**	**−1.3**	**—**	**−0.3**
Food	1.0	1.8	−9.6	−0.9	2.3	−1.3	5.1	8.1	12.2	−12.0	−1.4
Beverages	−3.9	−17.2	−12.7	−6.5	−13.9	6.3	74.9	0.9	−17.4	12.1	−11.0
Agricultural raw materials	5.2	3.3	2.8	−3.6	2.7	16.2	10.1	3.7	−3.0	8.7	2.6
Metals	6.4	−5.7	−10.7	−14.3	−2.3	−14.2	16.6	19.5	−11.9	1.9	0.4
Fertilizers	3.6	2.1	−4.5	3.2	−5.0	−15.4	8.0	10.6	13.7	0.4	−3.0
Advanced economies	**3.3**	**0.7**	**−4.7**	**−6.0**	**2.0**	**3.1**	**8.6**	**6.6**	**2.6**	**0.2**	**0.5**
Developing countries	**0.9**	**−3.2**	**−5.7**	**−3.4**	**−2.8**	**3.0**	**19.0**	**7.6**	**−4.7**	**2.2**	**−2.4**
Regional groups											
Africa	−0.3	−3.9	−3.4	−5.3	−6.5	2.8	22.1	5.9	−6.3	4.7	−3.0
Sub-Sahara	−0.6	−4.5	−3.4	−5.8	−6.7	4.6	23.1	5.5	−7.8	5.2	−3.0
Asia	1.1	−0.7	−5.5	−0.5	3.2	10.4	13.8	8.6	−4.7	1.0	0.8
Excluding China and India	1.2	−1.4	−5.7	0.3	4.5	11.9	14.5	8.7	−5.9	1.9	0.7
Middle East and Europe	2.6	2.0	−2.6	−6.2	−5.6	−11.2	17.5	10.4	−2.8	1.1	1.4
Western Hemisphere	1.3	−5.3	−7.1	−4.9	−6.2	−3.3	23.3	7.3	−4.0	2.4	−5.5
Analytical groups											
By source of export earnings											
Fuel	3.2	−16.9	−10.2	−11.1	−1.1	16.7	11.3	6.6	−9.5	5.2	3.1
Manufactures	0.5	−3.5	−6.0	−0.5	−1.0	7.6	12.3	7.6	−1.9	−0.5	−0.2
Primary products	0.9	−3.0	−4.7	−6.6	−5.1	−3.7	23.9	11.3	−10.4	4.0	−4.9
Services, factor income, and private transfers	1.7	−1.0	−2.6	−6.8	−8.1	−0.3	18.1	9.4	−5.9	1.9	0.2
Diversified	1.1	−2.0	−6.2	−3.4	−2.6	1.6	24.6	5.2	−3.4	4.0	−3.8
By external financing source											
Net creditor countries	6.1	−20.5	−13.9	−18.0	−2.9	−6.3	25.2	18.8	−13.7	4.7	3.6
Net debtor countries	0.9	−3.2	−5.7	−3.4	−2.8	3.0	18.9	7.6	−4.7	2.2	−2.4
Official financing	0.2	1.2	−3.2	−3.9	−8.7	0.5	24.6	7.0	−8.1	4.5	−3.8
Private financing	1.2	−3.9	−6.6	−3.1	−2.6	2.8	16.8	8.1	−3.3	0.5	−2.7
Diversified financing	0.7	−4.0	−4.7	−3.8	1.1	5.4	21.1	6.7	−6.0	5.4	−0.7
Net debtor countries by debt-servicing experience											
Countries with recent difficulties	0.6	−5.1	−6.2	−4.2	−5.2	−0.5	20.1	5.9	−2.5	2.4	−3.6
Countries without recent difficulties	1.2	−1.5	−5.3	−2.8	−0.8	5.8	18.1	8.9	−6.2	2.1	−1.5
Other groups											
Heavily indebted poor countries	−1.2	−7.5	−4.6	−5.6	−8.1	6.5	28.7	5.3	−10.2	6.9	−3.8
Least developed countries	1.3	−1.8	−4.3	−6.2	−9.3	−1.6	30.3	10.0	−13.2	7.1	−5.9
Middle East and north Africa	2.9	0.3	−2.0	−3.7	−7.8	−11.7	14.4	14.4	—	1.2	−0.1
Memorandum											
Average oil spot price[2]	. . .	21.2	28.7	−15.8	−1.6	−11.6	−5.5	8.0	18.9	−3.6	−6.7
In U.S. dollars a barrel	. . .	17.84	22.97	19.33	19.03	16.82	15.89	17.17	20.42	19.69	18.36
Export unit value of manufactures[3]	4.7	−0.6	9.9	−0.4	3.6	−5.7	3.1	11.2	−2.8	−2.1	1.4

[1]Averages of world market prices for individual commodities weighted by 1987–89 exports as a share of world commodity exports and total commodity exports for the indicated country group, respectively.

[2]Average of U.K. Brent, Dubai, and West Texas Intermediate crude oil spot prices.

[3]For the manufactures exported by the advanced economies.

Table A24. Advanced Economies: Export Volumes, Import Volumes, and Terms of Trade

(Annual percent change)

	Average 1979–88	1989	1990	1991	1992	1993	1994	1995	1996	1997	1998
Trade in goods and services											
Export volume											
Advanced economies	**5.0**	**7.8**	**6.7**	**5.7**	**5.2**	**3.4**	**8.9**	**8.4**	**5.0**	**6.9**	**6.7**
Major industrial countries	4.4	9.0	7.4	5.5	4.5	1.9	8.1	7.9	4.3	6.7	6.4
United States	5.5	11.7	8.5	6.3	6.6	2.9	8.2	8.9	6.5	7.3	6.8
Japan	5.7	9.1	6.9	5.4	4.9	1.2	4.6	5.4	2.2	8.1	7.8
Germany[1]	4.0	10.2	10.4	12.8	−0.3	−4.9	8.0	5.9	4.9	6.8	6.0
France	3.4	10.3	5.4	4.1	4.9	−0.4	6.0	6.0	3.5	6.8	6.4
Italy	3.1	8.9	6.8	−0.8	5.9	9.1	10.5	11.6	0.2	5.0	5.6
United Kingdom	2.8	4.7	5.0	−0.7	4.1	3.5	9.2	8.0	6.3	6.6	6.0
Canada	5.6	0.8	4.1	1.4	7.6	10.4	14.7	12.0	4.5	4.0	4.6
Other advanced economies	6.2	5.4	5.3	6.2	6.4	6.1	10.4	9.3	6.1	7.2	7.3
Memorandum											
Industrial countries	4.5	8.1	6.8	5.1	4.4	2.3	8.3	7.3	4.7	6.6	6.3
European Union	3.9	7.8	6.5	5.0	3.4	1.6	8.9	7.2	4.5	6.4	6.0
Newly industrialized Asian economies	11.3	4.5	6.3	12.5	11.4	11.9	12.8	15.4	7.2	8.8	9.3
Import volume											
Advanced economies	**5.0**	**8.5**	**5.7**	**3.1**	**4.7**	**1.8**	**9.7**	**8.7**	**5.3**	**5.9**	**6.1**
Major industrial countries	4.8	8.1	5.5	1.8	4.1	1.2	9.2	8.1	5.0	5.8	5.7
United States	5.5	3.9	3.9	−0.7	7.5	9.2	12.0	8.0	6.4	8.2	6.9
Japan	3.8	18.6	7.9	−4.7	−1.1	1.8	8.9	14.3	10.3	2.0	1.8
Germany[1]	3.1	8.4	9.4	13.7	2.0	−5.7	7.6	6.4	2.6	4.5	5.1
France	4.0	8.3	6.1	3.0	1.2	−3.5	6.7	5.3	2.2	4.8	5.1
Italy	4.7	9.1	8.9	2.7	5.4	−8.1	8.9	9.6	−1.7	4.8	8.8
United Kingdom	5.3	7.4	0.5	−5.2	6.6	3.0	5.4	4.4	7.8	7.8	6.9
Canada	6.9	6.3	2.0	3.3	5.6	8.8	11.5	8.7	5.1	5.5	4.4
Other advanced economies	5.4	9.2	6.0	5.6	5.8	3.0	10.7	9.7	5.8	6.3	6.8
Memorandum											
Industrial countries	4.7	8.4	5.1	1.9	3.9	0.6	9.2	7.8	5.0	5.9	5.8
European Union	4.2	8.5	5.8	4.1	3.6	−3.2	7.8	6.6	3.6	5.6	6.3
Newly industrialized Asian economies	9.7	10.9	11.5	15.1	12.2	11.1	13.2	14.6	7.3	6.6	7.9
Terms of trade											
Advanced economies	**—**	**−0.3**	**−0.4**	**0.5**	**0.6**	**1.1**	**—**	**—**	**−0.1**	**−1.0**	**−0.4**
Major industrial countries	—	−1.3	−0.7	0.9	0.9	1.6	0.1	0.1	—	−1.2	−0.6
United States	−0.8	−0.6	−1.7	1.9	−0.3	1.3	0.2	0.4	0.1	−0.1	−0.1
Japan	−1.0	−3.0	−6.1	0.8	1.4	3.8	1.4	−0.5	−3.7	−3.9	−3.9
Germany[1]	—	−2.3	0.7	−1.0	2.5	1.7	0.1	1.1	−0.3	−0.2	−0.2
France	—	−1.6	0.1	0.7	1.0	0.9	0.5	−0.2	−0.1	−0.6	—
Italy	−0.6	−1.3	3.0	3.5	−0.5	−0.7	−1.6	−1.5	3.1	−1.4	0.8
United Kingdom	0.4	1.6	1.0	1.2	1.7	0.3	−2.1	−2.4	1.1	−2.0	−0.1
Canada	1.2	2.1	−2.1	−1.5	−0.5	0.3	0.5	2.1	2.4	1.2	0.1
Other advanced economies	−0.1	1.7	0.2	−0.2	0.2	0.2	−0.2	−0.2	−0.2	−0.7	−0.1
Memorandum											
Industrial countries	—	−0.7	−0.3	0.5	0.7	1.2	0.1	0.4	—	−1.0	−0.4
European Union	—	−0.5	0.9	0.3	1.3	0.5	−0.5	−0.1	0.5	−0.8	0.1
Newly industrialized Asian economies	−0.3	3.1	0.1	0.3	0.4	0.7	−1.0	−2.0	−0.9	−1.2	−0.4
Memorandum											
Trade in goods											
Advanced economies											
Export volume	5.5	7.7	6.3	5.6	5.0	2.8	9.5	8.8	5.1	6.6	7.3
Import volume	5.4	7.8	5.2	4.1	5.2	2.1	10.8	9.1	4.8	6.2	6.2
Terms of trade	—	−1.2	−0.7	1.5	1.5	1.9	0.4	0.4	−1.0	−0.7	−0.9

[1]Data through 1991 apply to west Germany only.

Table A25. Developing Countries—by Region: Total Trade in Goods

(Annual percent change)

	Average 1979–88	1989	1990	1991	1992	1993	1994	1995	1996	1997	1998
Developing countries											
Value in U.S. dollars											
Exports	4.4	14.7	16.7	0.7	8.9	3.8	14.4	19.0	7.9	10.5	8.0
Imports	5.3	9.2	13.2	8.8	13.7	9.0	9.2	18.7	8.2	11.9	9.5
Volume											
Exports	1.4	8.2	7.3	3.6	10.1	7.1	12.4	11.7	6.0	11.3	8.0
Imports	3.0	6.5	5.5	6.5	14.3	10.5	7.7	12.1	7.2	11.3	9.1
Unit value in U.S. dollars											
Exports	3.9	10.4	9.3	−2.0	0.5	−2.9	2.2	6.7	2.0	−0.6	0.5
Imports	3.2	5.7	7.4	2.6	1.1	−0.7	1.4	6.0	1.1	0.4	0.6
Terms of trade	0.8	4.4	1.8	−4.5	−0.6	−2.2	0.8	0.7	0.9	−1.0	—
Memorandum											
Real GDP growth in developing country trading partners	3.7	4.1	3.6	2.5	3.1	2.6	3.9	3.3	3.5	3.6	3.6
Market prices of nonfuel commodities exported by developing countries	0.9	−3.2	−5.7	−3.4	−2.8	3.0	19.0	7.6	−4.7	2.2	−2.4
Regional groups											
Africa											
Value in U.S. dollars											
Exports	3.4	8.5	16.4	−3.4	−0.7	−3.1	1.7	16.3	10.4	6.4	6.3
Imports	2.2	5.7	10.1	−2.0	6.9	−3.2	6.2	17.4	2.7	7.8	6.9
Volume											
Exports	0.6	7.4	4.6	1.1	0.8	5.2	3.3	9.7	10.5	7.1	6.5
Imports	0.1	3.8	0.6	−3.1	3.7	3.1	5.6	8.4	5.4	6.7	5.6
Unit value in U.S. dollars											
Exports	4.1	1.9	11.3	−3.7	−0.5	−7.1	1.2	6.3	2.4	−0.8	0.1
Imports	3.8	2.8	10.0	1.7	4.8	−4.5	2.1	8.5	−0.1	−0.2	1.0
Terms of trade	0.3	−0.9	1.2	−5.3	−5.1	−2.7	−0.8	−2.0	2.5	−0.6	−0.9
Sub-Sahara											
Value in U.S. dollars											
Exports	3.1	7.0	13.6	−4.8	0.5	−3.5	2.2	15.6	9.7	6.6	6.6
Imports	2.0	1.4	7.8	2.1	5.4	−3.9	4.4	17.8	3.7	8.3	7.9
Volume											
Exports	0.4	8.2	3.6	−1.5	3.1	3.7	4.4	10.0	12.2	6.2	6.5
Imports	0.2	—	−1.0	0.6	2.9	1.8	4.9	9.4	7.7	6.1	6.6
Unit value in U.S. dollars											
Exports	4.5	—	9.7	−2.5	−1.3	−6.0	1.8	5.6	0.8	—	0.4
Imports	3.9	2.6	9.6	2.4	4.8	−3.5	1.6	7.9	−0.4	0.2	1.0
Terms of trade	0.6	−2.6	—	−4.8	−5.8	−2.5	0.1	−2.1	1.2	−0.2	−0.6

Table A25 *(concluded)*

	Average 1979–88	1989	1990	1991	1992	1993	1994	1995	1996	1997	1998
Asia											
Value in U.S. dollars											
Exports	10.5	14.0	16.1	13.4	15.2	11.8	23.5	23.2	3.8	10.7	10.9
Imports	10.6	14.3	13.2	11.8	14.4	18.8	16.6	24.1	6.3	10.8	11.8
Volume											
Exports	7.6	11.8	10.7	11.9	11.0	11.5	19.4	15.8	2.9	11.1	11.2
Imports	7.7	13.3	5.4	10.5	10.8	18.1	14.3	17.1	5.2	10.8	12.0
Unit value in U.S. dollars											
Exports	3.4	1.9	5.1	1.4	3.8	0.3	3.4	6.3	0.9	−0.3	−0.3
Imports	3.0	1.8	7.2	1.4	3.3	0.7	2.0	6.0	1.0	0.1	−0.2
Terms of trade	0.4	0.1	−2.0	—	0.5	−0.4	1.4	0.4	−0.1	−0.4	−0.2
Excluding China and India											
Value in U.S. dollars											
Exports	9.1	18.0	15.4	15.1	15.3	12.7	18.1	22.6	5.5	9.7	11.9
Imports	8.4	20.9	27.5	14.1	9.7	13.7	18.9	27.5	7.0	8.6	11.6
Volume											
Exports	6.5	14.7	9.4	14.2	9.8	11.3	15.0	14.5	5.3	10.4	11.7
Imports	6.2	21.2	17.1	12.9	5.4	12.0	16.9	18.7	6.5	9.3	11.5
Unit value in U.S. dollars											
Exports	3.3	2.9	5.8	0.9	5.2	1.3	2.7	7.0	0.3	−0.7	0.1
Imports	2.3	1.4	9.2	1.5	4.3	1.6	1.8	7.5	0.4	−0.8	0.1
Terms of trade	1.0	1.6	−3.1	−0.6	0.9	−0.3	0.9	−0.4	−0.1	0.1	—
Middle East and Europe											
Value in U.S. dollars											
Exports	−1.1	24.8	24.2	−9.4	10.0	−5.4	5.3	9.7	12.2	14.9	2.8
Imports	3.8	6.4	15.9	5.2	9.8	1.4	−10.6	17.8	12.1	17.2	5.9
Volume											
Exports	−3.5	14.3	3.4	−5.7	13.1	−1.3	7.1	4.3	7.9	15.6	0.2
Imports	2.1	5.0	6.9	−2.4	22.0	2.0	−11.4	6.2	10.7	17.4	4.6
Unit value in U.S. dollars											
Exports	2.9	10.4	20.9	−3.4	0.5	−4.0	−1.1	5.5	4.1	−0.4	3.4
Imports	2.1	2.1	8.6	7.7	−5.7	1.2	0.3	12.8	1.7	0.2	1.3
Terms of trade	0.8	8.1	11.3	−10.3	6.5	−5.1	−1.3	−6.5	2.3	−0.7	2.0
Western Hemisphere											
Value in U.S. dollars											
Exports	6.9	10.4	9.9	−1.3	4.7	5.6	15.3	21.2	11.0	8.5	8.4
Imports	3.7	6.9	12.4	16.5	21.1	7.8	16.9	10.1	11.9	11.6	9.4
Volume											
Exports	5.8	−1.2	8.8	5.4	11.8	10.3	10.7	11.8	8.4	10.2	8.4
Imports	0.7	−0.7	7.9	17.4	18.5	11.0	15.4	9.2	9.6	10.1	7.8
Unit value in U.S. dollars											
Exports	2.2	26.3	1.1	−3.7	−3.8	−4.3	4.0	8.6	2.4	−1.4	0.2
Imports	4.1	18.7	4.2	−1.1	2.6	−2.8	1.1	−0.1	1.5	1.4	1.3
Terms of trade	−1.8	6.4	−3.0	−2.6	−6.2	−1.6	2.8	8.7	0.9	−2.7	−1.1

Table A26. Developing Countries—by Source of Export Earnings: Total Trade in Goods

(Annual percent change)

	Average 1979–88	1989	1990	1991	1992	1993	1994	1995	1996	1997	1998
Fuel											
Value in U.S. dollars											
Exports	−1.8	26.6	28.9	−11.0	6.7	−6.5	0.8	9.9	16.3	12.1	1.9
Imports	1.1	3.3	8.7	8.1	12.0	−6.3	−11.2	11.5	4.6	21.2	6.5
Volume											
Exports	−3.8	14.9	6.7	−4.1	11.0	−1.3	6.0	3.8	9.2	14.6	0.6
Imports	−0.7	2.4	0.9	−1.4	25.2	−6.3	−8.6	1.7	2.3	21.8	5.6
Unit value in U.S. dollars											
Exports	2.6	11.3	21.5	−6.4	−1.2	−5.3	−3.7	6.4	6.5	−1.5	2.1
Imports	2.2	0.9	7.9	9.3	−5.6	1.1	−2.8	12.3	2.4	—	0.8
Terms of trade	0.4	10.2	12.6	−14.4	4.7	−6.3	−0.9	−5.3	4.1	−1.5	1.3
Nonfuel											
Value in U.S. dollars											
Exports	8.5	10.2	11.4	6.6	9.8	8.0	19.2	21.7	5.7	10.1	9.9
Imports	7.3	11.1	14.5	9.0	14.1	13.3	13.9	20.0	8.8	10.4	10.1
Volume											
Exports	6.4	5.7	7.5	7.5	9.7	10.4	14.6	14.1	5.2	10.5	9.8
Imports	4.5	7.9	6.9	8.7	11.2	15.2	11.5	14.0	8.0	9.8	9.6
Unit value in U.S. dollars											
Exports	3.0	10.0	4.0	0.2	1.2	−1.9	4.3	6.8	0.8	−0.4	0.1
Imports	3.7	7.2	7.2	0.6	3.0	−1.2	2.4	4.8	0.9	0.4	0.5
Terms of trade	−0.7	2.6	−3.1	−0.4	−1.8	−0.7	1.9	1.8	−0.1	−0.8	−0.4
Manufactures											
Value in U.S. dollars											
Exports	12.0	10.4	10.4	12.1	14.7	11.1	24.2	22.0	1.5	9.6	10.1
Imports	10.2	15.1	10.8	11.8	13.0	21.0	17.7	27.6	4.4	9.2	10.3
Volume											
Exports	9.9	9.3	8.0	9.8	11.4	12.1	19.7	14.8	1.0	10.2	10.1
Imports	5.8	11.5	3.3	11.8	9.9	21.4	16.1	20.6	3.4	9.3	10.8
Unit value in U.S. dollars											
Exports	2.1	1.0	2.0	2.0	3.1	−0.9	3.7	6.2	0.5	−0.5	—
Imports	4.6	3.3	6.9	0.2	2.9	−0.3	1.3	5.7	0.9	0.3	−0.2
Terms of trade	−2.4	−2.2	−4.6	1.8	0.2	−0.6	2.4	0.5	−0.3	−0.8	0.3
Nonfuel primary products											
Value in U.S. dollars											
Exports	4.0	11.9	1.8	0.7	3.6	1.0	18.9	24.2	2.9	5.6	9.0
Imports	3.0	7.8	8.9	4.7	10.2	2.6	9.9	24.6	10.9	5.5	7.6
Volume											
Exports	1.7	12.0	1.8	4.0	4.5	8.8	6.2	9.6	8.6	8.5	8.6
Imports	−0.2	11.7	−1.7	2.7	4.6	6.1	5.1	15.4	8.9	3.6	6.0
Unit value in U.S. dollars											
Exports	3.9	1.3	0.8	−2.1	0.1	−6.0	14.1	13.8	−4.8	−2.2	0.5
Imports	5.6	2.0	11.8	3.4	7.7	−1.0	5.8	8.5	1.9	2.1	1.6
Terms of trade	−1.6	−0.7	−9.8	−5.3	−7.1	−5.1	7.9	4.9	−6.6	−4.3	−1.1

165

Table A26 *(concluded)*

	Average 1979–88	1989	1990	1991	1992	1993	1994	1995	1996	1997	1998
Services, factor income, and private transfers											
Value in U.S. dollars											
Exports	2.3	21.6	8.2	−1.2	2.1	1.1	13.9	16.2	6.6	6.7	6.2
Imports	6.2	−1.1	15.7	2.8	4.0	4.6	6.1	13.2	9.3	8.0	6.3
Volume											
Exports	1.3	3.4	2.5	−4.7	28.7	−1.9	5.3	11.8	0.7	4.1	2.4
Imports	3.4	0.9	5.8	—	−3.6	3.5	−0.8	7.1	5.1	5.9	3.6
Unit value in U.S. dollars											
Exports	2.4	20.9	7.1	26.3	2.8	4.3	7.4	2.5	5.7	0.9	3.3
Imports	3.5	−0.2	9.7	3.2	7.5	2.7	6.8	5.4	1.9	1.4	2.5
Terms of trade	−1.0	21.2	−2.4	22.5	−4.4	1.5	0.6	−2.7	3.7	−0.4	0.8
Diversified											
Value in U.S. dollars											
Exports	7.7	8.5	15.5	3.0	6.4	6.5	13.4	21.2	12.1	11.9	10.1
Imports	6.4	11.4	19.8	8.8	18.6	9.8	12.3	11.6	14.1	13.3	11.0
Volume											
Exports	5.6	0.4	8.9	7.0	7.4	9.8	10.7	14.2	10.8	11.7	10.2
Imports	5.1	5.0	13.4	9.0	17.5	13.4	10.2	7.3	14.4	12.4	9.8
Unit value in U.S. dollars											
Exports	3.3	21.0	6.6	−3.6	−0.8	−2.8	2.6	6.2	2.2	—	—
Imports	2.4	14.9	5.8	−0.1	1.1	−2.9	2.0	3.0	0.6	0.1	1.0
Terms of trade	0.9	5.4	0.8	−3.4	−1.8	0.1	0.6	3.2	1.6	−0.1	−1.0

8>8>

Table A27. Summary of Payments Balances on Current Account
(In billions of U.S. dollars)

	1989	1990	1991	1992	1993	1994	1995	1996	1997	1998
Advanced economies	**−60.9**	**−96.5**	**−27.4**	**−28.4**	**52.5**	**8.3**	**21.4**	**−6.0**	**−12.5**	**−0.3**
United States	−105.6	−94.7	−9.5	−62.6	−99.9	−148.4	−148.2	−165.1	−186.5	−200.3
European Union	−6.9	−31.5	−81.6	−80.5	11.2	25.9	57.3	86.9	84.5	88.0
Japan	57.2	35.8	68.4	112.3	132.0	130.6	111.4	65.8	77.7	90.0
Other advanced economies	−5.6	−6.1	−4.7	2.3	9.2	0.2	0.8	6.4	11.8	22.0
Developing countries	**−39.9**	**−24.0**	**−96.8**	**−79.0**	**−116.7**	**−87.0**	**−93.3**	**−98.0**	**−112.5**	**−133.6**
Regional groups										
Africa	−7.9	−3.7	−5.6	−9.7	−9.4	−11.4	−15.5	−7.7	−8.1	−8.2
Asia	−22.7	−16.4	−11.4	−12.8	−33.5	−22.2	−40.3	−49.6	−56.3	−65.8
Middle East and Europe	−3.9	−2.6	−63.1	−22.1	−29.1	−4.2	−4.7	−1.3	0.3	−6.0
Western Hemisphere	−5.4	−1.3	−16.8	−34.4	−44.7	−49.2	−32.8	−39.4	−48.3	−53.6
Analytical groups										
By source of export earnings										
Fuel	−1.6	14.7	−58.1	−24.1	−22.2	−3.4	1.9	24.3	23.6	17.3
Nonfuel	−38.3	−38.7	−38.7	−54.9	−94.5	−83.6	−95.2	−122.3	−136.1	−150.9
By external financing source										
Net creditor countries	5.5	10.8	−49.2	−11.2	−13.8	−6.6	0.3	8.7	9.9	0.2
Net debtor countries	−45.3	−34.8	−47.6	−67.8	−102.8	−80.3	−93.6	−106.7	−122.4	−133.8
Official financing	−11.5	−9.7	−12.2	−14.2	−16.1	−13.2	−16.2	−14.6	−14.6	−14.9
Private financing	−12.4	2.4	−22.1	−42.7	−73.7	−51.5	−54.8	−64.5	−79.5	−91.0
Diversified financing	−21.5	−27.5	−13.3	−10.9	−13.0	−15.6	−22.6	−27.6	−28.3	−27.9
Net debtor countries by debt-servicing experience										
Countries with recent difficulties	−18.4	−10.9	−22.6	−25.8	−34.5	−25.5	−40.9	−37.8	−44.0	−41.3
Countries without recent difficulties	−26.9	−24.0	−25.0	−42.0	−68.3	−54.8	−52.7	−68.9	−78.4	−92.5
Countries in transition	**−7.3**	**−21.9**	**2.8**	**−2.1**	**−6.6**	**5.1**	**−3.1**	**−9.4**	**−18.7**	**−25.6**
Central and eastern Europe	...	...	−6.7	0.5	−8.4	−4.3	−5.9	−15.9	−18.8	−16.8
Excluding Belarus and Ukraine	...	...	1.6	0.9	−6.4	−2.3	−4.1	−13.9	−15.8	−14.6
Russia	...	...	4.1	−1.2	2.6	10.4	4.8	9.6	3.8	−4.8
Transcaucasus and central Asia	...	...	5.3	−1.5	−0.8	−1.1	−1.9	−3.1	−3.7	−4.1
Total[1]	**−108.1**	**−142.4**	**−121.5**	**−109.6**	**−70.7**	**−73.6**	**−75.0**	**−113.5**	**−143.7**	**−159.5**
In percent of sum of world exports and imports of goods and services	−1.4	−1.7	−1.4	−1.2	−0.8	−0.7	−0.6	−0.9	−1.1	−1.1

[1]Reflects errors, omissions, and asymmetries in balance of payments statistics on current account, as well as the exclusion of data for international organizations and a limited number of countries. See "Classification of Countries" in the introduction to this Statistical Appendix.

Table A28. Advanced Economies: Balance of Payments on Current Account

	1989	1990	1991	1992	1993	1994	1995	1996	1997	1998
	In billions of U.S. dollars									
Advanced economies	**−60.9**	**−96.5**	**−27.4**	**−28.4**	**52.5**	**8.3**	**21.4**	**−6.0**	**−12.5**	**−0.3**
Major industrial countries	−67.2	−91.9	−26.7	−33.7	0.5	−35.4	−27.9	−56.3	−66.3	−66.7
United States	−105.6	−94.7	−9.5	−62.6	−99.9	−148.4	−148.2	−165.1	−186.5	−200.3
Japan	57.2	35.8	68.4	112.3	132.0	130.6	111.4	65.8	77.7	90.0
Germany[1]	57.2	48.9	−18.0	−19.4	−13.5	−19.7	−21.0	−17.6	−10.9	−8.2
France	−4.6	−9.8	−6.2	3.8	9.2	7.0	16.6	19.7	22.9	25.7
Italy	−11.8	−17.0	−23.6	−28.6	11.3	15.1	27.4	42.1	42.4	41.3
United Kingdom	−36.7	−33.5	−14.1	−17.9	−16.2	−3.7	−5.9	—	−11.8	−15.9
Canada	−22.8	−21.6	−23.6	−21.4	−22.3	−16.2	−8.2	−1.2	−0.1	0.6
Other advanced economies	6.3	−4.6	−0.7	5.3	52.0	43.7	49.2	50.3	53.8	66.4
Spain	−11.5	−17.9	−19.8	−21.1	−5.5	−6.8	1.3	2.9	3.2	3.1
Netherlands	10.0	9.2	7.7	7.3	13.6	17.9	17.9	20.6	16.2	16.5
Belgium-Luxembourg	3.6	3.6	4.9	6.6	11.2	12.7	14.2	13.9	13.0	13.2
Sweden	−3.4	−6.6	−4.8	−8.7	−3.8	0.8	4.9	6.2	10.0	12.6
Austria	0.2	1.2	0.1	−0.1	−0.7	−1.8	−4.7	−4.0	−3.3	−3.1
Denmark	−1.1	1.3	2.0	4.1	4.8	3.2	1.7	2.0	2.3	2.5
Finland	−5.7	−6.9	−6.6	−4.9	−1.1	1.3	5.3	4.2	4.1	4.2
Greece	−2.6	−3.4	−2.8	−2.1	−0.4	0.2	−1.7	−1.7	−2.7	−2.8
Portugal	0.1	−0.2	−0.7	—	0.3	−1.5	−0.3	−2.1	−2.0	−1.9
Ireland	−0.5	−0.4	0.3	0.5	1.8	1.4	1.5	0.7	1.0	0.7
Switzerland	6.8	8.5	10.6	15.1	19.5	17.8	21.1	19.2	16.8	17.2
Norway	0.2	3.9	5.1	4.7	3.5	3.0	4.5	11.2	13.5	15.5
Israel	1.3	0.5	−0.4	0.2	−1.1	−2.3	−3.9	−4.9	−4.0	−3.9
Iceland	−0.1	−0.1	−0.3	−0.2	—	0.1	0.1	−0.1	−0.2	−0.1
Korea	5.1	−2.2	−8.7	−4.5	0.4	−4.5	−8.9	−23.8	−20.0	−17.2
Australia	−17.0	−14.3	−9.3	−9.9	−9.7	−16.2	−18.5	−14.5	−15.2	−16.3
Taiwan Province of China	11.4	10.8	12.0	8.2	6.7	6.2	4.8	7.3	6.8	8.2
Hong Kong	8.0	6.7	6.1	5.8	8.6	2.6	−2.8	2.1	2.0	3.7
Singapore	2.9	3.1	4.9	5.6	4.2	11.3	15.1	14.6	16.2	18.8
New Zealand	−1.6	−1.2	−0.9	−1.1	−0.5	−1.5	−2.5	−3.5	−4.0	−4.6
Memorandum										
Industrial countries	−89.6	−115.4	−41.2	−43.6	33.8	−4.9	17.1	−1.4	−13.6	−9.9
European Union	−6.9	−31.5	−81.6	−80.5	11.2	25.9	57.3	86.9	84.5	88.0
Newly industrialized Asian economies	27.4	18.4	14.2	15.0	19.9	15.5	8.2	0.3	5.1	13.5
	In percent of GDP									
United States	−1.9	−1.6	−0.2	−1.0	−1.5	−2.1	−2.0	−2.2	−2.3	−2.4
Japan	2.0	1.2	2.0	3.0	3.1	2.8	2.2	1.4	1.8	2.0
Germany[1]	4.8	3.3	−1.0	−1.0	−0.7	−1.0	−0.9	−0.7	−0.5	−0.4
France	−0.5	−0.8	−0.5	0.3	0.7	0.5	1.1	1.3	1.6	1.7
Italy	−1.4	−1.6	−2.1	−2.3	1.1	1.5	2.5	3.5	3.7	3.5
United Kingdom	−4.3	−3.4	−1.4	−1.7	−1.7	−0.4	−0.5	—	−0.9	−1.2
Canada	−4.1	−3.8	−4.0	−3.8	−4.0	−3.0	−1.4	−0.2	—	0.1
Spain	−3.0	−3.6	−3.7	−3.7	−1.1	−1.4	0.2	0.5	0.6	0.5
Netherlands	4.4	3.2	2.6	2.3	4.3	5.3	4.5	5.2	4.4	4.3
Belgium-Luxembourg	2.3	1.9	2.5	3.0	5.3	5.5	5.3	5.3	5.3	5.3
Sweden	−1.8	−2.9	−2.0	−3.5	−2.0	0.4	2.1	2.5	4.3	5.3
Austria	0.2	0.8	—	−0.1	−0.4	−0.9	−2.0	−1.8	−1.6	−1.4
Denmark	−1.1	1.0	1.6	2.9	3.6	2.2	1.0	1.1	1.4	1.5
Finland	−5.1	−5.1	−5.4	−4.6	−1.3	1.3	4.3	3.4	3.4	3.4
Greece	−3.8	−4.1	−3.1	−2.2	−0.4	0.2	−1.5	−1.4	−2.0	−2.1
Portugal	0.3	−0.3	−1.0	—	0.4	−1.7	−0.2	−2.0	−2.0	−1.8
Ireland	−1.4	−0.8	0.7	1.1	3.9	2.7	2.4	1.1	1.3	0.9
Switzerland	3.8	3.7	4.6	6.3	8.4	6.9	6.9	6.6	6.2	6.2
Norway	0.2	3.3	4.3	3.7	3.0	2.4	3.1	7.2	8.5	9.5
Israel	2.8	0.9	−0.7	0.3	−1.7	−3.1	−4.5	−5.2	−3.8	−3.4
Iceland	−1.4	−2.2	−4.7	−3.1	0.1	1.9	0.8	−1.8	−3.2	−1.5
Korea	2.3	−0.9	−3.0	−1.5	0.1	−1.2	−2.0	−4.9	−4.1	−3.3
Australia	−6.0	−4.8	−3.2	−3.4	−3.4	−5.0	−5.3	−3.7	−3.6	−3.7
Taiwan Province of China	7.6	6.7	6.7	3.8	3.0	2.6	1.9	2.7	2.4	2.6
Hong Kong	12.0	8.9	7.1	5.7	7.4	2.0	−2.0	1.3	1.1	1.9
Singapore	9.6	8.3	11.2	11.3	7.2	15.9	17.7	15.7	15.8	16.8
New Zealand	−3.7	−2.8	−2.2	−2.7	−1.2	−3.0	−4.3	−5.5	−5.8	−6.3

[1]Data through June 1990 apply to west Germany only.

Table A29. Advanced Economies: Current Account Transactions

(In billions of U.S. dollars)

	1989	1990	1991	1992	1993	1994	1995	1996	1997	1998
Exports	2,362.2	2,706.1	2,788.7	2,990.5	2,938.7	3,302.4	3,930.4	4,057.0	4,121.8	4,398.4
Imports	2,386.0	2,742.0	2,799.3	2,966.3	2,850.0	3,232.0	3,843.5	3,997.9	4,081.7	4,353.6
Trade balance	−23.7	−35.9	−10.6	24.2	88.7	70.4	87.0	59.0	40.1	44.8
Services, credits	588.1	710.7	758.0	839.7	841.2	908.8	1,026.3	1,077.3	1,084.9	1,154.5
Services, debits	572.0	693.1	716.8	790.7	782.8	847.8	966.6	1,015.4	1,011.1	1,069.1
Balance on services	16.1	17.5	41.3	49.0	58.4	60.9	59.8	61.9	73.8	85.5
Balance on goods and services	0.1	−21.6	23.1	60.0	141.5	110.7	121.0	95.5	99.6	116.0
Factor income, net	7.7	−3.2	−7.6	−13.2	−5.6	−20.6	−25.8	−25.5	−14.3	−14.3
Current transfers, net	−61.0	−75.0	−50.5	−88.4	−89.0	−102.4	−99.6	−101.5	−112.1	−116.3
Current account balance	**−60.9**	**−96.5**	**−27.4**	**−28.4**	**52.5**	**8.3**	**21.4**	**−6.0**	**−12.5**	**−0.3**
Balance on goods and services										
Advanced economies	**−7.6**	**−18.4**	**30.6**	**73.2**	**147.1**	**131.3**	**146.8**	**120.9**	**113.9**	**130.3**
Major industrial countries	−23.5	−32.9	12.0	42.7	78.4	61.3	74.1	42.5	29.9	32.5
United States	−91.8	−80.3	−29.9	−38.3	−72.0	−104.4	−105.1	−114.2	−130.9	−140.5
Japan	37.9	18.0	54.3	80.7	96.5	96.4	74.7	21.2	30.3	39.0
Germany[1]	65.7	56.1	−0.5	−1.4	10.0	11.9	21.9	30.3	38.9	44.9
France	3.3	2.2	7.0	21.5	24.5	26.1	30.4	32.0	34.4	38.3
Italy	−1.9	—	−0.1	−0.4	33.9	37.4	45.7	63.4	58.7	55.8
United Kingdom	−35.0	−27.0	−11.9	−14.4	−11.9	−9.3	−7.4	−8.7	−20.7	−25.8
Canada	−1.8	−2.0	−6.9	−5.0	−2.5	3.2	13.9	18.5	19.2	20.8
Other advanced economies	15.9	14.6	18.6	30.5	68.7	70.1	72.6	78.5	84.0	97.8
Memorandum										
Industrial countries	−33.0	−30.7	24.5	67.2	134.7	123.2	146.5	128.8	114.0	122.6
European Union	25.6	25.7	−10.0	10.6	91.4	109.2	144.0	176.2	168.7	174.7
Newly industrialized Asian countries	27.3	16.0	11.8	11.8	19.1	15.7	11.5	4.6	11.3	19.1
Factor income, net										
Advanced economies	**7.7**	**−3.2**	**−7.6**	**−13.2**	**−5.6**	**−20.6**	**−25.8**	**−25.5**	**−14.3**	**−14.3**
Major industrial countries	25.0	24.6	20.7	20.9	18.3	8.3	1.1	4.9	17.1	19.2
United States	13.9	20.9	15.8	11.2	9.7	−4.2	−8.0	−8.4	−11.0	−12.9
Japan	23.4	23.2	25.9	35.4	40.6	40.3	44.4	53.6	57.4	61.2
Germany[1]	11.1	16.8	19.4	16.8	11.9	7.0	−2.0	−12.6	−7.6	−8.2
France	−0.3	−3.9	−5.7	−8.7	−9.1	−11.0	−7.5	−7.9	−7.4	−8.0
Italy	−7.8	−15.1	−18.2	−22.8	−17.9	−17.1	−16.1	−15.3	−14.1	−13.3
United Kingdom	5.7	2.3	0.3	5.5	3.3	13.3	12.5	16.1	19.8	21.2
Canada	−21.2	−19.6	−16.7	−16.5	−20.2	−20.1	−22.3	−20.5	−20.1	−20.9
Other advanced economies	−17.3	−27.8	−28.3	−34.2	−23.9	−28.9	−26.9	−30.4	−31.4	−33.5
Memorandum										
Industrial countries	5.3	−6.4	−11.0	−17.1	−7.4	−21.9	−26.8	−26.5	−13.5	−12.9
European Union	−3.1	−21.6	−26.0	−39.3	−32.3	−26.5	−30.7	−39.5	−27.8	−27.6
Newly industrialized Asian economies	2.4	3.2	3.4	3.9	1.8	1.3	1.0	1.0	−0.8	−1.3

[1]Data through June 1990 apply to west Germany only.

Table A30. Developing Countries: Payments Balances on Current Account

	1989	1990	1991	1992	1993	1994	1995	1996	1997	1998
					In billions of U.S. dollars					
Developing countries	**−39.9**	**−24.0**	**−96.8**	**−79.0**	**−116.7**	**−87.0**	**−93.3**	**−98.0**	**−112.5**	**−133.6**
Regional groups										
Africa	−7.9	−3.7	−5.6	−9.7	−9.4	−11.4	−15.5	−7.7	−8.1	−8.2
Sub-Sahara	−5.7	−4.6	−7.5	−9.4	−8.6	−8.4	−11.2	−6.7	−6.6	−7.4
Excluding Nigeria and South Africa	−7.4	−9.2	−9.8	−10.6	−9.5	−6.8	−7.2	−9.0	−8.4	−7.6
Asia	−22.7	−16.4	−11.4	−12.8	−33.5	−22.2	−40.3	−49.6	−56.3	−65.8
Excluding China and India	−10.1	−18.8	−20.9	−16.2	−20.2	−23.3	−37.1	−42.1	−42.7	−45.7
Middle East and Europe	−3.9	−2.6	−63.1	−22.1	−29.1	−4.2	−4.7	−1.3	0.3	−6.0
Western Hemisphere	−5.4	−1.3	−16.8	−34.4	−44.7	−49.2	−32.8	−39.4	−48.3	−53.6
Analytical groups										
By source of export earnings										
Fuel	−1.6	14.7	−58.1	−24.1	−22.2	−3.4	1.9	24.3	23.6	17.3
Manufactures	−15.1	−11.1	−4.8	−0.7	−26.8	−14.9	−43.8	−56.7	−61.2	−66.4
Nonfuel primary products	−7.8	−9.7	−9.5	−11.7	−12.0	−9.1	−10.3	−16.0	−16.5	−16.8
Services, factor income, and private transfers	−4.8	−5.9	−5.3	−3.9	−5.5	−6.0	−7.5	−9.2	−11.5	−13.1
Diversified	−10.6	−12.0	−19.1	−38.6	−50.2	−53.6	−33.6	−40.5	−46.9	−54.6
By external financing source										
Net creditor countries	5.5	10.8	−49.2	−11.2	−13.8	−6.6	0.3	8.7	9.9	0.2
Net debtor countries	−45.3	−34.8	−47.6	−67.8	−102.8	−80.3	−93.6	−106.7	−122.4	−133.8
Official financing	−11.5	−9.7	−12.2	−14.2	−16.1	−13.2	−16.2	−14.6	−14.6	−14.9
Private financing	−12.4	2.4	−22.1	−42.7	−73.7	−51.5	−54.8	−64.5	−79.5	−91.0
Diversified financing	−21.5	−27.5	−13.3	−10.9	−13.0	−15.6	−22.6	−27.6	−28.3	−27.9
Net debtor countries by debt-servicing experience										
Countries with recent difficulties	−18.4	−10.9	−22.6	−25.8	−34.5	−25.5	−40.9	−37.8	−44.0	−41.3
Countries without recent difficulties	−26.9	−24.0	−25.0	−42.0	−68.3	−54.8	−52.7	−68.9	−78.4	−92.5
Other groups										
Heavily indebted poor countries	−8.7	−9.7	−11.4	−12.2	−12.9	−8.8	−9.6	−13.2	−12.8	−12.0
Least developed countries	−6.3	−7.6	−8.8	−9.1	−8.1	−6.0	−7.1	−9.6	−10.0	−9.9
Middle East and north Africa	−8.0	−0.4	−63.1	−22.8	−24.8	−10.9	−7.3	3.2	3.8	−1.5

Table A30 *(concluded)*

	Average 1979–88	1989	1990	1991	1992	1993	1994	1995	1996	1997	1998
					In percent of exports of goods and services						
Developing countries	**−7.6**	**−7.0**	**−3.6**	**−14.5**	**−10.8**	**−15.3**	**−10.0**	**−9.1**	**−8.7**	**−9.1**	**−10.0**
Regional groups											
Africa	−12.9	−8.8	−3.5	−5.6	−9.6	−9.6	−11.4	−13.4	−6.1	−6.0	−5.8
Sub-Sahara	−13.6	−8.2	−5.9	−9.9	−12.4	−11.6	−11.1	−12.8	−7.1	−6.6	−6.8
Excluding Nigeria and South Africa	−23.3	−20.7	−23.7	−25.8	−28.3	−26.5	−17.6	−16.2	−18.9	−16.6	−14.0
Asia	−13.8	−13.2	−8.1	−5.0	−4.8	−11.4	−6.1	−9.0	−10.4	−10.6	−11.1
Excluding China and India	−15.0	−9.7	−15.3	−15.1	−10.1	−11.2	−10.9	−14.0	−14.8	−13.7	−13.1
Middle East and Europe	0.5	−2.5	−1.4	−35.7	−11.4	−15.5	−2.1	−2.2	−0.5	0.1	−2.1
Western Hemisphere	−16.2	−3.7	−0.8	−10.3	−20.0	−24.3	−23.5	−13.2	−14.4	−16.3	−16.8
Analytical groups											
By source of export earnings											
Fuel	0.6	−1.0	7.2	−31.8	−12.4	−12.0	−1.8	1.0	10.4	9.0	6.5
Manufactures	−16.4	−9.2	−6.0	−2.3	−0.3	−10.2	−4.6	−10.9	−13.6	−13.3	−13.1
Nonfuel primary products	−32.7	−18.5	−22.5	−21.4	−25.2	−25.6	−16.4	−15.1	−22.4	−21.7	−20.4
Services, factor income, and private transfers	−18.5	−16.1	−17.4	−14.9	−10.1	−13.7	−13.5	−15.0	−17.4	−20.5	−22.2
Diversified	−13.1	−6.4	−6.2	−9.6	−17.9	−21.9	−20.7	−10.9	−11.7	−12.1	−12.9
By external financing source											
Net creditor countries	9.6	6.4	9.7	−46.2	−9.5	−12.5	−6.0	0.2	6.2	6.9	0.1
Net debtor countries	−13.8	−9.4	−6.3	−8.5	−11.1	−15.7	−10.6	−10.3	−10.9	−11.2	−11.2
Official financing	−23.4	−20.6	−14.9	−19.0	−21.4	−23.5	−18.3	−19.1	−15.2	−14.6	−13.8
Private financing	−10.1	−4.0	0.7	−5.8	−10.1	−16.3	−9.6	−8.5	−9.4	−10.5	−11.1
Diversified financing	−23.1	−19.0	−23.1	−11.7	−8.8	−9.8	−10.3	−12.8	−14.0	−11.7	−10.3
Net debtor countries by debt-servicing experience											
Countries with recent difficulties	−19.2	−9.5	−5.0	−11.3	−12.3	−16.1	−10.9	−15.2	−12.6	−12.8	−11.1
Countries without recent difficulties	−16.4	−9.4	−7.2	−7.0	−10.4	−15.5	−10.5	−8.3	−10.1	−10.4	−11.2
Other groups											
Heavily indebted poor countries	−34.4	−27.6	−28.5	−34.3	−36.1	−39.2	−23.8	−21.3	−27.4	−24.4	−20.9
Least developed countries	−40.3	−32.1	−36.7	−44.3	−46.1	−38.3	−24.7	−25.2	−31.9	−30.9	−28.0
Middle East and north Africa	−0.9	−5.0	−0.2	−35.9	−12.0	−13.6	−5.8	−3.6	1.4	1.5	−0.6
Memorandum											
Median											
Developing countries	−19.1	−13.5	−13.7	−14.6	−15.9	−17.6	−13.5	−12.9	−12.4	−11.7	−10.9

Table A31. Developing Countries—by Region: Current Account Transactions

(In billions of U.S. dollars)

	1989	1990	1991	1992	1993	1994	1995	1996	1997	1998
Developing countries										
Exports	464.0	541.6	545.2	593.6	616.2	704.9	838.7	905.2	1,000.7	1,081.1
Imports	431.6	488.6	531.8	604.4	658.8	719.6	853.9	924.3	1,034.3	1,132.9
Trade balance	32.3	53.0	13.4	−10.8	−42.6	−14.7	−15.2	−19.1	−33.6	−51.8
Services, net	−26.9	−27.5	−45.5	−38.5	−32.7	−24.1	−23.4	−28.3	−24.1	−26.2
Balance on goods and services	5.4	25.5	−32.1	−49.3	−75.2	−38.8	−38.6	−47.3	−57.7	−78.1
Factor income, net	−63.7	−62.8	−61.1	−57.7	−65.3	−71.5	−84.6	−78.4	−82.1	−82.6
Current transfers, net	18.4	13.2	−3.7	28.0	23.8	23.3	29.6	27.8	27.8	27.0
Current account balance	**−39.9**	**−24.0**	**−96.8**	**−79.0**	**−116.7**	**−87.0**	**−93.3**	**−98.0**	**−112.5**	**−133.6**
Memorandum										
Exports of goods and services	566.7	660.9	666.5	730.5	763.8	868.8	1,030.6	1,121.6	1,239.6	1,340.9
Interest payments	81.9	86.8	82.0	81.0	81.5	87.8	98.7	103.3	109.2	114.2
Oil trade balance	116.2	152.7	129.7	135.8	118.0	116.1	125.1	162.6	168.6	170.5
Regional groups										
Africa										
Exports	76.8	89.4	86.4	85.8	83.1	84.5	98.2	108.5	115.4	122.7
Imports	70.5	77.6	76.0	81.2	78.6	83.4	97.9	100.5	108.4	115.9
Trade balance	6.4	11.8	10.4	4.5	4.5	1.0	0.3	7.9	7.1	6.9
Services, net	−8.5	−10.0	−10.0	−10.0	−9.4	−8.7	−10.2	−9.9	−9.5	−10.0
Balance on goods and services	−2.2	1.8	0.3	−5.4	−4.9	−7.7	−9.9	−2.0	−2.5	−3.1
Factor income, net	−16.1	−17.4	−17.6	−16.6	−16.1	−15.0	−17.3	−17.5	−17.0	−16.5
Current transfers, net	10.4	11.9	11.7	12.3	11.7	11.4	11.7	11.8	11.4	11.4
Current account balance	**−7.9**	**−3.7**	**−5.6**	**−9.7**	**−9.4**	**−11.4**	**−15.5**	**−7.7**	**−8.1**	**−8.2**
Memorandum										
Exports of goods and services	88.8	103.3	99.9	101.0	98.1	100.0	115.3	126.6	134.6	143.0
Interest payments	15.2	16.6	16.8	15.9	15.1	14.5	16.2	16.2	16.6	17.4
Oil trade balance	17.4	28.0	25.5	25.4	22.4	19.4	22.4	27.7	29.7	30.1
Asia										
Exports	146.4	169.9	192.6	221.8	248.0	306.2	377.2	391.4	433.4	480.6
Imports	160.7	181.9	203.3	232.6	276.4	322.2	399.9	425.2	471.2	526.9
Trade balance	−14.4	−12.0	−10.7	−10.7	−28.4	−16.0	−22.7	−33.7	−37.9	−46.3
Services, net	−3.4	−0.7	0.3	−3.3	−8.0	−9.1	−14.9	−14.8	−16.2	−17.8
Balance on goods and services	−17.8	−12.7	−10.3	−14.0	−36.5	−25.0	−37.6	−48.6	−54.1	−64.1
Factor income, net	−10.9	−9.5	−12.4	−11.0	−9.8	−13.5	−20.9	−18.7	−19.3	−19.5
Current transfers, net	6.0	5.8	11.3	12.2	12.7	16.3	17.9	17.7	17.5	17.8
Current account balance	**−22.7**	**−16.4**	**−11.4**	**−12.8**	**−33.5**	**−22.2**	**−40.3**	**−49.6**	**−56.3**	**−65.8**
Memorandum										
Exports of goods and services	171.8	202.3	227.4	263.5	294.6	363.8	449.8	479.1	531.6	591.1
Interest payments	16.3	17.2	18.7	20.4	19.8	23.5	27.0	29.4	31.7	33.7
Oil trade balance	1.0	—	−1.1	−2.7	−4.3	−5.1	−7.5	−10.8	−13.1	−14.1

Table A31 *(concluded)*

	1989	1990	1991	1992	1993	1994	1995	1996	1997	1998
Middle East and Europe										
Exports	124.2	154.2	139.7	153.7	145.5	153.2	168.1	188.5	216.7	222.8
Imports	110.4	127.9	134.5	147.7	149.7	133.9	157.7	176.7	207.0	219.3
Trade balance	13.8	26.3	5.3	6.0	−4.2	19.4	10.4	11.8	9.6	3.5
Services, net	−16.1	−17.2	−32.3	−23.3	−15.4	−6.8	−1.9	0.6	2.4	3.7
Balance on goods and services	−2.3	9.1	−27.1	−17.2	−19.6	12.5	8.5	12.4	12.0	7.2
Factor income, net	3.4	2.8	1.5	3.8	2.3	0.5	1.6	1.6	4.2	4.0
Current transfers, net	−5.1	−14.4	−37.5	−8.7	−11.8	−17.1	−14.8	−15.3	−15.9	−17.2
Current account balance	**−3.9**	**−2.6**	**−63.1**	**−22.1**	**−29.1**	**−4.2**	**−4.7**	**−1.3**	**0.3**	**−6.0**
Memorandum										
Exports of goods and services	158.9	192.0	176.9	194.5	187.4	195.3	217.8	242.9	277.6	287.6
Interest payments	9.5	11.2	9.0	8.1	8.5	9.1	10.3	10.2	10.6	10.5
Oil trade balance	84.2	106.0	90.9	99.4	87.5	88.1	95.2	123.8	129.4	132.4
Western Hemisphere										
Exports	116.6	128.1	126.4	132.3	139.7	161.0	195.2	216.8	235.2	254.9
Imports	90.1	101.2	117.9	142.9	154.1	180.1	198.4	221.9	247.7	270.8
Trade balance	26.5	26.9	8.4	−10.6	−14.4	−19.1	−3.2	−5.1	−12.5	−15.9
Services, net	1.2	0.5	−3.5	−2.0	0.2	0.5	3.6	−4.1	−0.7	−2.1
Balance on goods and services	27.7	27.4	5.0	−12.6	−14.2	−18.6	0.4	−9.2	−13.2	−18.0
Factor income, net	−40.2	−38.7	−32.6	−33.8	−41.7	−43.4	−48.0	−43.8	−49.9	−50.6
Current transfers, net	7.1	10.0	10.8	12.1	11.2	12.8	14.8	13.6	14.7	15.0
Current account balance	**−5.4**	**−1.3**	**−16.8**	**−34.4**	**−44.7**	**−49.2**	**−32.8**	**−39.4**	**−48.3**	**−53.6**
Memorandum										
Exports of goods and services	147.3	163.3	162.3	171.5	183.7	209.7	247.7	272.9	295.8	319.1
Interest payments	40.8	41.8	37.4	36.5	38.1	40.6	45.3	47.5	50.2	52.5
Oil trade balance	13.6	18.7	14.4	13.7	12.5	13.8	15.0	21.9	22.6	22.1

Table A32. Developing Countries—by Analytical Criteria: Current Account Transactions
(In billions of U.S. dollars)

	1989	1990	1991	1992	1993	1994	1995	1996	1997	1998
By source of export earnings										
Fuel										
Exports	141.5	182.4	162.2	173.1	161.9	163.2	179.5	208.6	233.9	238.3
Imports	100.1	108.8	117.7	131.7	123.4	109.6	122.1	127.8	154.9	164.9
Trade balance	41.4	73.5	44.6	41.4	38.5	53.7	57.3	80.8	78.9	73.3
Services, net	−27.2	−32.8	−48.3	−42.4	−31.0	−24.3	−22.1	−29.2	−25.1	−25.1
Balance on goods and services	14.2	40.7	−3.8	−1.0	7.5	29.4	35.2	51.7	53.8	48.2
Factor income, net	−1.9	−0.8	−4.4	−3.0	−7.4	−8.2	−10.2	−4.2	−6.3	−5.4
Current transfers, net	−13.8	−25.3	−50.0	−20.2	−22.3	−24.6	−23.1	−23.2	−24.0	−25.4
Current account balance	**−1.6**	**14.7**	**−58.1**	**−24.1**	**−22.2**	**−3.4**	**1.9**	**24.3**	**23.6**	**17.3**
Memorandum										
Exports of goods and services	164.1	204.6	182.6	194.0	184.4	183.7	202.4	233.3	262.6	268.2
Interest payments	12.9	13.2	10.4	10.4	9.9	9.9	12.0	11.3	11.9	12.5
Oil trade balance	116.0	153.2	132.3	140.0	125.3	122.6	133.6	171.5	176.8	174.0
Nonfuel exports										
Exports	322.5	359.3	382.9	420.5	454.3	541.7	659.2	696.6	766.8	842.8
Imports	331.5	379.8	414.1	472.6	535.4	610.1	731.8	796.5	879.4	968.0
Trade balance	−9.0	−20.5	−31.2	−52.2	−81.1	−68.4	−72.5	−99.9	−112.6	−125.2
Services, net	0.3	5.3	2.9	3.8	−1.7	0.2	−1.3	0.9	1.0	−1.1
Balance on goods and services	−8.7	−15.2	−28.3	−48.3	−82.8	−68.2	−73.8	−99.0	−111.6	−126.2
Factor income, net	−61.8	−62.1	−56.7	−54.7	−57.8	−63.3	−74.5	−74.3	−75.8	−77.1
Current transfers, net	32.2	38.5	46.3	48.2	46.1	47.9	52.7	51.0	51.8	52.5
Current account balance	**−38.3**	**−38.7**	**−38.7**	**−54.9**	**−94.5**	**−83.6**	**−95.2**	**−122.3**	**−136.1**	**−150.9**
Memorandum										
Exports of goods and services	402.6	456.3	483.9	536.5	579.4	685.1	828.2	888.3	977.0	1,072.6
Interest payments	69.0	73.6	71.6	70.6	71.6	77.9	86.8	92.0	97.3	101.7
Oil trade balance	0.3	−0.5	−2.6	−4.2	−7.3	−6.5	−8.5	−8.8	−8.2	−3.5
Manufactures										
Exports	142.8	157.6	176.7	202.7	225.3	279.9	341.5	346.7	380.1	418.6
Imports	138.3	153.2	171.3	193.5	234.1	275.4	351.3	366.7	400.5	441.7
Trade balance	4.5	4.4	5.3	9.2	−8.8	4.5	−9.9	−20.0	−20.5	−23.1
Services, net	−2.1	−0.4	0.7	−1.8	−6.2	−8.0	−13.0	−11.3	−11.3	−11.2
Balance on goods and services	2.4	4.0	6.1	7.4	−14.9	−3.5	−22.8	−31.3	−31.8	−34.3
Factor income, net	−20.6	−18.6	−20.1	−18.4	−22.1	−25.3	−37.3	−40.1	−44.4	−47.2
Current transfers, net	3.1	3.5	9.2	10.3	10.2	13.9	16.4	14.7	15.0	15.1
Current account balance	**−15.1**	**−11.1**	**−4.8**	**−0.7**	**−26.8**	**−14.9**	**−43.8**	**−56.7**	**−61.2**	**−66.4**
Memorandum										
Exports of goods and services	164.0	185.2	204.7	235.9	263.7	326.8	402.3	417.6	459.1	507.2
Interest payments	20.2	20.9	20.7	21.8	22.1	24.0	29.2	32.5	36.3	38.5
Oil trade balance	−3.6	−5.5	−5.9	−6.8	−8.1	−8.5	−11.9	−15.3	−17.7	−18.2

Table A32 *(continued)*

	1989	1990	1991	1992	1993	1994	1995	1996	1997	1998
Nonfuel primary products										
Exports	35.4	36.1	36.3	37.6	38.0	45.2	56.1	57.7	60.9	66.4
Imports	34.0	37.0	38.8	42.7	43.9	48.2	60.0	66.6	70.2	75.6
Trade balance	1.4	−1.0	−2.5	−5.1	−5.9	−3.0	−3.9	−8.8	−9.3	−9.2
Services, net	−6.6	−6.5	−5.6	−6.2	−6.1	−5.9	−6.8	−6.6	−6.6	−7.0
Balance on goods and services	−5.2	−7.4	−8.0	−11.4	−11.9	−8.9	−10.7	−15.5	−15.9	−16.1
Factor income, net	−7.7	−8.0	−8.0	−8.0	−7.2	−7.5	−7.1	−8.1	−8.6	−9.0
Current transfers, net	5.2	5.7	6.6	7.7	7.2	7.4	7.5	7.6	8.0	8.3
Current account balance	**−7.8**	**−9.7**	**−9.5**	**−11.7**	**−12.0**	**−9.1**	**−10.3**	**−16.0**	**−16.5**	**−16.8**
Memorandum										
Exports of goods and services	41.9	43.1	44.2	46.3	47.0	55.4	68.4	71.3	75.9	82.7
Interest payments	9.2	9.1	9.0	9.0	8.7	8.6	9.0	8.7	9.3	9.7
Oil trade balance	−2.8	−3.5	−3.5	−2.9	−2.4	−2.5	−3.1	−3.8	−3.6	−3.3
Services, factor income, and private transfers										
Exports	13.6	14.7	14.5	14.8	15.0	17.1	19.9	21.2	22.6	24.0
Imports	32.2	37.2	38.3	39.8	41.7	44.2	50.0	54.7	59.1	62.8
Trade balance	−18.6	−22.5	−23.7	−25.0	−26.7	−27.1	−30.2	−33.5	−36.5	−38.8
Services, net	7.2	8.8	8.5	10.7	10.6	12.9	14.7	16.1	16.7	17.4
Balance on goods and services	−11.3	−13.7	−15.2	−14.3	−16.1	−14.2	−15.5	−17.4	−19.7	−21.4
Factor income, net	−3.8	−3.8	−2.5	−2.4	−2.0	−2.2	−2.9	−2.6	−2.6	−2.7
Current transfers, net	10.3	11.6	12.4	12.8	12.6	10.4	10.8	10.7	10.9	11.0
Current account balance	**−4.8**	**−5.9**	**−5.3**	**−3.9**	**−5.5**	**−6.0**	**−7.5**	**−9.2**	**−11.5**	**−13.1**
Memorandum										
Exports of goods and services	29.9	34.0	35.7	38.6	40.0	44.6	50.2	53.0	55.9	59.2
Interest payments	5.3	6.4	5.8	4.8	4.6	4.7	4.9	4.7	4.6	4.6
Oil trade balance	−0.4	−0.6	−0.6	−0.8	−0.7	−0.1	0.7	1.4	3.9	10.7
Diversified										
Exports	130.7	150.9	155.4	165.3	176.0	199.5	241.8	271.0	303.3	333.8
Imports	127.1	152.3	165.7	196.6	215.8	242.2	270.4	308.6	349.6	387.9
Trade balance	3.6	−1.4	−10.3	−31.2	−39.8	−42.7	−28.5	−37.6	−46.3	−54.1
Services, net	1.9	3.4	−0.8	1.2	−0.1	1.2	3.7	2.7	2.1	−0.3
Balance on goods and services	5.4	2.0	−11.1	−30.0	−39.8	−41.5	−24.8	−34.8	−44.2	−54.4
Factor income, net	−29.6	−31.7	−26.1	−26.0	−26.4	−28.2	−27.2	−23.5	−20.2	−18.2
Current transfers, net	13.6	17.7	18.1	17.4	16.1	16.2	18.0	17.9	17.9	18.1
Current account balance	**−10.6**	**−12.0**	**−19.1**	**−38.6**	**−50.2**	**−53.6**	**−33.6**	**−40.5**	**−46.9**	**−54.6**
Memorandum										
Exports of goods and services	166.7	194.0	199.4	215.6	228.7	258.2	307.3	346.4	386.2	423.6
Interest payments	34.4	37.2	36.1	35.1	36.2	40.7	43.8	46.1	47.1	48.8
Oil trade balance	7.1	9.0	7.4	6.3	3.9	4.6	5.9	8.8	9.1	7.3

Table A32 (continued)

	1989	1990	1991	1992	1993	1994	1995	1996	1997	1998
By external financing source										
Net debtor countries										
Exports	394.7	446.0	453.7	490.9	520.6	607.3	730.9	782.7	873.3	956.7
Imports	387.5	439.3	473.6	534.8	590.4	655.0	782.4	847.4	954.6	1,048.8
Trade balance	7.1	6.7	−19.9	−43.8	−69.8	−47.8	−51.5	−64.7	−81.2	−92.1
Services, net	−14.3	−10.6	−10.3	−10.1	−11.5	−7.5	−7.9	−11.8	−7.2	−8.7
Balance on goods and services	−7.2	−3.9	−30.2	−53.9	−81.3	−55.2	−59.3	−76.5	−88.4	−100.8
Factor income, net	−72.0	−71.0	−65.7	−64.3	−70.2	−75.7	−89.8	−83.8	−87.9	−88.1
Current transfers, net	33.8	40.1	48.2	50.4	48.7	50.6	55.2	53.7	54.4	55.1
Current account balance	**−45.3**	**−34.8**	**−47.6**	**−67.8**	**−102.8**	**−80.3**	**−93.6**	**−106.7**	**−122.4**	**−133.8**
Memorandum										
Exports of goods and services	481.1	549.3	560.0	612.6	653.1	757.9	907.2	982.3	1,095.3	1,199.6
Interest payments	80.9	85.8	81.1	80.1	80.3	86.6	97.3	102.2	108.3	113.2
Oil trade balance	59.7	73.8	54.9	53.4	44.3	42.6	45.7	72.0	78.3	84.5
Official financing										
Exports	44.5	52.3	50.9	51.1	52.6	55.2	65.6	74.7	78.3	84.0
Imports	53.9	60.2	61.8	66.2	67.9	69.9	82.6	89.6	93.8	100.3
Trade balance	−9.4	−7.9	−10.9	−15.1	−15.3	−14.7	−16.9	−14.9	−15.5	−16.3
Services, net	−4.3	−4.7	−4.7	−4.4	−6.1	−5.1	−4.3	−4.9	−4.1	−3.8
Balance on goods and services	−13.7	−12.6	−15.6	−19.6	−21.4	−19.8	−21.2	−19.8	−19.6	−20.1
Factor income, net	−8.6	−10.0	−12.8	−12.1	−11.3	−10.6	−13.3	−13.3	−13.2	−13.2
Current transfers, net	10.7	13.0	16.2	17.5	16.6	17.2	18.4	18.6	18.2	18.4
Current account balance	**−11.5**	**−9.7**	**−12.2**	**−14.2**	**−16.1**	**−13.2**	**−16.2**	**−14.6**	**−14.6**	**−14.9**
Memorandum										
Exports of goods and services	56.0	65.3	64.4	66.4	68.4	72.2	84.6	95.5	100.3	107.7
Interest payments	11.2	12.2	12.3	12.2	11.8	11.5	12.7	12.7	13.3	14.0
Oil trade balance	7.2	10.9	9.2	9.7	8.4	6.5	7.8	10.4	11.5	11.0
Private financing										
Exports	260.8	300.6	316.6	345.9	367.6	438.0	531.5	561.4	612.5	666.6
Imports	236.5	269.9	310.5	357.4	402.5	447.5	533.3	571.8	635.7	698.6
Trade balance	24.3	30.7	6.1	−11.5	−34.9	−9.5	−1.7	−10.4	−23.2	−32.0
Services, net	−2.2	0.1	−4.6	−6.0	−4.3	−1.2	−1.5	−3.7	1.8	1.4
Balance on goods and services	22.1	30.8	1.6	−17.5	−39.2	−10.7	−3.2	−14.1	−21.4	−30.6
Factor income, net	−46.9	−43.1	−40.1	−43.0	−51.8	−59.0	−71.9	−69.5	−78.5	−81.4
Current transfers, net	12.5	14.7	16.4	17.8	17.2	18.2	20.2	19.0	20.4	21.0
Current account balance	**−12.4**	**2.4**	**−22.1**	**−42.7**	**−73.7**	**−51.5**	**−54.8**	**−64.5**	**−79.5**	**−91.0**
Memorandum										
Exports of goods and services	312.1	364.8	381.8	421.4	452.2	534.6	646.5	689.9	754.1	821.1
Interest payments	50.9	53.6	51.0	52.4	52.5	58.2	66.8	70.9	75.0	78.7
Oil trade balance	34.0	50.9	43.8	42.6	36.7	36.7	39.0	48.4	47.2	47.2

Table A32 (continued)

	1989	1990	1991	1992	1993	1994	1995	1996	1997	1998
Diversified financing										
Exports	89.4	93.1	86.2	93.9	100.3	114.1	133.8	146.5	182.5	206.0
Imports	97.1	109.2	101.3	111.1	119.9	137.6	166.5	185.9	225.0	249.9
Trade balance	−7.8	−16.1	−15.1	−17.2	−19.6	−23.5	−32.8	−39.4	−42.5	−43.8
Services, net	−7.8	−5.9	−1.0	0.3	−1.1	−1.1	−2.1	−3.2	−4.9	−6.3
Balance on goods and services	−15.5	−22.0	−16.1	−16.9	−20.7	−24.7	−34.9	−42.6	−47.4	−50.1
Factor income, net	−16.5	−17.9	−12.7	−9.1	−7.2	−6.1	−4.6	−1.0	3.8	6.5
Current transfers, net	10.6	12.3	15.6	15.1	14.9	15.2	16.6	16.0	15.8	15.6
Current account balance	**−21.5**	**−27.5**	**−13.3**	**−10.9**	**−13.0**	**−15.6**	**−22.6**	**−27.6**	**−28.3**	**−27.9**
Memorandum										
Exports of goods and services	113.1	119.2	113.8	124.8	132.5	151.0	176.2	196.8	240.9	270.8
Interest payments	18.7	20.0	17.8	15.4	16.0	16.8	17.9	18.6	20.1	20.5
Oil trade balance	18.6	12.0	2.0	1.2	−0.7	−0.7	−1.1	13.2	19.6	26.4
Net debtor countries by debt-servicing experience										
Countries with recent difficulties										
Exports	162.9	180.4	163.9	168.4	170.6	186.9	214.5	239.6	273.8	296.9
Imports	141.1	156.0	161.5	175.7	180.3	193.3	234.4	255.6	298.4	322.0
Trade balance	21.8	24.4	2.4	−7.2	−9.8	−6.4	−19.8	−16.0	−24.5	−25.1
Services, net	−18.5	−19.0	−15.7	−14.2	−14.9	−13.0	−14.0	−21.1	−18.2	−19.5
Balance on goods and services	3.3	5.4	−13.3	−21.5	−24.7	−19.5	−33.8	−37.1	−42.8	−44.6
Factor income, net	−40.8	−38.2	−33.9	−30.2	−34.8	−30.2	−33.6	−25.3	−26.3	−22.6
Current transfers, net	19.0	22.0	24.7	25.9	25.0	24.2	26.1	24.6	25.5	25.9
Current account balance	**−18.4**	**−10.9**	**−22.6**	**−25.8**	**−34.5**	**−25.5**	**−40.9**	**−37.8**	**−44.0**	**−41.3**
Memorandum										
Exports of goods and services	194.7	216.1	200.1	209.1	213.7	234.3	268.6	300.6	343.7	373.0
Interest payments	45.4	46.1	40.7	36.7	35.6	35.6	41.9	42.6	46.5	48.1
Oil trade balance	55.5	70.0	53.8	53.4	47.6	46.4	50.6	76.2	82.7	83.2
Countries without recent difficulties										
Exports	231.7	265.6	289.9	322.5	350.0	420.4	516.4	543.1	599.5	659.8
Imports	246.4	283.3	312.2	359.1	410.1	461.7	548.0	591.8	656.2	726.7
Trade balance	−14.7	−17.7	−22.3	−36.6	−60.1	−41.3	−31.6	−48.7	−56.7	−67.0
Services, net	4.2	8.5	5.4	4.1	3.4	5.6	6.1	9.3	11.0	10.8
Balance on goods and services	−10.5	−9.3	−16.8	−32.4	−56.6	−35.8	−25.5	−39.4	−45.7	−56.2
Factor income, net	−31.2	−32.8	−31.7	−34.0	−35.4	−45.5	−56.3	−58.5	−61.7	−65.5
Current transfers, net	14.8	18.1	23.6	24.5	23.7	26.5	29.1	29.1	28.9	29.2
Current account balance	**−26.9**	**−24.0**	**−25.0**	**−42.0**	**−68.3**	**−54.8**	**−52.7**	**−68.9**	**−78.4**	**−92.5**
Memorandum										
Exports of goods and services	286.4	333.3	359.9	403.5	439.4	523.6	638.6	681.7	751.6	826.6
Interest payments	35.4	39.6	40.4	43.3	44.7	51.0	55.5	59.6	61.8	65.1
Oil trade balance	4.3	3.8	1.2	—	−3.3	−3.8	−4.9	−4.2	−4.5	1.3

Table A32 (concluded)

	1989	1990	1991	1992	1993	1994	1995	1996	1997	1998
Other groups										
Heavily indebted poor countries										
Exports	26.1	28.2	26.6	26.7	26.0	29.7	36.2	38.8	41.9	46.0
Imports	28.2	30.3	30.4	32.0	32.3	33.9	40.8	45.9	49.1	53.1
Trade balance	−2.1	−2.1	−3.8	−5.3	−6.3	−4.2	−4.6	−7.1	−7.2	−7.1
Services, net	−5.6	−6.2	−5.5	−6.2	−5.7	−4.8	−5.1	−5.8	−5.5	−5.4
Balance on goods and services	−7.7	−8.3	−9.2	−11.5	−12.0	−9.0	−9.6	−12.9	−12.7	−12.5
Factor income, net	−7.4	−7.3	−8.4	−7.6	−7.7	−6.9	−7.3	−7.6	−7.5	−7.2
Current transfers, net	6.5	5.8	6.2	6.9	6.9	7.1	7.4	7.3	7.5	7.7
Current account balance	**−8.7**	**−9.7**	**−11.4**	**−12.2**	**−12.9**	**−8.8**	**−9.6**	**−13.2**	**−12.8**	**−12.0**
Memorandum										
Exports of goods and services	31.4	34.2	33.1	33.7	33.0	37.1	45.1	48.3	52.4	57.5
Interest payments	6.8	7.2	7.9	7.5	7.7	7.2	7.6	7.7	7.4	7.0
Oil trade balance	3.2	3.9	3.5	3.9	3.0	3.3	4.1	3.7	5.2	5.4
Least developed countries										
Exports	16.3	16.6	15.8	15.3	16.3	19.2	22.2	23.7	25.2	27.7
Imports	23.8	25.8	26.0	26.6	27.3	28.6	32.7	35.9	37.9	40.7
Trade balance	−7.5	−9.2	−10.2	−11.2	−10.9	−9.4	−10.5	−12.3	−12.7	−13.0
Services, net	−3.3	−3.1	−3.0	−3.2	−3.1	−2.4	−2.7	−2.8	−2.6	−2.4
Balance on goods and services	−10.8	−12.3	−13.1	−14.5	−14.1	−11.7	−13.2	−15.1	−15.2	−15.4
Factor income, net	−3.2	−2.4	−3.0	−2.8	−2.3	−2.9	−2.9	−2.9	−3.0	−2.8
Current transfers, net	7.7	7.2	7.3	8.2	8.3	8.6	9.0	8.3	8.3	8.2
Current account balance	**−6.3**	**−7.6**	**−8.8**	**−9.1**	**−8.1**	**−6.0**	**−7.1**	**−9.6**	**−10.0**	**−9.9**
Memorandum										
Exports of goods and services	19.8	20.6	19.9	19.7	21.0	24.4	28.2	30.2	32.2	35.4
Interest payments	3.6	3.5	3.8	3.8	3.6	3.7	3.9	4.0	4.1	3.7
Oil trade balance	−0.7	−0.9	−1.2	−1.1	−1.2	−0.6	−0.5	−0.7	−0.5	−0.5
Middle East and north Africa										
Exports	127.7	160.3	145.1	156.7	147.8	152.7	167.0	186.9	212.7	218.0
Imports	111.6	124.8	130.3	142.5	138.3	131.4	145.1	155.1	181.8	191.6
Trade balance	16.1	35.5	14.9	14.2	9.5	21.3	21.9	31.9	30.9	26.3
Services, net	−21.1	−23.1	−38.5	−29.5	−22.5	−14.4	−12.1	−11.2	−11.4	−10.9
Balance on goods and services	−5.0	12.4	−23.6	−15.3	−13.0	6.9	9.8	20.7	19.5	15.4
Factor income, net	1.2	1.1	−1.3	0.9	−0.5	−1.5	−2.2	−2.4	0.2	0.3
Current transfers, net	−4.1	−13.9	−38.2	−8.5	−11.3	−16.2	−15.0	−15.1	−15.9	−17.2
Current account balance	**−8.0**	**−0.4**	**−63.1**	**−22.8**	**−24.8**	**−10.9**	**−7.3**	**3.2**	**3.8**	**−1.5**
Memorandum										
Exports of goods and services	158.2	192.6	176.0	190.8	181.9	186.9	205.3	228.2	258.3	266.0
Interest payments	−11.6	−12.7	−10.4	−9.4	−9.3	−9.5	−11.2	−11.1	−11.3	−11.4
Oil trade balance	93.4	121.6	105.5	113.1	100.5	99.8	108.4	139.7	146.5	150.5

Table A33. Summary of Balance of Payments and External Financing

(In billions of U.S. dollars)

	1989	1990	1991	1992	1993	1994	1995	1996	1997	1998
Developing countries										
Balance of payments										
Balance on current account	−39.9	−24.0	−96.8	−79.0	−116.7	−87.0	−93.3	−98.0	−112.5	−133.6
Balance on capital and financial account	39.9	24.0	96.8	79.0	116.7	87.0	93.3	98.0	112.5	133.6
By balance of payments component										
Capital transfers[1]	3.6	12.4	2.1	−3.4	1.8	1.8	−1.5	1.1	4.0	2.5
Net financial flows	59.3	60.2	156.9	143.1	165.1	138.3	182.1	196.5	171.9	188.7
Errors and omissions, net	−7.2	−3.9	−12.4	−15.0	−10.2	−11.0	−26.5	−17.3	−8.3	1.5
Change in reserves (− = increase)	−15.8	−44.6	−49.7	−45.7	−40.0	−42.2	−60.7	−82.3	−55.1	−59.1
By type of financing flow										
Nonexceptional financing flows	17.9	8.5	106.3	83.5	117.0	108.0	135.9	170.4	170.3	190.8
Exceptional financing flows	37.8	60.1	40.2	41.2	39.7	21.2	18.1	9.9	−2.7	1.9
Arrears on debt service	9.7	15.4	13.5	4.6	13.0	−4.0	−4.1	−7.3	. . .	. . .
Debt forgiveness	3.5	13.6	1.0	0.2	1.5	1.1	2.5	0.4	. . .	. . .
Rescheduling of debt service	24.0	14.0	13.8	14.8	19.2	14.7	15.1	12.0	. . .	. . .
Change in reserves (− = increase)	−15.8	−44.6	−49.7	−45.7	−40.0	−42.2	−60.7	−82.3	−55.1	−59.1
External financing										
Balance on current account	−39.9	−24.0	−96.8	−79.0	−116.7	−87.0	−93.3	−98.0	−112.5	−133.6
Change in reserves (− = increase)[2]	−15.8	−44.6	−49.7	−45.7	−40.0	−42.2	−60.7	−82.3	−55.1	−59.1
Asset transactions, including net errors and omissions[3]	−17.7	−27.9	27.9	−14.7	−20.1	−18.6	−33.8	−33.3	−33.3	−12.8
Total, net external financing[4]	**73.4**	**96.6**	**118.6**	**139.4**	**176.8**	**147.8**	**187.8**	**213.6**	**200.9**	**205.5**
Non-debt-creating flows, net	24.1	31.9	34.6	37.0	79.4	92.6	82.4	110.0	111.5	107.5
Capital transfers[1]	3.6	12.4	2.1	−3.4	1.8	1.8	−1.5	1.1	4.0	2.5
Direct investment and other equity flows	20.6	19.4	32.6	40.4	77.6	90.8	83.9	108.8	107.5	104.9
Net credit and loans from IMF[5]	−1.5	−1.9	1.1	−0.4	−0.1	−0.8	12.6	−1.0	. . .	. . .
Net external borrowing[6]	50.8	66.6	82.9	102.8	97.5	56.0	92.8	104.6	93.2	103.2
Borrowing from official creditors[7]	27.2	13.0	20.8	14.3	23.3	20.4	31.0	−3.8	−5.5	−0.6
Borrowing from banks[8]	8.0	17.4	18.5	19.8	17.8	−32.8	11.4	9.8	18.7	18.7
Other borrowing[9]	15.6	36.3	43.6	68.8	56.3	68.4	50.3	98.7	80.1	85.1
Memorandum										
Balance on goods and services in percent of GDP[10]	0.2	0.8	−1.0	−1.4	−1.9	−0.9	−0.8	−0.9	−0.9	−1.1
Scheduled amortization of external debt	83.8	91.5	93.9	111.7	125.3	128.9	144.3	159.4	139.0	135.8
Gross external financing[11]	157.2	188.1	212.6	251.1	302.1	276.6	332.0	372.9	340.0	341.3
Gross external borrowing[11]	134.6	158.2	176.8	214.5	222.8	184.9	237.1	264.0	232.3	238.9
Countries in transition										
Balance of payments										
Balance on current account	−7.3	−21.9	2.8	−2.1	−6.6	5.1	−3.1	−9.4	−18.7	−25.6
Balance on capital and financial account	7.3	21.9	−2.8	2.1	6.6	−5.1	3.1	9.4	18.7	25.6
By balance of payments component										
Capital transfers[1]	0.4	—	0.9	2.5	2.7	0.3	0.5	0.2	−0.1	—
Net financial flows	9.3	10.8	−0.1	7.1	14.1	5.1	37.9	10.7	25.6	35.0
Errors and omissions, net	4.1	4.2	−3.9	−1.1	2.7	−2.3	−1.7	−2.0	−0.7	−0.8
Change in reserves (− = increase)	−6.4	6.8	0.4	−6.3	−12.9	−8.3	−33.6	0.5	−6.2	−8.6

Table A33 (concluded)

	1989	1990	1991	1992	1993	1994	1995	1996	1997	1998
By type of financing flow										
Nonexceptional financing flows	11.1	−2.3	−17.6	−12.3	−4.3	−18.2	20.1	0.8	23.0	32.4
Exceptional financing flows	2.7	17.3	14.5	20.7	23.8	21.3	16.6	8.2	1.8	1.9
Arrears on debt service	0.8	9.0	6.1	8.5	3.4	3.4	−13.9	−0.5	...	...
Debt forgiveness	0.4	—	0.9	2.4	2.1	—	—	—	...	...
Rescheduling of debt service	1.5	8.3	7.2	9.7	16.6	15.6	26.8	8.8	...	...
Change in reserves (− = increase)	−6.4	6.8	0.4	−6.3	−12.9	−8.3	−33.6	0.5	−6.2	−8.6
External financing										
Balance on current account	−7.3	−21.9	2.8	−2.1	−6.6	5.1	−3.1	−9.4	−18.7	−25.6
Change in reserves (− = increase)[2]	−6.4	6.8	0.4	−6.3	−12.9	−8.3	−33.6	0.5	−6.2	−8.6
Asset transactions, including										
net errors and omissions[3]	1.2	−1.1	−2.2	−1.3	11.2	−0.8	−1.1	−2.4	−1.0	−1.2
Total, net external financing[4]	**12.5**	**16.1**	**−0.9**	**9.7**	**8.3**	**4.0**	**37.8**	**11.3**	**25.9**	**35.5**
Non-debt-creating flows, net	0.6	—	3.2	6.6	8.4	5.4	13.4	11.3	13.2	16.5
Capital transfers[1]	0.4	—	0.9	2.5	2.7	0.3	0.5	0.2	−0.1	—
Direct investment and other										
equity flows	0.2	—	2.3	4.1	5.7	5.1	12.9	11.1	13.3	16.5
Net credit and loans from IMF[5]	−0.3	0.3	2.4	1.6	3.7	2.4	4.7	2.2	...	...
Net external borrowing[6]	12.2	15.8	−6.5	1.5	−3.8	−3.8	19.6	−2.3	7.9	16.7
Borrowing from official										
creditors[7]	−1.9	6.6	1.5	—	3.2	−10.3	8.8	−8.8	2.9	9.5
Borrowing from banks[8]	12.4	−0.6	−4.5	−0.5	4.5	2.8	−0.6	0.5	0.5	—
Other borrowing[9]	1.7	9.8	−3.6	2.0	−11.5	3.6	11.4	6.0	4.6	7.2
Memorandum										
Balance on goods and services										
in percent of GDP[10]	−0.1	−0.7	0.1	—	−1.6	1.3	0.2	−0.1	−0.6	−1.1
Scheduled amortization										
of external debt	17.1	29.1	28.0	27.5	24.4	26.5	24.3	21.5	15.3	18.8
Gross external financing[11]	29.7	45.2	27.1	37.2	32.7	30.5	62.1	32.8	41.2	54.3
Gross external borrowing[11]	29.3	44.8	21.5	29.0	20.6	22.6	43.9	19.3	23.3	35.5

[1]Comprise debt forgiveness as well as all other identified transactions on capital account as defined in the 5th edition of the IMF's *Balance of Payments Manual.*

[2]Positioned here to reflect the discretionary nature of many countries' transactions in reserves.

[3]Include changes in recorded private external assets (mainly portfolio investment), export credit, the collateral for debt-reduction operations, and the net change in unrecorded balance of payments flows (net errors and omissions).

[4]Equals, with opposite sign, the sum of transactions listed above. It is the amount required to finance the deficit on goods and services, factor income, and current transfers; the increase in the official reserve level; the net asset transactions; and the transactions underlying net errors and omissions.

[5]Comprise use of IMF resources under the General Resources Account, Trust Fund, Structural Adjustment Facility (SAF), and Enhanced Structural Adjustment Facility (ESAF). For further detail, see Table A37.

[6]Net disbursement of long- and short-term credits (including exceptional financing) by both official and private creditors.

[7]Net disbursements by official creditors (other than monetary authorities) based on directly reported flows, and flows derived from statistics on debt stocks. The estimates include the increase in official claims caused by the transfer of officially guaranteed claims to the guarantor agency in the creditor country, usually in the context of debt rescheduling.

[8]Net disbursements by commercial banks based on directly reported flows and on cross-border claims and liabilities reported in the International Banking section of the IMF's *International Financial Statistics.*

[9]Includes primary bond issues and loans on the international capital markets. Since the estimates are residually derived, they also reflect any underrecording or misclassification of official and commercial bank credits above.

[10]This is often referred to as the "resource balance" and, with opposite sign, the "net resource transfer."

[11]Net external financing/borrowing (see footnotes 4 and 6, respectively) plus amortization due on external debt.

Table A34. Developing Countries—by Region: Balance of Payments and External Financing[1]

(In billions of U.S. dollars)

	1989	1990	1991	1992	1993	1994	1995	1996	1997	1998
Africa										
Balance on current account	−7.9	−3.7	−5.6	−9.7	−9.4	−11.4	−15.5	−7.7	−8.1	−8.2
Change in reserves (− = increase)	−2.5	−3.9	−3.2	2.4	−1.0	−5.8	−2.2	−4.4	−5.3	−4.6
Asset transactions, including net errors and omissions	−3.0	−2.2	−3.5	−2.3	−0.5	−1.8	−0.4	−4.1	−0.5	0.9
Total, net external financing	**13.3**	**9.7**	**12.4**	**9.6**	**10.8**	**19.0**	**18.1**	**16.1**	**13.9**	**11.9**
Non-debt-creating flows, net	3.5	2.4	2.3	−2.9	0.9	4.0	2.5	5.0	7.0	5.9
Net credit and loans from IMF	0.1	−0.6	0.2	−0.2	0.2	0.9	0.8	0.6	...	...
Net external borrowing	9.7	7.9	9.9	12.8	9.8	14.1	14.8	10.6	7.1	7.5
From official creditors	7.2	4.4	5.9	8.6	6.2	5.5	4.0	6.4	0.1	0.3
From banks	1.7	4.3	0.9	2.4	−1.4	−1.1	3.1	−0.1	0.7	0.2
Other	0.9	−0.9	3.1	1.8	4.9	9.7	7.8	4.3	6.3	7.0
Memorandum										
Net financial flows	12.1	7.3	11.4	14.2	10.9	18.2	17.6	15.4	10.2	11.2
Exceptional financing	14.8	20.3	15.2	21.3	14.0	17.7	19.0	12.0	1.2	0.3
Sub-Sahara										
Balance on current account	−5.7	−4.6	−7.5	−9.4	−8.6	−8.4	−11.2	−6.7	−6.6	−7.4
Change in reserves (− = increase)	−2.5	−3.1	−1.8	2.8	−0.9	−3.8	−3.2	−2.2	−3.8	−3.3
Asset transactions, including net errors and omissions	−2.3	−0.7	−3.2	−2.6	−0.9	−1.5	−0.4	−4.1	−0.5	0.9
Total, net external financing	**10.4**	**8.4**	**12.5**	**9.2**	**10.4**	**13.7**	**14.8**	**13.0**	**11.0**	**9.8**
Non-debt-creating flows, net	3.2	−0.6	1.9	−3.9	—	2.8	1.6	4.0	5.7	4.2
Net credit and loans from IMF	−0.4	−0.3	—	—	0.7	0.5	0.6	0.1	...	...
Net external borrowing	7.7	9.3	10.7	13.1	9.7	10.5	12.6	8.9	6.0	6.8
From official creditors	5.5	6.2	4.7	7.4	4.3	5.9	2.8	5.5	−0.8	−0.4
From banks	2.6	5.4	0.7	2.5	1.3	1.7	1.7	−0.9	—	−0.3
Other	−0.4	−2.3	5.3	3.3	4.1	2.9	8.1	4.4	6.7	7.5
Memorandum										
Net financial flows	9.2	8.7	11.5	13.8	10.5	12.8	14.3	12.3	7.3	9.0
Exceptional financing	13.5	15.9	14.2	20.7	14.0	12.0	12.7	7.2	−2.3	−0.7
Asia										
Balance on current account	−22.7	−16.4	−11.4	−12.8	−33.5	−22.2	−40.3	−49.6	−56.3	−65.8
Change in reserves (− = increase)	−4.7	−19.1	−26.7	−15.1	−25.3	−47.4	−28.3	−43.2	−33.8	−33.8
Asset transactions, including net errors and omissions	−1.9	−0.2	−8.0	−13.2	−14.6	−6.3	−31.7	−18.9	−18.9	−13.6
Total, net external financing	**29.2**	**35.7**	**46.1**	**41.1**	**73.4**	**75.9**	**100.3**	**111.7**	**109.0**	**113.1**
Non-debt-creating flows, net	9.2	10.8	13.1	18.6	34.9	44.5	50.5	55.8	54.3	53.2
Net credit and loans from IMF	−1.1	−2.4	1.9	1.3	0.6	−0.8	−1.5	−1.0	...	...
Net external borrowing	21.2	27.3	31.1	21.3	38.0	32.3	51.3	56.9	55.6	60.9
From official creditors	9.1	6.4	10.6	10.7	10.1	6.2	5.6	7.2	7.3	7.4
From banks	6.3	12.0	10.6	7.6	9.8	9.4	13.3	15.0	14.1	13.8
Other	5.7	8.8	9.9	3.0	18.1	16.7	32.4	34.6	34.2	39.6
Memorandum										
Net financial flows	27.9	33.8	43.0	33.9	63.5	69.0	94.7	101.4	95.5	98.0
Exceptional financing	1.8	2.3	2.4	2.2	1.7	1.6	0.1	0.2	0.2	0.2

Table A34 (concluded)

	1989	1990	1991	1992	1993	1994	1995	1996	1997	1998
Asia excluding China and India										
Balance on current account	−10.1	−18.8	−20.9	−16.2	−20.2	−23.3	−37.1	−42.1	−42.7	−45.7
Change in reserves (− = increase)	−6.2	−8.7	−10.2	−15.8	−16.7	−11.0	−6.8	−12.6	−12.3	−15.1
Asset transactions, including										
net errors and omissions	−2.5	1.2	−1.5	−2.3	−7.6	−4.7	−15.3	−11.6	−12.0	−13.0
Total, net external financing	**18.8**	**26.4**	**32.7**	**34.3**	**44.5**	**39.0**	**59.2**	**66.2**	**67.0**	**73.7**
Non-debt-creating flows, net	6.3	8.0	9.5	11.1	11.2	11.5	14.7	18.0	20.5	24.3
Net credit and loans from IMF	—	−1.0	0.2	0.1	0.1	0.4	−0.3	−0.2	...	...
Net external borrowing	12.5	19.4	23.0	23.1	33.1	27.1	44.8	48.4	46.7	49.9
From official creditors	5.1	3.9	6.6	4.7	4.2	2.7	3.7	4.3	5.0	4.8
From banks	1.7	9.6	6.9	3.5	2.1	7.2	10.5	12.5	9.8	8.8
Other	5.7	5.8	9.6	14.8	26.8	17.1	30.6	31.6	31.9	36.3
Memorandum										
Net financial flows	17.4	25.1	30.1	30.6	34.4	30.1	51.2	54.3	53.4	59.2
Exceptional financing	1.8	2.3	2.4	2.2	1.7	1.6	0.1	0.2	0.2	0.2
Middle East and Europe										
Balance on current account	−3.9	−2.6	−63.1	−22.1	−29.1	−4.2	−4.7	−1.3	0.3	−6.0
Change in reserves (− = increase)	−9.8	−4.4	−4.3	−11.7	6.1	−0.1	−6.5	−13.9	−4.1	−10.3
Asset transactions, including										
net errors and omissions	−3.2	−9.6	52.4	10.2	−0.4	10.4	9.7	5.7	−6.7	4.6
Total, net external financing	**17.0**	**16.5**	**14.9**	**23.6**	**23.4**	**−6.1**	**1.5**	**9.5**	**10.5**	**11.7**
Non-debt-creating flows, net	4.1	11.8	2.0	2.0	2.1	0.7	−2.2	0.9	2.6	2.3
Net credit and loans from IMF	−0.2	−0.1	—	0.1	—	0.4	0.4	0.1	...	...
Net external borrowing	13.1	4.9	13.0	21.5	21.3	−7.2	3.3	8.5	7.8	9.5
From official creditors	3.0	−6.2	1.1	−3.0	5.9	10.3	−1.3	−5.8	−7.4	−6.6
From banks	−0.3	4.4	2.1	11.0	5.0	−9.2	−8.0	−3.7	0.5	0.9
Other	10.4	6.7	9.7	13.4	10.4	−8.4	12.5	18.1	14.7	15.2
Memorandum										
Net financial flows	13.5	0.4	74.3	41.5	27.9	7.9	11.3	13.6	4.3	15.8
Exceptional financing	1.2	14.6	7.3	6.4	14.7	−5.4	−1.4	−0.2	0.9	0.5
Western Hemisphere										
Balance on current account	−5.4	−1.3	−16.8	−34.4	−44.7	−49.2	−32.8	−39.4	−48.3	−53.6
Change in reserves (− = increase)	1.1	−17.3	−15.5	−21.3	−19.9	11.2	−23.6	−20.8	−12.0	−10.4
Asset transactions, including										
net errors and omissions	−9.6	−16.0	−13.0	−9.4	−4.6	−20.9	−11.4	−16.0	−7.2	−4.7
Total, net external financing	**13.9**	**34.6**	**45.2**	**65.1**	**69.1**	**58.9**	**67.8**	**76.2**	**67.5**	**68.7**
Non-debt-creating flows, net	7.2	6.7	11.5	13.3	14.2	22.1	20.1	30.1	32.0	32.1
Net credit and loans from IMF	−0.2	1.2	−1.0	−1.6	−0.9	−1.3	12.9	−0.7	...	...
Net external borrowing	6.9	26.8	34.8	53.4	55.8	38.1	34.8	46.8	38.4	39.3
From official creditors	7.9	8.3	3.2	−2.0	1.1	−1.7	22.7	−11.6	−5.5	−1.8
From banks	0.3	−3.4	4.8	−1.2	4.3	−31.9	3.1	−1.5	3.5	3.8
Other	−1.3	21.9	26.7	56.6	50.4	71.7	9.1	59.9	40.4	37.3
Memorandum										
Net financial flows	5.8	18.6	28.2	53.5	62.8	43.2	58.4	66.0	62.0	63.6
Exceptional financing	20.0	22.9	15.3	11.4	9.3	7.3	0.4	−2.2	−5.0	0.9

[1]For definitions, see footnotes to Table A33.

Table A35. Developing Countries—by Analytical Criteria: Balance of Payments and External Financing[1]

(In billions of U.S. dollars)

	1989	1990	1991	1992	1993	1994	1995	1996	1997	1998
By source of export earnings										
Fuel										
Balance on current account	−1.6	14.7	−58.1	−24.1	−22.2	−3.4	1.9	24.3	23.6	17.3
Change in reserves (− = increase)	−7.8	−7.6	−1.4	2.1	10.8	−0.7	−2.0	−21.6	−17.0	−18.6
Asset transactions, including										
net errors and omissions	−0.6	−18.4	45.4	7.0	3.8	4.5	7.9	1.4	−7.4	3.5
Total, net external financing	**10.1**	**11.3**	**14.1**	**15.0**	**7.7**	**−0.4**	**−7.9**	**−4.1**	**0.8**	**−2.3**
Non-debt-creating flows, net	—	−3.6	0.7	−6.5	−2.6	−0.4	−3.8	1.2	5.3	4.1
Net credit and loans from IMF	1.7	1.9	0.5	−0.5	−0.8	0.4	−0.2	0.4	...	...
Net external borrowing	8.4	13.0	12.8	22.0	11.0	−0.5	−3.9	−5.7	−4.5	−5.6
From official creditors	3.8	3.6	1.7	2.1	2.9	11.2	1.2	0.9	−4.8	−3.1
From banks	3.9	−12.4	2.9	13.1	3.6	−10.0	−3.4	−3.4	−0.5	0.5
Other	0.8	21.8	8.2	6.8	4.5	−1.6	−1.7	−3.2	0.7	−3.1
Memorandum										
Net financial flows	12.2	7.6	78.6	40.0	17.2	11.1	4.1	2.2	−5.3	2.2
Exceptional financing	9.4	11.1	8.4	15.9	17.7	5.7	11.1	8.3	4.4	2.1
Nonfuel										
Balance on current account	−38.3	−38.7	−38.7	−54.9	−94.5	−83.6	−95.2	−122.3	−136.1	−150.9
Change in reserves (− = increase)	−8.0	−37.0	−48.3	−47.8	−50.8	−41.5	−58.7	−60.7	−38.1	−40.5
Asset transactions, including										
net errors and omissions	−17.1	−9.5	−17.5	−21.6	−23.8	−23.1	−41.7	−34.7	−26.0	−16.3
Total, net external financing	**63.4**	**85.3**	**104.5**	**124.4**	**169.1**	**148.2**	**195.7**	**217.7**	**200.2**	**207.8**
Non-debt-creating flows, net	24.0	35.3	28.1	37.4	54.5	71.6	74.7	90.6	90.6	89.3
Net credit and loans from IMF	−3.2	−3.8	0.6	—	0.6	−1.2	12.8	−1.4	...	...
Net external borrowing	42.5	53.8	75.9	86.9	113.9	77.8	108.2	128.5	113.3	122.9
From official creditors	23.4	9.4	19.1	12.1	20.4	9.2	29.8	−4.7	−0.8	2.4
From banks	4.1	29.8	15.5	6.7	14.2	−22.8	14.9	13.1	19.1	18.2
Other	15.0	14.6	41.2	68.1	79.3	91.3	63.4	120.1	94.9	102.2
Memorandum										
Net financial flows	47.1	52.6	78.3	103.1	147.9	127.3	177.9	194.3	177.3	186.4
Exceptional financing	28.4	49.1	31.8	25.4	21.9	15.5	7.0	1.6	−7.1	−0.1
By external financing source										
Net creditor countries										
Balance on current account	5.5	10.8	−49.2	−11.2	−13.8	−6.6	0.3	8.7	9.9	0.2
Change in reserves (− = increase)	−1.1	0.8	−0.2	−3.2	9.6	0.9	−0.2	−10.1	−5.0	−4.2
Asset transactions, including										
net errors and omissions	−3.6	−12.1	48.3	7.8	3.9	5.1	8.4	4.2	−6.5	3.8
Total, net external financing	**−0.8**	**0.4**	**1.2**	**6.7**	**0.2**	**0.7**	**−8.5**	**−2.8**	**1.6**	**0.2**
Non-debt-creating flows, net	−0.7	−0.1	−0.1	−1.0	−0.7	−0.5	−3.7	−0.7	−0.2	−0.9
Net credit and loans from IMF	—	—	—	—	—	—	—	—	...	...
Net external borrowing	—	0.5	1.3	7.6	1.0	1.3	−4.8	−2.1	1.8	1.1
From official creditors	−0.2	—	0.1	−0.2	0.2	0.3	0.1	0.3	0.4	0.6
From banks	0.1	—	1.1	6.6	−0.4	1.3	−6.1	−3.3	—	0.1
Other	0.1	0.5	0.1	1.2	1.1	−0.4	1.2	0.9	1.4	0.4
Memorandum										
Net financial flows	−3.5	−5.3	63.2	24.6	7.4	11.0	1.7	1.3	−5.4	3.6
Exceptional financing	—	—	—	—	—	—	—	—	—	—

183

Table A35 (continued)

	1989	1990	1991	1992	1993	1994	1995	1996	1997	1998
Net debtor countries										
Balance on current account	−45.3	−34.8	−47.6	−67.8	−102.8	−80.3	−93.6	−106.7	−122.4	−133.8
Change in reserves (− = increase)	−14.7	−45.5	−49.5	−42.5	−49.7	−43.0	−60.5	−72.3	−50.1	−55.0
Asset transactions, including										
net errors and omissions	−14.1	−15.9	−20.4	−22.5	−24.0	−23.7	−42.2	−37.4	−26.8	−16.6
Total, net external financing	**74.2**	**96.2**	**117.5**	**132.7**	**176.5**	**147.0**	**196.3**	**216.4**	**199.4**	**205.3**
Non-debt-creating flows, net	24.7	31.8	28.9	31.9	52.7	71.8	74.6	92.5	96.1	94.3
Net credit and loans from IMF	−1.5	−1.9	1.1	−0.4	−0.1	−0.8	12.6	−1.0	. . .	. . .
Net external borrowing	51.0	66.3	87.5	101.3	124.0	76.0	109.1	124.9	107.1	116.1
From official creditors	27.5	12.9	20.7	14.4	23.1	20.1	31.0	−4.1	−5.9	−1.2
From banks	7.9	17.4	17.4	13.1	18.2	−34.1	17.5	13.1	18.7	18.6
Other	15.7	36.0	49.3	73.7	82.7	90.1	60.5	116.0	94.3	98.8
Memorandum										
Net financial flows	62.8	65.5	93.7	118.5	157.7	127.3	180.3	195.2	177.3	185.1
Exceptional financing	37.8	60.1	40.2	41.2	39.7	21.2	18.1	9.9	−2.7	1.9
Official financing										
Balance on current account	−11.5	−9.7	−12.2	−14.2	−16.1	−13.2	−16.2	−14.6	−14.6	−14.9
Change in reserves (− = increase)	−2.0	−4.6	−4.5	1.8	−0.1	−5.3	−2.1	−2.8	−3.2	−3.8
Asset transactions, including										
net errors and omissions	−0.4	0.6	1.7	2.4	3.7	1.5	1.3	−2.7	1.3	2.6
Total, net external financing	**13.9**	**13.7**	**15.0**	**9.9**	**12.5**	**17.0**	**16.9**	**20.0**	**16.5**	**16.0**
Non-debt-creating flows, net	3.8	3.8	3.4	−1.3	3.0	5.0	5.0	7.6	10.0	9.0
Net credit and loans from IMF	—	−0.8	0.2	0.3	−0.3	0.8	0.6	—	. . .	. . .
Net external borrowing	10.1	10.6	11.4	10.9	9.9	11.2	11.3	12.4	6.4	8.0
From official creditors	10.0	6.2	8.3	9.7	6.9	7.7	4.4	8.0	2.6	2.1
From banks	−2.3	5.0	0.1	1.9	2.0	1.8	2.0	−0.5	−0.6	—
Other	2.4	−0.5	3.0	−0.7	0.9	1.6	4.9	4.9	4.3	6.0
Memorandum										
Net financial flows	12.5	10.6	13.7	14.4	12.0	15.8	15.9	19.4	12.9	15.3
Exceptional financing	14.3	19.7	15.5	20.5	14.1	13.2	12.1	7.2	2.0	−1.0
Private financing										
Balance on current account	−12.4	2.4	−22.1	−42.7	−73.7	−51.5	−54.8	−64.5	−79.5	−91.0
Change in reserves (− = increase)	−9.5	−34.7	−31.3	−29.7	−35.7	−25.0	−58.0	−59.3	−34.1	−34.2
Asset transactions, including										
net errors and omissions	−9.9	−21.5	−25.4	−32.4	−32.0	−29.9	−38.4	−34.2	−28.8	−21.1
Total, net external financing	**31.7**	**53.7**	**78.8**	**104.8**	**141.5**	**106.3**	**151.3**	**158.0**	**142.4**	**146.4**
Non-debt-creating flows, net	13.3	13.6	20.7	27.2	43.7	59.2	59.4	72.0	70.9	68.8
Net credit and loans from IMF	−0.2	0.5	−1.2	−1.9	−0.4	−0.2	13.7	0.2	. . .	. . .
Net external borrowing	18.6	39.7	59.3	79.5	98.2	47.3	78.1	85.9	74.2	80.9
From official creditors	8.9	7.9	7.0	0.1	8.6	8.3	24.9	−13.7	−9.5	−4.8
From banks	4.7	3.8	12.9	9.3	17.7	−40.5	8.9	4.2	11.6	12.7
Other	5.1	28.0	39.5	70.2	71.8	79.5	44.3	95.4	72.0	72.9
Memorandum										
Net financial flows	23.8	36.3	58.3	84.3	120.9	84.2	134.9	136.1	122.2	124.6
Exceptional financing	18.4	22.4	14.7	12.6	18.4	4.9	3.6	1.6	−1.2	2.2

Table A35 (continued)

	1989	1990	1991	1992	1993	1994	1995	1996	1997	1998
Diversified financing										
Balance on current account	−21.5	−27.5	−13.3	−10.9	−13.0	−15.6	−22.6	−27.6	−28.3	−27.9
Change in reserves (− = increase)	−3.3	−6.2	−13.6	−14.6	−13.9	−12.8	−0.5	−10.2	−12.8	−17.0
Asset transactions, including										
net errors and omissions	−3.8	5.0	3.3	7.6	4.3	4.7	−5.1	−0.5	0.7	2.0
Total, net external financing	**28.6**	**28.7**	**23.6**	**18.0**	**22.6**	**23.7**	**28.1**	**38.3**	**40.4**	**42.9**
Non-debt-creating flows, net	7.6	14.4	4.7	6.0	6.0	7.5	10.2	12.8	15.2	16.5
Net credit and loans from IMF	−1.3	−1.6	2.2	1.2	0.6	−1.4	−1.7	−1.1	...	...
Net external borrowing	22.3	16.0	16.7	10.8	15.9	17.5	19.6	26.6	26.5	27.2
From official creditors	8.6	−1.1	5.5	4.6	7.6	4.0	1.7	1.6	0.9	1.4
From banks	5.5	8.6	4.4	2.0	−1.5	4.6	6.7	9.4	7.6	5.9
Other	8.2	8.4	6.9	4.2	9.9	9.0	11.3	15.7	18.0	19.9
Memorandum										
Net financial flows	26.5	18.6	21.7	19.8	24.9	27.4	29.6	39.7	42.2	45.2
Exceptional financing	5.1	18.1	10.0	8.1	7.2	3.1	2.4	1.0	−3.5	0.7
Net debtor countries by debt-servicing experience										
Countries with recent difficulties										
Balance on current account	−18.4	−10.9	−22.6	−25.8	−34.5	−25.5	−40.9	−37.8	−44.0	−41.3
Change in reserves (− = increase)	−7.6	−15.9	−12.7	−20.7	−15.6	−9.9	−13.2	−23.8	−17.2	−22.0
Asset transactions, including										
net errors and omissions	−10.1	−4.3	−6.6	−3.3	1.0	−15.9	−11.2	−19.4	−7.4	−2.2
Total, net external financing	**36.1**	**31.0**	**41.9**	**49.8**	**49.2**	**51.3**	**65.3**	**81.0**	**68.6**	**65.5**
Non-debt-creating flows, net	10.3	16.2	8.3	7.1	11.0	13.3	14.1	23.7	31.1	30.6
Net credit and loans from IMF	−0.2	−0.2	−0.8	−1.2	−0.1	1.1	1.8	0.6	...	...
Net external borrowing	26.0	15.0	34.4	43.9	38.3	36.9	49.4	56.7	37.5	36.7
From official creditors	17.4	2.4	6.3	2.7	10.0	14.7	6.5	3.0	−4.1	−4.4
From banks	1.8	−6.4	−0.2	3.3	−1.0	−48.8	4.8	1.2	1.8	1.7
Other	6.8	19.0	28.3	37.9	29.4	71.0	38.1	52.5	39.9	39.4
Memorandum										
Net financial flows	29.5	13.8	28.4	46.4	45.9	40.0	56.9	71.2	60.6	61.4
Exceptional financing	36.7	57.1	38.5	39.8	38.2	20.5	19.3	12.3	−3.0	1.6
Countries without recent difficulties										
Balance on current account	−26.9	−24.0	−25.0	−42.0	−68.3	−54.8	−52.7	−68.9	−78.4	−92.5
Change in reserves (− = increase)	−7.1	−29.6	−36.7	−21.8	−34.0	−33.2	−47.3	−48.5	−33.0	−33.0
Asset transactions, including										
net errors and omissions	−4.1	−11.6	−13.8	−19.2	−25.0	−7.7	−31.0	−18.0	−19.4	−14.3
Total, net external financing	**38.1**	**65.1**	**75.6**	**83.0**	**127.3**	**95.7**	**131.0**	**135.4**	**130.8**	**139.8**
Non-debt-creating flows, net	14.4	15.5	20.6	24.8	41.7	58.5	60.5	68.8	65.0	63.7
Net credit and loans from IMF	−1.3	−1.7	1.9	0.8	−0.1	−1.9	10.9	−1.6	...	...
Net external borrowing	25.0	51.3	53.1	57.3	85.7	39.1	59.6	68.2	69.5	79.5
From official creditors	10.0	10.5	14.5	11.8	13.1	5.4	24.5	−7.2	−1.8	3.2
From banks	6.1	23.8	17.6	9.8	19.3	14.7	12.7	11.9	16.9	16.9
Other	8.9	17.0	21.0	35.7	53.3	19.1	22.4	63.4	54.5	59.4
Memorandum										
Net financial flows	33.3	51.7	65.3	72.1	111.8	87.4	123.5	124.0	116.7	123.7
Exceptional financing	1.1	3.1	1.7	1.4	1.4	0.7	−1.2	−2.4	0.3	0.3

Table A35 *(concluded)*

	1989	1990	1991	1992	1993	1994	1995	1996	1997	1998
Other groups										
Heavily indebted poor countries										
Balance on current account	−8.7	−9.7	−11.4	−12.2	−12.9	−8.8	−9.6	−13.2	−12.8	−12.0
Change in reserves (− = increase)	−0.5	0.4	−1.4	0.2	1.1	−3.0	−2.2	−1.8	−1.6	−1.6
Asset transactions, including										
net errors and omissions	−2.5	−1.1	1.8	1.7	3.3	1.0	1.6	1.2	0.9	2.3
Total, net external financing	**11.6**	**10.5**	**10.9**	**10.3**	**8.5**	**10.8**	**10.2**	**13.9**	**13.4**	**11.4**
Non-debt-creating flows, net	3.2	2.0	4.5	4.1	3.5	4.0	4.5	6.6	7.7	6.4
Net credit and loans from IMF	−0.3	−0.3	0.1	—	−0.2	0.5	0.6	0.2	...	...
Net external borrowing	8.8	8.7	6.4	6.2	5.2	6.2	5.0	7.0	5.7	5.7
From official creditors	7.6	8.3	4.2	5.8	2.5	4.2	2.6	4.5	2.1	1.3
From banks	1.3	0.6	0.3	0.7	−1.0	0.4	−0.1	−0.5	0.4	—
Other	—	−0.1	1.9	−0.3	3.7	1.6	2.5	3.1	3.1	4.4
Memorandum										
Net financial flows	8.4	7.8	7.8	7.8	6.4	8.9	8.0	11.3	9.5	10.3
Exceptional financing	9.7	10.3	11.3	12.3	11.4	10.4	8.5	3.9	−1.2	0.2
Least developed countries										
Balance on current account	−6.3	−7.6	−8.8	−9.1	−8.1	−6.0	−7.1	−9.6	−10.0	−9.9
Change in reserves (− = increase)	−0.8	−0.2	−1.9	−0.6	−1.3	−2.4	−1.2	−0.1	−1.2	−1.5
Asset transactions, including										
net errors and omissions	−1.9	−0.9	1.3	0.7	1.9	0.7	1.3	0.1	1.1	2.6
Total, net external financing	**9.1**	**8.7**	**9.4**	**9.0**	**7.5**	**7.7**	**6.9**	**9.5**	**10.1**	**8.8**
Non-debt-creating flows, net	3.0	2.8	3.7	3.9	3.2	3.3	3.2	4.1	5.7	4.5
Net credit and loans from IMF	−0.3	−0.4	0.1	0.2	−0.1	0.2	0.5	0.1	...	...
Net external borrowing	6.4	6.3	5.6	4.8	4.3	4.2	3.2	5.4	4.3	4.8
From official creditors	4.4	4.8	3.1	3.0	2.4	2.1	1.1	1.7	1.4	0.7
From banks	0.4	—	0.4	0.5	−0.9	−0.6	0.4	0.3	0.1	0.1
Other	1.6	1.4	2.1	1.4	2.8	2.8	1.7	3.4	2.8	4.0
Memorandum										
Net financial flows	3.7	2.2	3.4	2.7	1.4	2.0	2.7	7.8	8.5	11.1
Exceptional financing	4.7	5.5	5.4	6.2	5.8	5.5	4.1	1.5	1.4	−1.2
Middle East and north Africa										
Balance on current account	−8.0	−0.4	−63.1	−22.8	−24.8	−10.9	−7.3	3.2	3.8	−1.5
Change in reserves (− = increase)	−7.0	−3.9	−6.7	−10.8	6.5	−1.4	−1.2	−12.2	−7.4	−12.4
Asset transactions, including										
net errors and omissions	−5.3	−10.3	54.4	15.6	6.6	6.0	8.9	5.5	−5.4	5.9
Total, net external financing	**20.3**	**14.6**	**15.5**	**18.0**	**11.7**	**6.3**	**−0.4**	**3.5**	**9.1**	**8.0**
Non-debt-creating flows, net	4.0	14.3	1.7	2.4	2.3	1.3	−2.2	1.1	3.2	3.1
Net credit and loans from IMF	0.5	−0.3	0.2	−0.1	−0.5	0.5	0.2	0.6	...	...
Net external borrowing	15.8	0.6	13.6	15.7	9.9	4.5	1.6	1.9	5.3	5.0
From official creditors	6.0	−9.5	0.2	−1.4	4.9	10.5	0.8	−1.9	−2.9	−1.8
From banks	−3.3	2.2	2.9	9.1	−0.2	−12.4	−5.1	−2.9	0.2	0.2
Other	13.0	7.9	10.4	8.0	5.2	6.3	5.9	6.7	8.0	6.6
Memorandum										
Net financial flows	16.2	−3.7	77.2	38.9	19.9	17.6	10.2	8.8	3.3	12.7
Exceptional financing	3.9	20.4	9.4	8.2	15.8	1.4	6.1	5.8	5.5	2.6

[1]For definitions, see footnotes to Table A33.

Table A36. Developing Countries: Reserves[1]

	1989	1990	1991	1992	1993	1994	1995	1996	1997	1998
					In billions of U.S. dollars					
Developing countries	**153.2**	**193.4**	**248.4**	**264.3**	**311.8**	**364.5**	**429.5**	**499.4**	**555.3**	**615.1**
Regional groups										
Africa	12.7	17.5	21.3	18.1	19.5	24.5	26.6	30.3	35.5	40.0
Sub-Sahara	10.1	13.6	15.6	11.9	13.2	15.6	19.0	20.7	24.4	27.6
Asia	50.9	68.1	95.2	87.1	109.9	158.2	184.4	227.5	261.3	295.1
Excluding China and India	28.0	35.8	46.7	59.6	76.1	84.3	89.8	101.5	113.8	128.9
Middle East and Europe	56.3	59.3	65.8	70.0	73.3	76.6	88.4	91.1	96.0	107.1
Western Hemisphere	33.4	48.5	66.2	89.1	109.2	105.2	130.1	150.5	162.4	172.9
Analytical groups										
By source of export earnings										
Fuel	50.1	56.1	60.5	52.3	51.4	52.8	55.2	65.5	83.2	102.5
Manufactures	48.7	63.6	85.9	88.9	117.7	169.2	206.4	248.4	274.5	303.9
Nonfuel primary products	11.4	15.2	18.7	22.2	23.1	31.9	37.0	36.6	40.3	41.5
Services, factor income, and private transfers	8.1	10.8	15.3	20.3	24.7	28.1	32.4	32.9	32.4	30.7
Diversified	34.8	47.7	68.1	80.5	94.9	82.5	98.5	116.0	124.8	136.5
By external financing source										
Net creditor countries	31.1	27.0	29.1	26.3	25.3	25.1	29.2	29.2	34.2	38.3
Net debtor countries	122.1	166.5	219.3	238.0	286.5	339.4	400.3	470.2	521.1	576.7
Official financing	9.1	14.2	17.6	16.0	18.7	24.2	23.6	26.0	29.2	33.0
Private financing	82.8	118.6	153.2	161.8	197.7	231.4	289.5	347.2	382.2	417.2
Diversified financing	30.2	33.6	48.5	60.1	70.1	83.8	87.1	97.0	109.7	126.5
Net debtor countries by debt-servicing experience										
Countries with recent difficulties	41.0	58.8	75.7	97.9	115.0	130.7	145.8	169.3	187.1	209.8
Countries without recent difficulties	81.1	107.7	143.7	140.1	171.6	208.7	254.4	301.0	334.0	366.9
Other groups										
Heavily indebted poor countries	4.3	4.7	6.0	6.3	5.9	7.7	10.0	11.6	13.0	14.5
Least developed countries	7.6	9.0	10.9	11.1	12.2	14.1	15.5	16.1	17.4	18.9
Middle East and north Africa	51.6	54.2	63.6	67.7	70.8	75.0	81.0	82.0	90.3	103.5

Table A36 *(concluded)*

	1989	1990	1991	1992	1993	1994	1995	1996	1997	1998
					Ratio of reserves to imports of goods and services[2]					
Developing countries	**27.3**	**30.4**	**35.6**	**33.9**	**37.2**	**40.2**	**40.2**	**42.7**	**42.8**	**43.3**
Regional groups										
Africa	13.9	17.3	21.3	17.0	18.9	22.7	21.2	23.6	25.9	27.4
Sub-Sahara	14.6	18.0	20.3	14.6	16.8	19.5	20.4	21.5	23.7	25.0
Asia	26.8	31.6	40.1	31.4	33.2	40.7	37.8	43.1	44.6	45.0
Excluding China and India	24.8	25.3	29.4	33.6	37.4	35.0	29.3	30.4	31.3	31.7
Middle East and Europe	34.9	32.4	32.3	33.0	35.4	41.9	42.2	39.5	36.2	38.2
Western Hemisphere	27.9	35.7	42.0	48.4	55.2	46.1	52.6	53.3	52.6	51.3
Analytical groups										
By source of export earnings										
Fuel	33.4	34.2	32.5	26.8	29.0	34.2	33.0	36.1	39.9	46.6
Manufactures	30.1	35.1	43.3	38.9	42.3	51.2	48.6	55.3	55.9	56.1
Nonfuel primary products	24.2	30.0	35.8	38.5	39.2	49.6	46.8	42.2	43.9	41.9
Services, factor income, and private transfers	19.7	22.7	30.0	38.2	44.1	47.8	49.3	46.8	42.9	38.1
Diversified	21.6	24.8	32.3	32.8	35.3	27.5	29.6	30.4	29.0	28.6
By external financing source										
Net creditor countries	42.6	32.8	26.8	23.2	24.2	26.5	28.4	26.5	30.1	32.3
Net debtor countries	25.0	30.1	37.2	35.7	39.0	41.7	41.4	44.4	44.0	44.3
Official financing	13.0	18.2	22.0	18.7	20.8	26.3	22.4	22.5	24.4	25.8
Private financing	28.6	35.5	40.3	36.9	40.2	42.4	44.6	49.3	49.3	49.0
Diversified financing	23.5	23.8	37.3	42.4	45.8	47.7	41.3	40.5	38.0	39.4
Net debtor countries by debt-servicing experience										
Countries with recent difficulties	21.4	27.9	35.5	42.5	48.2	51.5	48.2	50.1	48.4	50.2
Countries without recent difficulties	27.3	31.4	38.1	32.1	34.6	37.3	38.3	41.7	41.9	41.6
Other groups										
Heavily indebted poor countries	11.0	11.0	14.2	13.9	13.1	16.7	18.4	18.9	19.9	20.7
Least developed countries	24.9	27.3	32.9	32.4	34.7	39.1	37.4	35.6	36.6	37.2
Middle East and north Africa	31.6	30.1	31.9	32.8	36.3	41.6	41.5	39.5	37.8	41.3

[1]In this table, official holdings of gold are valued at SDR 35 an ounce. This convention results in a marked underestimate of reserves for countries that have substantial gold holdings.

[2]Reserves at year-end in percent of imports of goods and services for the year indicated.

Table A37. Net Credit and Loans from IMF[1]

(In billions of U.S. dollars)

	1988	1989	1990	1991	1992	1993	1994	1995	1996
Developing countries	**−3.6**	**−1.5**	**−1.9**	**1.1**	**−0.4**	**−0.1**	**−0.8**	**12.6**	**−1.0**
Regional groups									
Africa	−0.3	0.1	−0.6	0.2	−0.2	0.2	0.9	0.8	0.6
Sub-Sahara	−0.2	−0.4	−0.3	—	—	0.7	0.5	0.6	0.1
Asia	−1.9	−1.1	−2.4	1.9	1.3	0.6	−0.8	−1.5	−1.0
Excluding China and India	−0.6	—	−1.0	0.2	0.1	0.1	0.4	−0.3	−0.2
Middle East and Europe	−0.5	−0.2	−0.1	—	0.1	—	0.4	0.4	0.1
Western Hemisphere	−0.9	−0.2	1.2	−1.0	−1.6	−0.9	−1.3	12.9	−0.7
Analytical groups									
By source of export earnings									
Fuel	0.2	1.7	1.9	0.5	−0.5	−0.8	0.4	−0.2	0.4
Manufactures	−2.3	−2.0	−2.6	1.4	0.9	−0.1	−0.9	−1.2	−0.9
Nonfuel primary products	−0.5	−0.4	−0.5	−0.3	—	−0.1	0.2	0.4	0.1
Services, factor income, and private transfers	−0.3	−0.1	−0.3	0.1	0.1	0.1	—	−0.1	—
Diversified	−0.6	−0.7	−0.5	−0.6	−1.0	0.7	−0.5	13.7	−0.6
By external financing source									
Net creditor countries	—	—	—	—	—	—	—	—	—
Net debtor countries	−3.6	−1.5	−1.9	1.1	−0.4	−0.1	−0.8	12.6	−1.0
Official financing	−0.5	—	−0.8	0.2	0.3	−0.3	0.8	0.6	—
Private financing	−1.4	−0.2	0.5	−1.2	−1.9	−0.4	−0.2	13.7	0.2
Diversified financing	−1.7	−1.3	−1.6	2.2	1.2	0.6	−1.4	−1.7	−1.1
Net debtor countries by debt-servicing experience									
Countries with recent difficulties	−0.9	−0.2	−0.2	−0.8	−1.2	−0.1	1.1	1.8	0.6
Countries without recent difficulties	−2.7	−1.3	−1.7	1.9	0.8	−0.1	−1.9	10.9	−1.6
Other groups									
Heavily indebted poor countries	−0.2	−0.3	−0.3	0.1	—	−0.2	0.5	0.6	0.2
Least developed countries	−0.2	−0.3	−0.4	0.1	0.2	−0.1	0.2	0.5	0.1
Middle East and north Africa	−0.2	0.5	−0.3	0.2	−0.1	−0.5	0.5	0.2	0.6
Countries in transition	**−0.5**	**−0.3**	**0.3**	**2.4**	**1.6**	**3.7**	**2.4**	**4.7**	**2.2**
Central and eastern Europe	. . .	. . .	. . .	2.4	0.5	2.0	0.5	−1.3	−0.1
Excluding Belarus and Ukraine	. . .	. . .	. . .	2.4	0.5	2.0	0.2	−2.7	−0.4
Russia	. . .	. . .	. . .	—	1.0	1.5	1.5	5.5	2.1
Transcaucasus and central Asia	. . .	. . .	. . .	—	—	0.2	0.3	0.6	0.2
Memorandum									
Total, nonindustrial countries									
Net credit provided under:									
General Resources Account	−3.932	−2.542	−1.885	2.520	0.393	3.374	0.594	15.735	0.989
Trust Fund	−0.669	−0.509	−0.365	−69	—	−60	−14	−15	—
SAF/ESAF	0.551	1.232	0.688	1.070	0.733	0.253	0.998	1.619	0.237
Disbursements at year-end under:[2]									
General Resources Account	31.996	28.639	29.028	31.821	30.971	34.258	37.015	53.109	52.356
Trust Fund	1.177	0.627	0.296	0.226	0.217	0.157	0.153	0.141	0.137
SAF/ESAF	1.205	2.440	3.363	4.499	5.041	5.285	6.635	8.343	8.305

[1]Excludes industrial countries' net credit from IMF. Includes net disbursements from programs under the General Resources Account, Trust Fund, Structural Adjustment Facility (SAF), and Enhanced Structural Adjustment Facility (ESAF). The data are on a transactions basis, with conversions to U.S. dollar values at annual average exchange rates.

[2]Converted to U.S. dollar values at end-of-period exchange rates.

Table A38. Summary of External Debt and Debt Service

	1989	1990	1991	1992	1993	1994	1995	1996	1997	1998
					In billions of U.S. dollars					
External debt										
Developing countries	**1,125.4**	**1,227.9**	**1,298.1**	**1,373.6**	**1,488.0**	**1,609.7**	**1,732.2**	**1,783.3**	**1,853.4**	**1,949.2**
Regional groups										
Africa	216.5	236.8	242.9	240.2	246.5	266.7	282.9	286.8	285.7	288.9
Asia	293.7	332.6	365.7	404.3	450.2	499.9	545.0	563.7	598.3	648.0
Middle East and Europe	197.8	221.3	230.6	240.2	257.4	266.5	274.2	274.3	281.2	290.6
Western Hemisphere	417.3	437.2	459.0	488.8	533.8	576.5	630.1	658.4	688.2	721.6
Analytical groups										
By external financing source										
Net creditor countries	13.9	13.7	14.0	20.8	21.9	24.0	19.4	16.7	17.5	18.6
Net debtor countries	1,111.4	1,214.2	1,284.1	1,352.8	1,466.1	1,585.7	1,712.8	1,766.6	1,835.9	1,930.6
Official financing	200.0	220.5	227.6	230.7	241.1	257.7	271.3	277.1	279.8	284.8
Private financing	577.0	623.2	667.9	722.9	812.8	883.2	982.4	1,024.4	1,079.2	1,147.8
Diversified financing	334.5	370.6	388.6	399.2	412.3	444.8	459.1	465.1	476.9	498.1
Net debtor countries by debt-servicing experience										
Countries with recent difficulties	629.2	673.0	697.4	711.8	743.9	798.4	856.0	888.3	910.0	936.5
Countries without recent difficulties	482.2	541.2	586.7	641.0	722.2	787.2	856.9	878.3	926.0	994.2
Countries in transition	**153.0**	**202.6**	**210.6**	**212.2**	**230.3**	**247.0**	**260.4**	**271.8**	**280.7**	**299.5**
Central and eastern Europe	...	...	114.3	104.8	115.0	119.9	130.9	137.2	149.1	159.2
Excluding Belarus and Ukraine	...	...	114.3	100.6	109.7	111.5	121.1	126.4	135.3	143.3
Russia	...	...	95.3	105.4	110.4	119.8	120.4	124.1	118.6	123.7
Transcaucasus and central Asia	...	...	0.9	2.1	4.9	7.3	9.1	10.5	13.0	16.6
Debt-service payments[1]										
Developing countries	**135.8**	**137.0**	**147.4**	**170.9**	**179.7**	**201.6**	**234.2**	**257.8**	**245.6**	**246.1**
Regional groups										
Africa	26.4	30.2	30.5	30.7	26.9	24.3	25.8	30.1	34.5	36.4
Asia	35.9	36.2	38.9	47.4	52.3	58.2	69.1	77.8	79.3	81.2
Middle East and Europe	20.3	18.7	17.5	22.3	23.3	31.4	31.9	29.1	26.6	28.2
Western Hemisphere	53.3	51.9	60.4	70.4	77.2	87.7	107.4	120.9	105.1	100.3
Analytical groups										
By external financing source										
Net creditor countries	1.3	1.3	0.8	0.9	1.4	4.2	7.4	5.6	2.9	3.1
Net debtor countries	134.5	135.7	146.6	170.0	178.3	197.4	226.8	252.1	242.7	243.0
Official financing	15.6	17.2	18.4	18.4	17.2	20.6	20.7	21.9	25.9	26.2
Private financing	86.0	86.2	96.7	111.2	119.4	135.4	162.6	181.2	167.4	167.5
Diversified financing	32.9	32.3	31.4	40.4	41.7	41.3	43.6	49.0	49.3	49.3
Net debtor countries by debt-servicing experience										
Countries with recent difficulties	62.9	63.4	65.7	70.6	74.3	75.3	87.9	84.8	98.1	98.1
Countries without recent difficulties	71.6	72.3	80.9	99.4	104.0	122.0	139.0	167.4	144.6	144.9
Countries in transition	**28.3**	**36.4**	**37.1**	**23.8**	**16.6**	**18.7**	**25.8**	**30.5**	**30.3**	**35.2**
Central and eastern Europe	...	...	20.8	11.1	11.3	15.8	18.4	19.7	19.8	22.7
Excluding Belarus and Ukraine	...	...	20.8	11.1	11.1	13.8	16.7	18.0	17.9	20.4
Russia	...	...	16.3	12.6	5.0	2.3	6.0	9.8	9.1	11.1
Transcaucasus and central Asia	...	...	—	0.1	0.3	0.6	1.4	1.0	1.4	1.4

Table A38 (concluded)

	1989	1990	1991	1992	1993	1994	1995	1996	1997	1998
					In percent of exports of goods and services					
External debt[2]										
Developing countries	**198.6**	**185.8**	**194.8**	**188.0**	**194.8**	**185.3**	**168.1**	**159.0**	**149.5**	**145.4**
Regional groups										
Africa	243.8	229.2	243.1	237.8	251.4	266.7	245.4	226.5	212.3	202.1
Asia	170.9	164.4	160.8	153.4	152.8	137.4	121.2	117.7	112.6	109.6
Middle East and Europe	124.5	115.3	130.4	123.5	137.3	136.5	125.9	112.9	101.3	101.0
Western Hemisphere	283.4	267.7	282.7	285.0	290.6	274.9	254.4	241.2	232.7	226.1
Analytical groups										
By external financing source										
Net creditor countries	16.3	12.3	13.2	17.6	19.8	21.7	15.7	12.0	12.1	13.1
Net debtor countries	231.0	221.0	229.3	220.8	224.5	209.2	188.8	179.8	167.6	160.9
Official financing	357.3	337.4	353.3	347.6	352.2	356.9	320.8	290.1	279.0	264.4
Private financing	184.9	170.8	174.9	171.5	179.7	165.2	152.0	148.5	143.1	139.8
Diversified financing	295.8	310.9	341.6	319.8	311.2	294.5	260.6	236.4	198.0	183.9
Net debtor countries by debt-servicing experience										
Countries with recent difficulties	323.1	311.5	348.6	340.4	348.1	340.7	318.6	295.5	264.8	251.1
Countries without recent difficulties	168.4	162.4	163.0	158.9	164.3	150.4	134.2	128.8	123.2	120.3
Countries in transition	**72.8**	**104.0**	**118.6**	**135.7**	**127.6**	**121.8**	**100.4**	**98.2**	**93.8**	**93.9**
Central and eastern Europe	...	...	144.6	118.7	114.1	107.0	87.5	85.4	85.9	83.9
Excluding Belarus and Ukraine	...	...	160.6	128.2	133.9	118.3	94.1	92.6	91.6	88.5
Russia	...	...	154.8	183.4	167.6	152.4	128.2	126.4	112.4	115.6
Transcaucasus and central Asia	...	...	2.5	19.7	35.6	60.2	57.8	58.4	64.5	74.7
Debt-service payments										
Developing countries	**24.0**	**20.7**	**22.1**	**23.4**	**23.5**	**23.2**	**22.7**	**23.0**	**19.8**	**18.4**
Regional groups										
Africa	29.7	29.2	30.5	30.4	27.5	24.3	22.4	23.7	25.6	25.4
Asia	20.9	17.9	17.1	18.0	17.7	16.0	15.4	16.2	14.9	13.7
Middle East and Europe	12.8	9.7	9.9	11.5	12.4	16.1	14.7	12.0	9.6	9.8
Western Hemisphere	36.2	31.8	37.2	41.0	42.0	41.8	43.4	44.3	35.5	31.4
Analytical groups										
By external financing source										
Net creditor countries	1.6	1.2	0.7	0.8	1.3	3.8	6.0	4.0	2.0	2.2
Net debtor countries	28.0	24.7	26.2	27.8	27.3	26.0	25.0	25.7	22.2	20.3
Official financing	27.9	26.3	28.6	27.8	25.1	28.6	24.5	23.0	25.9	24.3
Private financing	27.6	23.6	25.3	26.4	26.4	25.3	25.1	26.3	22.2	20.4
Diversified financing	29.1	27.1	27.6	32.4	31.5	27.4	24.7	24.9	20.5	18.2
Net debtor countries by debt-servicing experience										
Countries with recent difficulties	32.3	29.3	32.8	33.8	34.8	32.2	32.7	28.2	28.5	26.3
Countries without recent difficulties	25.0	21.7	22.5	24.6	23.7	23.3	21.8	24.6	19.2	17.5
Countries in transition	**13.4**	**18.7**	**20.9**	**15.2**	**9.2**	**9.2**	**10.0**	**11.0**	**10.1**	**11.0**
Central and eastern Europe	...	...	26.3	12.5	11.2	14.1	12.3	12.2	11.4	11.9
Excluding Belarus and Ukraine	...	...	29.2	14.1	13.5	14.6	13.0	13.2	12.1	12.6
Russia	...	...	26.5	21.9	7.6	2.9	6.4	10.0	8.6	10.4
Transcaucasus and central Asia	...	...	—	0.9	2.2	5.0	8.9	5.7	6.9	6.4

[1]Debt-service payments refer to actual payments of interest on total debt plus actual amortization payments on long-term debt. The projections incorporate the impact of exceptional financing items.

[2]Total debt at year-end in percent of exports of goods and services in year indicated.

191

Table A39. Developing Countries—by Region: External Debt, by Maturity and Type of Creditor

(In billions of U.S. dollars)

	1989	1990	1991	1992	1993	1994	1995	1996	1997	1998
Developing countries										
Total debt	**1,125.4**	**1,227.9**	**1,298.1**	**1,373.6**	**1,488.0**	**1,609.7**	**1,732.2**	**1,783.3**	**1,853.4**	**1,949.2**
By maturity										
Short-term	163.2	185.3	219.9	259.6	294.2	294.4	304.9	335.1	337.9	362.7
Long-term	962.1	1,042.7	1,078.2	1,113.9	1,193.8	1,315.3	1,427.3	1,448.2	1,515.5	1,586.5
By type of creditor										
Official	547.0	579.3	627.0	639.7	681.0	744.6	791.4	757.7	745.4	745.9
Banks	391.9	386.7	399.0	410.1	424.3	404.6	422.1	425.0	434.9	453.8
Other private	186.4	262.0	272.2	323.8	382.7	460.5	518.6	600.6	673.1	749.5
Regional groups										
Africa										
Total debt	**216.5**	**236.8**	**242.9**	**240.2**	**246.5**	**266.7**	**282.9**	**286.8**	**285.7**	**288.9**
By maturity										
Short-term	25.9	27.8	31.7	35.6	42.7	46.9	58.0	60.9	33.4	26.0
Long-term	190.6	209.0	211.2	204.6	203.8	219.8	224.9	225.9	252.3	263.0
By type of creditor										
Official	136.2	153.5	161.1	167.5	176.2	188.1	196.5	198.2	195.6	195.7
Banks	41.5	42.9	43.2	38.3	35.9	34.3	37.0	37.8	35.0	35.7
Other private	38.7	40.4	38.5	34.4	34.5	44.3	49.4	50.8	55.1	57.6
Sub-Sahara										
Total debt	**163.6**	**180.5**	**186.6**	**185.6**	**193.2**	**207.0**	**219.4**	**223.5**	**222.2**	**225.0**
By maturity										
Short-term	23.1	24.7	29.1	33.2	40.5	44.7	55.8	58.2	31.1	23.5
Long-term	140.5	155.8	157.5	152.5	152.7	162.3	163.6	165.3	191.1	201.5
By type of creditor										
Official	107.9	124.3	130.6	136.3	143.8	155.3	162.5	164.6	162.1	161.6
Banks	19.6	20.9	20.9	16.8	16.8	17.4	17.6	18.3	15.0	15.1
Other private	36.0	35.3	35.1	32.6	32.6	34.3	39.3	40.7	45.1	48.4
Asia										
Total debt	**293.7**	**332.6**	**365.7**	**404.3**	**450.2**	**499.9**	**545.0**	**563.7**	**598.3**	**648.0**
By maturity										
Short-term	38.3	45.9	58.2	68.1	73.4	75.2	95.7	112.5	130.0	148.8
Long-term	255.4	286.7	307.5	336.2	376.9	424.8	449.3	451.3	468.3	499.2
By type of creditor										
Official	148.3	172.4	193.5	209.0	235.2	259.7	268.3	262.1	265.4	273.7
Banks	83.7	100.5	103.1	114.8	125.1	146.3	165.4	175.3	187.5	201.6
Other private	61.7	59.8	69.1	80.5	89.9	93.8	111.3	126.3	145.5	172.7
Middle East and Europe										
Total debt	**197.8**	**221.3**	**230.6**	**240.2**	**257.4**	**266.5**	**274.2**	**274.3**	**281.2**	**290.6**
By maturity										
Short-term	37.5	38.9	42.5	52.7	62.2	47.7	52.4	61.9	67.9	74.5
Long-term	160.3	182.4	188.1	187.5	195.1	218.8	221.9	212.5	213.3	216.1
By type of creditor										
Official	138.8	109.8	114.8	105.8	109.2	126.9	128.8	118.4	111.1	104.7
Banks	42.6	45.1	54.1	63.9	66.4	58.6	50.2	45.4	45.8	46.7
Other private	16.5	66.4	61.6	70.5	81.8	81.0	95.2	110.5	124.3	139.2
Western Hemisphere										
Total debt	**417.3**	**437.2**	**459.0**	**488.8**	**533.8**	**576.5**	**630.1**	**658.4**	**688.2**	**721.6**
By maturity										
Short-term	61.5	72.7	87.5	103.2	115.8	124.6	98.8	99.8	106.6	113.3
Long-term	355.8	364.5	371.5	385.6	418.0	451.9	531.3	558.6	581.6	608.3
By type of creditor										
Official	123.7	143.5	157.5	157.4	160.5	169.8	197.8	179.0	173.4	171.8
Banks	224.1	198.3	198.6	193.0	197.0	165.3	169.6	166.5	166.6	169.7
Other private	69.5	95.4	102.9	138.4	176.4	241.4	262.7	313.0	348.2	380.1

Table A40. Developing Countries—by Analytical Criteria: External Debt, by Maturity and Type of Creditor

(In billions of U.S. dollars)

	1989	1990	1991	1992	1993	1994	1995	1996	1997	1998
By source of export earnings										
Fuel										
Total debt	**182.8**	**199.6**	**206.5**	**217.0**	**228.3**	**243.2**	**242.3**	**231.9**	**225.6**	**219.1**
By maturity										
Short-term	37.2	37.1	44.7	53.2	63.2	57.2	56.9	56.2	36.5	36.6
Long-term	145.7	162.5	161.8	163.8	165.1	186.1	185.4	175.6	189.2	182.6
By type of creditor										
Official	95.5	66.2	68.3	69.0	73.8	93.3	97.5	94.6	88.6	85.2
Banks	68.5	49.2	59.5	62.5	64.4	51.2	44.6	41.1	40.3	40.8
Other private	18.8	84.2	78.7	85.5	90.1	98.7	100.2	96.2	96.7	93.2
Nonfuel										
Total debt	**942.5**	**1,028.3**	**1,091.6**	**1,156.6**	**1,259.7**	**1,366.4**	**1,489.9**	**1,551.4**	**1,627.8**	**1,730.1**
By maturity										
Short-term	126.1	148.1	175.3	206.4	230.9	237.3	248.0	278.9	301.5	326.1
Long-term	816.5	880.2	916.4	950.1	1,028.7	1,129.2	1,241.9	1,272.6	1,326.3	1,404.0
By type of creditor										
Official	451.5	513.1	558.7	570.7	607.2	651.2	694.0	663.1	656.8	660.7
Banks	323.4	337.5	339.5	347.5	359.9	353.4	377.5	383.9	394.6	413.0
Other private	167.6	177.8	193.5	238.3	292.6	361.8	418.4	504.4	576.3	656.4
Manufactures										
Total debt	**289.2**	**319.8**	**343.6**	**377.8**	**422.1**	**467.8**	**532.4**	**569.2**	**612.9**	**666.8**
By maturity										
Short-term	36.7	52.0	63.6	67.0	73.7	74.9	98.3	116.1	131.9	147.6
Long-term	252.5	267.8	280.1	310.8	348.4	392.9	434.1	453.1	481.0	519.2
By type of creditor										
Official	105.8	118.2	134.2	141.5	151.7	164.7	167.9	164.4	167.4	173.0
Banks	116.1	128.7	128.0	136.1	144.5	124.9	137.4	140.5	148.0	158.1
Other private	67.2	72.9	81.5	100.3	125.9	178.1	227.0	264.2	297.5	335.7
Nonfuel primary products										
Total debt	**147.8**	**161.7**	**168.2**	**176.7**	**184.4**	**196.9**	**204.0**	**209.4**	**209.9**	**214.0**
By maturity										
Short-term	24.8	20.7	22.0	26.7	27.0	29.8	35.4	39.0	30.6	24.4
Long-term	122.9	141.0	146.1	150.0	157.4	167.1	168.7	170.4	179.3	189.6
By type of creditor										
Official	99.9	114.5	120.4	125.8	132.2	141.4	146.0	146.8	147.5	148.0
Banks	27.6	28.5	28.8	29.6	29.9	31.8	33.5	33.8	29.7	30.7
Other private	20.3	18.7	19.0	21.2	22.3	23.7	24.5	28.8	32.7	35.3
Services, factor income, and private transfers										
Total debt	**87.0**	**95.6**	**95.5**	**89.2**	**84.5**	**90.5**	**95.6**	**96.6**	**102.5**	**108.7**
By maturity										
Short-term	11.5	10.3	10.4	10.9	9.7	11.8	15.2	14.0	16.7	19.5
Long-term	75.5	85.4	85.1	78.3	74.8	78.7	80.4	82.6	85.8	89.2
By type of creditor										
Official	67.1	74.6	75.5	66.9	65.7	68.7	69.9	66.4	66.2	66.1
Banks	13.5	13.9	13.1	13.7	9.3	9.1	9.0	9.5	10.0	10.3
Other private	6.4	7.1	6.9	8.6	9.5	12.8	16.7	20.7	26.3	32.3
Diversified										
Total debt	**418.7**	**451.2**	**484.3**	**512.8**	**568.6**	**611.3**	**657.9**	**676.3**	**702.5**	**740.6**
By maturity										
Short-term	53.1	65.1	79.2	101.8	120.5	120.8	99.1	109.8	122.3	134.6
Long-term	365.6	386.1	405.1	411.0	448.1	490.5	558.7	566.5	580.2	606.0
By type of creditor										
Official	178.8	205.8	228.6	236.4	257.6	276.4	310.2	285.5	275.7	273.7
Banks	166.2	166.3	169.6	168.1	176.2	187.7	197.5	200.1	206.9	213.8
Other private	73.7	79.1	86.1	108.3	134.9	147.2	150.2	190.7	219.8	253.2

Table A40 *(continued)*

	1989	1990	1991	1992	1993	1994	1995	1996	1997	1998
By external financing source										
Net creditor countries										
Total debt	**13.9**	**13.7**	**14.0**	**20.8**	**21.9**	**24.0**	**19.4**	**16.7**	**17.5**	**18.6**
By maturity										
Short-term	10.0	9.9	9.5	9.7	10.9	11.7	8.1	8.2	8.7	9.0
Long-term	3.9	3.8	4.5	11.1	11.0	12.4	11.3	8.5	8.8	9.6
By type of creditor										
Official	1.4	1.4	1.4	1.6	2.0	2.6	2.7	2.9	3.2	3.9
Banks	5.9	5.0	11.6	13.6	13.9	14.8	8.2	4.8	4.8	4.9
Other private	6.7	7.4	1.0	5.5	5.9	6.6	8.5	9.0	9.5	9.8
Net debtor countries										
Total debt	**1,111.4**	**1,214.2**	**1,284.1**	**1,352.8**	**1,466.1**	**1,585.7**	**1,712.8**	**1,766.6**	**1,835.9**	**1,930.6**
By maturity										
Short-term	153.2	175.3	210.4	249.9	283.3	282.8	296.8	326.8	329.2	353.7
Long-term	958.2	1,038.9	1,073.7	1,102.9	1,182.8	1,302.9	1,416.0	1,439.7	1,506.7	1,577.0
By type of creditor										
Official	545.6	577.9	625.6	638.0	679.0	741.9	788.8	754.8	742.2	742.0
Banks	386.0	381.8	387.4	396.5	410.4	389.8	413.9	420.2	430.2	448.9
Other private	179.7	254.5	271.2	318.3	376.7	453.9	510.2	591.6	663.6	739.7
Official financing										
Total debt	**200.0**	**220.5**	**227.6**	**230.7**	**241.1**	**257.7**	**271.3**	**277.1**	**279.8**	**284.8**
By maturity										
Short-term	13.7	15.6	19.3	21.2	26.1	30.3	39.1	43.3	29.0	21.9
Long-term	186.3	204.8	208.3	209.6	214.9	227.4	232.2	233.7	250.8	262.9
By type of creditor										
Official	159.9	179.2	187.1	195.7	206.8	223.2	233.2	234.8	233.3	235.2
Banks	23.5	23.7	22.6	18.1	18.3	18.7	20.0	20.7	21.2	21.7
Other private	16.6	17.6	17.9	16.9	16.0	15.8	18.2	21.6	25.3	27.9
Private financing										
Total debt	**577.0**	**623.2**	**667.9**	**722.9**	**812.8**	**883.2**	**982.4**	**1,024.4**	**1,079.2**	**1,147.8**
By maturity										
Short-term	100.2	117.0	143.5	174.2	203.8	196.3	190.0	204.1	225.5	249.1
Long-term	476.8	506.2	524.4	548.8	608.9	686.8	792.4	820.3	853.7	898.6
By type of creditor										
Official	158.6	186.0	209.5	212.7	225.9	253.5	287.4	260.8	250.5	246.2
Banks	295.1	283.3	287.2	296.3	314.6	287.7	304.7	302.6	309.7	322.1
Other private	123.2	153.9	171.3	213.8	272.3	342.0	390.4	461.0	519.1	579.5
Diversified financing										
Total debt	**334.5**	**370.6**	**388.6**	**399.2**	**412.3**	**444.8**	**459.1**	**465.1**	**476.9**	**498.1**
By maturity										
Short-term	39.4	42.7	47.6	54.6	53.3	56.1	67.6	79.4	74.8	82.6
Long-term	295.1	327.8	341.0	344.5	359.0	388.6	391.4	385.7	402.1	415.5
By type of creditor										
Official	227.2	212.7	229.0	229.5	246.3	265.2	268.2	259.2	258.4	260.6
Banks	67.4	74.8	77.6	82.1	77.5	83.4	89.3	96.9	99.2	105.1
Other private	39.9	83.1	82.0	87.6	88.5	96.1	101.6	109.0	119.2	132.4

Table A40 *(concluded)*

	1989	1990	1991	1992	1993	1994	1995	1996	1997	1998
Net debtor countries by debt-servicing experience										
Countries with recent difficulties										
Total debt	**629.2**	**673.0**	**697.4**	**711.8**	**743.9**	**798.4**	**856.0**	**888.3**	**910.0**	**936.5**
By maturity										
Short-term	84.9	92.6	108.3	119.7	122.7	120.4	135.7	146.4	123.8	122.6
Long-term	544.3	580.4	589.1	592.1	621.2	678.0	720.3	741.8	786.1	813.9
By type of creditor										
Official	341.3	340.0	365.6	364.3	384.2	421.4	436.9	426.2	419.5	415.2
Banks	213.5	189.9	192.6	191.2	180.5	131.1	132.0	133.1	128.7	130.6
Other private	74.3	143.2	139.3	156.2	179.3	246.0	287.1	328.9	361.8	390.7
Countries without recent difficulties										
Total debt	**482.2**	**541.2**	**586.7**	**641.0**	**722.2**	**787.2**	**856.9**	**878.3**	**926.0**	**994.2**
By maturity										
Short-term	68.3	82.7	102.1	130.3	160.5	162.3	161.1	180.4	205.4	231.1
Long-term	413.9	458.5	484.6	510.8	561.6	624.9	695.7	697.9	720.5	763.1
By type of creditor										
Official	204.3	237.9	260.0	273.7	294.8	320.6	351.9	328.6	322.7	326.8
Banks	172.5	191.8	194.8	205.2	229.9	258.7	281.9	287.1	301.5	318.4
Other private	105.4	111.4	131.9	162.1	197.4	207.9	223.1	262.6	301.8	349.0
Other groups										
Heavily indebted poor countries										
Total debt	**141.2**	**159.5**	**166.1**	**172.5**	**181.1**	**193.3**	**199.9**	**203.2**	**204.6**	**207.6**
By maturity										
Short-term	13.3	14.1	18.3	22.1	27.0	28.6	35.6	36.8	24.1	16.8
Long-term	127.9	145.5	147.8	150.4	154.1	164.7	164.3	166.4	180.5	190.8
By type of creditor										
Official	113.4	131.2	136.5	143.6	151.4	162.8	167.8	169.4	171.2	172.7
Banks	15.8	16.7	16.0	15.6	15.6	16.4	16.5	17.3	14.2	14.4
Other private	12.0	11.6	13.6	13.4	14.1	14.1	15.6	16.5	19.1	20.5
Least developed countries										
Total debt	**97.0**	**110.4**	**115.9**	**119.2**	**124.5**	**133.3**	**138.7**	**140.9**	**143.8**	**146.9**
By maturity										
Short-term	7.2	7.4	9.2	10.1	11.6	13.5	17.2	18.8	18.4	11.5
Long-term	89.8	103.0	106.7	109.1	112.9	119.8	121.4	122.1	125.4	135.4
By type of creditor										
Official	83.0	96.3	100.9	104.5	109.3	119.8	123.7	122.9	122.8	123.7
Banks	6.5	7.0	7.0	6.6	6.7	6.0	5.8	6.6	6.9	7.4
Other private	7.5	7.1	8.0	8.1	8.5	7.5	9.2	11.5	14.1	15.7
Middle East and north Africa										
Total debt	**223.3**	**243.7**	**252.2**	**256.2**	**261.5**	**280.1**	**284.9**	**280.5**	**284.1**	**289.0**
By maturity										
Short-term	35.1	32.8	36.4	42.9	46.2	38.9	39.9	43.7	47.4	51.3
Long-term	188.2	210.9	215.8	213.4	215.3	241.3	245.0	236.8	236.7	237.8
By type of creditor										
Official	160.1	130.7	135.5	128.3	131.7	147.7	149.9	143.8	139.8	138.1
Banks	51.0	52.6	62.3	69.5	66.3	55.0	50.3	46.5	46.5	46.7
Other private	12.2	60.4	54.4	58.5	63.5	77.4	84.7	90.3	97.8	104.2

Table A41. Developing Countries: Ratio of External Debt to GDP[1]

	1989	1990	1991	1992	1993	1994	1995	1996	1997	1998
Developing countries	**39.9**	**39.2**	**39.9**	**38.3**	**38.6**	**37.0**	**34.9**	**32.3**	**30.2**	**28.5**
Regional groups										
Africa	62.2	61.4	65.1	62.7	65.3	74.2	66.1	62.3	66.2	62.0
Sub-Sahara	63.1	62.8	64.6	63.0	67.4	74.0	65.3	62.2	68.6	64.1
Asia	29.8	31.2	33.1	32.8	34.4	32.0	29.1	26.3	24.9	24.1
Excluding China and India	47.8	47.1	47.0	44.6	44.6	42.3	40.2	37.0	35.1	34.4
Middle East and Europe	38.6	36.9	37.2	34.3	33.7	33.2	28.7	24.8	20.9	17.8
Western Hemisphere	42.7	40.5	39.7	38.6	37.9	35.5	37.1	36.3	35.2	34.9
Analytical groups										
By source of export earnings										
Fuel	37.3	37.4	38.8	36.5	36.7	35.8	28.7	23.5	19.6	15.5
Manufactures	23.8	25.5	28.5	29.6	31.4	28.2	26.0	25.2	25.0	25.0
Nonfuel primary products	78.9	80.6	77.6	73.1	69.0	67.4	57.3	51.0	44.3	40.0
Services, factor income, and private transfers	90.8	90.2	85.0	70.7	59.7	57.0	57.3	55.0	53.8	53.2
Diversified	50.1	43.6	40.8	38.2	38.4	39.3	42.6	39.9	37.5	36.6
By external financing source										
Net creditor countries	7.8	6.5	6.4	8.7	9.2	9.8	7.5	5.9	5.9	6.1
Net debtor countries	42.0	41.6	42.3	40.4	40.5	38.7	36.4	33.7	31.4	29.5
Official financing	77.8	80.5	81.8	80.0	82.4	84.6	74.0	67.0	73.2	68.5
Private financing	32.5	31.5	31.9	31.2	32.7	31.6	31.2	29.5	28.2	27.5
Diversified financing	54.6	55.2	58.4	53.9	48.9	44.3	38.8	34.4	29.2	25.5
Net debtor countries by debt-servicing experience										
Countries with recent difficulties	53.8	53.4	54.9	51.3	48.4	44.4	39.6	36.9	33.7	30.3
Countries without recent difficulties	32.7	32.6	33.3	32.7	34.7	34.2	33.8	31.0	29.5	28.9
Other groups										
Heavily indebted poor countries	87.5	91.8	93.2	90.0	87.0	89.5	80.9	70.8	60.2	53.3
Least developed countries	72.1	71.5	68.6	59.7	51.7	48.6	44.6	38.4	33.0	28.9
Middle East and north Africa	44.4	44.2	45.9	40.9	39.0	37.4	32.5	27.3	22.4	18.6

[1]Debt at year-end in percent of GDP in year indicated.

Table A42. Developing Countries: Debt-Service Ratios[1]

(In percent of exports of goods and services)

	1989	1990	1991	1992	1993	1994	1995	1996	1997	1998
Interest payments[2]										
Developing countries	**11.6**	**9.4**	**9.7**	**9.3**	**9.2**	**8.5**	**8.6**	**9.0**	**8.8**	**8.4**
Regional groups										
Africa	12.8	12.0	12.3	11.5	10.5	10.5	10.5	10.5	11.3	11.8
Sub-Sahara	11.2	10.9	11.0	10.0	8.9	9.6	9.4	9.6	10.8	11.5
Asia	9.3	8.3	7.9	7.5	6.9	6.4	5.8	6.1	6.0	5.7
Excluding China and India	10.1	8.8	8.0	6.8	6.2	6.0	5.7	6.2	6.1	5.9
Middle East and Europe	5.7	4.0	4.3	5.0	5.2	4.3	4.3	4.4	3.8	3.6
Western Hemisphere	19.9	15.6	16.6	15.6	16.0	15.4	16.6	17.6	17.6	16.3
Analytical groups										
By source of export earnings										
Fuel	7.1	5.8	5.0	4.8	4.4	3.9	4.2	4.1	4.4	4.5
Manufactures	9.8	7.4	8.4	8.2	8.3	7.1	7.4	7.8	7.9	7.6
Nonfuel primary products	12.7	11.2	12.2	10.1	9.6	10.3	8.2	8.1	12.7	10.3
Services, factor income, and private transfers	11.9	7.0	11.0	15.3	12.9	8.6	8.0	13.9	7.9	7.7
Diversified	17.5	15.3	14.7	13.3	13.2	13.3	13.3	13.4	12.3	11.6
By external financing source										
Net creditor countries	1.0	0.6	0.3	0.4	0.6	0.7	0.5	0.8	0.6	0.7
Net debtor countries	13.5	11.2	11.5	11.0	10.6	9.7	9.7	10.2	9.9	9.3
Official financing	13.6	12.2	13.6	11.9	10.3	11.6	9.4	10.0	11.4	12.1
Private financing	13.0	10.4	10.6	10.3	10.2	9.2	9.8	10.5	10.2	9.6
Diversified financing	14.7	13.1	13.4	13.0	12.1	10.6	9.7	9.2	8.2	7.5
Net debtor countries by debt-servicing experience										
Countries with recent difficulties	14.9	11.9	13.7	13.5	13.1	11.9	13.4	13.4	13.5	12.4
Countries without recent difficulties	12.6	10.8	10.3	9.7	9.4	8.7	8.2	8.8	8.3	7.9
Other groups										
Heavily indebted poor countries	10.2	9.8	11.9	9.1	10.0	13.5	9.7	12.6	10.3	10.0
Least developed countries	9.2	7.9	9.1	8.3	6.6	6.4	8.1	11.2	7.9	8.3
Middle East and north Africa	6.1	4.2	4.5	5.3	5.4	4.1	4.4	4.6	4.0	3.9

Table A42 *(concluded)*

	1989	1990	1991	1992	1993	1994	1995	1996	1997	1998
Amortization[2]										
Developing countries	**12.4**	**11.3**	**12.4**	**14.1**	**14.4**	**14.6**	**14.1**	**13.9**	**11.0**	**9.9**
Regional groups										
Africa	16.9	17.2	18.2	18.9	17.0	13.8	11.9	13.2	14.3	13.7
Sub-Sahara	12.2	10.4	10.9	12.2	9.9	10.8	9.5	12.3	13.5	12.0
Asia	11.6	9.6	9.2	10.5	10.8	9.6	9.5	10.1	9.0	8.0
Excluding China and India	11.9	10.6	10.7	11.0	11.8	10.8	10.5	10.6	10.3	9.4
Middle East and Europe	7.1	5.7	5.6	6.5	7.2	11.8	10.4	7.5	5.8	6.2
Western Hemisphere	16.3	16.2	20.6	25.5	26.0	26.4	26.8	26.7	17.9	15.1
Analytical groups										
By source of export earnings										
Fuel	7.1	7.4	8.4	7.5	8.9	12.6	10.0	7.5	6.4	6.8
Manufactures	12.2	9.2	9.3	10.7	11.0	7.9	9.2	9.5	9.7	8.5
Nonfuel primary products	11.5	9.6	13.0	11.2	12.2	14.3	20.2	17.3	11.0	8.8
Services, factor income, and private transfers	14.5	8.7	8.6	16.9	16.4	11.0	6.6	12.5	6.5	6.0
Diversified	17.6	18.1	19.8	23.9	22.7	25.3	23.2	23.1	16.3	14.4
By external financing source										
Net creditor countries	0.6	0.5	0.4	0.3	0.7	3.1	5.5	3.2	1.4	1.5
Net debtor countries	14.5	13.5	14.7	16.7	16.7	16.3	15.3	15.5	12.2	10.9
Official financing	14.3	14.1	15.1	15.9	14.8	17.0	15.1	12.9	14.5	12.2
Private financing	14.5	13.2	14.7	16.1	16.2	16.1	15.4	15.7	12.0	10.8
Diversified financing	14.3	14.0	14.3	19.4	19.4	16.8	15.1	15.7	12.2	10.7
Net debtor countries by debt-servicing experience										
Countries with recent difficulties	17.4	17.5	19.2	20.3	21.7	20.2	19.3	14.8	15.1	13.9
Countries without recent difficulties	12.5	10.9	12.2	14.9	14.3	14.6	13.6	15.7	11.0	9.6
Other groups										
Heavily indebted poor countries	15.0	13.1	16.2	12.8	14.0	19.3	17.4	14.4	13.1	9.9
Least developed countries	16.2	13.3	14.0	14.1	11.3	10.9	13.2	14.9	13.1	9.9
Middle East and north Africa	8.6	8.6	9.0	8.9	9.9	12.0	9.9	7.0	5.4	5.8

[1]Excludes service payments to the IMF.

[2]Interest payments on total debt and amortization on long-term debt. Estimates through 1996 reflect debt-service payments actually made. The estimates for 1997 and 1998 take into account projected exceptional financing items, including accumulation of arrears and rescheduling agreements. In some cases, amortization on account of debt-reduction operations is included.

Table A43. IMF Charges and Repurchases to the IMF[1]

(In percent of exports of goods and services)

	1989	1990	1991	1992	1993	1994	1995	1996
Developing countries	**1.6**	**1.5**	**1.3**	**1.0**	**0.9**	**0.7**	**0.9**	**0.4**
Regional groups								
Africa	2.1	1.6	1.3	1.1	1.1	0.8	2.6	0.5
Sub-Sahara	2.1	1.4	1.1	0.9	0.7	0.5	3.0	0.3
Asia	1.4	1.4	1.0	0.5	0.3	0.5	0.4	0.3
Excluding China and India	1.1	1.2	0.8	0.5	0.3	0.2	0.2	0.1
Middle East and Europe	0.2	0.1	0.1	—	—	—	0.1	—
Western Hemisphere	2.9	3.2	3.0	2.7	2.6	1.5	1.6	0.8
Analytical groups								
By source of export earnings								
Fuel	—	0.1	0.3	0.4	0.5	0.4	0.5	0.2
Nonfuel	2.2	2.1	1.7	1.2	1.0	0.8	1.0	0.4
By external financing source								
Net creditor countries	—	—	—	—	—	—	—	—
Net debtor countries	1.8	1.8	1.5	1.2	1.1	0.8	1.0	0.4
Official financing	3.2	2.6	1.8	1.5	1.4	0.7	3.3	0.5
Private financing	1.5	1.5	1.3	1.1	1.1	0.6	0.6	0.3
Diversified financing	2.1	2.0	2.0	1.3	0.7	1.4	1.3	0.7
Net debtor countries by debt-servicing experience								
Countries with recent difficulties	2.3	2.2	2.2	2.0	1.9	1.1	1.9	0.6
Countries without recent difficulties	1.5	1.5	1.2	0.8	0.6	0.6	0.6	0.4
Other groups								
Heavily indebted poor countries	4.4	3.6	2.4	2.0	1.7	1.1	5.8	0.6
Least developed countries	4.6	3.8	2.8	1.7	1.3	0.9	8.5	0.5
Middle East and north Africa	0.3	0.3	0.3	0.3	0.4	0.3	0.3	0.2
Countries in transition	**0.2**	**0.2**	**0.1**	**0.5**	**0.4**	**1.1**	**1.4**	**0.5**
Central and eastern Europe	...	...	0.3	0.8	0.5	1.9	2.3	0.4
Excluding Belarus and Ukraine	...	...	0.3	0.9	0.7	2.3	2.6	0.4
Russia	...	...	—	—	0.1	0.2	0.3	0.7
Transcaucasus and central Asia	...	...	—	—	—	0.1	0.3	0.2
Memorandum								
Total, in billions of U.S. dollars								
General Resources Account	9.316	10.119	8.768	8.059	7.533	8.270	12.806	5.588
Charges	2.316	2.530	2.431	2.291	2.215	1.724	2.847	2.151
Repurchases	7.000	7.589	6.337	5.768	5.319	6.546	9.960	3.438
Trust Fund	0.513	0.367	0.070	—	0.063	0.015	0.015	0.001
Interest	0.004	0.002	0.001	—	0.003	—	—	0.001
Repayments	0.509	0.365	0.069	—	0.060	0.014	0.015	—
SAF/ESAF	0.007	0.013	0.021	0.055	0.151	0.329	0.586	0.596
Interest	0.007	0.013	0.021	0.022	0.025	0.024	0.034	0.039
Repayments	—	—	—	0.033	0.126	0.305	0.552	0.557

[1]Excludes advanced economies. Charges on, and repurchases (or repayments of principal) for, use of IMF credit.

Table A44. Summary of Sources and Uses of World Saving

(In percent of GDP)

	Averages 1975–82	Averages 1983–90	1991	1992	1993	1994	1995	1996	1997	1998	Average 1999–2002
World											
Saving	24.1	22.5	22.7	22.2	21.8	22.6	22.9	23.3	23.6	24.0	24.6
Investment	24.5	23.4	23.5	23.3	23.3	23.4	23.7	24.0	24.6	25.1	25.7
Advanced economies											
Saving	22.5	21.0	21.2	20.1	19.7	20.2	20.7	21.1	21.3	21.7	22.1
Private	21.1	19.8	19.7	19.9	19.7	19.7	20.2	20.0	19.6	19.7	19.8
Public	1.4	1.2	1.5	0.3	—	0.5	0.5	1.1	1.7	1.9	2.4
Investment	22.7	21.6	21.4	20.7	20.1	20.6	20.9	20.9	21.5	21.7	22.2
Private	18.2	17.6	17.4	16.6	15.9	16.6	16.9	16.9	17.6	17.9	18.3
Public	4.6	4.0	4.0	4.1	4.2	4.0	4.0	4.0	3.8	3.8	3.8
Net lending	−0.2	−0.6	−0.2	−0.6	−0.4	−0.4	−0.1	0.2	−0.2	−0.1	—
Private	2.9	2.2	2.3	3.3	3.8	3.1	3.3	3.1	1.9	1.8	1.4
Public	−3.2	−2.8	−2.5	−3.9	−4.2	−3.6	−3.5	−2.9	−2.1	−1.8	−1.5
Current transfers	−0.5	−0.4	−0.2	−0.4	−0.4	−0.5	−0.4	−0.4	−0.5	−0.4	−0.5
Factor income	—	—	−0.1	−0.4	−0.5	−0.4	−0.1	0.3	−0.1	−0.1	—
Resource balance	0.2	−0.2	—	0.2	0.5	0.4	0.4	0.4	0.4	0.4	0.4
United States											
Saving	19.7	17.1	15.8	14.5	14.3	15.2	15.9	16.8	16.6	16.8	17.1
Private	17.9	16.4	15.8	15.6	14.7	14.5	14.8	15.3	15.0	15.1	15.3
Public	1.8	0.6	0.1	−1.1	−0.4	0.7	1.1	1.5	1.5	1.7	1.7
Investment	20.3	19.5	15.8	16.0	16.5	17.7	17.7	17.8	18.6	18.8	19.1
Private	16.9	16.0	12.4	12.7	13.3	14.6	14.7	14.7	15.6	15.9	16.2
Public	3.4	3.5	3.4	3.3	3.2	3.1	3.1	3.1	3.0	3.0	2.9
Net lending	−0.6	−2.4	—	−1.5	−2.2	−2.5	−1.9	−1.0	−2.1	−2.1	−2.1
Private	1.1	0.5	3.3	2.9	1.4	−0.1	0.1	0.6	−0.6	−0.8	−0.9
Public	−1.6	−2.9	−3.3	−4.4	−3.6	−2.3	−2.0	−1.6	−1.5	−1.3	−1.2
Current transfers	−0.3	−0.5	0.1	−0.6	−0.6	−0.6	−0.5	−0.6	−0.6	−0.6	−0.6
Factor income	0.4	0.6	0.4	−0.3	−0.6	−0.4	0.1	1.1	0.1	0.2	0.1
Resource balance	−0.6	−2.4	−0.5	−0.6	−1.1	−1.5	−1.4	−1.5	−1.6	−1.7	−1.6
European Union											
Saving	22.2	20.9	20.1	19.0	18.4	19.3	20.2	19.9	20.3	20.7	21.1
Private	21.9	21.1	21.1	21.2	21.4	21.9	22.5	21.5	20.8	21.1	20.7
Public	0.3	−0.2	−1.0	−2.2	−3.0	−2.6	−2.3	−1.6	−0.6	−0.4	0.4
Investment	22.0	20.5	21.2	20.1	18.2	18.8	19.3	18.7	19.2	19.7	20.4
Private	17.8	17.3	18.0	16.9	15.2	16.0	16.6	16.1	16.8	17.3	18.1
Public	4.2	3.3	3.2	3.2	3.1	2.9	2.7	2.6	2.4	2.3	2.3
Net lending	0.2	0.4	−1.1	−1.1	0.2	0.5	0.9	1.2	1.0	1.1	0.7
Private	4.1	3.8	3.1	4.3	6.2	6.0	5.9	5.4	4.0	3.7	2.6
Public	−3.9	−3.4	−4.2	−5.3	−6.1	−5.5	−5.0	−4.2	−3.0	−2.7	−1.9
Current transfers	−0.8	−0.4	−0.6	−0.6	−0.6	−0.7	−0.5	−0.5	−0.6	−0.6	−0.6
Factor income	−0.3	−0.1	−0.3	−0.5	−0.5	−0.3	−0.2	−0.3	−0.4	−0.3	−0.2
Resource balance	1.3	1.0	−0.3	—	1.2	1.4	1.7	2.0	2.0	2.0	1.6
Japan											
Saving	31.9	32.0	34.2	33.8	32.8	31.4	30.7	31.3	31.3	31.4	31.3
Private	28.6	25.6	24.4	25.0	25.8	25.7	27.1	26.7	26.0	26.0	25.6
Public	3.3	6.4	9.8	8.8	6.9	5.7	3.5	4.6	5.3	5.4	5.7
Investment	31.5	29.3	32.2	30.8	29.7	28.7	28.5	29.8	29.6	29.4	29.0
Private	22.1	22.3	25.6	23.3	21.1	20.0	19.9	20.7	21.2	21.1	20.4
Public	9.4	7.0	6.6	7.5	8.5	8.7	8.6	9.1	8.4	8.3	8.6
Net lending	0.4	2.7	2.0	3.0	3.1	2.8	2.2	1.4	1.7	1.9	2.3
Private	6.4	3.3	−1.2	1.7	4.7	5.7	7.2	5.9	4.8	4.9	5.2
Public	−6.1	−0.6	3.2	1.3	−1.6	−3.0	−5.1	−4.5	−3.0	−2.9	−2.9
Current transfers	−0.1	−0.1	−0.3	−0.1	−0.1	−0.1	−0.2	−0.2	−0.2	−0.2	−0.2
Factor income	—	0.6	0.8	1.0	0.9	0.9	0.8	1.2	1.2	1.3	1.4
Resource balance	0.4	2.3	1.6	2.2	2.3	2.1	1.5	0.5	0.7	0.9	1.1

Table A44 *(continued)*

	Averages		1991	1992	1993	1994	1995	1996	1997	1998	Average 1999–2002
	1975–82	1983–90									

Newly industrialized Asian economies											
Saving	...	34.2	34.2	33.3	33.3	33.1	33.6	33.3	33.4	33.8	34.3
Private	...	28.4	25.1	28.0	27.1	26.0	26.6	27.0	27.3	27.2	27.7
Public	...	5.8	9.0	5.3	6.2	7.1	7.0	6.3	6.1	6.6	6.6
Investment	...	27.8	32.1	31.7	31.0	31.4	32.4	33.3	33.0	32.8	32.8
Private	...	21.7	25.0	24.7	24.0	24.6	25.6	26.2	26.0	25.8	25.7
Public	...	6.1	7.1	7.0	7.0	6.8	6.8	7.0	7.0	7.0	7.1
Net lending	...	6.4	2.1	1.6	2.3	1.6	1.2	—	0.4	1.0	1.5
Private	...	6.6	0.1	3.3	3.1	1.4	1.0	0.8	1.3	1.4	2.0
Public	...	−0.2	2.0	−1.7	−0.8	0.2	0.1	−0.8	−0.9	−0.4	−0.5
Current transfers	...	—	−0.1	−0.1	−0.1	−0.2	−0.5	−0.5	−0.5	−0.4	−0.3
Factor income	...	−0.3	0.4	0.2	0.1	0.3	0.9	0.6	0.5	0.4	0.3
Resource balance	...	6.7	1.8	1.5	2.4	1.5	0.8	—	0.4	1.0	1.6
Developing countries											
Saving	25.4	22.6	24.0	25.0	25.1	26.3	26.4	27.0	27.2	27.5	27.9
Investment	25.7	24.5	25.7	26.6	28.3	27.7	28.3	28.9	29.4	29.8	30.2
Net lending	−0.3	−1.9	−1.8	−1.7	−3.2	−1.4	−1.9	−1.9	−2.2	−2.2	−2.2
Current transfers	0.9	1.0	1.1	1.5	1.3	1.2	1.1	1.0	0.9	0.9	0.7
Factor income	−0.5	−2.0	−1.5	−1.5	−1.7	−1.6	−2.0	−1.7	−1.9	−1.5	−1.4
Resource balance	−0.7	−0.9	−1.3	−1.6	−2.8	−1.0	−1.0	−1.3	−1.3	−1.6	−1.6
Memorandum											
Acquisition of foreign assets	2.4	0.5	1.7	1.6	2.1	2.6	2.6	2.6	1.8	1.3	1.1
Change in reserves	1.1	0.2	2.0	1.2	1.2	2.2	1.6	2.0	1.2	1.0	0.8
Regional groups											
Africa											
Saving	27.2	17.6	18.2	17.1	15.0	16.2	16.4	17.1	18.1	19.1	20.6
Investment	31.6	21.3	20.9	20.8	19.2	20.8	21.6	20.9	20.8	21.0	22.0
Net lending	−4.4	−3.7	−2.7	−3.7	−4.1	−4.6	−5.3	−3.8	−2.6	−1.9	−1.4
Current transfers	2.0	3.2	4.3	4.6	4.6	4.7	4.1	3.8	3.6	3.4	3.1
Factor income	−1.5	−5.0	−5.0	−4.6	−5.1	−4.8	−5.2	−5.2	−5.6	−4.4	−3.8
Resource balance	−4.8	−2.0	−2.1	−3.7	−3.6	−4.5	−4.2	−2.3	−0.6	−1.0	−0.8
Memorandum											
Acquisition of foreign assets	−0.3	0.6	1.3	−1.4	−0.1	2.1	0.2	1.8	1.4	1.1	1.2
Change in reserves	−0.2	0.3	0.9	−1.2	0.4	2.2	0.8	1.5	1.4	1.2	1.2
Asia											
Saving	26.0	26.7	29.9	30.3	31.9	32.5	32.2	32.9	33.0	33.0	32.9
Investment	25.2	28.6	30.3	31.1	34.6	33.5	33.9	35.0	35.4	35.4	35.2
Net lending	0.8	−1.9	−0.3	−0.8	−2.7	−1.1	−1.8	−2.1	−2.3	−2.4	−2.2
Current transfers	1.3	0.8	1.0	1.0	1.0	1.1	1.0	0.9	0.8	0.8	0.6
Factor income	1.6	−0.6	−0.9	−0.9	−0.7	−1.0	−1.3	−1.2	−1.3	−1.1	−1.0
Resource balance	−2.0	−2.1	−0.5	−0.9	−3.0	−1.2	−1.4	−1.8	−1.8	−2.1	−1.9
Memorandum											
Acquisition of foreign assets	8.5	0.7	3.5	2.2	3.1	4.3	3.6	3.2	2.3	1.8	1.4
Change in reserves	3.8	0.5	2.7	0.9	1.7	3.8	1.8	2.3	1.6	1.4	1.0
Middle East and Europe											
Saving	32.0	19.3	16.3	22.5	19.1	22.0	22.4	21.0	20.2	20.1	19.9
Investment	25.8	23.1	23.9	24.9	24.0	21.0	22.5	21.3	21.5	21.7	22.2
Net lending	6.2	−3.8	−7.6	−2.5	−4.9	1.0	−0.1	−0.3	−1.3	−1.6	−2.3
Current transfers	0.7	0.6	−1.5	1.3	0.6	−0.4	−0.4	−0.4	−0.5	−0.6	−0.6
Factor income	−0.3	−0.5	1.3	0.5	−0.8	−0.1	−0.2	−0.2	−0.6	0.2	−0.2
Resource balance	5.8	−3.9	−7.3	−4.3	−4.7	1.5	0.5	0.4	−0.3	−1.3	−1.5
Memorandum											
Acquisition of foreign assets	8.5	−0.3	−6.1	0.6	0.1	−0.7	0.5	1.1	0.5	−0.4	—
Change in reserves	3.8	−0.8	1.4	3.1	—	0.5	1.4	1.8	—	0.1	0.3

Table A44 (continued)

	Averages 1975–82	Averages 1983–90	1991	1992	1993	1994	1995	1996	1997	1998	Average 1999–2002
Western Hemisphere											
Saving	20.3	19.8	18.7	18.4	17.5	18.2	18.0	18.7	19.1	19.6	20.1
Investment	23.8	19.9	19.8	20.6	20.5	20.4	20.0	20.3	21.2	21.8	22.6
Net lending	−3.5	−0.1	−1.1	−2.3	−3.0	−2.3	−1.9	−1.5	−2.1	−2.2	−2.5
Current transfers	0.2	0.6	1.2	1.2	1.0	1.0	1.1	1.0	0.9	0.9	0.8
Factor income	−2.3	−4.0	−2.7	−2.6	−3.1	−2.5	−3.4	−2.3	−2.7	−2.3	−2.4
Resource balance	−1.4	3.2	0.4	−0.9	−0.9	−0.8	0.4	−0.1	−0.4	−0.8	−0.9
Memorandum											
Acquisition of foreign assets	1.4	0.6	2.4	2.0	1.6	0.8	2.3	2.3	1.3	0.9	0.7
Change in reserves	—	0.2	1.6	1.7	1.3	−0.7	1.5	1.4	0.8	0.6	0.5
Analytical groups											
By source of export earnings											
Fuel											
Saving	38.8	19.8	18.0	21.8	18.4	21.6	23.2	24.2	23.2	23.5	23.9
Investment	30.5	22.2	25.1	26.7	23.0	21.1	23.2	20.9	20.9	21.3	22.0
Net lending	8.3	−2.3	−7.1	−4.9	−4.6	0.4	0.1	3.3	2.3	2.2	1.8
Current transfers	−2.3	−2.2	−6.3	−2.0	−2.3	−2.3	−2.2	−2.1	−1.8	−1.9	−1.7
Factor income	0.7	−0.9	0.1	−2.0	−2.6	−2.6	−2.8	−1.9	−3.7	−1.8	−1.5
Resource balance	9.9	0.8	−1.0	−0.9	0.3	5.4	5.1	7.2	7.9	5.9	5.0
Memorandum											
Acquisition of foreign assets	8.8	−0.1	−5.5	−2.2	−2.1	−0.1	−0.5	3.4	2.9	1.2	1.0
Change in reserves	3.5	−1.1	0.3	−1.2	−1.5	0.6	0.6	3.6	2.2	1.5	1.3
Nonfuel											
Saving	22.2	23.0	24.8	25.4	26.0	26.8	26.7	27.3	27.7	28.0	28.3
Investment	24.5	24.9	25.8	26.6	29.0	28.5	28.9	29.8	30.4	30.7	31.0
Net lending	−2.3	−1.8	−1.0	−1.2	−3.0	−1.7	−2.1	−2.5	−2.7	−2.7	−2.6
Current transfers	1.6	1.5	2.1	1.9	1.7	1.6	1.5	1.4	1.2	1.2	1.0
Factor income	−0.8	−2.2	−1.7	−1.4	−1.6	−1.5	−1.9	−1.6	−1.7	−1.5	−1.4
Resource balance	−3.2	−1.1	−1.4	−1.7	−3.2	−1.8	−1.7	−2.2	−2.2	−2.4	−2.2
Memorandum											
Acquisition of foreign assets	0.9	0.6	2.7	2.1	2.6	3.0	3.0	2.5	1.7	1.3	1.1
Change in reserves	0.5	0.4	2.3	1.5	1.6	2.4	1.7	1.8	1.1	1.0	0.8
By external financing source											
Net creditor countries											
Saving	47.4	20.6	−3.1	14.4	15.8	16.1	17.7	20.2	18.0	18.9	17.5
Investment	25.1	22.0	21.1	21.4	22.5	20.0	19.2	18.2	18.4	19.0	17.8
Net lending	22.2	−1.4	−24.2	−7.0	−6.7	−3.9	−1.5	1.9	−0.3	−0.1	−0.2
Current transfers	−8.7	−8.8	−24.2	−9.6	−10.7	−11.6	−10.4	−9.7	−9.5	−9.6	−9.5
Factor income	1.8	3.0	2.2	1.6	2.0	1.1	1.0	0.8	−1.5	1.9	2.0
Resource balance	29.0	4.4	−2.1	1.1	1.9	6.6	8.0	10.8	10.7	7.6	7.2
Memorandum											
Acquisition of foreign assets	21.2	−1.1	−23.6	−3.0	−6.5	−2.8	−4.0	2.0	4.0	0.2	—
Change in reserves	6.0	−4.2	0.2	1.4	−4.3	−0.2	—	3.9	1.7	1.5	1.2
Net debtor countries											
Saving	24.3	22.6	24.9	25.4	25.5	26.6	26.6	27.2	27.5	27.8	28.2
Investment	25.7	24.6	25.9	26.8	28.5	28.0	28.6	29.2	29.7	30.1	30.5
Net lending	−1.4	−1.9	−1.0	−1.5	−3.1	−1.3	−1.9	−2.0	−2.3	−2.3	−2.3
Current transfers	1.4	1.4	2.0	1.8	1.7	1.6	1.5	1.3	1.2	1.2	1.0
Factor income	−0.6	−2.2	−1.6	−1.6	−1.9	−1.7	−2.1	−1.7	−1.9	−1.6	−1.5
Resource balance	−2.2	−1.1	−1.3	−1.7	−2.9	−1.3	−1.3	−1.6	−1.6	−1.9	−1.8
Memorandum											
Acquisition of foreign assets	1.4	0.6	2.6	1.8	2.4	2.8	2.8	2.6	1.8	1.3	1.1
Change in reserves	0.8	0.4	2.1	1.2	1.4	2.3	1.7	1.9	1.2	1.0	0.8

Table A44 *(continued)*

	Averages		1991	1992	1993	1994	1995	1996	1997	1998	Average 1999–2002
	1975–82	1983–90									
Official financing											
Saving	21.8	13.6	14.4	14.2	12.7	13.7	13.0	12.9	14.4	15.7	17.9
Investment	26.0	18.0	18.7	19.4	18.6	18.6	18.4	18.7	18.5	19.2	20.5
Net lending	−4.2	−4.4	−4.2	−5.2	−6.0	−4.8	−5.4	−5.8	−4.1	−3.5	−2.6
Current transfers	4.1	4.5	6.4	6.6	6.4	6.2	5.7	5.2	4.8	4.6	3.9
Factor income	−0.4	−1.8	−3.5	−3.6	−3.6	−3.3	−4.1	−4.1	−4.3	−3.4	−3.0
Resource balance	−8.0	−7.1	−7.1	−8.2	−8.7	−7.7	−7.0	−7.0	−4.7	−4.6	−3.5
Memorandum											
Acquisition of foreign assets	0.2	0.4	0.5	−1.9	−1.3	1.4	−0.2	0.6	0.3	0.4	0.7
Change in reserves	—	0.2	1.5	−0.8	0.4	2.2	0.7	0.6	0.8	0.9	0.8
Private financing											
Saving	26.0	25.7	27.7	27.7	28.5	29.8	29.5	30.3	30.3	30.4	30.4
Investment	26.8	26.2	27.7	28.8	31.7	30.5	30.9	31.6	32.1	32.3	32.4
Net lending	−0.8	−0.5	—	−1.1	−3.1	−0.7	−1.4	−1.3	−1.8	−1.9	−2.0
Current transfers	0.4	0.5	0.7	0.7	0.7	0.7	0.6	0.5	0.5	0.5	0.4
Factor income	−0.3	−2.2	−1.1	−1.5	−1.8	−1.7	−2.4	−1.9	−2.2	−1.9	−1.9
Resource balance	−1.0	1.2	0.4	−0.3	−2.0	0.3	0.5	0.1	−0.2	−0.5	−0.5
Memorandum											
Acquisition of foreign assets	1.4	0.9	3.4	2.6	3.2	3.6	4.0	3.5	2.3	1.8	1.4
Change in reserves	0.5	0.5	2.2	1.0	1.3	2.4	2.4	2.4	1.3	1.1	0.7
Diversified financing											
Saving	21.4	19.2	22.6	24.0	22.6	23.3	24.3	24.5	25.2	25.5	26.1
Investment	22.7	23.7	24.5	24.9	24.4	25.0	26.3	27.0	27.8	28.3	29.1
Net lending	−1.3	−4.5	−1.9	−0.9	−1.7	−1.7	−2.0	−2.5	−2.7	−2.9	−3.0
Current transfers	2.3	2.1	3.2	2.6	2.4	2.2	2.1	1.9	1.7	1.6	1.3
Factor income	−1.5	−2.6	−2.0	−1.1	−1.4	−0.9	−0.5	−0.4	−0.3	—	0.1
Resource balance	−2.2	−3.9	−3.1	−2.4	−2.8	−3.0	−3.7	−4.0	−4.1	−4.5	−4.5
Memorandum											
Acquisition of foreign assets	2.3	−0.2	1.6	1.3	1.7	1.4	0.8	1.2	0.8	0.5	0.7
Change in reserves	2.1	0.2	2.2	2.7	2.3	2.0	0.2	1.2	1.1	0.8	1.0
Net debtor countries by debt-servicing experience											
Countries with recent difficulties											
Saving	24.4	18.0	19.1	19.9	17.2	19.1	18.5	18.7	19.2	19.5	20.5
Investment	27.1	20.9	20.7	21.6	20.5	20.2	20.8	20.4	21.1	21.4	22.3
Net lending	−2.8	−2.9	−1.6	−1.7	−3.3	−1.0	−2.3	−1.7	−2.0	−1.9	−1.8
Current transfers	1.6	2.1	3.4	3.1	2.9	2.6	2.3	2.0	1.9	1.8	1.6
Factor income	−1.9	−3.6	−2.3	−2.2	−3.4	−2.0	−2.1	−1.4	−1.7	−1.1	−0.9
Resource balance	−2.5	−1.4	−2.7	−2.6	−2.9	−1.6	−2.4	−2.3	−2.2	−2.7	−2.6
Memorandum											
Acquisition of foreign assets	2.2	0.2	1.1	1.0	1.0	1.9	1.4	2.4	1.4	0.9	0.9
Change in reserves	0.8	0.2	1.4	1.7	1.2	1.0	0.8	1.6	1.0	0.8	0.8
Countries without recent difficulties											
Saving	24.2	25.4	27.8	27.9	29.1	29.7	29.9	30.5	30.7	30.9	30.9
Investment	24.5	26.8	28.4	29.2	32.1	31.2	31.7	32.7	33.0	33.3	33.4
Net lending	−0.3	−1.3	−0.6	−1.4	−3.0	−1.5	−1.8	−2.1	−2.4	−2.4	−2.4
Current transfers	1.2	0.9	1.3	1.2	1.1	1.2	1.2	1.1	1.0	0.9	0.8
Factor income	0.4	−1.4	−1.3	−1.3	−1.2	−1.5	−2.1	−1.9	−2.0	−1.8	−1.7
Resource balance	−2.0	−0.9	−0.7	−1.3	−3.0	−1.2	−0.8	−1.3	−1.4	−1.6	−1.5
Memorandum											
Acquisition of foreign assets	0.8	0.7	3.3	2.1	2.9	3.2	3.4	2.7	1.9	1.5	1.2
Change in reserves	0.8	0.5	2.5	1.0	1.5	2.8	2.0	2.0	1.3	1.1	0.8

Table A44 *(concluded)*

	Averages		1991	1992	1993	1994	1995	1996	1997	1998	Average 1999–2002
	1975–82	1983–90									
Countries in transition											
Saving	...	...	29.7	26.2	21.3	22.2	20.5	18.9	18.5	19.9	21.2
Investment	...	...	31.1	28.8	24.7	22.2	21.3	21.0	21.5	23.1	24.5
Net lending	...	...	−1.4	−2.5	−3.4	−0.1	−0.8	−2.1	−3.0	−3.3	−3.3
Current transfers	...	...	0.8	2.1	1.4	0.9	0.6	0.5	0.5	0.4	0.4
Factor income	...	...	−3.1	−2.6	−1.4	−0.9	−1.1	−1.1	−1.6	−1.6	−1.8
Resource balance	...	...	0.9	−2.1	−3.5	−0.1	−0.3	−1.5	−1.9	−2.1	−1.9
Memorandum											
Acquisition of foreign assets	...	...	1.5	2.8	1.1	1.5	4.3	0.3	0.6	0.8	0.5
Change in reserves	...	...	−0.6	1.5	2.9	1.8	4.0	0.1	0.5	0.7	0.5

Note: The estimates in this table are based on individual countries' national accounts and balance of payments statistics. For many countries, the estimates of national saving are built up from national accounts data on gross domestic investment and from balance-of-payments-based data on net foreign investment. The latter, which is equivalent to the current account balance, comprises three components: current transfers, net factor income, and the resource balance. The mixing of data sources, which is dictated by availability, implies that the estimates for national saving that are derived incorporate the statistical discrepancies. Furthermore, errors, omissions, and asymmetries in balance of payments statistics affect the estimates for net lending; at the global level, net lending, which in theory would be zero, equals the world current account discrepancy. Notwithstanding these statistical shortcomings, flow of funds estimates, such as those presented in this table, provide a useful framework for analyzing development in saving and investment, both over time and across regions and countries. Country group composites are weighted by GDP valued at purchasing power parities (PPPs) as a share of total world GDP.

Table A45. Summary of World Medium-Term Baseline Scenario

	Eight-Year Averages		Four-Year Average					Four-Year Average
	1979–86	1987–94	1995–98	1995	1996	1997	1998	1999–2002
	Annual percent change unless otherwise noted							
World real GDP	**3.1**	**3.3**	**4.1**	**3.7**	**4.0**	**4.4**	**4.4**	**4.5**
Advanced economies	2.6	2.7	2.7	2.5	2.5	2.9	2.9	2.9
Developing countries	4.1	5.4	6.4	6.0	6.5	6.6	6.5	6.5
Countries in transition	2.8	–3.6	1.8	–0.8	0.1	3.0	4.8	5.4
Memorandum								
Potential output								
Major industrial countries	2.5	2.6	2.2	2.2	2.2	2.3	2.3	2.3
World trade, volume[1]	**3.5**	**6.2**	**7.2**	**9.2**	**5.6**	**7.3**	**6.8**	**6.7**
Imports								
Advanced economies	4.1	6.3	6.5	8.7	5.3	5.9	6.1	6.3
Developing countries	2.1	6.7	9.8	11.6	8.3	10.7	8.4	7.8
Countries in transition	2.1	—	10.0	15.9	7.7	9.8	6.8	7.8
Exports								
Advanced economies	4.5	6.5	6.7	8.4	5.0	6.9	6.7	6.5
Developing countries	0.1	8.5	9.3	11.2	7.0	11.0	8.0	7.9
Countries in transition	3.1	–0.2	8.0	13.5	4.7	6.9	7.0	8.3
Terms of trade								
Advanced economies	–0.3	0.4	–0.4	—	–0.1	–1.0	–0.4	–0.3
Developing countries	1.7	–1.1	0.3	2.0	0.4	–0.9	–0.3	–0.1
Countries in transition	–0.3	—	–0.4	–1.1	2.2	0.5	–3.2	–0.3
World prices in U.S. dollars								
Manufactures	3.4	3.6	1.8	11.2	–2.8	–2.1	1.4	1.4
Oil	0.8	1.4	3.7	8.0	18.9	–3.6	–6.7	1.1
Nonfuel primary commodities	–0.5	4.0	1.6	8.2	–1.3	—	–0.3	1.8
Consumer prices								
Advanced economies	7.7	3.8	2.5	2.6	2.4	2.5	2.5	2.3
Developing countries	28.6	49.2	13.0	21.3	13.1	9.7	8.5	7.1
Countries in transition	6.0	120.4	45.9	117.7	42.7	30.7	11.6	7.2
Interest rates (in percent)								
Real six-month LIBOR[2]	5.7	3.1	3.6	3.6	3.6	3.9	3.4	3.4
World real long-term interest rate[3]	4.1	4.4	3.9	4.3	3.8	3.5	3.9	4.3
	In percent of GDP							
Balances on current account								
Advanced economies	–0.4	–0.2	—	0.1	—	–0.1	—	–0.1
Developing countries	–1.3	–2.0	–1.9	–1.9	–1.8	–1.8	–2.0	–1.8
Countries in transition	0.2	–0.2	–1.1	–0.4	–0.9	–1.4	–1.7	–1.7
Total external debt								
Developing countries	29.1	39.4	31.5	34.9	32.3	30.2	28.5	24.4
Countries in transition	7.0	23.2	24.6	31.5	26.3	20.9	19.6	17.5
Debt service								
Developing countries	4.1	4.6	4.2	4.7	4.7	4.0	3.6	3.0
Countries in transition	1.4	2.5	2.7	3.1	2.9	2.3	2.3	2.4

[1]Data refer to trade in goods and services.

[2]London interbank offered rate on U.S. dollar deposits less percent change in U.S. GDP deflator.

[3]GDP-weighted average of ten-year (or nearest maturity) government bond rates for the United States, Japan, Germany, France, Italy, the United Kingdom, and Canada.

Table A46. Developing Countries—Medium-Term Baseline Scenario: Selected Economic Indicators

	Eight-Year Averages		Four-Year Average					Four-Year Average
	1979–86	1987–94	1995–98	1995	1996	1997	1998	1999–2002
	Annual percent change							
Developing countries								
Real GDP	4.1	5.4	6.4	6.0	6.5	6.6	6.5	6.5
Export volume[1]	0.1	8.5	9.3	11.2	7.0	11.0	8.0	7.9
Terms of trade[1]	1.7	−1.1	0.3	2.0	0.4	−0.9	−0.3	−0.1
Import volume[1]	2.1	6.7	9.8	11.6	8.3	10.7	8.4	7.8
Regional groups								
Africa								
Real GDP	2.3	2.2	4.3	2.9	5.0	4.7	4.8	4.7
Export volume[1]	1.2	3.7	7.9	8.4	9.9	6.3	6.8	4.6
Terms of trade[1]	—	−1.9	−0.5	−1.7	2.6	−0.6	−2.1	−0.1
Import volume[1]	−0.7	1.7	6.1	7.3	6.3	6.1	4.6	4.9
Asia								
Real GDP	6.3	7.9	8.3	8.9	8.2	8.3	7.7	7.7
Export volume[1]	6.4	12.8	10.4	15.3	4.6	10.8	11.1	10.6
Terms of trade[1]	0.2	−0.6	−0.1	0.7	−0.5	−0.4	—	−0.3
Import volume[1]	6.7	11.0	11.4	17.7	5.9	10.7	11.7	9.9
Middle East and Europe								
Real GDP	2.1	3.4	4.0	3.8	4.5	3.9	3.9	3.8
Export volume[1]	−5.6	6.9	6.9	1.1	10.0	16.2	1.3	2.3
Terms of trade[1]	4.4	−2.3	1.7	3.6	4.8	−2.5	1.0	0.3
Import volume[1]	2.7	0.9	9.4	6.0	14.1	14.4	3.6	3.1
Western Hemisphere								
Real GDP	2.8	2.8	3.6	1.3	3.5	4.4	5.1	5.0
Export volume[1]	4.4	7.4	9.7	14.1	7.5	9.5	8.0	7.9
Terms of trade[1]	−2.3	−0.1	—	4.8	−2.4	−0.8	−1.4	—
Import volume[1]	−1.5	10.1	8.5	7.4	9.3	10.2	7.2	7.5
Analytical groups								
Net debtor countries by debt-servicing experience								
Countries with recent difficulties								
Real GDP	2.4	2.4	4.3	3.2	3.8	4.8	5.2	4.9
Export volume[1]	−0.2	5.7	8.5	5.3	6.2	14.1	8.5	6.4
Terms of trade[1]	−0.1	−1.8	0.1	3.1	—	−1.3	−1.4	0.2
Import volume[1]	−1.1	2.2	9.5	11.7	6.9	13.5	6.2	6.3
Countries without recent difficulties								
Real GDP	5.5	7.0	7.4	7.4	7.6	7.5	7.1	7.3
Export volume[1]	5.6	10.3	10.5	15.1	6.5	10.7	9.8	9.4
Terms of trade[1]	−0.2	−0.3	0.2	1.9	−0.6	−0.5	−0.2	−0.3
Import volume[1]	4.7	10.6	10.4	13.2	7.8	10.6	10.2	9.0

Table A46 (concluded)

	1986	1990	1994	1995	1996	1997	1998	2002
	In percent of exports of goods and services							
Developing countries								
Current account balance	−18.8	−3.6	−10.0	−9.1	−8.7	−9.1	−10.0	−9.9
Total external debt	243.5	185.8	185.3	168.1	159.0	149.5	145.4	129.3
Debt-service payments[2]	29.5	20.7	23.2	22.7	23.0	19.8	18.4	15.7
Interest payments	16.2	9.4	8.5	8.6	9.0	8.8	8.4	7.2
Amortization	13.3	11.3	14.6	14.1	13.9	11.0	9.9	8.6
Regional groups								
Africa								
Current account balance	−15.8	−3.5	−11.4	−13.4	−6.1	−6.0	−5.8	−6.0
Total external debt	249.8	229.2	266.7	245.4	226.5	212.3	202.1	168.7
Debt-service payments[2]	31.8	29.2	24.3	22.4	23.7	25.6	25.4	23.0
Interest payments	12.6	12.0	10.5	10.5	10.5	11.3	11.8	9.2
Amortization	19.2	17.2	13.8	11.9	13.2	14.3	13.7	13.8
Asia								
Current account balance	−19.8	−8.1	−6.1	−9.0	−10.4	−10.6	−11.1	−9.4
Total external debt	221.6	164.4	137.4	121.2	117.7	112.6	109.6	97.7
Debt-service payments[2]	25.2	17.9	16.0	15.4	16.2	14.9	13.7	11.7
Interest payments	12.2	8.3	6.4	5.8	6.1	6.0	5.7	4.9
Amortization	13.0	9.6	9.6	9.5	10.1	9.0	8.0	6.8
Middle East and Europe								
Current account balance	−21.6	−1.4	−2.1	−2.2	−0.5	0.1	−2.1	−6.8
Total external debt	135.1	115.3	136.5	125.9	112.9	101.3	101.0	105.5
Debt-service payments[2]	12.4	9.7	16.1	14.7	12.0	9.6	9.8	7.5
Interest payments	6.6	4.0	4.3	4.3	4.4	3.8	3.6	3.2
Amortization	5.8	5.7	11.8	10.4	7.5	5.8	6.2	4.3
Western Hemisphere								
Current account balance	−16.8	−0.8	−23.5	−13.2	−14.4	−16.3	−16.8	−14.6
Total external debt	379.5	267.7	274.9	254.4	241.2	232.7	226.1	194.6
Debt-service payments[2]	50.8	31.8	41.8	43.4	44.3	35.5	31.4	27.0
Interest payments	32.9	15.6	15.4	16.6	17.6	17.6	16.3	13.9
Amortization	17.9	16.2	26.4	26.8	26.7	17.9	15.1	13.1
Analytical groups								
Net debtor countries by debt-servicing experience								
Countries with recent difficulties								
Current account balance	−33.7	−5.0	−10.9	−15.2	−12.6	−12.8	−11.1	−9.2
Total external debt	374.6	311.5	340.7	318.6	295.5	264.8	251.1	213.9
Debt-service payments[2]	43.5	29.3	32.2	32.7	28.2	28.5	26.3	23.9
Interest payments	24.0	11.9	11.9	13.4	13.4	13.5	12.4	10.4
Amortization	19.5	17.5	20.2	19.3	14.8	15.1	13.9	13.6
Countries without recent difficulties								
Current account balance	−11.6	−7.2	−10.5	−8.3	−10.1	−10.4	−11.2	−10.7
Total external debt	222.7	162.4	150.4	134.2	128.8	123.2	120.3	109.8
Debt-service payments[2]	29.0	21.7	23.3	21.8	24.6	19.2	17.5	14.2
Interest payments	15.6	10.8	8.7	8.2	8.8	8.3	7.9	6.8
Amortization	13.3	10.9	14.6	13.6	15.7	11.0	9.6	7.5

[1]Data refer to trade in goods and services.

[2]Interest payments on total debt plus amortization payments on long-term debt only. Projections incorporate the impact of exceptional financing items. Excludes service payments to the IMF.

World Economic and Financial Surveys

This series (ISSN 0258-7440) contains biannual, annual, and periodic studies covering monetary and financial issues of importance to the global economy. The core elements of the series are the *World Economic Outlook* report, usually published in May and October, and the annual report on *International Capital Markets*. Other studies assess international trade policy, private market and official financing for developing countries, exchange and payments systems, export credit policies, and issues discussed in the *World Economic Outlook*.

World Economic Outlook: A Survey by the Staff of the International Monetary Fund

The *World Economic Outlook*, published twice a year in English, French, Spanish, and Arabic, presents IMF staff economists' analyses of global economic developments during the near and medium term. Chapters give an overview of the world economy; consider issues affecting industrial countries, developing countries, and economies in transition to the market; and address topics of pressing current interest.

ISSN 0256-6877.
$35.00 (academic rate: $24.00; paper)
1997 (May). ISBN 1-55775-648-1. **Stock #WEO-197.**
1996 (Oct.). ISBN 1-55775-610-4. **Stock #WEO-296.**
1996 (May). ISBN 1-55775-567-1. **Stock #WEO-196.**
1995 (Oct.). ISBN 1-55775-467-5. **Stock #WEO-295.**

International Capital Markets: Developments, Prospects, and Key Policy Issues
by a staff team led by Takatoshi Ito and David Folkerts-Landau

The current issue provides a comprehensive survey of recent developments in international financial markets in 1995 and 1996, including developments in emerging capital markets, bond markets, major currency markets, and derivative markets. The report focuses on efforts by the major industrial countries to strengthen the management of financial risk and prudential oversight over the international banking system.

$20.00 (academic rate: $12.00; paper).
1996. ISBN 1-55775-609-0. **Stock #WEO-696.**
1995. ISBN 1-55775-516-7. **Stock #WEO-695.**

Staff Studies for the World Economic Outlook
by the IMF's Research Department

These studies, supporting analyses and scenarios of the *World Economic Outlook*, provide a detailed examination of theory and evidence on major issues currently affecting the global economy.

$20.00 (academic rate: $12.00; paper).
1995. ISBN 1-55775-499-3. **Stock #WEO-395.**
1993. ISBN 1-55775-337-7. **Stock #WEO-393.**

Issues in International Exchange and Payments Systems
by a staff team from the IMF's Monetary and Exchange Affairs Department

The global trend toward liberalization in countries' international exchange and payments systems has been widespread in both industrial and developing countries and most dramatic in Central and Eastern Europe. Countries in general have brought their exchange systems more in line with market principles and moved toward more flexible exchange rate arrangements in recent years.

$20.00 (academic rate: $12.00; paper).
1995. ISBN 1-55775-480-2. **Stock #WEO-895.**

Private Market Financing for Developing Countries
by a staff team from the IMF's Policy Development and Review Department under the direction of Steven Dunaway

The latest study surveys recent trends in flows to developing countries through banking and securities markets. It also analyzes the institutional and regulatory framework for developing country finance; institutional investor behavior and pricing of developing country stocks; and progress in commercial bank debt restructuring in low-income countries.

$20.00 (academic rate: $12.00; paper).
1995. ISBN 1-55775-526-4. **Stock #WEO-1595.**
1995. ISBN 1-55775-456-X. **Stock #WEO-995.**

International Trade Policies
by a staff team led by Naheed Kirmani

The study reviews major issues and developments in trade and their implications for the work of the IMF. Volume I, *The Uruguay Round and Beyond: Principal Issues*, gives an overview of the principal issues and developments in the world trading system. Volume II, *The Uruguay Round and Beyond: Background Papers*, presents detailed background papers on selected trade and trade-related issues. This study updates previous studies published under the title *Issues and Developments in International Trade Policy*.

$20.00 (academic rate: $12.00; paper).
1994. *Volume I. The Uruguay Round and Beyond: Principal Issues*
ISBN 1-55775-469-1. **Stock #WEO-1094.**
1994. *Volume II. The Uruguay Round and Beyond: Background Papers*
ISBN 1-55775-457-8. **Stock #WEO-1494.**
1992. ISBN 1-55775-311-1. **Stock #WEO-1092.**

Official Financing for Developing Countries
by a staff team from the IMF's Policy Development and Review Department under the direction of Anthony R. Boote

This study provides information on official financing for developing countries, with the focus on low- and lower-middle-income countries. It updates and replaces *Multilateral Official Debt Rescheduling: Recent Experience* and reviews developments in direct financing by official and multilateral sources.

$20.00 (academic rate: $12.00; paper)
1995. ISBN 1-55775-527-2. **Stock #WEO-1395.**
1994. ISBN 1-55775-378-4. **Stock #WEO-1394.**

Officially Supported Export Credits: Recent Developments and Prospects
by Michael G. Kuhn, Balazs Horvath, Christopher J. Jarvis

This study examines export credit and cover policies in major industrial countries.

$20.00 (academic rate: $12.00; paper).
1995. ISBN 1-55775-448-9. **Stock #WEO-595.**

Available by series subscription or single title (including back issues); academic rate available only to full-time university faculty and students.

Please send orders and inquiries to:
International Monetary Fund, Publication Services, 700 19th Street, N.W.
Washington, D.C. 20431, U.S.A.
Tel.: (202) 623-7430   Telefax: (202) 623-7201
E-mail: publications@imf.org
Internet: http://www.imf.org